# Sigmund Freud on the Way to Paris, 1873–1885

*Sigmund Freud on the Way to Paris, 1873–1885* poses a question: where does psychoanalysis begin?

Giosuè Ghisalberti considers how Freud's own development – in terms of both his formal education and his personal growth – influenced the development of psychoanalysis. Rather than a beginning to psychoanalysis, this book instead traces four convergent influences: one, the nature of Freud's "Jewishness" as determined by the Hebrew language, the Torah, and the man Moses; two, his interdisciplinary scientific studies in medicine, laboratory research, and clinical internship; three, the foundational aspect of Anna O.'s illness; and four, the time he spent in Paris observing hysterics at the Salpêtrière hospital. Rather than a beginning to psychoanalysis, the book instead traces several influences, beginning with the "archaic heritage" he drew from an ancient culture as he presented it in the third and last part of *Moses and Monotheism*.

*Sigmund Freud on the Way to Paris, 1873–1885* will be of great interest to students and scholars of psychoanalysis, the humanities, and the sciences looking to trace four origins of psychoanalysis.

**Giosuè Ghisalberti** received his PhD from the Department of Social and Political Thought, York University, Canada. He has written on several interdisciplinary subjects, including the ancient world, religion, philosophy, and psychoanalysis.

# History of Psychoanalysis
Series Editor
Peter L. Rudnytsky

This series seeks to present outstanding new books that illuminate any aspect of the history of psychoanalysis from its earliest days to the present, and to reintroduce classic texts to contemporary readers.

Other titles in the series:

**The Marquis de Puysegur and Artificial Somnambulism**
Memoirs to Contribute to the History and Establishment of Animal Magnetism
*Edited and translated by Adam Crabtree and Sarah Osei-Bonsu*

**The Subversive Edge of Psychoanalysis**
*David James Fisher*

**The Vicissitudes of Psychoanalysis in Soviet Russia, 1930–1980**
*Lizaveta van Munsteren*

**Freud's British Family**
Reclaiming Lost Lives in Manchester and London
*Roger Willoughby*

**Sigmund Freud's Inner Divisions**
Personal and Theoretical
*Ken Fuchsman*

**Sigmund Freud on the Way to Paris, 1873–1885**
Foundations of Psychoanalysis
*Giosuè Ghisalberti*

For further information about this series please visit https://www.routledge.com/The-History-of-Psychoanalysis-Series/book-series/KARNHIPSY

# Sigmund Freud on the Way to Paris, 1873–1885

Foundations of Psychoanalysis

Giosuè Ghisalberti

LONDON AND NEW YORK

Designed cover image: © Giosuè Ghisalberti

First published 2026
by Routledge
4 Park Square, Milton Park, Abingdon, Oxon OX14 4RN

and by Routledge
605 Third Avenue, New York, NY 10158

*Routledge is an imprint of the Taylor & Francis Group, an informa business*

© 2026 Giosuè Ghisalberti

The right of Giosuè Ghisalberti to be identified as author of this work has been asserted in accordance with sections 77 and 78 of the Copyright, Designs and Patents Act 1988.

All rights reserved. No part of this book may be reprinted or reproduced or utilised in any form or by any electronic, mechanical, or other means, now known or hereafter invented, including photocopying and recording, or in any information storage or retrieval system, without permission in writing from the publishers.

For Product Safety Concerns and Information please contact our EU representative GPSR@taylorandfrancis.com. Taylor & Francis Verlag GmbH, Kaufingerstraße 24, 80331 München, Germany.

*Trademark notice*: Product or corporate names may be trademarks or registered trademarks, and are used only for identification and explanation without intent to infringe.

*British Library Cataloguing-in-Publication Data*
A catalogue record for this book is available from the British Library

ISBN: 978-1-041-12322-4 (hbk)
ISBN: 978-1-041-12321-7 (pbk)
ISBN: 978-1-003-66415-4 (ebk)

DOI: 10.4324/9781003664154

Typeset in Times New Roman
by Deanta Global Publishing Services, Chennai, India

# Contents

| | | |
|---|---|---|
| Introduction: Psychoanalysis of Neurotic Perceptions | | 1 |
| 1 | Jewish Transferences | 23 |
| | *Freud's Archaic Heritage   23* | |
| | *The Hebrew Language, the Torah, and Interpretation   37* | |
| | *The Revelations of Moses   49* | |
| 2 | Science, Medicine, and the Laboratory | 69 |
| | *Freud's Idea of Wissenschaft   69* | |
| | *Francis Bacon and the Idols of the Mind   85* | |
| | *The Microscope as an Allegory of Perception   99* | |
| 3 | Anna O.'s "Private Theatre" | 116 |
| | *The Splitting of Consciousness   116* | |
| | *Phenomenology of an Illness Called Hysteria   131* | |
| | *Memories of Anna O.   146* | |
| 4 | Jean-Martin Charcot's Neurology | 163 |
| | *Freud's Obituary of Charcot   163* | |
| | *Hysterics at the Salpêtrière   176* | |
| | *Before Freud's Return to Vienna   187* | |
| | *Works Cited* | *203* |
| | *Bibliography* | *205* |
| | *Index* | *218* |

# Introduction

## Psychoanalysis of Neurotic Perceptions

"In consequence of the special character of our discoveries, our scientific work in psychology will consist in translating unconscious processes into conscious ones, and thus filling in the gaps in conscious perception."

(Some Elementary Lessons on Psychoanalysis)

In one of the last articles Freud wrote in 1938 before its posthumous publication, the last sentence highlights two inter-related themes and their importance for the history of psychoanalysis even before its full-fledged creation, as originally named or in practice after the beginning of Josef Breuer's cathartic method in 1880–1882 and Anna O.'s self-described "chimney-sweeping" and "talking cure." Throughout his life, Freud maintained, one, a consistent self-understanding of "scientific work in psychology" and, two, the recognition of the incompleteness of conscious perception due to the innumerable ways the psyche could distort the self, others, and reality. The science of psychoanalysis, as a unique *Wissenschaft*, was concerned, above all, with consciousness and perception. Despite the incompleteness of the late work, two insights were something other than "elementary lessons." The intellectual and psychotherapeutic challenge of making the dynamics of the unconscious known (more than cognitively, which was a superficial form of knowledge) could begin from a consequential intent later summed up by the memorable phrase, "where the id was, there the ego shall be." One act, of translation – from ideations to interpretation and understanding, and then life – had in part defined the psychological project from Freud's earliest intuitions and, in time, discoveries. The psychoanalysis of neurotic perceptions evolved over a significant period of time and according to a number of Freud's experiences – inevitably, first, from his childhood intuitions and imagination. A defining statement in *An Autobiographical Study*, which encompasses his life as a whole up until that time, is revealing and, going forward, consequential for our specific interests in his early development. Recalling his time as a Gymnasium student, Freud writes:

> Neither at that time, nor indeed in my later life, did I feel any particular predilection for the career of a doctor. I was moved, rather, by a sort of curiosity, which was, however, directed more towards human concerns that towards

natural objects; nor had I grasped the importance of observation as one of the best means of gratifying it. My deep engrossment in the Bible story (almost as soon as I learned the art of reading) had, as I recognized much later, an enduring effect upon the direction of my thinking.

(SE 20:8)

*Human concerns, observations, reading* that began, *formally*, as a medical student and then moved, due to interests and circumstances, in a few simultaneous directions that would be unified as both a character disposition and a method. His earliest discoveries will be traced from our specific time-period (from 1873, when he began his studies at the University of Vienna, to 1885, when he travelled to Paris to work with Jean-Martin Charcot at the Salpêtrière) and how a still-undefined interest had been drawn to the complicated nature of consciousness. Once he recognized, with Breuer, a "split" between the conscious psyche and a more disguised and elusive aspect of the self, Freud set himself towards presenting perhaps the most important change in perspective of all: the necessity of recognizing the limits and dynamics of human perception beyond the physiological consensus of his day. For if one analysis proved to be essential – "parts of the self are split off and projected unto objects where they permanently reside, remaining unavailable to the self"[1] – Freud's discoveries were to be fundamental for the binding relationship between the self and the world.

The particular topic was still on his mind late in his life, as attested by another 1938 unfinished piece, "Splitting of the Ego in the Process of Defense." "I find myself for a moment in the interesting position of not knowing whether what I have to say should be regarded as something long and familiar and obvious or something entirely new and puzzling. But I am inclined to think the latter" (SE 23:275). *New and puzzling*: after almost six decades, the innovations of psychoanalysis were still being processed; the power of reason and intelligence and the imagination were still working towards the enigma of the psyche and mental illness, as an everyday neurosis for an individual or a more serious pathology in the social world. To appreciate Freud's thinking in 1938, and his sense of the split consciousness discussed, first, in relation to Anna O., a return to his beginnings can be attempted and partially traced in order to understand just how important this one piece of psychoanalytic insight remained. "The synthetic function of the ego, though it is of such extraordinary importance, is subject to particular conditions and is liable to a whole number of disturbances." How neurotic disturbances were first analyzed, as symptoms – of repression or defence, projection or reaction formation – was foundational for the creation of psychoanalysis. Although a split consciousness was incomplete because, as an image, only divisive and topographical, its complex effects could be diagnosed according to their manifested variables. The intellectual and psychotherapeutic objective – to come to terms with "the gaps in conscious perception" – did indeed require a particular kind of translation. How the translation and *transference* took place over an extended period of time can be, at least in part, reconstructed from a number of Freud's experiences, both cultural and professional and beginning with a particular relationship to Judaism.

Overall, his cultural and professional experiences will involve us in four distinct influences and early periods in Freud's life: one, an inherited cultural Judaism in terms of the Hebrew language, scripture as a "Bible story," and Moses the individual who, in the Decalogue and then in the writing of Exodus, made everyone conscious of the possible pathology of the image; two, his education into the world of 19th-century German *Wissenschaft* and particularly in the fields of medicine, laboratory research, and a clinical internship; three, the case of Anna O. and the symptoms that were, initially, described under the category of hysteria and then understood by Freud to be more significant because of the nature of her somnambulistic and hypnoid *absences*, her disturbances of vision, and the creation of her "private theatre;" and, four, during his stay in Paris and as an observer of Jean-Martin Charcot's anatomo-clinical method, Freud's beginning of the arduous theoretical task of unifying his impressions over a considerable length of time and realizing how each of his distinct experiences was necessary to the creation of a new relationship to psychological illness.

In one encyclopedia article, Freud was clear about a starting point. "The best way of understanding psycho-analysis is still by tracing its origin and development" (SE 18:235). He has done so on numerous occasions, each time with the emphasis on inter-related elements. They will be taken into consideration while at the same time laying stress on some others he may have neglected or omitted for his own reasons. One origin is unquestioned – though it cannot be circumscribed by the date he gives us in a paper he wrote for the Australasian Medical Congress. "Psycho-analysis started with researches into hysteria, but in the course of years it has extended far beyond that field of work. *The Studies on Hysteria* by Breuer and myself, published in 1895, were the beginnings of psychoanalysis" (SE 12:207). Beginnings: the plural is extensive and will be examined according to four different foundational experiences, all of them more than a decade before the co-written work. Freud's "start" has a long history before 1895.

The title of the previously mentioned writing, "Some Elementary Lessons in Psychoanalysis," might deceptively appear as one more introduction, a summary of sorts as Freud reached the end of his life. There were to be many, all of them insistent on the connection between the recognized methods of science and psychoanalysis. Although he expects some or most of his readers to be familiar with his subject – "which, though they are known to him, he has so far neglected or insufficiently appreciated" (SE 23:281) – he calls our attention to an oversight and, perhaps, something more serious. "Psycho-analysis," Freud writes, "is a part of the mental science of psychology." His belief has been challenged from innumerable sides and perspectives. The for and against has been exhaustively documented. And yet, nothing has been settled, in his lifetime or in the present especially during a *revival* of neurobiology; rather than revisit a traditional opposition, another reason has to be found to *return to Freud* – to mention Jacques Lacan's unnecessary call, which has always been known, intimately, by researchers and/or analysands. When, in the final lessons, Freud gives us one of the characteristics of the psychical, the first is essentially the only one to be emphasized and for reasons that take us to his origins, as an individual, and as someone who *formed himself* according to a number of elements, personal and intellectual, as a culture heritage and a self-conscious *Bildung*. "If someone asks what the 'the psychical' means, it is easy to reply by enumerating its constituents." There are many. The *first* one in his list? "Our perceptions." The nature of our perceptions has always been tied to our consciousness. The taken-for-granted reality was, in essence, no different than the traditional view of the cosmos as they appeared, as it were, to "the naked eye." The sensual *image*, we first learnt about analytically – from Moses in the Decalogue, by philosophers since Plato, through mathematical calculations, and then by the use of the telescope – was deceptive. Our perceptions and assumptions about the nature of cosmological reality were wrong and illusory. The consequence of a logic was not always extended; our immediate reality, for everyday experience, could be equally distorted– or, worse, deluded and pathological. Our reality was an assumed one, taken for granted as if immediate to the senses and, more particularly, the evidence of our sight. Freud reminded us that we have internalized a false image, as seen from the perspective of the earth or from our own self-evident eyesight; the admission of one kind of perceptual error, of physical reality, also required us to turn to the depths of our human interiority and, from there, begin an exhaustive task. "Consciousness is only a *quality* or attribute of what is psychical, and moreover an inconstant one" (SE 23:286). Inconstant and incomplete. This one defining statement serves for us to return to the beginning of a period in Freud's life and to see how many ideas, and experiences, led him to think about the nature of consciousness and human perception as determined by elements far more complex than a self or ego. Michael Robbins believes that Freud's psychology of consciousness has been "neglected." In my estimate, no analysand ever has, or could, since consciousness, in the most immediate *and* disguised way, in life and dreams, words and ideations, has always been omnipresent in the analytic situation. Robbins's call on "subsequent generations of analysts to make psychoanalysis less Freudian and more a science-like edifice of conceptual building blocks"[2] seems misguided, for reasons that will be presented at length and, to begin with, because of Freud's relationship to Judaism *and* science. Why not *more Freudian* once we find ourselves in the closest proximity to him, that is, in a shared transference and for the benefit of our knowledge and conscious perception of *ourselves*?

In "An Outline of Psychoanalysis," another unfinished work from 1938, Freud wrote:

> We many now venture on the assertion that the psychology of consciousness was no better capable of understanding the normal functioning of the mind than of understanding dreams. The date of conscious self-perception, which alone were at its disposal [to the ego] have proved in every respect inadequate.
>
> (SE 23:195–6)

By "inadequate," Freud does not at all mean in terms of our *knowledge*. Psychoanalysis is distinct since the appearance of a merely epistemological problem is, more importantly, an existential one; the inadequacy turns out to be one where a compromised consciousness leads to all kinds of debilitations, illnesses, and then serious limits to our freedom. "The normal and abnormal manifestations observed by us (that is, the phenomenology of the subject) need to be described from the point of view of their dynamics and economics" (SE 23:156). *The phenomenology of the subject*. The philosophical language should not be a surprise. In this one summing-up, one of many, Freud takes himself, and us, back to beginnings. His investigation has to be, necessarily, our own if we are to understand how Freud arrived at the discoveries he made. He continues, "The starting-point for this investigation is provided by a fact without parallel, which defies all explanation or description – the fact of consciousness." Our starting point (which is also his) takes us back to 1938 and then to a period that requires our recollection and analysis, of our relationship to Freud no less than for ourselves.

In one final late work, especially Section III of *Moses and Monotheism*, which will take up some of our attention in due time and to set out one cultural foundation to his thinking, Freud turns to the figure of the individual Moses to make a statement that we can also apply to psychoanalysis and, therefore, return to "preliminaries." One passage alerts us to a connection:

> A fresh complication arises when we become aware of the probability that what may be operative in an individual's psychical life may also include not only what he has experienced himself but also things that were innately present in him at his birth, elements with a phylogenetic origin – an archaic heritage. The questions then arise of what this consists in, what it contains and what is the evidence for it.
>
> (SE 23:98)

Without necessarily interpreting the passage in terms of a *contradiction*, two concepts are (at least originally, and seemingly) incompatible. The biology of phylogenesis and the historical culture of an archaic heritage are each unique and defined according to different disciplines. Freud's language, in Section (E) called "Difficulties," has divergent meanings.

> The immediate and most certain answer is that it contains in certain [innate] dispositions such as are characteristic of all living organisms: in the capacity and tendency, that is, to enter particular lines of development and to react in a particular manner to certain excitations, impressions and stimuli. Since experience shows that there are distinctions in this respect between individuals of the human species, the archaic heritage must include these distinctions; they represent what we recognize as the constitutional factor in the individual.
>
> (SE 23:98)

The biological language does not make the task any easier, though "disposition" is ambiguous enough to be open-ended. At the moment, being undecided is not an obstacle; one problem has been established and makes for our interest in consciousness divided, at our beginning, between innate biology and acquired history, or, to use other language, heredity and culture. Three works from the late 1930's have been mentioned, each of them allowing us to take note of a conflict and its relevance for our understanding of perception and consciousness and, therefore, our sense of reality. To emphasize them prepares us for a specific kind of return to origins and to an examination that will require us to unify disparate interests and experiences.[3]

*One* origin was a decisive one. In *Moses and Monotheism*, Freud writes, "Every novelty must have its preliminaries and preconditions in something earlier" (SE 23:21). *Preconditions*, in the plural; tracing the origin of every single one is nearly impossible, certainly impractical from the perspective of one project with well-defined parameters. The more workable endeavour seems to me to be able to trace only a few of the most important and most especially to see how they are interrelated in the whole schema of Freud's life and psychoanalytic writing at their formative stages. Arriving at the end of the first quarter of the 21st century makes for a more complete assessment of the interest in Freud and psychoanalysis. The scholarship is immense; and as one prepares to write a project on only a few of the origins of psychoanalysis, beginning from Freud's cultural childhood, education, and *Bildung*, one recognizes the prior efforts and the impossibility of providing the reader with anything exhaustive. "The breadth of Freud's personal culture ensures that his thinking on many topics does not lack antecedents."[4] Both Freud's culture and the "antecedents" require, first, to be identified, and then placed in a context hopefully capable of recognizing his creativity and originality.

One fairly recent effort starts out with: "the book poses the question: where does psychoanalysis begin?"[5] One is tempted to answer, with a measure of caution and self-consciousness, and with a number of other questions, the ones given to us quite a few times from Freud – and then others. An older work of scholarship, which has one part of the subtitle "From the Beginnings (1886–1900)," is itself both out of date and seriously misled – for more reasons than the ones mentioned by Reuben Fine when he writes (in 1973), and surprisingly: "about forty years have passed since the publication of Freud's last major book *The Problem of Anxiety* (1926)."[6] Any project that attempts to trace the origin of psychoanalysis can only do so by self-consciously limiting the various possibilities – some which may be self-evident, others more disguised and obscure. In any case, as Freud reminds us, "each event seems to be overdetermined and proves to be the effect of several convergent causes" (SE 23:107). The concept of overdetermination reminds us of being attentive to our omissions and, in Fine's case, simply wrong. *Several convergent causes* are Freud's own words. The ambition of writing a "new historiography of psychoanalysis"[7] is beyond the scope of the following project since the innumerable connections and influences are overdetermined to a dynamic degree. The only manageable effort is to choose only a few of the aspects of the history before the invention of psychoanalysis and see how they led to a unique kind of knowledge of human beings and the reality they have made, both rationally and unconsciously. There can be no singular "new," not unless, in emulation of Freud, one can immerse oneself in a cultural world and be discerning enough to unify his own affinities and professional occupations.

Victor Schermer, writing a decade ago, believes that "psychoanalysis is now in crisis and requires a thorough rethinking of what it is about."[8] An analysand, and a reader, does not think so at all. There is, indeed, a crisis at the present; we had better look at ourselves and the world of our own making, first and foremost, before being certain about any cultural creation like psychoanalysis and *its* supposed crisis. Our social situation at the moment seems much more precarious and for reasons evident in all of Freud's major works of the 1920's.[9] To return to Freud's origins and concentrating on only four aspects of his biography and intellectual formation, one has in mind to present a neglected problem, neurotic perception and its distortion of reality, and its commitment from Freud as a matter of research and, ultimately, therapy at the individual and cultural level. Our discontents have become much graver a century after. How will the project to come be ordered; or rather, how will the four overlapping themes of Freud's life and experiences during the foundations of psychoanalysis be organized when we make the attempt to inter-relate a Jewish heritage, the sciences beginning with medicine, the case of Anna O., and Freud's short but formative time when he travelled to Paris to study with Jean-Martin Charcot?

There are more than a few possibilities, each of them with their own distinctions. "In its great days, psychoanalysis stood at the confluence of two distinct currents," Eli Zaretsky writes in the Epilogue to *Secrets of the Soul*. "One was strictly scientific ... the other stream was humanistic ... This stream drew on literary sources such as the Hebrew Bible."[10] He adds a final comment: "Freud fused these two currents into an extraordinary new synthesis, neither wholly scientific nor wholly humanistic." No different than a split in consciousness, a "fusion" or "synthesis" of science and humanism seems adequate as a start but incomplete. Mentioning Moses, once again, only makes the task ahead more challenging since one decision takes us to a history that is not at all certain except in its form in the Torah and, later, in the midrash interpretations by the rabbis at Yavneh as well as later developments related to the Kabbalah, each moment with its own pertinence for Freud, directly or indirectly. No question, science and humanism both will take up much of our attention, for a number of reasons, including that once anxiety-filled definition of psychoanalysis as a "Jewish science." While some effort will be devoted to thinking about Judaism *and* science as a relationship, and one with unexpected connections (for one, to Francis Bacon's *Novum Organum* and to his definitions of the idols of the mind) we may come to the conclusion that science may no longer be important for psychoanalysis, in the present, as it was for Freud. His preoccupations are less significant in our time. If, during his life, Freud worried that "too much emphasis on Jewish influence might have been to the detriment of psychoanalysis as a science,"[11] that one issue has been consigned to history.

How can we best choose the earliest of influences in his life and make the argument for its long-lasting importance and, in many ways, as a foundation for his non-institutional education. Reasons for being circumspect about psychoanalysis as a "Jewish science"[12] will be revealed in due time. The reality of Freud's Jewish ethnicity has been much debated. His "Jewishness" may indeed be a factor in the development of psychoanalysis. *How* is the question and one that extends beyond a personal *identity*. We have to be able to separate our assumptions about identity and a broader connection to a history, a culture, and a scriptural writing.

Before doing so, however, Freud's self-understanding at different moments in his early life, as a student first, will have to be examined. Historians and biographers have, since Ernest Jones's three-volume biography, given us more and more *information*. Nothing replaces, however, our own return to Freud's writing. Our historical details are exhaustive; we are still confronted with our limitations, in ourselves and most especially because of our particular era. We are always forced to consider the extent of relations. Looking ahead, Ruth Golan anticipates a problem. "Whether or not psychoanalysis in itself constitutes a science is arguable, but there is no argument regarding the fact that it owes its existence to science."[13] The *debt*, if any, will have to be more precisely identified. One can, from necessity, examine scientific reason as well as that of "Jewish origins." Whether we do so while also considering Judaism as a way of life for Freud, indeed, as a *tovat hayim*, a "principle of life,"[14] will not be summarily dismissed without some considerations as he outlines them in our 1873–1886 time-frame.

Jean-Michael Quinodoz's approach,[15] for all its merit, will not be followed, certainly not according to any letter of the law since our beginning, here in in the Introduction, sets out from the end of Freud's productive life. It has been shared, in the same year of publication, by Edgar Levenson, who believes that "an overview of psychoanalytic theory and practice, pulling it into its chronological context, will bring order to the mélange of claims and counterclaims."[16] A *chronological* reading cannot take into consideration the intimations of Freud's thinking and how, according to the four principal themes of the project, all try to convey one aspect of his self-development. Consciousness is anything but chronological; the timelessness of the psyche forces us to maintain a number of events simultaneously in mind as we try to understand Freud's creative thinking.

A return to Freud gives us a vantage point from which to examine two different periods of history. We are not – are never – exempt from the necessity of analyzing ourselves. A brief look at his biographers, to start with, leaves us with information that may be biographically true (factually accurate) and still be incomplete – as Freud himself told us during his acceptance speech for the Goethe Prize. As far as all the biographies written on Freud go, one of his own reminders should serve us well when we consider all the biographies written on Freud.

> But what can these biographies achieve for us? Even the best and fullest of them could not answer the two questions which alone seem worth knowing about.

It would not throw any light on the miraculous gift that makes an artist, and it could not help us to comprehend any better the value and the effect of his works.
(SE 21:211)

As far as the latter go, we can indeed comprehend both the value and the effect of Freud's invention of psychoanalysis before it came to define itself and long after. The former is, today, a matter of dispute; because if (most) academics are to be followed, then the 19th-century belief in remarkable individuals has been replaced by an over-emphasis on historicity. The idea of a "miraculous gift" might sound hyperbolic to many who have been persuaded by the categories of history and, for example, structure or *discourse*. Aversions are to be expected most especially from historicist orthodoxies. The power of structures and discourses and knowledge has, perhaps, run its course. In any event, if the few examples presented are any indication, none of them are going to satisfy us because Freud remains, like psychoanalysis, in a history that cannot be closed off, in the classical past or the present, as far back as the confluence of different civilizations and their persistence into our time. How the archaic, the period known as the Renaissance, and the modern was represented remarkably in "The Moses of Michelangelo" can be shown in Freud's superlative description of Moses and "the nature of a superman [*Übermensch*]" (SE 13:221).

How, then, can we present a study on a period of Freud's development and consciously choose only four defining experiences? Doing so is done, first of all, to present an idea of a *trans-historical transference* that occurs in a prolonged period of a specific kind of reception, what Freud calls (in *Moses and Monotheism*) an archaic heritage. Our first origin is Jewish as a cultural heritage and transference that cannot be reduced to ethnicity or identity. In *The Discovery of the Unconscious*, Henri Ellenberger presented the "ancestry" of what he called "dynamic psychiatry."[17] His beginning, in 1775 and with the conflict of individuals who each had different motivations, is much, much too late. Our beginning, in Judaism, will take us to one specific foundation; one tenth of the Decalogue, on the imperative to be aware of "graven images," once interpreted from its extra-theological meaning, makes for one association between Freud and a specific culture. Once an image and an idol is understood to be the epitome of the neurotic psyche, then a theological commandment can be interpreted, in our saeculum, according to Moses's *psychological* acuity. The transcendental finds its place in the most immanent place possible, in our selves, individually and within a culture, exerting considerable pressure on us and our capacity for independence of mind. One connection, from the archaic to the modern will be made and, in particular, when science (in 1620) was not yet disciplined; for when Francis Bacon wrote the *Novum Organum* and exposed the idols of the mind, he was advancing the archaic into the modern, just as Freud would do and so maintain *our* lineage to Judaism.

Although the coming project on Freud's period between 1873 and 1886 could be viewed as a small part of a genre known as "intellectual biography," there are enough elements in the themes to be discussed to be prudent about our assumptions about his life. Scholars can, of course, pursue "Freud's intellectual biography – that is, the relations between the unfolding of his thinking and crucial development in his life history,"[18] as long as care as taken not to over-extend ourselves, as does Joel Whitebook when he returns to Freud's early childhood and then a *wild* analysis about one incident and then our assumptions about its "trauma." A psychobiography of Freud should be avoided; we are in no position to evaluate his own analysis. On the other hand, Ernst Falzeder asks a still-relevant question: "is there still an unknown Freud?"[19] We are ourselves too incomplete to be able to know the whole. "The judgement of contemporary witnesses is biased by their own interests, their involvement, and their lack of distance ... In the present controversies each of the parties or camps seem to have construed a 'Freud' of its own." Needless to say, unless we have been persuaded by a muddle-headed relativism, not all "parties or camps" are equal. Freud and psychoanalysis make relativism a peculiar kind of cultural neurosis; we should avoid it unless ambiguity and ambivalence is turned into an ideal. Peter Loewenberg has a highly satisfying quote. "Whoever knows only one thing about Freud knows something wrong."[20] We are obligated, then, to both suspend anything we might "know" and then pursue a specific kind of inquiry that makes the attempt to see the force of convergences and how, together, each with their own sense, lead to a new way of seeing the depth of human beings and the meaning of a world.

Franz Rosensweig makes a proposal. Our own direction will make it possible to read his encouragement and relate it more specifically, and according to both Freud the individual and his ability to recognize a historical event of the highest importance (the Sinai testament – without the burden of its revelatory theology) and see its relevance for everyone, that is, universally.

> The state of the world today may force us to postpone many desirable things, not for a better day but for a better century. It could hardly be asserted that the great urgency of the present moment is to organize the science of Judaism [*Wissenschaft des Judentums*] or to prompt both Jews and non-Jews to the endless writing of books on Jewish subjects.[21]

Judaism will here be presented in such a way as to overcome that once disparaging term, psychoanalysis as a "Jewish science," and instead trace a history of perception from the Sinai to the origins of modern science and its method not so much as an epistemological problem, as it ordered its knowledge, but first and foremost as it self-consciously understood itself and its perception of a world. Our effort will be dedicated towards showing how the sensibility of Jewish consciousness to the image was shared by the methodology of science in terms of its observation – in Freud's case, as a physician and, more importantly, as both a scientist working in a laboratory and then discussing the symptoms of Anna O.'s illness. One of our digressions will attempt to connect the Biblical world of Moses and the Jews to an individual (Francis Bacon) who in his *Novum Organum* organized the possibility of a new kind of knowledge and did so, one way, by exposing the mendacity of four idols of the mind – the ones Freud confronted on several occasions, each with works on the nature of the tribe, the cave, the market-place, and the theatre.

One persistent problem has continued since the early days of psychoanalysis; the problems have been several and interconnected, beginning with psychoanalysis as a Jewish invention, a preoccupation that was hardly taken lightly, either by Freud or by those who exploited an ethnic fantasy for their own purposes. The issue of anti-Semitism will not be pursued here, at any time in Freud's life, as a student or, more seriously, after the *Anschluss*. Revisiting the intractable historical problem of anti-Semitism when discussing psychoanalysis will only be incidental to the project as a whole; rather than focusing on a certain conception of *Jewishness* – as ethnic and a matter of identity – another examination can be undertaken. David Herman believes that a majority of early biographers "downplayed the significance of Freud's Jewishness ... and the culture of antisemitism in the world in explaining the origins, nature, and practice of psychoanalysis."[22] My interpretation will not "downplay" Freud's Jewishness; but it will also not overdetermine one factor by misunderstanding its extent or minimizing its multi-dimensional connection with other historical developments. One way to imagine Freud's *culture*, which can be defined according to a word coined by a Stoic philosopher, comes down to understanding him and psychoanalysis in "its general European context" of classical antiquity[23] and as a *cosmopolitan* – which is an alternative to the very inaccurate *assimilationist*. The over-emphasis, by some, of his Jewish identity will be supplemented by a number of other significant experiences that, together, eventually led him to create psychoanalysis. The project ahead simply outlines four experiences based on distinct periods of his life – his culture, to begin with (which was Jewish *and* European) and then a number of life-forming experiences as an adult. Rosensweig's *Wissenschaft* is one among others.

The issue of ethnicity can, however, be treated as an inheritance among others. For as long as psychoanalysis was organized into a society of physicians, and then, lay-analysts, its standing in the scientific community has been an uncertain one. Up until the end, Freud never tired of arguing for its legitimacy as a scientific practice. One of my doubts can be expressed in the beginning and by being, on purpose, with purpose, *undecided* – which is not the same as ambivalent. *For Freud's sake*, some of my efforts will be dedicated to defending the scientific status of psychoanalysis, even though my position (as an analysand) needs no science whatsoever. On the contrary, and allowing myself one moment of polemic, psychoanalysis does not need scientific legitimacy because it transcends the limits of science and the age-old ideals of empiricism and "objectivity."

And yet, one has no difficulty in not only defining psychoanalysis as a science, it fulfils something much more ambitious and as first defined by Thomas Kuhn. A few selected comments from his classical work *The Structure of Scientific Revolutions* are enough.

The early developmental stages of most sciences have been characterized by continual competition between a number of distinct views of nature, each partially derived from, and roughly compatible with, the dictates of scientific observation and method. What differentiated these various schools was not only or another failure of method – they were all "scientific" – but what we shall come to call their incommensurable ways of seeing the world and of practicing science in it.[24]

The so-called "objectivity" of scientific observation is inseparable from "ways of seeing," our main preoccupation, for psychoanalysis, for us, as it influences perception and the nature of reality beyond the direction of the anatomists and physiologists of an age. Psychoanalysis, in the 21st century, no longer needs the approval or the legitimacy of science. According to Kuhn, psychoanalysis fulfills the obligation of being revolutionary because, in many ways, the acknowledged experts at the time (among them, Jean-Martin Charcot) in principle rejected anything that was considered "vitalist," a word discredited in order to be replaced by biological mechanisms. Kuhn continues, "Sometimes a normal problem, one that ought to be solved by known rules and procedures, resists the reiterated onslaught of the ablest members of the group within those competence it falls." No one, then or today, will say that hysteria is a "normal problem," in itself or as the subject of science, medicine, and neurology. It was observed and explained with the assumptions of an age. The physicalists had built more or less a consensus. So what made Freud (in more ways than the archaic heritage of his Judaism) open-minded enough to resist traditional explanations and professional assessments of his time? That one objective follows; and we preface only a few of the early episodes of Freud's life with an affirmation about psychoanalysis as a scientific revolution. There comes a time when, as Kuhn writes,

> the purpose of normal research fails to perform in the anticipated manner, revealing an anomaly that cannot, despite repeated effort, be aligned with professional expectations. In these and other ways besides, normal science repeatedly goes astray. And when it does – when, that is, the profession can no longer evade anomalies that subvert the existing tradition of scientific practice – then begins the extraordinary investigations that lead the profession at last to a new set of commitments, a new basis for the practice of science. The extraordinary episode in which the shift of professional commitments occurs are the ones known in this essay as scientific revolutions. They are the tradition-shattering complements to tradition-bound activity of normal science.

*A new basis for the practice of science.* Does psychoanalysis meet Kuhn's criteria, as seems to be the case, and in what ways was it a revolution as momentous as the ones Freud associated with the proper names of Copernicus (and, before him, Pythagoras) and Darwin? We are bound to revisit a relation since, as now seems more obvious, no consensus will be reached. None needs to be.²⁵ One fact we can all agree on: Freud was committed to scientific inquiry and remained so for his entire life. How *we respond* to his self-conception is a matter of interpretation. At the level of a transition in his experience and personal life, the time he spent in a laboratory doing minute research on aquatic specimens (using a microscope, which allowed him to think about a scientific instrument and its allegory of perception) left him with a certain ability to look and see beyond the visible appearance of the world. Can Freud be really defined as a "crypto-biologist," as does Frank Sulloway in his attempt to "bring both Freud and the history of psychoanalysis with the professional boundaries of the history of science."²⁶ The word "boundary" might be revealing enough for us to avoid; it echoes the limitations of groups – of which the scientific community is, necessarily, one. Our needs to set Freud and psychoanalysis within limits is an indication of some of our desires rather than a conceptual or historical reality. The evaluations are, in any event, so wide-ranging that the reader has no choice but to undertake the reading of Freud alone (to begin with) and come to one's own conclusion if he does, or does not, leave us a "scientific legacy."²⁷ He surely leaves us a legacy much more comprehensive than a scientific one and one that also includes his suspicions about the role of technological progress and scientism.

Our relationship to psychoanalysis – and to Freud over a lifetime of work – continues to be a mixed one, understandable more now when our knowledge of transferences and projections is unavoidable and so necessarily turned towards ourselves. The ongoing history has as many characteristics as there are individuals (analysts, analysands, scholars, academics) who perpetually return to Freud to trace origins to our present. All of them, together, will be incomplete since we are always trying to add more element to our understanding of how Freud *became*,²⁸ when and how. So we have all kinds of attempts, some that even go to the lengths of modifying Freud for contemporary sensibilities – as if our present deserved that much consideration and with the additional imperative of writing a "new" history of psychoanalysis, one with a "richer and more nuanced narrative."²⁹ Richer, more nuanced – or one more morally acceptable? It might ultimately be the case that, as Peter Rudnytsky writes, "each of us creates Freud in his or her image."³⁰ If so, then even before beginning *any* work on Freud and psychoanalysis it might be prudent to spend some time on ourselves and more extensively on the meaning of *image*, which is inseparable from our consciousness and our perception before seeing anything at all.

The many-sided influences on Freud's thinking as a whole reach one more decisive moment when his relationship with Breuer, and the manner of dealing with one patient, gives him the impetus away from the physicalism of his time and towards a perception of a depth-psychology that indicates how the self could be "split." How did his discussion with Breuer on the Anna O. case add one more element to his development that complemented a Jewish heritage and scientific knowledge, in a medical school, a laboratory, and a clinic? Beginning with the

"Preliminary Communication," though not published until 1893, gives us a sense of Freud's thinking about this one patient and how he understood a number of inter-related symptoms as well as the therapy defined, at the time, as cathartic. One later recollection is introduced to mark a difference. For us, the discovery of the transference is *not* the most important issue.

> The first difference between Breuer and myself came to light on a question concerning the finer psychical mechanism of hysteria. He gave preference to a theory which was still to some extent physiological, as one might say; he tried to explain the mental splitting in hysterical patients by the absence of communication between various mental states ('states of consciousness', as we called them at that time) ... I had taken the matter less scientifically; everywhere I seemed to discern motives and tendencies analogous to those of everyday life, and I looked upon psychical splitting itself.
>
> (SE 14:7)

How did Freud interpret the nature of Anna O.'s "psychical splitting" and long before his theory of an erotic transference? Her fragmentation was inseparable from her "disturbances of visions" (which were not, only, visual hallucinations but also ideations) and from what she termed her "private theatre." Freud understood the cathartic method to be much more than a kind of medical/psychotherapeutic "purgation." By turning to Aristotle's *Poetics* and tracing his concepts and placing them in the context of a neurotic imagination, we can introduce Freud's development during the time when he was working in a psychiatric clinic headed by Theodor Meynert and comparing the treatment of patients privately as opposed to an institution. At some indefinite, yet certain time, Freud made a connection that would establish one of the foundations of psychoanalysis; while we can acknowledge the centrality of the Oedipus Complex and its meaning for an individual in a family, his earlier reflections on tragedy for the understanding of neurotic acting-out would prepare him for the period of observation at the Salpêtrière in Paris.

In the section of the *Introductory Lectures on Psychoanalysis* called "The Sense of Symptoms," Freud writes, "Even before I went to Paris, Breuer told me about a case of hysteria which, between 1880 and 1882, he had treated in a peculiar manner which had allowed him to penetrate deeply into the causation and significance of hysterical symptoms" (SE 20:19). There are three points to emphasize: one, his knowledge *before* Paris, two, the invention of a particular treatment, and, three, his interpretation of Anna O.'s symptoms. A number of them will be traced as to their inter-relation and as examples of a general diagnosis. The diagnosis has been made, the effects of her condition recognized. "Two entirely distinct states of consciousness were present which alternated very frequently and without warning" (SE 2:24). *Two states of consciousness*. Once the condition was recognized, the experience had to be better understood. Anna O.'s ability to present her day-to-day experience in a form she called the "talking cure" was, in itself, a form of translation and a way for the immediacy of her perceptions to be analyzed. Her presentation allowed Freud to interpret a number of symptoms according to an emerging theory as well as an equally informative classical one. Once we complement the previous origins with his reflections on Anna O. we reach another turning point. The descriptions of her "severe disturbances of vision" (SE 2:22) were symptoms directly related to the projections of her psyche. One connection, if it did not occur to Freud *at the time*, would be added to his thinking (for reasons to be shown) in Paris. Before 1885–1886, however, he already sensed how the drama of Anna O.'s life and the cathartic method were inter-related, even if Breuer's own definition was one of chance rather than explicit intention. Returning to Aristotle's *Poetics* will add one more element to our understanding of a process that began with Breuer and developed even further in Paris. The tragic would, in the next decade, become one more foundation to psychoanalysis and one far more extensive than for the consequences of the Oedipus Complex in terms of a specifically familial dynamic.

As we move from the third to the final part of the study on the psychoanalysis of consciousness and perception by stressing the relationship of the psyche for the process of seeing, we can turn to Freud's experiences in Paris while observing the hysterical patients at the Salpêtrière. Analysts who have focused in particular on this one necessity have reminded us, time and again, of the role of the psyche in creating a distorted perception of reality and, consequently, an unsettled, and painful, relation with oneself. Julia Segal writes, "Phantasies make up the background to everything we do, think or feel: they determine our perceptions and in a sense *are* our perceptions."[31] The affirmation of a certain predicament could not be more important; because once we come to the realization that our unconscious (our phantasies, desires, drives) are often responsible for the "conscious" perception we see and experience every day, then psychoanalysis seems to be more relevant than ever in understanding the nature of human reality.

A dominant form of thought, in the third quarter of the 19th century, is equally true for us today; for that reason alone, Freud's life and thought in its beginnings needs to be revisited. He tells us that "the neurologists of that period had been brought up to have a high respect for chemico-physical and pathologico-anatomical facts ... and they seemed to have established an intimate and possibly exclusive connection between certain functions and particular parts of the brain." All in all, a remarkable statement – *for us* to think about much more than as a strictly historical problem. The return to Freud is at the same time a confrontation with *ourselves* and due to a very similar problem, one that ultimately comes down to a conception of the human and too-strictly defined according to a scientistic self-understanding. Whether we, too, are facing a scientistic self-conception cannot at all be excluded when we consider the influence of neurobiology and the persuasion of materialism, made even more determinate by technology. Whether the ends of "post-human" desires are neurotic and pathological remains to be seen. The back-and-forth will be a constant one in the project to come. A historical transference, between Freud and us as readers, will allow us to both follow some of his most formative experiences and compare them and, also, our own as we maintain the difference between consciousness and the brain. There will be a number of opportunities to read Freud and to see the nuances and subtleties of his statements. The Paris period is a transformative one and ultimately leads him to embark on his own personal direction.

In "A Short Account of Psychoanalysis," Freud takes us to Paris. From here, we will return to "the secrets of the neuroses" as he began to think about them.

> As late as 1885, when I was studying at the Salpêtrière, I found that people were content to account for hysterical paralyses by a formula which asserted that they were founded on slight functional disturbances of the same parts of the brain which, when they were severely damaged, led to the corresponding organic paralyses. Of course this lack of understanding affected the *treatment* of these pathological conditions as well.

The latter concern is hardly an incidental one. The "formula," especially considering its diagnosis of neurological disorders like Parkinson's disease (which Jean-Martin Charcot discovered along with other illnesses now common to us – like MLS) was a misleading one, theoretically, and for the therapeutic treatments of the ill, whether by a family physician or in a clinic as large as the Salpêtrière. Incidentally, the "Short Account" does not mention Charcot. Whatever the reason, this one article among many others that he wrote makes a definitive statement for our Introduction and for now setting down, in order, the principal themes of the project to come. As for Freud's period in Paris, his professional account of the experience (to his superiors in Vienna, some of whom had been responsible for the travel grant) gives us one sense of his personal impression of Charcot.

> One could see how, to begin with, he would stand undecided in the face of some new manifestation which was hard to interpret, one could follow the path along which he endeavoured to arrive at an understanding of it, one could study the way in which he took stock of difficulties and overcame them, and one could observe with surprise that he never grew tired of looking at the same phenomenon.
>
> (SE 1:10)

"New manifestation." The appearance of the nervous illness then called hysteria would become central to Freud's investigations – as they had since the case of Anna O. One more note from his report can be highlighted, for a number of reasons that will be related to Anna O.'s disturbances of vision and her private theatre. When Charcot gave lectures on his latest researches, "they produced the effect primarily by the constant references to the patients who were being demonstrated." The fantasies of the ur-patient of psychoanalysis, the appearances of the Salpêtrière hysterics on a medical stage, and, finally, how Freud understood

Aristotle's theory of tragedy, all converged to give him a new sense of the meaning of neurotic acting-out. The project to come attempts to bring together all of Freud's disparate experiences and how, over a period of time, he unified them as a way to move forward on his own, independently of major movements of the time and the individuals – like Charcot – who were then leaders in the field.

At the Salpêtrière and privy to the examination of hysterics by Jean-Martin Charcot, Freud came to initial conclusions that, when pursued more assiduously and over an extended period of time, led him to the creation of psychoanalysis – that is, a science of the psyche that was not grounded in either anatomy or heredity, neither a malady with physiological causes nor a familial biology. As he would soon discover, neurotic disorders are not inherited, biologically, genetically, from a family – though they can, indeed, be caused in part by the experiences of family life, which is to say, our human relationships, the closest and therefore the more fraught with emotional conflicts and complications. Paris has been chosen as a turning point for Freud because the specific experiences he had, and what he witnessed, in terms of the theatrical presentation of hysterics, were looked at by him with a different eye, a perception he had developed due to three fundamental experiences of his life – culturally as a Jew, working in the laboratory and looking under a microscope, and learning about Josef Breuer's cathartic method. In many ways, the study to follow can begin with the sense of Freud's psychoanalysis of neurotic perceptions and the dynamic of human consciousness; at the same time, we are going to also reflect on Freud, the individual, and trace how foundational experiences, when creatively understood and inter-connected, could engender entirely different ways of thinking both about neurotic patients and human beings as such. At the Salpêtrière, Freud experienced a wide array of individuals suffering from "psychical devastation." How he personally began thinking about their conditions and how they perceived themselves, others, and the world would mark one of his imminent discoveries. "The influences of unconscious forces on self-perception may be fruitfully studied in those patients who employ defensive altered states of consciousness because of the preponderance of periodic irruptions of disassociated, unconscious aspects of the self."[32] Freud taught himself how to recognize how "altered states of consciousness," deep, inaccessible, unconscious, could have the most profound effect on both self-perception and the perception of reality, the two criss-crossing to such an extent that reality could easily be transformed into a perpetual reconfirmation of a distorted world.

The conclusion that "Charcot turned him in a new direction"[33] after his experience in Paris will be questioned and judged to be misleading. If we return to the experience between 1880 and 1882 when Josef Breuer was treating Anna O., and then to his discussion with Freud at the same time as the physician-trained scientist and researcher was working as an intern in Theodor Meyner's clinic, an (almost) irreconcilable conflict was already apparent to him. Anatomy and physiology could not explain all the symptoms of Anna O.'s illness, whether we call it hysteria, conversion disorder, or anything else; a diagnosis, before any category, depends on being able to understand the nature of her symptoms. Freud's period in Paris was a formative one. Charcot did not, for all his influence, fundamentally alter Freud's own direction, which had been developing independently and with a number of directions. The theatrical display of patients at the Salpêtrière gave Freud the opportunity to think about hysterics as a living image and as embodiments of what Anna O. called her private theatre. How he then conceptualized the overly dramatized lives of hysterics with Aristotle's theory of tragedy in the *Poetics* was a step no one had taken before him.

At the end of our Introduction, and with lingering doubts (for example, about a supposed crisis in psychoanalysis) we can extend an earlier concern with a more general question – which, apparently, still needs to be asked. "What is psychoanalysis?"[34] No answer is forthcoming, not summarily in any case. Still, if at the end of the first quarter of the 21st century we are obliged to turn to Freud's writing as an origin, then one life and a biography will be, in part, one kind of access. The ongoing process was expressed by Freud in yet another late writing, "Analysis Terminable and Interminable." "The sharper our eye grows" (SE 23:243). The expression, with one metaphorical sense, will be more completely presented over the length of the project to come on psychoanalysis as the practice of enhancing consciousness and perception once the intrusions of the unconscious were sufficiently recognized and either diverted, converted, or eliminated depending on the therapeutic abilities of the individual. One seemingly random expression from one of the last papers written by Freud specifically on technique can both look ahead to the awareness of the interminability of psychoanalytic knowledge and, for the purpose of the upcoming project, take us back to his *Bildung*, the most accurate term for his early education. His experiences were multiple. They were cultural and scientific, personal and professional. One psychoanalytic ideal was already a motivation for him long before he began his own life as a therapist. How did Freud contribute to the "sharpening of our eyes" and how was the commonplace saying supported by a lifetime of analytic work and writing? Any attempt to answer the question comprehensively does so by returning to his inheritance of a Jewish culture, his university studies in medicine, science, and psychiatry, his association with Breuer and the cathartic method he developed with Anna O., and the observation of patients in a Paris hospital. Biographies have covered all of the most important facts; there are, as can be expected from a life and mind as complex as Freud's, other, less noted remnants that, when examined together, can give us one more piece towards our understanding of the creation and development of psychoanalysis during the formative period. In terms of laying out the development of Freud's understanding of psychological illness, the four distinct themes of the study are intended to be, as much as possible, overlapping; because instead of emphasizing *one* influence, all of them will be inter-related to a large degree. After the decisive period studying the nature of hysteria at the Salpêtrière and convinced of his own intuition as to the non-physiological causes of the ailment, his first of many confrontations with traditional assumptions in the truth of science will be deliberated and changed. They were not radically new. Freud had intimations of his own long before the decisive year of 1885–1886. His stay in Paris deserves renewed attention, both for the experience in itself and for being a culmination. In order for Freud to have reached his insights – on hysteria as a psychical debility instead of a hereditary one, an emphasis had to be completely altered, from the biological and familial to a more personal, more interior process that determined how any neurotic became bound to their symptoms. A note of uncertainty, or perhaps a resignation when it came to our desire to believe in absolute categories, can set us towards the project and its start with Judaism and science. A note from "The Question of Lay Analysis" has more than one reason for us.

> It will be objected at this point that whether psycho-analysis, regarded as a science, is a subdivision or medicine or of psychology is a purely academic question, and of no practical interest. The real point at issue, it will be said, is a different one, namely the application of analysis to the treatment of patients ... I only want to be assured that the therapy will not destroy the science.
> (SE 20:254)

Freud's worry now seems unfounded. Science, medicine, psychotherapy: could any of them be separated in the history of psychoanalysis even before its beginnings? Freud's thinking would only extend itself to virtually the whole history of culture as such, each time never forgetting or forsaking his first interests, beginning with the conscious transference of a Jewish archaic heritage.

An Introduction allows us to anticipate the themes of the project and to begin a process of selection, downplaying some, emphasizing others. Mikita Brottman tells us that psychoanalysis has had "a shaky relationship with academia and a particularly fraught and anxious connection to science."[35] As to the former, Freud almost never mentioned "academia." The earlier reference to psychoanalysis in (or out of) the university was clear enough. Our times, however, make this one relationship, especially critical theory academics, unavoidable; and so, highlighting the history of mental illness, as a malady and in its institutional context, will be part of the discussion to come.

The Introduction has set out to anticipate the main themes of the project and their inter-relationship for Freud's development from the time he was a young, seventeen-year-old student in 1873 to the spring of 1886 when he returns from Paris to open his private practice. The previously mentioned chronology cannot hope to adequately understand Freud's thinking, which was anything but linear and reflected the intricacies of the psyche. Nor can we, finally, accept the historicist fallacy of "context." Steven Beller believes that

> It is from the results in that domain – the context both of Vienna 1900 and of Jewish Vienna – that Freud's explorations can begin to be properly understood and evaluated. They will eventually help us to answer another question about

psychoanalysis: at a time when psychoanalysis is increasingly beleaguered as being unscientific or no longer of theoretical worth, how valid does it remain?[36]

An answer will not be withheld; there will be more than a few. The validity of psychoanalysis and the "contexts" (plural) and, more importantly, Freud himself and how a number of experiences were, eventually, recognized for their complex connections, ultimately made it possible to create psychoanalysis. No single origin can explain the complexity of Freud's thinking as an individual; no context can easily contain him, a strictly historical one least of all. The assertion is insufficient; a brief examination of only a few of the cultural and intellectual transitions in his life can, one hopes by the end, confirm an argument or, at least, renew our interminable questions. One uncommon psychoanalyst, Neville Symington, writes: "a piece of knowledge may not be understood and its significance allowed to startle the mind unless it is within a pattern of understanding to which it is related."[37] How Freud taught us to think beyond a "pattern of understanding" should go some way to recognizing the particularity of a human characteristic he valued as highly as freedom, intelligence and its contribution to the advancement of human thought and life. If we were to read Freud's writing *back to him*, we could certainly do worse than to use a memorable phrase by Leo Strauss: "It is our duty as scholars and perhaps our duty as human beings to combine open-mindedness with intransigence."[38] Are there any who exceeded Freud in this double duty? As for us, thinking about our convictions, as opposed to intransigence, might be a better reflection of how (and how long it took) to come to our affinity to Freud personally and to psychoanalysis. Following Freud in the earliest phase of his life, education, and thinking will present some of the most important, and enduring, aspects of his *Bildung*, beginning with an archaic heritage that will be interpreted, more analytically, as a form of *Übertragung*, a transference that will be trans-historical and as effective today as during *any time* in the past.

## Notes

1. Steiner, John. *Psychic Retreats: Pathological Organizations in Psychotic, Neurotic and Borderline Patients*. London: Routledge, 1993, 54.
2. Robbins, Michael. "The Primary Process: Freud's Profound yet Neglected Contribution to the Psychology of Consciousness," 186–197 *Psychoanalytic Inquiry* 38 (3), 2018, 187.
3. The theme of perception and consciousness could have led to a more academic (or, more specifically, philosophical) study on the relationship between phenomenology and psychoanalysis. In *Psychoanalysis in a New Light* (Cambridge: Cambridge University Press), Gunnar Karlsson writes: "there is common ground of values between them in order for psychoanalysis to benefit from taking part in phenomenological reflection," 20. However productive such a study may be, psychoanalysis does not actually need any "benefit" from phenomenology at all since it has always been guided by an interest, and then a therapeutic concern, in the dynamics of consciousness and its relation to the perception of the normal and the pathological. Our period is in any case well prior to the definitive beginning of modern phenomenology in the work of Edmund Husserl and the publication of the two-volume *Logical Investigations* in 1900–1901. The date, for

a number of reasons, is not like any other. It also marks the publication – in November 1899 – of Freud's *The Interpretation of Dreams*. That Freud and Husserl were both students of Franz Brentano at the University of Vienna is a connection that has often been mentioned. Others who have pursued the thematic relation include David Snelling in *Philosophy, Psychoanalysis and the Origin of Meaning: Pre-Reflective Intentionality in the Psychoanalytic View of the Mind*. London: Routledge, 2017.
4 Mace, C.J. "Hysterical Conversion: I: A History," 369–377 *British Journal of Psychiatry* 161, 1992, 372.
5 Ffytche, Matt. *The Foundation of the Unconscious: Schelling, Freud, and the Birth of the Modern Psyche*. Cambridge: Cambridge University Press, 2011.
6 Fine, Reuben. *The Development of Freud's Thought*. New York: Jason Aronson, Inc., 1973, vii. Commenting on the latter assessment is misguided for more reason than one; the accurate title is *Inhibitions, Symptoms, and Anxiety*. No one, today, would call this his last major work. As for the first quote, on beginnings, 1886 turns out (for us) to be one kind of *end* and so returns us to another, much earlier beginning.
7 Cotti, Patrica. "Towards a New Historiography of Psychoanalysis: In Defense of Psychoanalysis as a Science – An Essay on George Makari's *Revolution in Mind*," 133–146 *Psychoanalysis and History* 14 (1), 2012.
8 Schermer, Victor L. *Meaning, Mind, and Self-Transformation: Psychoanalytic Interpretations and the Interpretation of Psychoanalysis*. London: Karnac, 2014.
9 See *Freud, the Contemporary Super-Ego, and Western Morality*. London: Routledge, 2023.
10 Zaretsky, Eli. *Secrets of the Soul: A Social and Cultural History of Psychoanalysis*. New York: Alfred A. Knopf, 2004, 332.
11 Schneider, Stanley and Joseph H. Berke. "Freud's Meeting with Rabbi Alexander Safran," 1–15 *Psychoanalysis and History* 12 (1), 2010, 8.
12 The topic has been endlessly presented and debated. One article can be cited for its question. Michael P. Donner's writing is titled: "Is Psychoanalysis a Jewish Science? Why Do You Ask?" *Psycritiques*, 55 (40), 2010. Both questions could be answered – the latter with too many possibilities. The first, however, deserves attention. At the risk of being evasive, the answer is best left up to the reader. My own response will be demonstrated in the whole.
13 Golan, Ruth. *Loving Psychoanalysis: Looking at Culture with Freud and Lacan*. London: Routledge, 2006, xii–xiii.
14 Bielik-Robson, Agata. "Psychoanalysis as Tovat Hayim: In Promise Salvation," 55–70 *European Judaism* 55 (1), Mar, 2022.
15 Quinodoz, Jean-Michel. *Reading Freud: A Chronological Exploration of Freud's Writings*. Tr. David Alcorn. London: Routledge, 2005.
16 Levenson, Edgar A. *The Fallacy of Understanding and the Ambiguity of Change*. Hillsdale N.J.: Routledge, 2005, 8.
17 Ellenberger, Henri F. *The Discovery of the Unconscious: The History and Evolution of Dynamic Psychiatry*. New York: Basic Books, 1970.
18 Whitebook, Joel. *Freud An Intellectual Biography*. Cambridge: Cambridge University Press, 2007, 16.
19 Falzeder, Ernst. *Psychoanalytic Filiations: Mapping the Psychoanalytic Movement*. London: Routledge, 2015, 149 and 172.
20 Loewenberg, Peter. *Fantasy and Reality in History*. Oxford: Oxford University Press, 1995, 33. The quote comes from the chapter on "Freud's Psychosocial Identity."
21 Rosenzweig, Franz. *On Jewish Learning*. Ed. N.N. Glatzer. New York: Schocken Books, 1955, 55.
22 Herman, David. "Psychoanalysis, Jews and History," 8697 *European Judaism* 55 (1), Mar, 2022, 90–91.

23 Armstrong, Richard H. *A Compulsion for Antiquity: Freud and the Ancient World*. Ithaca: Cornell University Press, 2005.
24 Kuhn, Thomas. *The Structure of Scientific Revolutions*. Second Edition. Chicago: The University of Chicago Press, 1970, 4.
25 Petocz, Agnes. "The Scientific Status of Psychoanalysis Revisited," 145. *Philosophy, Science, and Psychoanalysis: A Critical Meeting*. Ed. Simon Boag, Linda A.W. Brakel, Vesa Talvitie. London: Routledge, 2015.
26 Sulloway, Frank J. *Freud, Biologist of the Mind: Beyond the Psychoanalytic Legend*. Cambridge, Mass.: Harvard University Press, 1979, 1.
27 Westen, Drew. "The Scientific Legacy of Sigmund Freud: Toward a Psychodynamically Informed Psychological Science," 333–371 *Psychological Bulletin* 124 (3), 1998.
28 Phillips, Adam. *Becoming Freud: The Making of a Psychoanalyst*. New Haven: Yale University Press, 2014.
29 Shapira, Michal. "The New History of Psychoanalysis: Towards a Richer and More Nuanced Narrative," 227–231 *Modern Intellectual History* 17(1), 2020.
30 Rudnytsky, Peter L. *Rescuing Psychoanalysis from Freud and other Essays on Re-vision*. London: Karnac, 2011, 3.
31 Segal, Julia. *Phantasy in Everyday Life: A Psychoanalytic Approach to Understanding Ourselves*. London: Karnac, 1995, 22.
32 Brenner, Ian. *Dark Matters: Exploring the Reality of Psychic Destitution*. London: Karnac, 2014, 58.
33 Schorske, Carl. E. "Freud: The Psychoarchaeology of Civilizations," 5–24 *The Cambridge Companion to Freud*. Ed. Jerome Neu. Cambridge: Cambridge University Press, 1991, 13.
34 The question is posed by Richard D. Chessick's *The Future of Psychoanalysis*. Albany: SUNY Press, 2007.
35 Brottman, Mikita. *Phantoms of the Clinic: Thought-Transference to Projective Identification*. London: Routledge, 2011, xii.
36 Beller, Steven. "Solving Riddles: Freud, Vienna and the Historiography of Madness," 27–42 *Journeys into Madness: Mapping Mental Illness in the Austro-Hungarian Empire*. Ed. Gemma Blackshaw and Sabine Wieber. New York: Berghahn Books, 2012, 28.
37 Symington, Neville. *A Healing Conversation: How Healing Happens*. London: Routledge, 2006, 12.
38 Strauss, Leo. *Jewish Philosophy and the Crisis of Modernity: Essays and Lectures in Modern Jewish Thought*. Albany: SUNY, 1997, 285.

# Chapter 1

# Jewish Transferences

> Among the precepts of the Moses religion there is one that is of greater importance than appears to begin with. This is the prohibitions against making an image of God ... For it meant that a sensory perception was given second place to what may be called an abstract idea – triumph of intellectuality over sensuality.
>
> *(Moses and Monotheism)*

## Freud's Archaic Heritage

Freud's historical, cultural, and intellectual relationship to Judaism has been an inseparable aspect of our attempts to understand his personal "formation," to use both a relevant German term (*Bildung*) and a more esoteric one in our considerations of the *Sefer Yetzirah* (the "Book of Formation" – or "Creation"), a title whose ambiguity does not present a dilemma of interpretation but rather an acceptance of its wide range of meanings, including the divine/human relation as contemplated by the kabbalists as necessary towards our sense of "repair." Any thinking about Freud's own individual development and *formal* education in medicine, scientific research, and 19th-century neurology is also a reflection of psychoanalysis and its conception of the nature of human being, individually and socially – which takes us immediately to areas that will be highlighted in this opening on Jewish themes as transferences and his relationship to an inheritance, in general and across civilizations, and then a more focused set of personal interests.

While retaining a concept of limits, our primary themes of a cultural transference and inheritance will include the Hebrew language, the reading and interpretation of the Torah and, finally, the significance (for Freud personally, as a matter of identification) of Moses the man and the individual who was chosen to be the receiver of a revelation – a perception of an event that for psychoanalysis occurs as an experience in and of the world without any metaphysical origins. Psychical revelations are, in principle, equally binding; the prototypical one, dreaming, later came to be defining and, for one reason, according to the manifest/latent distinction, the seen and the disguised. The examination of Freud's Jewish identity, scholarly and otherwise, as well as the problem of psychoanalysis as a "Jewish science," has been part of its history, in its inception and later at a particular historical period

DOI: 10.4324/9781003664154-2

during the writing of the first two essays of *Moses and Monotheism* and the social and political realities for the Jewish people in the 1930's and after. These remain central for one kind of analysis in order to understand anti-Semitism, historically and at a particularly grave time; there are others that will be, for us, more informative, and more significant, in our ongoing attempts to understand Freud as an individual and then psychoanalysis as an original creation in accordance with an access to interior depths, for their inter-relationships and effects.

The opening of Freud's third essay, written in 1938, should be heard for our benefit and for a modern predicament. "We are living in a specially remarkable period, we find to our astonishment that progress has allied itself with barbarism" (SE 23:54). To understand him, within the strict closure of a historical context, deprives us of analyzing ourselves and how *our* barbarism may be precisely intertwined with a perverse sense of "progress." The idolatry of "graven images," in the Sinai at an indeterminate time, remains perhaps even more relevant in our contemporary situation and so makes psychoanalysis essential to our self-understanding in the 21st century. Adding scientific and, more specifically, biological concepts – for example, phylogenesis and ontogenesis – prepares us for a connection between the intellectual disciplines of Judaism and a conception of science that will be examined from a number of perspectives: the medical in a university, the experimental in a laboratory, and the neurological in a clinic – to mention but three and still without being restricted by *bios* as one conception of life, of the body and the psyche. An archaic heritage is also inseparable from the history of science since its origins and according to disciplines, such as biology, and then theories of heredity and degeneration – the latter defined by Freud as a *psychical regression*. Biological heredity, cultural heritage; they are effectively historical and still split as decisively as consciousness. Eric Smadja stresses one interpretation. "For Freud, the notion of archaic heritage seems to represent an agent of liaison between phylogenesis and ontogenesis."[1] How so will have to be addressed and in ways that extend beyond the original grounds of such a distinction – which was biological and according to the definitions invented by Ernst Haeckel, the German scientist who became one of the world's foremost exponents of Darwinism and influenced more than a generation of researchers, including Freud's teachers.[2] The idea of a "liaison" serves our purpose since Freud's personal relationship to both Judaism *and* science will be constant in tracing the specific period of our attention. Freud's archaic heritage, defined explicitly as such in *Moses and Monotheism*, has a long and complex history. The transferences are linear (from/to) and dynamic when Freud becomes its specific recipient. There are, in effect, two strands of an archaic heritage.

> It contains in certain [innate] dispositions such as are characteristics of all living organisms: in the capacity and tendency, that is, to enter particular lines of development and to react in a particular manner to certain excitations, impressions and stimuli. Since experience shows that there are distinctions in his respect between individuals and the human species, the archaic heritage must

include these distinctions; they represent what we as recognize the *constitutional* factor in the individual.

(SE 23:98)

The theory, as presented here, involves us in several issues: one, the biology of inheritance as formulated by Haeckel, a cultural inheritance as witnessed in the history of Judaism and, for us who are attempting to understand Freud's formation, a certain constitution (or, better, character) and the essential mystery of how an individual *forms himself* from all the resources available to him, including ones that are ineffable and hard to either identify or quantify.

Given the choices to be made, one emphasis can be stated at the outset: despite the working concept of the phylogeny/ontogeny relation as conceived by the science of biology, another can act (for us) as a better substitute since it is culturally more deliberate. The biological is not negated; nor can it be. The ontogenetic may be a recapitulation of the phylogenetic; one continuity, at the biological level and according to the genealogy of generations, however, does not compare with another kind of inheritance and then its multi-faceted interpretation as worked out, consciously, by individuals. The complexity of Freud's *Übertragung*, as both a transference and a transmission, is a dynamic and layered one; the historical and the conceptual overlap, more so when the fact of "constitution" is analyzed. In "The Dynamics of Transference," he writes, "One might venture to regard constitution itself as a precipitate from the accidental effects produced on the endless, long chain of our ancestors" (SE 12:99).

We are, at this one starting point, driven to a side and a preference, though not at all towards an either/or. The conflict and controversy is a well-known one in the endless debate between the sciences – "hard" or "human," which, parenthetically, the German *Wissenschaft* does not share, even if preceded by *Natur*. The American philosopher Adrian Johnston is right to point out how Freud "repeatedly appeals to a phylogenetic "archaic heritage,"[3] – to again re-quote Freud's own words – but how we interpret the meaning of such a reality is not at all certain until an examination is carried out that suspends immediate judgements of belief or conviction. Johnston's neurobiological interests, alone and with a co-author (Catherine Malabou) have attempted to establish relatively new connections.[4] How pertinent they are will be determined and by anyone interested in comparing any affinity between psychoanalysis and neurobiology. Here, insofar as a selected few foundations of psychoanalysis are chosen, there will be none at all.

For us, the history of biology and culture diverge to a qualitative degree, as they will for Freud when the physicalist direction of 19th-century science encounters nothing less than a form of writing prior to the emerging sense of the natural world, in its history and conception. How Judaism and science intersect, for Freud, will require details from his cultural inheritances as well as his prolonged period of study at the University of Vienna beginning in 1873 and extending until his trip to Paris in 1885. For the moment, the transference comes first; and it does so from the ancient world that is not, in essence, past but remains effective as a remnant within *consciousness*. Jacob Neusner mentions one of our orientations. "Philosophy proved uniquely important to Jews living in close contact with other cultures and traditions."[5] The statement, true for the classical and Hellenistic world, for example, was no less true in the 19th century. Freud's own relationship to the *discipline* of philosophy or to the human sciences more generally, did not prevent him from developing a unique contribution to humanistic thought and, in particular, a profound *metaphysical* reflection on human reality that, in one writing, provides the one distinct reference to Immanuel Kant explicitly for the nature of consciousness. As soon as Freud tells us that "portions of the ego are unconscious," (SE 23:96) our previous complacency about perception and reality is forever unsettled. Kant's Enlightenment principle, "dare to know," becomes *more necessary* with Freud and much more extensive since it expands well beyond the rational, the cognitive, or the epistemological.

The assessment of Jewish education in the classical world, whether the place is Babylon or in Jerusalem during its Hellenistic, Roman, or Christian phases, was no less important for someone like Freud; he did not study Judaism as a theological but rather for its "intellectual forces – forces, that is, which cannot be grasped by the senses (particularly by the sight) but which none the less produce undoubted and indeed extremely powerful effects" (SE 23:114). These forces, or drives, were part of his early pursuit and essential to early questions – the ones that were already present in him as a Gymnasium student and where Samuel Hammerschlag, the librarian of the Jewish community library in Vienna, was one of his teachers.[6] One question, on Freud's Jewish identity, will be part of a prudent inquiry. There are, for some, many reasons to insist on his "Jewishness." The extent is no small matter and can easily lead to a fixation rather than the need to think of interpretation and overdetermination together. *One* interpretation, at the outset, can be mentioned; how persuasive the argument is can only be assessed at the end. David Herman believes that early biographers, for example, Ernest Jones, "downplayed the significance of Freud's Jewishness." The contentious point can be disputed in principle; reasons were given or rationalized, depending on the objectives. Freud acknowledged his heritage; and yet one can understand, for a number of reasons (for one, not to be, simply, categorized with the complacent limits of others) his own attitude.

Arnold Richards *asks a question*. "Just what did it mean to Freud that psychoanalysis was founded by a Jew?"[7] One answer, presuming to be conclusive, can never suffice. "The science that psychoanalysis became was therefore founded on personal identity, and for Freud the personal identity is deeply rooted in Judaism."[8] Herman's summary should not immediately persuade us. Others are more emphatic. "The culture of antisemitism in the world can explain the origins, nature, and practice of psychoanalysis."[9] The assertion is overstated; to be true, that would present Freud as essentially driven by resentment and the creation of psychoanalysis as a reactive endeavour to a particular historical situation. Turning away from one of our 20th-century obsessions – identity as conceived by social and political theory – Freud presents us with nuances that do not easily fit into our modern desires, or our ready-made assumptions that have often been all-too moral. Does it not seem as if *our* projections have never been more insistent? Shifting to another historical period, not one among others for Freud, allows us to establish another element of an archaic heritage.

Returning to one of the most transformative events in the history of Judaism, Freud also tells us about his own intellectual roots and his lifelong commitment to Judaism if not its *theology*. He writes:

> The Jews retained their intellectual interests. The nation's political misfortunes taught it to value at its true worth the one possession that remained to it – its literature. Immediately after the destruction of the Temple in Jerusalem by Titus, the Rabbi Jochanan ben Zakkai asked permission to open the first Torah school in Jabneh. From that time on, the Holy Writ and intellectual concern with it were what held the scattered people together.
> 
> (SE 23:115)

Bringing together "the Holy Writ and intellectual concern" we have Freud, near the end of his life, summing up one of the outstanding characteristics of the Jewish people and, we should not ignore, himself and his cultural formation as a *Jewish-European* and, to use a much more appropriate word than assimilation, *cosmopolitan*. The hyphen can remain even if we turn the first into European Jew and think about the transference between one and the other. Freud made sure to highlight a historical event, to be traced back to Sinai – "the triumph of intellectuality over sensuality" – and then a reminder for anyone stuck in a historicist frame.

> This may not seem obvious at first sight, and before it can carry conviction we must recall other processes of the same character in the development of human civilization ... The new realm of intellectuality was opened up, in which ideas, memories and inferences become decisive in contrast to the lower psychical activity which had direct perceptions by the sense-organs as its content. This was unquestionably one of the most important stages on the path to hominization.
> 
> (SE 23:113)

"The path to hominization." Its universality gives us the opportunity, before our *decision*, if there are to be any, to pay attention to Freud's thinking, in his present and historical recollection.

Any reference to Freud's Jewishness has to be more than matter-of-fact, of birth and family and identity. "Of his birthplace," Robert Kaplan writes in a short article on Freud's family, "there was a vigorous intellectual attitude to the Torah, epitomized by the famous yeshivot of the region."[10] The claim may be factually true; its meaning for Freud can be asserted, with qualifications. To understand only some aspects of his life around this issue, other avenues are also necessary: his individual biography, a more all-encompassing archaic heritage, and the many-sided consequences of him as a founder of a psychotherapeutic culture. The connection has sometimes been overstated; patterns are noticeable when they are personal.

> Psychoanalysis, in some respects like the Jewish tradition from which it emerged, represents a body of thoughts about man's relation to himself and to others and places a great value on the influence of memory, narrative, and history in creating meaning within the dyadic relationship of analyst and patient.[11]

Surely *a* "tradition" extends from the ancient world to the modern, with a number of historical eras (like the ancient Greeks, the Enlightenment, or German romanticism) that also allowed psychoanalysis to be invented. To concentrate, here, on the Jewish is but one of the many origins which can be followed. Our relationship – that is, *our transferences* – are just as important; however multi-dimensional they are, decisions will be unavoidably made. They are inevitable in a scholarly context. "Psychoanalysis, it might be said, owes its hybrid character in the history of Western thought to its continuation of the Jewish exegetic tradition."[12] It *might* be said. The hesitation leaves us with other considerations. While one fully agrees with the idea of psychoanalysis being "hybrid," there will be other facets of equal importance and on the way towards identifying not so much psychoanalysis, but one way to understand Freud's individual creativity and, equally as important, the substance of his character. To read, interpret, and to recognize the distinction between a literal appearance and an allegorical meaning, was present as an attitude in Freud and moved him across disciplines and experiences, from his university studies in medicine, science, and laboratory research, to the closeness of a depth-psychology that no contemporary theory of heredity could contain.

The many-sided inquiry into Freud's individual formation, in ways that are more elaborate than the *facts* of his identity, moves us from one of his historical markers towards a number of factors that are much more personal, more individual, and more intellectual. A *reader* has a reminder for us as we reflect on a personal Jewishness, even if we can also suspend the confidence of saying, about Freud, "more than he knew." The interpretative obligation is more pronounced than usual since, at the outset, how we understand Freud's Jewishness as well as his self-conscious independence from religion will be central in first setting out some of the foundations of psychoanalysis. It has always seemed to me highly precarious to point out that we know (or think we do) more than Freud knew about himself. Our present has become overly confident, to the point of narcissistic self-congratulations, about our perception of the past; nothing appears easier today than making moral judgements about individuals or history as a whole and from the vantage point of the present. Our present is no apex. Since Freud in part invented the art of demystification, we are in a collaborative if not, always, a dependent state. Harold Bloom writes, "Few questions of spiritual or intellectual history are as vexed as the

Jewishness of Freud. It mystified Freud, more than he knew, and we go on weakly misreading it."[13] Before trying to decide what Freud did not know (about himself), it might be more prudent to analyze ourselves first and see how we have misread and misunderstood him and, first, ourselves no matter how sophisticated our hermeneutics happen to be. Many have done so wilfully. Our main concern as we turn to a number of cumulative experiences in Freud's life and thinking involves an attempt to unify them, even as they might seem, at first glance, irreconcilable – like the relationship between Judaism and science or, more specifically, how the Jewish sensibility to the image, idolatry, and perception was essential to the emergence of modernity and science. Despite the inter-relationship of our first Jewish themes, and in an order that can certainly be rearranged, the ones that are personal should be first in priority. The consequences of an archaic heritage are more difficult, more varied, and involve us in a distinct relationship between the meaning of transference in a way that is independent of the analytic situation and brings us into contact with his idea of the psyche and history. History is also, if not primarily, psychical. Quite a few commentators have overextended themselves. When they presume to tell us about *Freud's unconscious*, the results are going to be debatable, at best.

Some have been tempted to *analyze Freud*: his individuality can certainly be looked at from a number of perspectives and with varying degrees of accuracy. Being circumspect, most especially when indulging in "wild" analysis, should be a requirement, whether one has joined the legions of detractors, or if one is sympathetic and something more, an analysand, for example. Declarations can be made; they are not always close to the truth or, more importantly, familiar enough with Freud to able to go beyond the obvious category of identity. What do we make, for example, of "Freud's Jewish unconscious"[14] and what can it possibly mean? One response to Jill Salberg's argument can be examined. "Surrounded by anti-Semitism, Freud's attitudes towards his Jewish identity was deeply ambivalent."[15] The analysis is *critical*; but is it accurate? Was he "ambivalent" about his Jewishness as a consequence of anti-Semitism? The connection is not an obvious one.

One soon and inevitably notices one strain of thought whenever Freud appears *in the consciousness of others*; to be enigmatic and to reference another great Jewish thinker, he appears in a mirror enigmatically. He is "covert," "hidden," "submerged," as if the figure himself became representative of the enigmatic psyche in need of being discovered. "A submerged Jewish tradition secretly influences, perhaps even unconsciously steers Freud's work."[16] There is no need, at all, to invoke the "submerged" or the unconscious. Three references, thus far, on an unconscious element in Freud personally or psychoanalysis as a theory and practice had better be quite clear about the parameters of such an inquiry. Doing Freud one better, unconsciously, is no easy task; it does require some self-confidence or recklessness and, at times, something worse when his critics *expose themselves*. There is more of them in the mirror than Freud. He would most probably demand some self-accounting when extreme situations are relied upon and motivations disavowed. In the case of Janine Chasseguet-Smirgel, no ordinary psychoanalytic writer,[17] she presents us with a problem and then, for each of us, a responsibility. "Generally speaking, there is ample material in his works demonstrating Freud's fidelity to his Jewish heritage. Yet one can point to other passages seemingly indicating an unconscious desire to deny his Jewishness."[18] To support or reject the claim – above all, of an "unconscious desire" – one would have to be thorough in a way that is out of reach; still, that would not be enough, not if our understanding of Freud's sympathies are analyzed closely, as they will when Moses the man becomes our focus. Psycho-speculations have been common; when Freud's "personal myth" of Moses is presented as "the disguised gratification of some unconscious wish,"[19] turning to *Moses and Monotheism*, most especially the third and final part, takes our interpretation as close to the origins as possible. Finally, we have a kind of summary and "the chiefly unconscious forces which shaped the formulation of a 'Jewish science' of the mind."[20] Any analysis of the unconscious kind will be suspended, thematically, to ensure that the Jewish and many other influences are considered together. Judaism *and* science will, in the project as a whole, be consistently presented. One more response can be stated here, in this case due to an argument made by co-editors; they are highly critical of one idea that should, first, not be misconstrued and, second, so easily dismissed. "Cosmopolitanism and its sister concept, nomadism, have taken on quite different meanings when their referent is the Jews."[21] But what if Freud actually saw himself as *cosmopolitan* – a word that, for me, has no "referent" or negative association to Jewish "nomadism" since its inventor was a Stoic philosopher. My preference for Freud as a conscious cosmopolitan is preferable to the inaccurate "assimilated." Acculturation is more acceptable as long as we understand the concept as Freud did. The idea of Freud as a European Jew can be repeated. Why would anyone deny the significant accomplishments of a German and European culture and the highly creative transference in the history of Judaism? So much for Freud's unconscious as others see it. What does *he* say?

In order to present instances of Freud's own declaration about himself that are, on the face of it, relatively uncomplicated, we can turn to three examples – beginning again with *An Autobiographical Study*. His method should not be overlooked. He calls it a "new proportion." What he implies, also, by "*combination*" should not be self-evident. His abilities to internalize and then process divergent ideas was, after all, one aspect of his outstanding intellectual work, both in terms of a discipline and himself.

> I must endeavour to construct a narrative in which the subjective and objective attitudes, biographical and historical interests, are combined in a new proportion. I was born on May 6th, 1856, at Freiberg in Moravia, a small town in what is now Czechoslovakia. My parents were Jews, and I have remained a Jew myself.
> (SE 20:7)

*I have remained a Jew myself.* What are we to make of his declaration in 1924 and during a decade of concentrated work on society and politics? Before we fall back on our traditional assumptions, Freud, again, reminds us just as he did in *The Future of an Illusion*:

> There is an element of grandeur about everything to do with the origin of religion, certainly including the Jewish one, and that is not matched by the explanation we have hitherto given. Some other factor must be involved to which there is little that is analogous and nothing that is of the same kind, something unique and something of the same order of magnitude as what has come out of it, as religion itself.
>
> (SE 23:128)

Paying attention, for a moment, to his language makes it impossible for us to be expedient and rely on the commonplace. Secularists have made Freud theirs, too easily. *Grandeur, unique, magnitude.* Since Freud admits that his "explanation" is incomplete, he leaves us with considerable reading and interpretation, with him as opposed to a simple against. One collaboration has to be ongoing.

He was certainly not a practicing Jew even in terms of cultural observances. *How*, then, was he a Jew? A childhood memory, and a phrase in particular, will remain with us; the biographical disclosure can be repeated. "I was moved," he tells us about his early education,

> by a sort of curiosity, which was, however, directed towards human concerns than towards natural objects ... My deep engrossment in *the Bible story* (almost as soon as I learnt the art of reading) had, as I recognized much later, an enduring effect upon the direction of my interest.
>
> (SE 20:8)

*The Bible story* is my emphasis. Three themes can be restated since they will be constant as long as no theology is inferred: human concerns, the Bible story, the art of reading. He was, to define his interests in a different way, a humanist, a mythographer, a reader. How so, and each as an expression of certain kind of extra-cultural Judaism, will be presented in the project to come and for a reason that is inseparable from a phenomenology of consciousness – a term (philosophically speaking) that connects Freud as a thinker with classical resources, for the time being restricted to the Jewish and with the particular emphasis on the image, idolatry, consciousness, and perception. "We notice that consciousness is a transient quality which attaches to a psychical process only in passing" (SE 23:96). His insight is not a specifically *religious* problem; the "transience," temporally speaking, is a fundamentally human one and in ways we can be deceived – as we all "know" *cognitively* – by appearances, visually in the world, in fantasy in ourselves. We should be unfazed by a theological assessment. "Freud's views," Isaac Lakritz writes, "are not inherently translatable to the field of ethics and morality. To reconcile this aspect of them with Judaism results in a degradation of both."[22] The theological position is an understandable one; but so is the psychoanalytic perspective and its unique ability to understand ethics and morality when it has been subjected to the imperious rules of the super-ego and so submits the self to demands both impossible to fulfil and, in society, exploitable for political ends. Freud will not be held to a theological standard, orthodox or not. Our criteria is, consciously, psychoanalytic and extra-aware of the temptations of dogma.

There is no way to adequately explain the meaning of Freud's "deep engrossment" except to proceed towards writings on specific Biblical themes and other indications which he gives us, in *Moses and Monotheism* and elsewhere. We can mention a few commentators who have, rightly, emphasized the fact. "Sigmund Freud read the Bible through one version of the Enlightenment, but he too was not immune from reading the Enlightenment through Jewish eyes."[23] How Freud read the Bible is hardly self-evident, and certainly not when we simply view him as an atheist. His religiosity was complicated. All his later writings on religion are revealing if they are, for us, textually specific. Still, at this point, the biographical testimonies need to be demonstrated before finding specific examples of a deeper, that is, transferential, relation. On the now much-debated subject of Freud's Jewishness and its importance for understanding the origin and the European context of psychoanalysis, the possibility of inquiry remains open. My preferences are not at all historical, strictly speaking; they are textual and based on the supposition of a transference occurring, as a matter of course, between individuals and ways of thinking. One demand will be met. "There should be evidence that Freud incorporated actual *content* from Jewish sources."[24] Surely, when it comes to the Torah (and Freud's personal relationship to Moses) the evidence is obvious. His reflections on Moses, for one, should make his interests (his *positive transference*) unequivocal and most especially when he describes him, in one moment, as "more than human," that is, as an *Übermensch*. The passage has not been mentioned often. Why not?

Returning to facts and speculation about a childhood, Joel Whitebook has presented evidence for the influence of Freud's father on his thinking, including the copy of the *Israelitische Bibel* in the household.[25] According to many commentators, Freud's statements about Judaism are not free of *ambivalence*, an often-repeated word used for the sake of criticism, or worse; less controversial is his internalization of a Judaism which does not necessarily have to be circumscribed by religious dogma but rather by an appreciation for the inheritance of tradition and its influence on character and intelligence and a personal culture. The Jewish awareness of the image and its regression into idolatry, which has one Biblical origin with Moses, has to be extracted from its archaic origin and made relevant for Freud in the 19th century and, equally if not more important, for us today at a time when images (of ourselves and everything else) are literally in the palm of our hands. Previously, his unconscious was the subject; now we have his testimony, first from his autobiography and then from other writings.

The Preface to the Hebrew translation of *Totem and Taboo*, written in 1930, is another autobiographical statement that deserves some attention for what Freud expressed, very personally, very poignantly, about being Jewish. He does not hide either his estrangement from Judaism as a dogmatic and ritualistic religion or his inability to share in any "nationalist ideals." Despite the admission, he also believed himself to be someone who "feels that he is in his essential nature a Jew and who has no desire to alter that nature" (SE 13:xv). *Essential nature*. Both terms, today, are not often well received; they are over-determined and beyond the references of historicists and relativists. Freud goes on to say that "he could not now express that essence clearly in words." Out of reluctance or inability is hard to say. Perhaps out of humility in not being able to adequately represent what *being Jewish* means, which leaves us with considerable responsibility when a train of thought will be followed that may be read as, in parts, highly speculative (for the history of an esoteric thought in the Kabbalah) and, at others, based on a particular reading of what Freud means by the "Bible story," and then, more personally, an identification with the meaning of *der Mann Moses*.

In his "Address to the Society of B'Nai Brith" and recalling his decision to join the organization, he writes: "That you were Jews could only be agreeable to me; for I was myself a Jew, and it had always seemed to me not only unworthy but positively senseless to deny the fact" (SE 20:273). Although he again admits, not without "shame" (his word) that he did not share either a sense of religious faith or national pride, there was, nevertheless, a sense of identification that he readily acknowledged – even as it remained, in some sense, distant, not wholly committed since he always reserved a necessary independence, from *everything*. Another segment of the letter can be cited.

> But plenty of other things remained over to make attraction to Jewry and Jews irresistible – many obscure emotional forces, which were the more powerful the less they could be expressed in words, as well as a clear *consciousness* of inner identity, the safe privacy of a common mental construction. And beyond this there was a *perception* that it was to my Jewish nature alone that I owed two characteristics that had become indispensable to me in the difficult course of my life. Because I was Jew I found myself free from many prejudices which restricted others in the use of their *intellect*; and as a Jew I was prepared to join the Opposition and to do without agreement with the "compact majority."
> (20:273–4)

*Consciousness, perception, intellect*: these are my italics and for reasons that are foundational for Freud's understanding of the nature (the essence) of human beings, both as individuals and in a society that, at times, required the deepest kind of opposition and, more positively, independence. His claims, as a thinker, are philosophical; calling them metaphysical, in the best sense of the word, despite any of *his* explicit objections, is today necessary if we are to pursue a number of neglected possibilities as to his formation, as an individual and then as a psychoanalyst. One rereads him with satisfaction when the word freedom is so often expressed as one of his therapeutic ideals.

None of the highlighted concepts, in themselves or together, are in any way particularly Jewish character traits. Consciousness, perception, and intellect are, of course, comprehensively human. Our challenge, at this juncture, is to develop his affirmations, as a Jew and as an individual, and see if any can be made more interrelated and less to do with a *strict* identity. To do that we have to turn to a concept he developed in *Moses and Monotheism* and in a discussion on the specificity of an archaic heritage. One argument presented by Eliza Slavet can be countered and then dismissed. She writes, "Freud insists that the Jewish tradition is *biologically* transmitted."[26] *Biologically* is her emphasis. Is this how Freud interprets an archaic heritage? Is it biological or, rather, an enduring *Übertragung* that is a peculiar kind of transference and transmission he first understood in the psychoanalytic situation, in the analyst-analysand relationship and then universally as a condition of our relationship with others? Did he remain essentially a Jew, self-consciously, because of a biological inheritance or due to a highly motivated cultural disposition that placed him both at the beginning of Judaism (for him, with Moses) and then because of an entire history of reading, interpretation, and one tradition that was inseparable from a psycho-therapeutic endeavour? He will, in due time, answer the question without ambivalence. Before turning to the specifics on an archaic heritage, one other assumption – or presumption – can be answered. To align Freud with a biological understanding of the self contradicts one of the most important turns he specifically made away from the 19th conception of heredity and towards an entirely different idea of inheritance – from the family to an individual experience. We can continue to reflect on both his identity and his ethnicity,[27] as long as our particular interests do not end up being exclusive and with a strict adherence to evolutionary biology.

The status of Freud and psychoanalysis in relation to Judaism are now part of the scholarly compendium of an entire discipline in its history. Given the opening here very specifically on Freud being "engrossed" in the "Bible story," one foundation is relevant unless it is given too much prominence. There are many ways to understand what "the Jewish origins of psychoanalysis"[28] actually means; it is not at all obvious once we move beyond the certainty of Freud's birth and family or, for that matter, his early followers and their ethnicity. Our initial sense of a *Bildung*, archaic heritage, and then a transference in the act of reading, requires us to think of a simultaneous overlap in *his* consciousness. These all contributed to Freud's personal vision and how he reflected on how the psyche could determine an unconscious perception and so the production of a consensus reality. For my part, one introduction can set the tone for what Freud's Jewishness means in a study on his observations and *his vision*; the enigmatic word *revelations* will by no means be ignored, either for Freud as an individual who is more than aware of the depth of what he has called "self-recourses," and to a meaning that may be significant for us as long as its metaphysical reference is not immediately imposed on it. The Greek *apokalypsis* implies a disclosure that, previously, had been concealed and disguised. No access to such a phenomenon could be made possible without a sophisticated theory on the nature of a multi-layered psyche and consciousness. We can allude to one work, from 1923, where our intimations from his early years are confirmed. One of the most intractable problems for the analysis of a patient involves the examination of the origins of a perception. In *The Ego and the Id*, Freud had come a long way from his earliest suspicions. Unknown, unconscious, "sensations and feelings," he writes,

> may be more primordial, more elementary, than perceptions arising externally and they can come about even when consciousness is clouded ... These sensations are multiocular, like external perceptions; they may come from different places simultaneously and may thus have different or even opposite qualities.
> (SE 19:22)

These remarkable insights will later be traced to the case history of Anna O. and, in particular, her "*absences*," her disturbances of vision, and her private theatre, the first instance of what he called a "multiocular" neurosis. The different "places" he alludes to (as topographical) are first recognized as dynamics of the psyche in the patient now known to us as Bertha Pappenheim and in the co-written "Preliminary Communication." An analysis of her symptoms is indispensable for understanding Freud's thinking at a particular time in his life – which we will reach after a number or preliminaries are put in place.

How do we respond to Freud's statement as being more than casual and think about the repeated phrase "Bible story" and, in this case, how it appears to be an example on the "story" being *historical*. He relies on the story for sustaining his argument about Moses. In itself – that is, the argument about Moses being an Egyptian – is for me irrelevant since his provenance, the fact of his birth, is less consequential to *who he became* either through the theological belief in his prophetic standing before God or as the entirely self-referential ability of a human being to exceed his historical time and place and transcend the conditions of the world. The creation of a law is a momentous achievement; when, more specifically, we analyze the phenomenology of the "graven image," one form of the psychoanalysis of perception begins to take shape beyond its theological origins. Moses can be presented, in principle, as infinite and without being called (directly) by God. If the idea of a *story* is thought as closely related to Plato's invention of the word *mythos*, then how a story is read allegorically, for its meaning(s), is one of Freud's intellectual foundations.

Any movement from the autobiographical to a more specific example has to take us again to *Moses and Monotheism*. An essential psychoanalytic concept is related to the discussion of what Freud calls an archaic heritage. Our repetition makes the concept an emphatic one. How does this occur, and what are the specific characteristics of this heritage that we can isolate for both Freud and the foundations of psychoanalysis? He has often relied on the concept of the phylogenetic/ontogenetic relation to explain human development. One argument – which, noticeably, will differ from Darwin's theory of evolution – is presented as a "connection with the experience of earlier generations" (SE 23:99). What are the specific aspects of the connection that will be of utmost importance for Freud and psychoanalysis? One "assertion" is primary: "the archaic heritage of human beings comprises not only dispositions but also subject-matter – memory-traces of the experience of earlier generations." If the claim is accepted, the next step has to involve identifying, as precisely as possible, the subjects and the memories. As he warned his readers in terms of an exposition he was ultimately dissatisfied with, his sense of an archaic heritage was a complicated one since it *defied* the theory of evolution as presented by Darwin. Biological inheritance was inadequate as an explanation. As Freud understands it, the theory of evolution and human history are incompatible. The later distinction between heredity and acquisition is already latent in him if not, while a Gymnasium student, fully conscious. Freud's archaic heritage, when traced to specific influences, cannot be thought as other than acquired characteristics that are, at first, unconscious, and only on deeper reflection recognized consciously for an individual who has reflected sufficiently on the matter.

> On further reflection I must admit that I have behaved for a long time as though the inheritance of memory-traces of the experience of our ancestors, independently of direct communication and of the influence of education by the setting of an example, were established beyond question. When I spoke of the survival of tradition among a people or of the formation of a people's character, I had mostly in mind an inherited tradition of this kind and not one transmitted by communication.

*Mostly in mind.* And yet, despite the care and perhaps hesitation of this one idea, the transmission by *direct* communication is uncertain. Will it be clarified or explained as *Moses and Monotheism* reaches a conclusion and then returns to his earliest formation as an individual when he was growing up in a Jewish household and then began studying at the University of Vienna? He concludes that an either/or cannot be chosen. The inheritance is both evident in "direct communication" (for example, in the Torah) and in ways that are more enigmatic and inherited in ways that are not so easy to trace. There are direct transferences of an archaic heritage in terms, for one, of writing, and there are also many other "memory-traces" that have been handed down to the individual indirectly and enigmatically.

The opening of Freud's personal and historical connections has served to connect us to a number of ancillary issues; they are introductory insofar as our continuity has to be more specific as well as more speculative, on the one hand, and textual on the other. Mirian Leonard's word, "identity" has been mentioned and suspended. Its contemporary reality forces us to be circumspect. She mentions one relation, "Freud's Jewish identity and its relationship to his commitment to Wissenschaft."[29] Rather than the limits of identity, another choice will be made – or, rather, two: first, how does Judaism and the German word *Wissenschaft* become complementary (in Freud's mind, as a science that cannot be reduced to the material) and, two, how can we return to Freud's education beyond its formalism and again stress how the process of self-formation included a particular kind of transference that, eventually, he would make pivotal to the psychoanalytic situation? Ken Friden believes that Freud "never acknowledged the pseudorabbinical elements of his work."[30] The rabbinical "elements," pseudo or not, have to be specifically defined. Freud had no interest in the minutiae of Halakah observances as they were codified in the Mishnah; he did, however, appreciate the nuances of the history of interpretation, which was *exegetical* as it was related to Jewish *midrash* and, finally, *hermeneutics*. Exegesis, midrash, hermeneutics. Rather than being so sure about his conscious intentions, or resistances, another exercise can be attempted instead: how was his psychoanalytic concept of a cultural *Übertragung* effective as part of his comprehensive *Bildung* and *Wissenschaft* as a German-speaking European? Did he inherit a sensibility towards the possible deception of perception (and the image) from Judaism *and* was it interpreted, for example, in a work that opened modernity to a particular kind of thinking we can call scientific, such as in the work of Francis Bacon's *Novum Organum*? Jean-Joseph Goux leaves us with a consideration. There is no question that "Jewish thought imposes a withdrawal on every image of divinity and an upmost importance to written records."[31] How did Freud come to the same conclusion with regards to the nature of perception and the image, first, and then how did create a method (following the cathartic and the "talking cure" ) that again emphasized the power of perception and of language to expose our self-deceptions? Forthcoming will be a number of internalizations, both Jewish and scientific, on how Freud reflected on the image – and any perception at all – and recognized the act as determined by a number of dynamic psychical forces. Exodus 20:4–5 remains, in theological terms, a commandment. "You must not make for yourself a carved image or a form ... You must not bow down to them nor be enticed to serve them." *The image*, for Freud, would be understood with an extraordinary latent significance; our enticement – our desire – would betray just how willing we were, and are, to worship things, in the world and in ourselves.

## The Hebrew Language, the Torah, and Interpretation

Our first concern has been outlined, beginning from Freud's own autobiographical statements on the essence (in his mind) of his Jewishness and its role in determining his character as someone who was independent and in opposition to what he called "the majority. His Judaism, as an archaic heritage, was essential to himself as an individual and for being able to internalize a particular kind of transference that was, in itself, multi-dimensional and part of what he called his disposition. The question of Freud's ethnicity is a settled question as far as *the bare facts* are concerned. The inquiry now turns to some specific aspects of Judaism and, to begin with, one in particular whose consequences for theory and practice of psychoanalysis are possible but speculative. The reality and possible *extent* of an inheritance will be examined.

The earlier, perhaps enigmatic reference to the *Sefer Yetzirah* is suggestive enough not to be strictly esoteric and to follow Freud's interpretations on what self-formation means, for an individual, more than the idea of cosmic creation. His interests in Judaism are consistent; how far they can be extended is one outstanding question that, in our brief context, can be analyzed from two sides – a highly speculative one and a more personal and practical one – in the complexity of the Kabbalah and in Freud's interpretation of Moses as a figure who, here, will not be examined in any way for his Egyptianism much less for the historical hypothesis of his murder. Neither his place nor his death-event is relevant. Rather, his significance turns out to be a highly personal one for Freud, for being "aware of his great capacities, ambitious and energetic; he may even have played with the notion of one day being the leader of his people," (SE 23:28) and then for one commandment in particular and its psychological consequences beyond its theological law.

In *Moses and Monotheism*, Freud makes a statement which opens our next section on the invention of Hebrew alphabet, scriptural writing, and his interpretation of "the Bible story." One origin is an intriguing one because of the relation of language to ontology, that is, a way of being that will be, originally, theological – as established in the Torah – but then relevant for his developing ideas about human perception and its connection to the image and *idolatry as a neurotic problem*. Once the image is inseparable from our projections, psyche and reality establish another kind of connection; distortions are then inevitable, in ourselves and in the world. For Freud, the Jewish religion is an *intellectual* problem. He feels no particular affinity to its rituals, for example, or to *mitzvot*, the Jewish duty to religious observances; and yet still feels drawn to its cultural meanings and its attempt to create a certain kind of human being over and above rules of the conduct for everyday life. Did he understand ethics as a psychological problem? And did he translate the Jewish obligation of *tikkum olan* – and, once more, with its sense of "repair" – in relation to individual rather than, abstractly, to the world? How Judaism influenced him is, again, our question. *His ontogeny* was certainly more than a "recapitulation." He was not a *repetition*, not in the singular and according to an easily recognized inheritance. Did he represent a concept of *originality*, one inseparable from a freedom that could not be, simply, mimetic? Did he, before entering the University of Vienna in 1873, perceive himself according to a different conception of both phylogeny and an archaic inheritance? The questions will have to span half our inquiry, from the Jewish to the scientific, each criss-crossing each other in ways that allow for a unique kind of relationship. For the moment, an argument can be considered. Whether it can be sustained is not a pressing yes or no; instead, a history can be recollected in order to enhance our understanding of Freud and the creation of psychoanalysis.

One etymology should be kept in mind: that the Greek word for mysticism is related to *muein* – which means closing and opening the lips and the eyes, for us, in terms of speaking and seeing[32] – takes us to very practical questions. Immediately dismissing "mystical" Judaism as an aspect of Freud's archaic heritage is ill-advised

– just as any convictions we may have about his atheism. Rereading *The Future of an Illusion*, for one, does leave us with unexpected impressions and, analytically, a provocation for us today (in general) and then specifically for the discussions to come. "It is in keeping with the course of human development that external coercion gradually becomes internalized; for a special mental agency, man's super-ego, takes it over and includes it among its commandments" (SE 21:11). One commandment, more important than all the others, will be isolated both in the context of Judaism as well as in the emergence of modern science.

David Bakan's original thesis on "the development of psychoanalysis as an expression of Jewish mysticism"[33] seems quite distant from what we know about Freud's intellectual interests, practical and otherwise; if the proposal is given some thought and made more general – more Jewish, perhaps less mystical, at least as the idea is commonly understood – then a re-appraisal of his knowledge can be hazarded. Taking one very specific example of Judaism does give us a strict bearing from which to make decisions. Bakan makes the claim that Freud knew about the Kabbalistic text *Zohar*. But how? More or less culturally and without any specific knowledge? Or more intimately, possibly from discussions with his father, friends, or teachers? Or, again, from one of its senses as the interpretation of Scripture and its hidden meanings, according to Gershom Scholem, the founder of modern Kabbalah scholarship.[34] These questions are not going to answered either way; we simply do not have the evidence for making a strict connection between the development of Freud's emerging ideas and any speculations of the Kabbalistic kind, on consciousness, perception, and the reality of a deeply layered world, in writing or cosmologically. Going forward, and due to my *overall* argument as opposed to a strict one, any association with Jewish *mystical tradition* – to use Bakan's language – will have to be much more indirect. The latent/manifest distinction is not, only, a Jewish one. Saint Augustine, for one, made it explicit in his *Confessions*. Our earlier emphasis of their effect on intelligence and creativity is central to the coming arguments on the debilitating effects of neurotic symptoms. The *Zohar* has been read as a source of authority, as sacred, mystical, national, and literary.[35] To draw any parallels between this collection of writings, only published in Italy (Mantua) in 1588, and Freud and psychoanalysis could only be done, effectively, by someone with expertise in both. The task at hand is, therefore, general.

If one then has to begin from Bakan's research and, in part, both agree and support a facet of his arguments, a few could be chosen: for one, his presentation of the word Kabbalah as *"that which is received"* – which, translated, is inseparable from a *revelation* – then one outstanding question will be to ask how Freud reinterpreted the idea of a divine epiphany and understood it as a strictly human achievement. Reception and revelation: a provenance is not assured. The distinction, between a divine revelation and a creatively inspired act of creation – with the main example being the writing of the Decalogue – will be central to the turn towards *Moses and Monotheism*. For Freud, the reception (even if a revelation is understood in terms of a *teshuvah* or "turn" towards a way of life) would have to be psychical and internal; there are internal resources for a revelation to take place, and in a place, a topography, where the imagination creates an original idea from out of itself. Whether a connection can be made between one theological interpretation of reception and Freud's *Übertragung* (as a psychical and written transmission) can be left, for now, unanswered. Suspending the religious is done to be closer, in principle, to Freud than anyone with a particular religiosity. Moshe Idel, for example, suggests one possibility when he discusses Jewish mysticism as a practice to alter states of consciousness.[36] Of course, these are thought, one way, as a path towards a *unio mystica* and have nothing to do with psychoanalysis – except insofar as both presuppose the possibility of altering interior life. Both can be translated; the direction is unavoidably different.

One original thesis can be followed up. "Freud's origin in an orthodox Jewish milieu impacted his psychological theories."[37] *How* is a difficult question, as are any possible extensions. His "milieu," which takes us a historical context with a long and extensive genealogy, was in any case equally if not more European, for his present and in the way he regarded himself as cultured. How does one, for example, easily separate the Hellenistic from the Jewish during one period and, in another – say, the occupation of Judaea by the Romans – and its branching off into 1st-century Christianity? When we move from the orthodox to the mystical, our situation is an even more difficult one; if we also makes the claim for his "historical roots," which, previously, have also been classical and multiple, one culture may prove to be too exclusive in Freud's case if we again believe he was cosmopolitan, a European Jew. Affirmations can be made; how much they can be defined is another matter. "Mystical Jewish influences affected Freud and led him to develop his psychological theories."[38] The authors mention *psychological theories*. Was one actually capable of "leading him?" Sustaining the argument will prove to be difficult, especially when the formative Judaism, before any formal university education, is then supplemented by the medical, scientific, and psychiatric. Mentioning others, like his comprehensive reading during his Gymnasium education, makes it impossible to determine all his influences. Some are certain – like his relationship to Goethe – others are unknown and are likely to remain that way.

The mystical is not a category among others, not when an attempt is made to associate Freud to a tradition that is, at least in some aspect, metaphysically esoteric and never an explicit interest, at least in any of his writings. The speculations go even further. "Freud himself may have been acquainted with Kabbalistic writings. Researchers have compared psychoanalysis to the principles and psychological construction of a major stream of Kabbalah."[39] The Judaism of our departure can, in principle, turn towards the religious, the orthodox and the mystical all the way to the Kabbalah as part of the literary history of Judaism. In order to limit the discussion, and to remain within our objectives, it seems more reasonable to, again, turn to Freud and his writings. Our interests will have to be narrow; otherwise, there would be no choice but to fully enter the more esoteric texts beyond the Torah and read, explicitly and closely, the major writing such as the *Zohar*, the book of *illumination*, a meaning also understood as a rational enlightenment. Freud will indicate the way in terms of our categories; they will not be followed according to the esotericism of the Kabbalah or its specific writings, whatever their origin, in second-century Judaea or medieval Spain. On the contrary, they will be in some sense practical and involve the invention of the Hebrew alphabet, writing, and interpretation, one origin that, at least, appears less demanding. Only then, in the context of the Book of Exodus, will we be able to turn to Freud's relationship to Moses and see the levels of both his intellectual interests and particular *identification*, one based on a transference with the idea of a founding individual. In other words, the man Moses – and one particular idea on the nature of idolatry (as a form of neurosis) – is the one relationship we can draw from much more than the history of Jewish theology. The Torah, according to the interpretations presented in the *Zohar*, may contain "sublime secrets." Highlighting the word "sublime," as that which cannot be represented, cannot be disassociated from Freud's own interpretations – of the unconscious and what it can (or cannot) project into the world. Being called a "secular kabbalist"[40] would certainly puzzle Freud to no end. However, a consideration, at the appropriate time and in relation to the invention of the Hebrew alphabet, written language, and the Torah, has potential to be complementary in our understanding of what Freud inherited, explicitly and, more importantly, how his multi-dimensional interpretation of Judaism, 19th-century science, the case of Anna O., and his period of observation at the Salpêtrière in Paris all converged towards the creation of a momentous edifice of thought.

Connections have been made; the relationship are, for Freud, personally tenuous. One scholarly tradition and its various directions has not been reluctant to pursue Jewish themes as they converge with psychoanalysis. Acknowledging them is done more for the historical record than as an argument that, for me, is binding. Rather, one can use perhaps the most extreme example (with the Kabbalah) and then juxtapose it with Freud's writing. Inferences can be made; one can be sceptical or drawn to them as sensibility allows. No one doubts how intriguing they are, nor how provocative. For an inquiry involving psychoanalysis, one should always be prepared for the unsettling. A first reaction is hardly an adequate measure – of the topic or of ourselves. Any associations cannot be confirmed once and for all; they have to be multiple. So before turning to Freud's presentation in *Moses and Monotheism*, on the alphabet, scriptural writing, and interpretation, suggestions can be taken into consideration. Free association can also be a principle of inquiry. As always, one has to know if one affect or another is misleading or the beginning of an unconscious insight.

Objections can also be made; the back-and-forth is a method for us to be aware of the demands made for certain arguments. "He [Freud] seems to have had little or no knowledge of the Talmud, for example."[41] Perhaps, but we cannot be entirely sure of this "knowledge," not if we consider his father's reading of the Talmud in the leisure of his retirement and if they possibly discussed, in passing or in detail, any specific ideas from extra-biblical writings. Michel Eigen has distinguished himself by examining the therapeutic practice of psychoanalysis and its exchange with other forms of thought. In the case of his interest in psychoanalysis and the Kabbalah, he has given us the thinking of a certain kind of *elevation*. For us, in this particular context of Freud before Paris, the Kabbalah has to be kept within certain limits: if we are to concentrate on the early period of Freud's thinking and writing, the temptation to speculate about the most metaphysical and mystical expressions of being are, for now, too far ahead. If we were to follow such a path, as Eigen has done, we would be forced to move from the psychopathology of everyday life towards quite exceptional aspirations in terms of understanding cosmology, being, and YHWH as conceived by Jewish creativity and piety. These are too remote. The concern at hand is more practical; or, as Eigen puts it, "one never recovers from being human" or from the "soul dramas" of our lives, in ourselves, with others, and in our relation to the world.[42] Was Freud exposed, in one way or another, to the residual ideas of the Kabbalah as they were lived by Jews in their everyday life, and can we then make the association between one sacred writing and the invention of psychoanalysis more immediate? Freud was simply too sober-minded to think at the level of the Kabbalah and its tendency towards the mystical and highly metaphysical. He was not so much interested in the *elevation* of consciousness as, first, the recognition of what was, precisely, lower and deeper and more confounding for psychological health. Even the faintest of familiarity with some of its fundamental ideas or a one-time and therefore superficial reading of, for instance, the *Zohar*, quickly tells us how much distance there is from this kind of contemplation and the mundane world. Our relation is other, and especially in the context of an opening chapter dedicated to the perception of the world at an accessible level *for everyone*. The psychoanalytic concept of *residue*, in relation to the levels of dreams (as manifest and latent – in its appearance and its deeper meaning) can also apply to the manner in which the transference and transmission is active for the history of a Jewish idea.

Any possible connection between the Kabbalah, and its meaning as "received tradition," and the foundations of psychoanalysis can proceed only on the condition of prudence. Given the emphasis of the project as a whole and the central importance of the concept of *Übertragung*, how the transference of a Kabbalistic sense may have occurred for Freud is not an indifferent question, most especially when considering the interdisciplinary origins of psychoanalysis. The reservation can be expressed at the outset so as to set our inquiry not only on firm ground; we do so to temper any possible misguided enthusiasm. "Psychoanalytic experts," David Helperin advises, "need to understand that the Judaic specialist will often have legitimate reservation."[43] Balance is called for, both for the sake of the specificity of the Kabbalah as a profoundly religious writing (and for its creation of communities of faith, from the Middle Ages to groups like the Hasidim) and for the ideas and objectives of psychoanalysis above all as a form of interpretation. For those who have dedicated their lives to the study of Judaism – with, understandably, special attention to its multi-faceted theology – their attitude to the psychoanalysis-Kabbalah relation will be guarded, and perhaps, impossible. The reservations, from the specialist in Judaism, can also be expressed by anyone else.

There is no need to make the claim, for example, that "the covert Freud took pleasure in the study of the soul, very much related to his hassidic roots, going back many generations."[44] There is not really anything "covert" about the study of the "soul." Making Freud a latter-day Hassid is not necessary, and perhaps too precisely fitting him into a cultural milieu, of pious Jews and ancestral rabbis, however suggestive such a possibility remains. At the outset, we can rely on a tradition of scholarship and re-emphasize both the facts and, then, deliberate on the assumptions and the arguments that may be too far of a reach. Once again, Michael Eigen has been sensitive to a "convergence" between the Kabbalah and psychoanalysis. "I am not a Kabbalah scholar," he writes, "but aspects of its teaching have become part of me, as has psychoanalytic work. The two have many parts of convergence."[45] The idea of a possible transference can be hypothetically considered; doing so will also lead to other, less controversial connections on a technique of reading and interpretation. *Our* creativity is our responsibility. If one objection can be raised, perhaps one that Freud considered, the ideas created from out of the Jewish tradition are not, in themselves, unique. After all, Biblical hermeneutics as practiced before and during Freud's lifetime was also influential at a more general level culturally.

The connections for Freud are many and worthy of consideration; they are as intricate and as varied as the history of Judaism itself. Anyone with fidelity to Freud on the inter-related themes of Judaism has choices to make, themes to emphasize, keeping in mind how the subject figures in with the rest of the work ahead. Some suggestions are so broad as to be overwhelming in their implications; each demands a separate study. "Freud was assuredly indebted to Maimonides through the general, nonspecific heritage of the kabbalah, Renaissance esotericism, and German romanticism. The seed of psychoanalysis was in Maimonides's cure of souls."[46] One example from the many simply allows me to respond and affirm that the "seeds" were as disparate as the three presented above. The best we can hope for is to renew our efforts and expand both the grounds of psychoanalysis as well as Freud's innovations. Some reservations are appropriate when the arguments are noticeable by their emphatic "assuredly indebted." To again call upon the Christian tradition, and the Catholic in particular in a city like Vienna, he would have "assuredly" been knowledgeable about St. Augustine and, if no other writings, letters, or sermons, the *Confessions*; after all, the first modern autobiography gives us innumerable intimations of the unconscious. Or, much more likely, how much did Freud know about the work of Jacob Hamburger (1826–1911) and his *Encyclopedia Judaica*? Without invoking the idea of indebtedness, what was the extent of his knowledge of the movement called *Wissenschaft in Judentums*?[47] Answers are not available except hypothetically. One resource are his personal letters; but given the nature of his personal relationship with his correspondents, a sentence or two does not guarantee anything but our continued interest.

Although more than one comparison between the Kabbalist's view of language and psychoanalysis could be drawn, in order to remain consistent in my presentation one point of view will be chosen. For the Kabbalists, language could not be interpreted only from a historical context since, in its "nature," how it appeared and what it meant, were entirely different – as was its use. The Kabbalists looked at the materiality of language, its visible figure, as only one of its elements. The Kabbalists sought a "sacralization of language ... Language was not an arbitrary means of communication, but a medium of revelation."[48] One of the defining events of the revelation of language occurred during the Sinai event, in the writing of the Decalogue. For Freud, however, a secular interpretation of the revelation of language happened in the transference of an experience, a memory, a dream, a fantasy, or any number of other human moments of a life that then became a subject of analysis. Kabbalistic philology: approaching the subject from our perspective, the sense of what philology stood for could be taken from its initial religious or, if one liked, mystical context, and transferred towards understanding the alphabet as the source of the perception of consciousness rather than any idea of the structure of the psyche as linguistic. In any case, two directions were both equally fruitful; inquiry depended on one's orientation. Maimonides has been one suggestion. So many others could be mentioned and pursued, briefly or at length. All of them – say, like the figure of Abraham Abulafia or Isaac Luria – would demand another kind of in-depth historical inquiry, impossible here for obvious reasons. Instead of *named* individuals in the history of Judaism, beginning with Freud's own origin with Johanan ben Zakkai and the Yavneh rabbis, another turn, to a momentous origin, can serve to bring us back in closer proximity to Freud himself.

One beginning, as Freud speculates in *Moses and Monotheism*, will not be a historical hypothesis on the origin of a religion and its ties to Egypt; rather, one possible origin will lead, if indirectly, to the language of psychoanalysis as it emerged in Freud's writing and interpretation. The intricacies of the Kabbalah can remain within our considerations, neither affirming them unconditionally nor dismissing them outright. Freud's return to another beginning, in language, makes for a different set of arguments that are at once practical and far-reaching. An archaic heritage can be traced, more specifically, in terms of a language, in fact and as an essential aspect of psychotherapeutic interpretation.

"The scribes of Moses," Freud writes, "may have had a share in the invention of the first alphabet."

(SE 23:43)

The speculation, whether true or not, leads us to a more immediate set of circumstances. Comments directed at Moses and monotheism will be visited more fully in a moment. One can begin our next inquiry – which is less, in this instance, about a man or a known individual as opposed to an invention; or, put it another way and as alluded to earlier, something on the side of a inspiration/revelation spectrum. Some believe that *Moses and Monotheism* is "a book whose historical claims seem like pure fantasy." That surely depends on the details we see, and the ones we ignore, at times, to confirm a hunch or belief or argument – like what Richard Bernstein adds, "a book that many have read as an expression of Freud's alleged Jewish self-hatred."[49] Alleged indeed. The accusation is typical for the "many," even if there is no basis in reality for making such a statement. Are we unable to recognize Freud's *analytic* argument because of our fixation on his historical hypothesis? Such arguments (again, psychological and extreme) are far from a less emotional analysis and one where the Hebrew alphabet leads to the Decalogue and the one law of most importance to us – *now*. The scholarly debates have to be set aside: specific dates – for the compilation attributed, by some, to Ezra, the writing of the Dead Sea Scrolls, or the Mishnah (circa 200 C.E.) – are specific; our interests here, as it concerns Freud's interpretation *in Moses and Monotheism* – is much more personally relevant. "The early history of the alphabet is a critical window into the history of Hebrew itself. Because the history of Hebrew is intimately tied to its writing system, the development of the alphabet is more important than has been generally recognized."[50]

How did Freud internalize a historical transference of, first, an alphabet as it was invented, a language as it was written, and a technique of interpretation initially defined as midrash and then supplemented by a number of modern techniques related to both philology and hermeneutics? The lifelong relationship to religion, as such, concludes with an assessment that is also more enigmatic than has been defined, most especially by those who have been on the side of Freud's so-called atheism. Suspending any judgement, as we set out, is a principle and a conviction. What does it mean, for Freud, that the "scribes of Moses" invented the alphabet? Whether it was the first or not is for us important. Historical priority does not address Freud's argument – which he only makes indirectly. The alphabet, language, writing. What is he piecing together over and above the presentation that has most unsettled his readers about his relationship to Judaism as they see it?

If the scribes of Moses invented the Hebrew alphabet, they did so (in terms of the 22 letters) as a profound difference from the image of Egyptian hieroglyphic writing. *Our* priority is more significant than the fact of a *first* alphabet. The writing of images was transformed into the shape of letters that, in themselves, had to be perceived beyond their appearance and then towards an intricate depth. Scholars have been attracted to the meaning of Jewish letters and how they have been interpreted, according to a long and complicated tradition, by Jewish thinkers – some of them categorized as "mystical" or, at least, rabbinical in their vocation or sensibility. To begin, then, on the Jewish alphabet, language, and writing and its possible transference to Freud personally and then to psychoanalysis, has not been alien to the scholarly imagination, both theological and secular. In the beginning of the chapter, the *Sefer Hetzirah*, as the book of "formation," was alluded to. The same line of thought can now be pursued in one history of Jewish thinking.

For the Kabbalists, the being of creation and the Hebrew alphabet are inseparable; when we then also add the Sephirotic Tree of Life as a representation of the human body (which Freud understood physically as well as according to psychical principles – illness as, also, psychosomatic) we have an admittedly hypothetical but nonetheless provocative idea for Freud to contemplate during a time when the insights of psychoanalysis were being noted and served as an emerging theory. Beginning from Freud's startling hypothesis that the newly freed Jews from Egypt created their own alphabet from an oral tradition of long standing – an alphabet created in distinction to hieroglyphics – the wanderers in the Sinai were able to both create the letters as signs of a spoken and written language. The particularity of the first letter (the silent *aleph*) can be understood from out of their self-conception: the first letter would not be pronounced and would remain silent as a testimony of a prior existence. The Jews of the Sinai, who as former slaves now began to think about and represent the experience of freedom, did so not only by *living* their condition. They gave symbolic representation to who they were by transcending the reality of hieroglyphics. By creating an alphabet capable of representing a new kind of existence, they then made real an unprecedented level of thinking that would be represented in the writing of the Ten Commandments and (for Moses) as a transference from God to human beings. The order of the commandments, beginning with the first two – there will only be one god; and no "graven images" will be made or worshipped – have a theological origin. But was the second, for Freud, a phenomenological truth and related to the possible distortions of the psyche in its misrepresentations of reality – which was, essentially, the predicament suffered by neurotics, as he will eventually learn with the case of Anna O.?

Freud's sober rationalism did not allow him to pursue either a religious or, more remote still, a mystical understanding of creation and the human; for him, the deeply metaphysical meanings of Judaism and of the Kabbalistic writings could be adopted for the sake of a new kind of understanding (as it was for the pious), or it could serve depth-psychology as one more way to understand the complications of human beings. One truth, in Jewish thought, was for Freud a universally human experience. "Symbols such as the Sephirot and the letters of the Hebrew alphabet serve as intermediaries between perception of the unknown and familiarity with the human mind and body."[51] One affirmation can be noted: there is no question as to the depth of Jewish thought in its scriptural or mystical tradition. But whether ideas can claim both originality and uniqueness is another matter and so forces us to think about Freud's own cosmopolitan thinking (as a cultured European whose affinity began with its classical foundations) and *any language* in its relation to the "perception of the unknown." Are we, then, minimizing Freud's Jewish archaic heritage in order to make him, as has been suggested earlier, a cosmopolitan – described one way as a European Jew with a number of genealogical influences that started with the Hebrew alphabet and then extended to one of the most important innovations of the Jewish people in terms of the psychology of the image and idolatry? One foundation of psychoanalysis is, from Freud himself, indisputable;

how the elements were associated to other forms of thought – the scientific, for example – was to take a significant period of time.

For our purposes, however, we can now diverge from the more esoteric history – such as the symbol of the Sephirot – and guide ourselves with a more practical, a more psychoanalytic, concern with perception, first, and then language as it was defined, as we'll see with Anna O., as the "talking cure" and specifically to counteract the images of what she called her "private theatre?" We can now withdraw from an esoteric history and return to Freud as he represented himself and then created a psychoanalytic *science* – which will have to define itself according to one of the first principles of the discipline, observation, and then a more developed understanding of consciousness and perception. The point in the chapter to come is not to argue against the idea of a "Jewish science." Rather, the question is: how is Freud an individual intermediary between the archaic heritage of Judaism and the history of science as they converged, specifically, with him and during the extended creation of psychoanalysis? The connection between Judaism and science can be established and in a way that has nothing to do with ethnicity. Rather, if we are to pursue the latent significance of one and the other, one intersecting point will be on the nature of perception and the image – in other words, an origin in the injunction against idols (first, as things) and then ideas. The meaning of Moses, for Freud, now becomes more immediate than anything as esoteric as rabbinical interpretations of the Hebrew alphabet or the Sephirot.

Scholarly speculations are not without interest; but, if our knowledge of Freud is an accurate one, then the esoteric possibilities are better substituted with other, more obvious relations as he made them known to us explicitly. We can, as a final example, make our case for a more practical attitude to Freud. He was surely not interested in the question of the creation of the world from out of the name of God or from the 22 letters of the Hebrew alphabet.[52] The challenges are considerable because, for one, any turn to the midrashic and especially kabbalistic understanding of the Hebrew alphabet immediately involves us in the most complex of *metaphysical* issues. The mystical, for all its attractions as a complex form of thought in the Kabbalah, is too enticing and therefore has to be set aside for more practical interests. The extent of Freud's internalization of Jewish culture is, in the end, based on his writings – which, if interpreted as a struggle, were indicative of one kind of religious sensibility. His emphatic statements, on his "godlessness," for example, are too spirited to be believed without considering not so much any theological adherence but his unquestionable interest in culture, *Kultur*, civilization from its earliest formative stages. We cannot, as a first detail in the interest in the Hebrew alphabet, enter into the minutiae of interpretation and wonder if the creation of the world comes from out of the divine name – from the letters of the ineffable name, the *tetragrammaton* of YHWH – or from the Hebrew alphabet in the Torah. The endless fascination of rabbinical questions are simply too demanding for us to take the time proper for their understanding – never mind any of the innumerable midrashic commentaries. However, on the question of the "abyss" as it has been conceived in the period (if it can be so called) of creation, Freud was indeed drawn to its creation insofar as it reflected not the cosmology of the world but the infinite dynamic of the psyche. Our associations are to be considered when a process of translation takes place, and we separate Freud from a tradition he was most likely uninformed about – at least explicitly, profoundly – and did not care enough to study. He was, to be succinct, *worldly*.

The title of an essay on Freud and Judaism in terms of an "event" gives us one opportunity to continue the study on the psychoanalysis of consciousness and perception by going back to origins and on an event that had a particular meaning for Freud which he expresses near the end of *Moses and Monotheism*. One typical interest in Freud and psychoanalysis has been to look into the milieu of his own time and the social and political circumstances of the late 19th century and beyond. The time is not without its interests; how much more we can learn is an open question when it comes to psychoanalysis proper. Another option can be chosen in order to stretch the boundaries of the historical. Freud's personal interests in antiquity are also well known, both for his fascination with its objects and its varied times. One event in particular gives us a moment of pause. Freud takes note of the event in *Moses and Monotheism* when, during the Jewish War against the Romans in 66–70 and the inevitable destruction of Jerusalem, the rabbi Johanan ben Zakkai and his followers left the city and, finding haven in Yavneh, do nothing less than initiate a new period in the history of Judaism, one that would be devoted to the book rather than the rituals of the temple, to reading and interpretation, writing and commentary. In what way can we begin our own turn to Freud's life as a thinker with this one exceptional event, specifically mentioned by him, and consider it as one reference among others? The years following the exile in Yavneh and the turn towards the remaking of Judaism led to a number of transformations in the nature of a people, their beliefs, and their way of life. The development of a practice of reading, interpretation, and commentary (Midrash Haggadah) has been noted as an analogue of psychoanalysis when it comes to speech and free association. "What Freud ingeniously did was to introduce this technique, or rather certain aspects of it, into the very heart of the psychological and psychiatric knowledge of his time."[53] In what way did this "technique" contribute to psychoanalysis? One answer has been given when it comes specifically to psychoanalytic speech and free association. Any particular interests in what Freud calls the "Holy Writ" is not due to its association with the speech of the analysand; instead, the more minute analysis of the Hebrew language, first of all, and the fascination with the "Bible story" and its influence on Freud's sensibilities – ones that transcended our sometimes narrow understanding of "religion" – is more significant for us now and going forward. There is no more productive way for me to reflect on Freud's Judaism, in the context of a study on consciousness and perception, than to turn and relate it to his scientific studies at the University of Vienna. The *remnant* of a cultural awareness, during one of the decisive events in the history of Judaism, can be inter-related to a scientific method based on observation and visuality. The connection is not, during this study, on language and speech; rather, the inter-relationship, in addition to being a transference (or, *positively* stated, a *transmission* from the ancient world to the modern), is to the interpretation, psychologically speaking, of the "Bible story." His Jewishness led us to a number of considerations; however provocative they may have been, some only as allusions, are now left behind for a more practical, because more human, transference. It is no doubt true that "Freud's approach to the mind aims at the conversion of images to verbal narratives. The cognitive-linguistic approach is reminiscent of Jewish modes of textual interpretation."[54] The creation of Jewish midrash in the interpretation of scripture has been undoubtedly one of the cultural influences on Freud's intelligence; no such reality can be denied. The image of the Hebrew alphabet has been regarded for its multiplicity of meanings. One cannot fail to mention, over and above the linguistic and interpretive schema, a form of teaching directly to be internalized for an understanding of life. Once we emphasize the importance of the creation of the Hebrew alphabet as a distinct alternative to the images of Egyptian hieroglyphics, we have to consider how the development of written language, in scriptural form and requiring interpretation, differed from the immediacy, and possible self-deception, of the image. The creation of the alphabet and the injunction against idols or "graven images" was a related phenomenon. How Freud identified with Moses is, now, the most pressing issue because the most human and the one with the most distinctive transference. Did the alphabet, language, and writing culminate with the biography of a single man and with the one commandment that, beyond its theological significance, was preeminent for the psychoanalysis of perception?

## The Revelations of Moses

Our last theme on Moses the individual and what Freud explicitly calls his "transcendent influence" is at once the most accessible and the one most personal and transferential for Freud as we unify our initial themes of Judaism, language, and interpretation for its relevance in understanding the many complex factors in the origins of psychoanalysis and, for one of our central themes, the problems of "sensory perception" insofar as they could be false because projected, for one, out of a neurotic psyche. Without simply dismissing the speculations as they related to Jewish mysticism and psychoanalysis, they were ultimately less significant since they had never been part of Freud's actual writing – or life. The connection Freud makes in *Moses and Monotheism* – the psychological problem of "sensory perception" and then the "triumph of intellectuality" (*geistigkeit*) – can be a guiding one as long as we continue to emphasize one fact: Freud's observations are not theological and are inseparable from a psychological evaluation of Biblical writing and the *consciousness* not so much of the manifest example of "graven images" and their implications for religious life, but rather the problem of sensory perception and the image of reality, comprehensively understood, as a possible projection from out of the unconscious. How one individual recognized the possible tragedy involved in the projection of images into the world is, in part, the indirect relation to the Book of Exodus.

Although the theological origin of the idea of essentially outlawing images of God from a community of worshippers is, in itself, of obvious interest – not least of all for its historical innovation for the Jewish people after their liberation from Egypt – Freud interprets the event for its implications for the psychoanalysis of perception as it effects neurotic projections and the ways the meaning of reality could be distorted. Without returning, at length, to some of the more important psychological arguments from *Totem and Taboo*, one stands out for being essential in understanding the developments Freud made in his reflections on *Moses and Judaism*. "The projection outwards of internal perceptions is a primitive mechanism, to which, for instance, our sense perceptions are subject, and which therefore normally plays a very large part in determining the form taken by our external world" (SE 13:64). Was not the injunction against images, at first theologically understood from the Sinai event, interpreted by Freud to be a profoundly psychological problem and indicative of how ideations and other psychical effects made their way into reality and formed it according to the unconscious? Projection and idolatry were part of a related psychical process. In *The Ego and Id*, Freud writes:

> By their interposition internal thought-processes are made into perceptions. It is like a demonstration of the theorem that all knowledge has its origin in internal perception. When a hyper-cathexis of the process of thinking takes place, thoughts are *actually* perceived – as if they came from without – and are consequently held to be true.
>
> (SE 19:23)

The discoveries Freud had made in and through the analysis of patients led him to make far-reaching arguments about the nature of a historical event that allowed the Jewish people as they emerged from Egypt to remake themselves according to a new understanding of the self and reality. They did so, as told in Exodus, out of the experiences of one man. Freud had a lifelong relationship with the figure of Moses. The nature of his proximity to him was first presented in "The Moses of Michelangelo." The discussion of a sculpture is more true for *two* human beings.

> This general character of the figure is further heightened by laying stress on the conflict which is bound to arise between a reforming genius and the rest of mankind. Emotions of anger, contempt and pain are typified in him. Without them it would not have been possible to portray the nature of a superman (*Übermensch*) of this kind. Michelangelo has created, not a historical figure, but a character-type, embodying an inexhaustible inner force which tames the recalcitrant world.
>
> (SE 13:221)

How noticeable that a concept associated, philosophically, with Nietzsche is used by Freud to describe Moses. In one description, Moses is, then, an *Übermensch* and a "reforming genius." How so?

Sensory perception made way for a specific kind of reason that was simultaneously linguistic and ontological. The *written* commandments, whether in fact, or metaphorically written "in stone," represented a momentous turn away from the immediacy of images and of a perception presumed to be naturally occurring. The immediate impression of a perception (which is so taken for granted, true, and as a correspondence with reality) has to be suspended and analyzed no different than the interpretation of textual meaning. Writing transformed consciousness. A perception may be so altered, for psychical reasons soon to be more specifically analyzed with the first case history of psychoanalysis with Anna O., that reality itself is distorted and, with it, the personality of the individual – transforming the present no less than the entirety of the past. The perception, for example, may be experienced as anxiety-filled, and yet its origins are always disguised in the very symptom it expresses. The Jewish theological insight, for Freud, creatively interpreted and then applied not so much in the context of an actual image – although they too, as we obviously know today, can lead to all kinds of pathologies – resulted in the ability to understand how neurotic phenomenology acted out in its way of imposing itself on reality and then seeing. Freud understood how one ancient situation, as recounted in a bible story, had to be understood from a much wider perspective, an ontological and social one. The early prohibition was, for Freud, less important for the laws of a community and its religious beliefs than for a psychoanalyst who could interpret the life and ailments of a patient from a similar point of view – that is, from the images they were creating, through perception, as a confirmation of their neurosis. Our preoccupation with psychoanalysis as a philosophy of consciousness can be given one more support, a final one for Judaism and, as we move towards 19th-century science, once we bring together the scholarship on Freud's Jewish identity and our more expansive sense of his many-layered transferences. The *reaction* to the publication of *Moses and Monotheism* – "reception" lacks the force required for its examination – concentrated too heavily on Freud's historical speculations (about Moses's identity and death) and so failed to read the third and final section as a psychoanalysis of historical perception. Can we really come to the conclusion that the book was intended to "answer the riddle of anti-semitism"?[55] Or was Freud, for a long time extending to 1914 and before, drawn to Moses for highly personal reasons, of identification and for relating to the "transcendent influence of a single personality" in history, and in himself? Why did readers misunderstand Freud – and for reasons he was explicit about? In a typical academic fashion, Paul Reitter notes: "*Moses and Monotheism* never had much scholarly credibility."[56] If that is true, then we have to, also, question scholars and academics at the same time as following Freud's ideas in this one culminating work. The statement says much more about "scholars" than Freud's thinking. Projecting our inadequacies on him has been part of a long and still pervasive tradition.

We are told that "the Hebrew press seethed and only with difficulty was able to provide space for all those who wanted to fulminate about the book."[57] His critics were numerous; the reasons were specific and inseparable from the long history of Jewish persecution and the perpetually insecure status of their existence. At this one beginning, to do justice to the whole of the confrontation would take considerable attention to the details – from two points: an interpretation of *Moses and Monotheism* as Freud intended, and the various reactions to its publication and during a time (the end of the 1930's) when Jews were more than justified to be aware of how precarious their social existence had become. For our purposes, and by immediately adopting a psychoanalytic attitude, neither the work as a whole nor the time of its appearance will take up any more of our time. Instead, the historical event which proved to be so important for Freud, as an analogue of his own individual experience, was understood to be *present* to him from precisely the time when Jews had no choice but to reinvent themselves.

Jan Assman uses the phrase "progress in intellectuality" for the title of one of his chapters. He writes of "the extraordinary moral achievements and facets of sublimation that the monotheistic (that is, Jewish) patriarchal religion demands."[58] Without neglecting the theme of sublimation, while downplaying morality, our concentration on the importance of perception forces us to see Freud's recognition of this "progress" not in moral terms unless we interpret *the ethical* (as we can and should) as free from neurotic perception. Given the drive of the super-ego, most especially today among the born-again moralists of liberal democracy, how one separates "ethics" from neurosis is a hazardous job. Ethics and morality, for Freud, is a psychical problem.

Assman adds: "In revisiting the ban on graven images, Freud reveals this striving for intellectual emancipation to be a deeply Jewish project and, at the same time, a tradition that he himself claims to inherit and takes a step further with his psychoanalysis." *A step further*. For some, the arguments made in the first two parts of *Moses and Monotheism*, published earlier and separately as essays, represents more than one objectionable aspect. For our purposes, the question of Moses's *ethnicity* is a non-issue. The matter of most concern is how Freud, in part, identifies with him as pivotal historical figure and then draws parallels. The "step further" occurs when the truth of theology as inaugurated by the Mosaic imperative is translated into everyday life and as the conscious awareness of how both perception (and the creation of images which, of course, would have been obvious to Freud in the 1930's and as an enduring aspect of the totalitarian mentality – their signs and symbols) can distort both individual lives and social and political reality. Individually speaking, the neurotic, as an individual, projects unconscious fantasies into the world and then perceives them as the truth of reality instead of recognizing them as the effects of a mentally compromised psyche.

At the present moment, then, we are conscious of Shaul Bar-Haim's reminder of "the Mosaic legacy of Sigmund Freud,"[59] one that is a specifically hermeneutic undertaking. The "legacy" can be understood in a number of different ways. Which ones will we need to emphasize as the first of other ones in the history of psychoanalysis? Are we going to be motivated by Freud's argument on Moses's origins, as an individual and as the founder of a religion, and of a people? Not at all. There are too many other indications in the three inter-related essays that are more relevant for a psychoanalytic interpretation. The opening sentence is, for Freud, one thesis. "To deprive a people of the man whom they take pride in as the greatest of their sons is not a thing to be gladly or carelessly undertaken, least of all by someone who is himself one of them" (SE 23: 7). Describing Moses as *a son* is, perhaps, to upset the proper chronology of a lineage. Freud's admission, of being "one of them" (a son) is no less self-evident. Because if the question was, initially, about Freud's Jewishness, now it must also be what it means beyond a self-evident ethnicity or any other cultural characteristics of which he shared. The name Mosheh is already a puzzle that Freud "solves" with some etymological research that leads him to see its meaning as "he who draws out." The meaning should not be taken for granted; we should not simply infer an obvious meaning, for example, in terms of leading the Israelites out of bondage from a geographical place. The psychoanalyst is also someone who "draws out" and in ways that are completely psychical and no less concerned with being free – that is, being emancipated from neurotic determinations and a self-made reality that is intended to perpetuate one condition of being. Are there insights in Freud's always exceptional writing that alerts us to a number of meanings that appear as latent? He makes his method, and his intentions, quite obvious by telling the reader how "the substance of what it has to contribute is an application of psycho-analysis. The argument arrived at in this way will undoubtedly impress that minority of readers who are familiar with analytic thinking and who are able to appreciate its findings" (SE 23:10). To take him at his word allows us to move from all the manifest content of the three essays, most especially the third and last one, and inquire into its latent significance: an autobiographical self-presentation as well as one more in-depth inquiry into psychoanalysis as a therapeutic philosophy of consciousness. Any observation Freud makes about Moses and his creation is, also, part *confession* – which is to say, a revelation he first has reached in himself. The self-involvement, going back at least as far as the many personal dreams he analyzed in the *Interpretation of Dreams*, continues to animate his thinking, in himself and as someone who (in the late 1930's) is quite assured of being a founder and, to use a discredited word, a patriarch, a *pater arche* as the "father of a beginning."

Still, Freud knows that "every novelty must have its preliminaries and preconditions in something earlier," (SE 23:21) which is certainly one way to sum up his own origins and their different preconditions. Judaism is one origin; the emphasis will be a matter of a decision by individual readers who, in their own way, will also be *drawn to*, that is, enticed by desire and an attachment – or its opposite. Freud's revelations, we know, have also resulted in revulsions. He remains a pivotal and divisive figure. Negative transferences have been intense. For my part, one of Freud's illustrations have had the most impact. The historical event, easily passed over by the reader who may be familiar with the period but not necessarily its consequences, have to be revisited since Freud seems to hint at its world-historical importance both for Jewish religion and psychotherapy. If the prohibition against the image had to be made complete, one had to also become aware of an equally dangerous *spectacle*. The perception of all constructed reality had to be analyzed according to a new sensibility; and, in the ancient world, one spectacle above all served as the *sine qua non* of religious worship. How Freud brings our attention to the destruction of the temple in Jerusalem by the Romans and then the foundation of the rabbinical centre in Yavneh (which abandoned the ritual of *animal sacrifice* in the temple for the religious responsibility of reading, interpretation, midrash, and the ultimate writing of the Mishnah and the Talmud) brings us to a defining moment in the history of Judaism as well as Freud's own intellectual formation. The moment can be recalled as another in the history of the Jewish people. Freud draws together the Mosaic event in Sinai and the destruction of the temple in Jerusalem by the Romans. His two examples means that *the image* (the statue of a golden calf) and *the spectacle* (a slaughtered bull) are both superseded by Judaism at two moments in its history, one during the exodus from Egypt, the other after the exile from Jerusalem in the aftermath of the city's destruction.

When it comes to the writing of *Moses and Monotheism*, we can admit that "nearly all commentators agree that its subject is Jewish identity."[60] The "agreement" is not unanimous and merits, at least, a reconsideration. Freud would appreciate some of us not being part of the "nearly all." Our imperatives, especially if they are social and political, may be appropriate and necessary. But if we are to understand Freud and his motivations, the pressing idea of identity is not at all necessary for him as a strict bind. The political response to the publication of *Moses and Monotheism*, and due to its historical context, has been, understandably, filled with all kinds of responses and reactions. Political and moral disappointment is a unique phenomenon. The critical attitude demands it. Motivations are many and mixed. One statement, not for the first time, will be phrased as a question: could we say, when *Moses and Monotheism* is considered as a whole, that the book "could be construed as a form of Jewish self-hatred?"[61] The extreme consideration is mentioned again. One could arrive at such a conclusion if one read the first two essays, one, from an extremely narrow perspective, two, completely ignored the third and final section published when he was in London in 1939, three, was insightful enough to be able to forego Freud's reasons, four, *analyzed him* for an ethnic pathology – the last being highly susceptible to personal perceptions which (given the consequences of a post-Shoah consciousness) could certainly sway one's view decisively. All kinds of examinations have been attempted. How relevant they are is by no means obvious to answer. The reader can decide.[62] The European politics of the 1930's is a separate issue. To forego one form of analysis is done for the sake of a completely different emphasis, one that begins with Judaism and soon leads, when we consider his formal university education, towards the study of science and medicine and laboratory research.

At the end of *Moses and Monotheism*, Freud sums up the work and, sensing the incompleteness of his task, writes:

> Our investigation may have perhaps thrown a little light on the question of how the Jewish people have acquired the characteristics which distinguish them. Less light has been thrown on the problem of how it is that they have been able to retain their individuality till the present day.
>
> (SE 23:136–7)

One is tempted to answer with a reminder of a religious revolution, one that moved from the spectacles as they were carried out by a sacrificial culture in a temple to a community of students and teachers who read, interpreted, and then wrote endless (infinite) commentaries which, if they were never completed as a self-conscious task, assured a continuity in the life of the religion as well as all the people who were associated with its heritage. The statement is actually a question for us; or, to recall some of his most autobiographical declarations, he himself has openly expressed his views on how someone retains their character and individuality despite the majority consensus of a culture. A cosmopolitan thinker has internalized a number of different origins and developments and history and, comprehensively, made them his own.

We can think about making one contribution with the creation of psychoanalysis itself and then another by returning with Freud to the man Moses and three insights from *Moses and Monotheism*; comprehensively, they have provided us with the principal themes of the chapter on the creation of the Hebrew alphabet, its historical actuality in the writing, reading, and interpretation of the Torah, and on Freud's relationship with Moses as the one individual who was called a prophet by virtue of his ability to be foundational, that is, to use Freud's words, an *Übermensch* in his essay on Michelangelo but "*der grosse Mann*" in *Moses and Monotheism*. In each of our interests, the attention to a feature of their particularity (and how they can be viewed as a unity) will be at the basis of the argument to come on only a few of the more intricate origins of psychoanalysis. His conclusion can be followed: first, we have a testimony of how Freud himself may have acquired the characteristics that were highly personal; second, we then have to also hear his perplexity on how the characteristics have endured. There are innumerable possibilities for an answer. For our interests, which have been very specific since the beginning, we now have to try to answer how Freud's individual perception turned into a vision – that is, a way of thinking and seeing the world that was unique and led to lifelong discoveries. We turn again to some of the scholarship on Freud's Jewishness and then, more specifically, to the reception of his late work on Moses – which is impossible to read without sensing some identification and not a little emulation for being, for one, a leader and a great innovator of a form of life. We have to emphasize the connection between a revelation and a graven image, which is understood both as a fake sign and symbol (a sacred calf) as well as a perception that has the possibility of being converted from an individual experience to a mass one and therefore infecting, like the metaphor of a contagion, a group and then society as a whole.

Assessing the reactions to the publication of *Moses and Monotheism* poses obstacles that are far more significant than intellectual disagreements. The consequences, *at the time of the work's publication*, were grave. There is no way to adequately deal with the reality at hand (and definitely not in a work whose aims stretch out in different directions), or, frankly, to be able to fathom Freud's motivations unless we press one issue over many others and make one particular interpretation – which was psychoanalytic, *not political*. Transmission has been a predominant reality in Freud's inheritance and the repeated words *legacy and heritage*; we stress, again, the double-meaning of *Übertragung* as a transference and transmission. Was there a unique relationship between Moses and Freud? Before answering, some more responses to Freud's work can be examined, both for their essential interest and for complementing earlier impressions.

The identity, as a Jew, is for Freud less significant than his identification. Moses was "undoubtedly aware of his great capacities, ambitious and energetic" (SE 23:28). One could read innumerable sentences, on Moses, that could just as readily refer to himself. Freud's own transmission to us, as readers, warns us about possible avenues of interpretation; and yet, for political reasons (and moral ones, which are seemingly always attached) many of his readers did not listen. Hans Blumenberg, among other notable individuals, writes that "it remains dismaying what Freud did in 1939." The word *inexcusable* is implied, as is the force of moral judgement – which has no place in psychoanalysis and even less when Freud is the sole subject. Blumenberg's feelings are not hidden. His sources, letters for example, are a matter of record. Anecdotal evidence is less trustworthy. Still, we have the testimony of a conversation between Arthur Koestler and Freud when he visited him in London in 1938. Apparently, Freud's view of the unfolding events in Europe did not in the least surprise him. Perhaps his analytic resignation was interpreted as indifference or callousness – towards his own people. "That is the fate of those who make such good theories that the by-product is a philosophy of history capable of explaining what has happened, and what is happening, but which in doing so *prohibits* any moral judgment."[63] What Freud was expected *to do* is not easily anticipated. His *feelings* appear to be in question – and, above all, his morality. Is he lacking in empathy for Jewish suffering? Any assessment of *Moses and Monotheism*, placing it firmly (and only) in the historical context of its writing, is a decision and not necessarily a correct one. Is there, at least, an alternative and one that can reorientate any ill-will towards Freud based on one kind of interpretation? For making a moral judgement, as we know all too well today, answers no questions at all and simply takes the most expedient, and surely the easiest, way of all. Today it has received all the sanctions in the world. Blumenberg, it seems, expected Freud to be judgmental and to condemn the European situation at the time; the resolve not to do so is one more indication of Freud's character and refusal to fulfil the expectations of others who eventually become the "many" and then make any original thinking not only impossible, but immoral. His social and political insights had been already made clear in the work of the 1920's and their culmination in *Civilization and Its Discontents*. The word "barbarism," mentioned before, was his. He was never going to opt for the easiest response or, worse, the most expected one. Freud was not the only one to be so judged. Other names need not be mentioned since they would only add to the force of one interpretation and be a deviation from the theme of this project. In any event, reading *Moses and Monotheism* without at the same remembering what he had written about the psychopathology of politics and of groups in the 1920's suffers from an incompleteness and, worse, realizing how Freud's psychoanalytic analysis of certain radical politics were characterized by a well-known form of *hybris* – the belief that human nature could be altered if only the objective conditions of the world could be rectified. That illusion was exposed for the ideological mendacity it in fact produced. There are now many examples of states-made attempts at revolutions and *Reichs*, each of them with corresponding slaughters. The 21st-century form of liberalism has learnt its historical lessons well, cognitively or unconsciously. Black boots are still worn; only now they are fashionable more than practical.

The previous discussions on the culture of Judaism of his youth and its persistence for the whole of his life culminated with a work whose themes (not all of them noticed with the same acuity) had been on his mind for a long period of time. What did he plan to say and why? Are we so certain that one argument – however central, and understood to be unsettling – was not for Freud its ultimate intent? Any words, here, are only going to be presented as a foundation for the equally important experiences for Freud when he entered the University of Vienna in 1873 with the plan of studying physiology and anatomy and with the goal of becoming a doctor. With that in mind, now pressing forward with the intimate relation between Judaism and science, Freud's results, many years later, can be anticipated. For one, should we not be aware of the preponderance of images to continue to make one reality absolute? While we could interpret the Mosaic prohibition against images as a direct commentary on the use of signs and symbols in society to proclaim one absolute, we will stay away from Freud's actual situation in Vienna. A historical interpretation would only serve to restrict Freud to being a political commentator; in any case, the publication of *Civilization and Its Discontents* should have made everyone aware of his social and political philosophy. The images of Europe are a historical fact. Freud's psychoanalysis of images, then, and now, are much more important for us than to assure ourselves of our historical knowledge as well as our moral standing – which is so prized today that one has had no reluctance at all in becoming the worst kind of image, that is, a spectacle, and a self-serving one at that. Groups have turned themselves into their own form of idolatry.

Josef Yerushalmi has been at the forefront of the reassessment of *Moses and Monotheism*. One of his conclusions is: "The real fulcrum of the book, especially of its third part, is the problem of Tradition itself, not only the question of its origin but also of its essential dynamics."[64] Heard otherwise then intended, the meaning could just as easily be applied to the "tradition" of the psyche – its history for an individual – no less than the origin of a possible neurotic illness as well as its *essential dynamics*. To so transform the meaning of *Moses and Monotheism* is necessary if another interpretation is to be offered. Yerushalmi's "fulcrum," when displaced from the specificity of its Jewishness, takes us to the possibility of a set of relations that, when outlined more or less in order, will be concerned with another and quite different tradition – the one in the history of science and how Freud inherited its principles and transformed them from within and by also rethinking its metaphoric potential. Origin, tradition, dynamics: applied equally to science as Freud inherited its history and self-understanding, each of Yerushalmi's concepts draw us into a completely, though related, set of historical experiences. As we move towards the second chapter on science, we can stress the argument as laid out in the Introduction: our problem is not to understand anything as restrictive as a "Jewish science." Rather, the interest involves us trying to understand the connection between Judaism and science once Freud's hermeneutics of the Torah are first presented. Freud's writing, when interpreted in isolation, have led to narrow-minded conclusions. Identifying *the* motivation for the writing of *Moses and Monotheism* is too ambitious. The simplest observation would be a psychoanalytic one: we are more likely to be satisfied with the idea of overdetermination than any one fixation. Statements, as a general rule, are acceptable. "Freud studies the biblical text in the same way he investigates the unconscious mechanisms of his clinical cases."[65] One should not forget, however, which came first. In the case of Moses, Freud is doing something other than psychoanalyzing either the text or the man. For one thing, the act of writing was, also, an act of identification with a foundational figure and someone who can rightly be recognized, as biblical prophets tend to be, in the role of inaugurating a new way of life. Freud's consciousness presents itself to us as the thinker and writer he has been for an entire life.

"If Freud was Moses, he was a Moses visited by revelations about human beings, and not by the Divine Word."[66] The word revelations, so determined by theological principles and beliefs, are going to be immanent for Freud – and double-sided, that is, determined from *the double-conscience* of a fragmented psyche. Freud returns to the "Bible story" which had fascinated him since his youth and, knowing he was approaching the end of his life, intent on writing as a witness. The short autobiography had been instrumental in laying out the history of psychoanalysis more than being personal, except when necessary. In *Moses and Monotheism*, the ongoing transference is explicit and perpetual. One section, not surprisingly, is called "The Great Man."[67] We are, here, at one turning point for Freud. Unless we read his words as a personal revelation, the historical will remain our precedent and so find ourselves in knowledge that has been all-too-often confirmed by the majority.

> How is it possible for a single man to evolve such extraordinary effectiveness that he can form a people out of random individuals and families, can stamp them with their definitive character and determine their fate for thousands of

years? Is not a hypothesis such as this a relapse into the mode of thought which led to myths of a creator and to the worship of heroes, into times in which the writing of history was nothing more than a report on the deeds and destinies of single individuals?

(SE 23:107)

Without hyperbole and simply admitting to an uncommon ambition, Freud himself must have wondered how he had become such an individual. *Moses and Monotheism* is, then, an interpretation with a double-consciousness, one historical, one autobiographical and one of the final testimonies on how psychoanalysis became guided by human reason, intelligence, freedom, and the acuity of perception necessary for the balanced, and healthy, understanding of the self, others, and the world. His return to Moses was, to use a phrase he had borrowed from a renowned biologist, Ernest Haeckel, his way of tracing the ontogenetic through the phylogenetic and back again. However, if we also wish to make a personal distinction between the biological and the intellectual, Freud knew how everything he had adopted from the world (both Jewish and secular) was part of his individual creativity and, in the end, a testament to his character. There are many unmistakable sources of his own self-understanding. How he related himself, very personally, to a form of historical writing was one attitude among many others. The nature of the transference and his views on individual defined as an *Übermensch* made it impossible for him to see that "a text draws from and adapts from the world in which its authors live."[68] Half-true, for we also have to consider what happens when a reader of Freud's capacities enters the text with an original kind of thinking that is not, simply, *already in the world*.

"The Bible narrative" (SE 23:40) is an expression Freud adds to the sometimes-used "story," both of them intended to disregard any specific transmission from the divine to the human and instead begin from the one certainty of the existence of the Torah and its significance for readers while being aware that its meanings "have been distorted by the influence of powerful tendentious purposes and embellished by the products of poetic invention." The "powerful purposes" he refers to are, above all, psychological; the psyche, as a drive in history, has had its share of influence and determinations. There are indications from many of his writings throughout his life that these "purposes" and "inventions" could be understood no differently than neurotic phenomena. There is, however, one sometimes neglected aspect of Freud's sense of self, as a Jew and a reader, that cannot so easily be dismissed. My attitude, here, has nothing to do with an either/or defence or critique of religion. The question is and remains: what can we learn from Freud's interpretation that may offer a different way to understand this one writing and how, in many ways, it was indeed a culmination and one much more variegated in its interests and implications than has sometimes been thought? In a work that has been widely misunderstood, he writes about *our illusions* and so our inability to recognize certain kinds of truth. "The truths contained in religious doctrine are after all so distorted and systematically disguised that the mass of humanity cannot recognize them as truth" (SE 21:44). How many times has this passage from *The Future of an Illusion* been cited by atheists or anyone else who would like to make Freud simple-minded about religion?

One truth was a Mosaic one: worshipping an image was both a literal and allegorical problem. Its allegorical problem was an entirely psychological one and could not be reduced to a theological aberration. In Section (G) of *Moses and Monotheism* called "Historical Truth," Freud writes that,

> there is an element of grandeur about everything to do with the origin of religion ... and this is not matched by the explanations we have hitherto given. Some other factor must be involved to which there is little that is analogous and nothing that is of the same kind, something unique and something of the same order of magnitude as what has come out of it, as religion itself.
> (SE 23:128)

One finds it difficult not to also read something *to which there is a lot that is analogous*. Is there, here, an overlap between the creation of the Jewish religion and psychoanalysis? At the risk of overstepping a boundary – and yet, in attempting to understand Freud's own uniqueness, originality, and creativity, are we so far from the truth when we see how his identification with Moses was far closer than we can imagine? One point Freud makes has often (almost always) been forsaken by our own lapses and complacency. Our "explanations," for religion, have not been at all adequate to its meanings; so when Freud asks us to consider "what has come out of it," and, without our traditional prejudices, are we then able to recover something so *unique* that is as unprecedented as the Mosaic event? The question is a rhetorical one; enough has been suggested, thus far, to merit consideration, both for itself and for the arguments to come in the rest of the project. When the historical interpretations, by commentators, are set aside and suspended, we come to one of Freud's most outstanding ideas. There is no shortage of them; this one gives us a sense of his own self-understanding.

Although historicists will no doubt reject Freud's ideas about "the transcendent influence of a single personality," (SE 23:108) we now have a superlative problem; there is no need for us to shy away from the affirmation of the individual Moses and, at least, Michelangelo's representation of him along with Freud's interpretation. Two possibilities and their consequences, and none of them are, strictly speaking, historical at all: Moses is the individual who receives a revelation as portrayed in the Book of Exodus, or he is that rare individual, a genius, who has the internal resources and inspiration to utterly transform the nature of reality as he presents it for others to believe in and find of supreme value for its commitment of life. Our modern academic certainties have been in part responsible for narrowing ourselves, in perception, and to then lead ourselves to a number of conclusions for the sake of morality and, it also seems, to undermine ourselves as subjects. Our civilizations, and our humanity, have suffered as well. Is there anyone who can seriously question Freud's *transcendent influence* in the history of psychoanalysis or, more comprehensively, in the history of thought? As we draw near to a conclusion on Jewish transferences and an archaic heritage, the main elements of Freud's mind as he expressed them, in their final form, in *Moses and Monotheism*, lead us to the singularity of an individual.

Freud asks himself, and us, a question: "how is it possible for a single man to evolve such extraordinary effectiveness" (SE 23:107)? The question does not need to be answered. Ignored or deferred, the one individual can remain with us the rest of the way and see if he has an influence on what follows from his archaic heritage to a dominant form of thought in 19th-century European science. One individual and a people: Freud had spent his entire life reflecting on both.

Nearing our conclusion here, we are more drawn to him and, due to our own transference – and his transmission, in writing and more – away from judgements made about him, even from people who knew him personally. Isidor Sadger wrote. "Particularly with respect to things related to Judaism Freud's character did not stand the test of time."[69] Testimonies, of course, run both ways. Instead of the personal as judged by others, there are other ways to approach Freud's relation to Judaism and without turning to the reality everyone believes is the most obvious – or the most important: the political. The reason to turn to *Moses and Monotheism*, from the standpoint of psychoanalysis – to see how some of his hermeneutic insights, as a reader and researcher, is relevant for an understanding of human beings and their perception – remains strictly orientated to individuals. One of the reasons for the project, as a whole, is to see how Judaism, science, neurotic patients, and the understanding of hysteria were all contributing factors in the formation of psychoanalysis up until 1886, a historical date serving as a limit of a period and the beginning of another when he returns to Vienna from Paris.

Earlier readings of *Moses and Monotheism* that insisted on either a strictly historical or theological interpretation were set aside; the personal was chosen to be more representative of Freud the individual and of his psychoanalytic perceptions. The contentions will no doubt continue. Some arguments will be made – accepted or rejected depending on our attitudes. Can we be satisfied with Moshe Gresser's argument: "when faced with death after 1923, Freud must return to vindicate Jewish religion?"[70] "Vindication" is the wrong word and even worse sentiment. The feeling, and the drive, are too-often neurotic and originating in a fundamental weakness of character.

> We can affirm that the invention of a particular way of practicing Judaism and of opposing the resistances of the West to the Jews, demanded from Freud the same kind of strength that he needed to face the patient's resistance to the cure, as well as the resistance of the enlightened culture and the positivistic science that rejected his discoveries.[71]

The personal struggles are one issue; they are not, for me, primary because he saw himself as more than someone with an identity that needs to affirm himself because of a social prejudice. There is no denying the fact, as he tells us when he began his university studies. However, in turning, as we've done briefly, to the question of Freud's Jewishness, one attitude was maintained that made it impossible to be wishful on a question of ethnicity. We defined Freud as a cosmopolitan, doing so to avoid the inaccurate "assimilated," which is simply inaccurate when thinking about him as an individual who was raised with a number of decisive cultural influences. He was a European Jew.

Betty Bernardo Fuks adds: "the Jewish reading of a text, psychoanalysis, and the very writing share the same openness: openness to the word that each one is called to say." *Called*: the word has never been used by Freud to describe himself, but if we are to end the chapter with one final reference to Moses, then the Book of Leviticus should be recalled from its Hebrew origin as *wayiqra, being called* – which for Freud would not be from a divine voice and as the unique privilege of the prophet but something far less metaphysical and emerging, simply, from the relationship to the world in as many different ways as possible and so to make combinations inhere in oneself. Freud's own *Qara*, as a proclamation on the nature of being, became a personal responsibility – his own personal calling and the calling to others *to themselves* and for the personal freedom he so valued as a psychical ideal never to be squandered for any reason whatsoever. The evaluations on the question of Freud's Jewishness has been directed (only) at three inter-related themes. One affirmation cannot be confirmed. In a chapter called "Freud's Bible," David Biale concludes. "The intellectual spirit that created psychoanalysis was at bottom the heritage of Biblical Judaism."[72] The "at bottom" is too complete. There are other, equally important experiences that would be just as foundational that, together, created psychoanalysis. His experience while studying medicine at the University of Vienna and his subsequent choice to engage in scientific research in a laboratory was just as meaningful for his interest in consciousness and perception. "Freud's attitude to Jews and his own Jewishness had more ingredients than the courage with which he acknowledged the emotional source of his identity with Jews and the intellectual and characterological indebtedness he owed to Judaism."[73] More ingredients: by all means let us acknowledge a personal courage as, in part, an element of his Judaism. But at this transition from Judaism to the history of science, his experience at the University of Vienna, as a student and laboratory researcher and medical professional, were equally influential on the way he developed his consciousness and perception. Indeed, by tracing one influence back to Francis Bacon's *Novum Organum*, we can see how one of the defining works of the modern world was an amalgamation, classical as it was, of a humanism that did not easily separate ways of thinking and being. Judaism, philosophy, and science were inter-connected at the beginning of the modern era.

Coming to the end of the chapter, on the meaning of Moses for Freud, and the transition into science, one of the many interlocutors who will be omnipresent gives us an anticipation. "In *Moses and Monotheism*, Freud gives us a sense of how and why he understood psychoanalysis to be so distinctively the contribution of a Jew ... *Moses and Monotheism* is Freud's final testament to the Jewishness of his creation."[74] And yet others believe that in his "final manifesto," Freud is intent on doing something more personal and more divisive. "It is certain that in this, his last work, he liberates himself from Moses."[75] A final argument need not be made, not here; the rest of the project will continue to reflect on his "testament." Freud's creation was, undoubtedly (like Moses), "drawn out." The sources were many, and they can be traced back, in addition to Judaism, to other sources from the classical world and no less in the modern scientific one. Freud tells us so himself in an article, not often cited and which first appeared in a general publication, *Die Gesundheit*, where he explicitly grounds psychoanalysis in the ancient world and in the earliest forms of therapy. "Psychical (or Mental) Treatment" should be read for at least one reason. Freud concludes: "It may safely be anticipated that systematic modern mental treatment, which is a quite recent revival of ancient therapeutic methods, will provide physicians with far more powerful weapons for the fight against illness" (SE 7:302). *Ancient therapeutic methods.* The reference is suggestive, for it does not define which ancient methods he means. Our final turning point, from Judaism to science, has now been reached. The transition, from one to the other, will hopefully also address a preoccupation of long standing, the question of psychoanalysis as a "Jewish science." We have, so far, responded to a few commentators. One last one is appropriate. Richard Rubenstein writes that "underneath the prose of scientific rationality, which Freud tells us not to take seriously, this bearded Jew was a 20th-century Rebbe intent on giving his people and the world a new Torah."[76] Freud never asked us to do any such thing. His life, beginning from his university studies, is a testament to his scientific rationality and how, inter-related with Judaism, became essential in the foundation of psychoanalysis. *A new Torah* is only acceptable if highly modified. One introduction to our next theme of medicine and science as related to Freud's university studies is, also, a firm reminder of his conscious exposure to a wider culture.

> As a student, Freud took part for five years (1873–8) in the activities of the *Leseverein der deutschen Studenten Wiens* (Reading Group of the German Students in Vienna), a society which had as its central purpose the stimulation of a strong sense of German nationalism.[77]

Our perspective of "nationalism" may, however, make it virtually impossible to sense Freud's participation as an individual and as a student – that is, someone continuing to learn and be devoted to the German ideal of *Bildung*, a "national" imperative that was also classical and European and reflective of an entire history of civilization. The "parallels between the humanistic concept of self-cultivation through *Bildung* and the ideal of character development inherent in psychoanalysis"[78] were drawn from the beginning and would only increase when his Jewish heritage was complemented, both ways, by 19th-century science and by his significant contributions in a number of pre-psychoanalytic areas of research.

## Notes

1 Smadja, Eric. *Freud and Culture*. London: Karnac, 2015, 167.
2 Richards, Robert J. *The Tragic Sense of Life: Ernest Haeckel and the Struggle Over Evolutionary Thought*. Chicago: The University of Chicago Press, 2008.
3 Johnston, Adrian. *Prolegomena to Any Future Materialism. Volume One: The Outcome of Contemporary French Philosophy*. Evanston: Northwestern University Press, 2013, 59.
4 See, for example, their *Self and Emotional Life: Philosophy, Psychoanalysis, and Neuroscience*. New York: Columbia University Press, 2013.
5 Neusner, Jacob. *The Way of Torah: An Introduction to Judaism*. Encino, California: Dickenson Publishing Company, Inc., 1974, 50.
6 Hartman, Evelyn T. "An Analysis of Freud's Jewish Identity," 612–616 *Contemporary Psychoanalysis* 47 (4), 2011. Given the prominence of "identity" as currently discussed, in and out of institutions of higher learning, we can here suspend our assumptions about its meaning (however correct or distorted they may be) and instead make the attempt to interpret something as complicated as a "Jewish identity" – from the classical world, to Freud's 19th-century Vienna, and no less to our fraught times – by ensuring our definitions are not restrictive. We are going to be just as conscientious in not limiting Freud as we are in not limiting ourselves. Hartman's view is one we can proceed from: "Freud's views on his Judaism at times contradict each other, at times elude us." Beginning from our inadequacy seems more prudent than being so certain about Freud's "contradictions."
7 Richards, Arnold D. "Freud's Jewish Identity and Psychoanalysis as a Science," 987–1003 *Journal of the American Psychoanalytic Association* 62 (6) 2014. For us, one answer requires additional research and therefore forces us to pursue all kinds of questions (on Freud's identity and of psychoanalysis as inherently a Jewish form of knowledge) that will end with a perennial concern – that is, the life of Moses. Richards uses a word that is preferable that personal identity. On *Moses and Monotheism*, he writes, "The book itself is a kind of coming-to-consciousness of a distinctive type of Jewish legacy," 1003. The legacy, then, will be traced not so much to a personal identity, much less to the too-vague "Jewish science," but to a particular kind of legacy that is linguistic, textual, and interpretive.
8 Frosh, Stephen. "Freud and Jewish Identity," 167–178 *Theory & Psychology* 18 (2), Apr. 2008, 177.
9 Herman, David. "Psychoanalysis, Jews and History," 86–97 *European Judaism* 55 (1), Mar. 2022, 90–91. This is not the only place were Herman overextends himself. Since we will consider the role of the Kabbalah on Freud's thought, Herman adds something that is, again, provocative but perhaps overstated. For the Jews of Freud's generation, the "formation with Judaism and the Kabbalah predisposed a younger generation to think differently about human nature and interpretation." The equation is too neat. One could say the exact some thing about, for example, reading Goethe, the German Romantics, or Nietzsche. Nevertheless, due to Herman's connection, made by others, the influence on Freud's thought by the Kabbalah will be considered.
10 Kaplan, Robert M. "Soaring on the Wings of Wind: Freud, Jews, and Judaism," 318–325 *Australasian Psychiatry* 17 (4), Aug. 2009.
11 Aaron, Lewis and Libby Henik. "Introduction" to their co-edited *Answering a Question with a Question: Contemporary Psychoanalysis and Jewish Thought*. Brighton, Mass: Academic Studies Press, 2010, 17.
12 Handelman, Susan A. *The Slayers of Moses: The Emergence of Rabbinic Interpretation in Modern Literary Theory*. Albany: SUNY, 1982, 131.
13 Bloom, Harold. "Freud: Frontier Concepts, Jewishness, and Interpretation," 135–152 *American Imago* 48 (1), Spring 1991, 138. Given the themes of the chapter, two more

comments by Bloom can be added – especially when it comes to the importance of *Moses and Monotheism*. "Freudian speculations may or may not be scientific or philosophical; what counts about it is its interpretative power."
14 Salberg, Jill. "Hidden in Plain Sight: Freud's Jewish Identify Revisited," 197–217 *Psychoanalytic Dialogues* 17 (2), 2007.
15 Lewis, Aaron. "Freud's Ironically Jewish Science: Commentary on Paper by Jill Salberg," 219–231 *Psychoanalytic Dialogues* 17 (2), 2007, 228.
16 De Mendelssohn, Felix. "The Jewish Tradition in Sigmund Freud's Work," 31–47 *Psychoanalysis, Monotheism, and Morality: The Sigmund Freud Symposia 2009–2011*. Ed. Wolfgang Müller et al. Leuven: Leuven University Press, 2013, 37.
17 One could start, given our context, with *The Ego Ideal: A Psychoanalytic Study on the Malady of the Ideal*. Tr. Paul Burrows. New York: W.W. Norton, 1985.
18 Chasseguet-Smirgel, Janine. "Some Thoughts on Freud's Attitude During the Nazi Period," in *Freud and Judaism*. Ed. David Meghnagi. London: Karnac, 1993, 76–77.
19 Carroll, Michael P. "'Moses and Monotheism' Revisited – Freud's 'Personal Myth'?" 15–35 *American Imago* 44 (1), Spring 1987, 32.
20 Halpern, Werner I. "Review" of Jerry Vitor Diller's *Freud's Jewish Identity: A Case Study in the Impact of Ethnicity*," 129–131 *Shofar* 12 (3), Spring 1994.
21 Gelbin, Cathy S., and Sander L. Gilman. "Introduction" to their co-edited *Cosmopolitanism and the Jews*. Ann Arbor: University of Michigan Press, 2017. Gilman has devoted himself to Freud and Judaism in other works. We can refer, for example, to *The Case of Sigmund Freud: Medicine and Identity at the Fin de Siècle*. Baltimore: Johns Hopkins University Press, 1993. Prior to reading, the title in itself merits thought: "case" is no ordinary word; when applied to identity, one wonders about Gilman's intent. Given the subject of the upcoming second section, on aspects of the Kabbalah and the Zohar, one response to the Gelbin/Gilman thesis would be to mention how the Zohar, in particular, should not be considered from the pejorative "nomadism" but quite the contrary. See, for example, the idea of the Zohar and its setting of "walking stories" as the particular topic of David Greenstein's *Roads to Utopia: The Walking Stories in the Zohar*. Stanford: Stanford University Press, 2014.
22 Lakritz, Isaac. "Judaism and Freud," 225–227 *Tradition: A Journal of Orthodox Jewish Thought* 15 (1–2), Spring/Summer 1975, 227.
23 Biale, David. *Not in the Heavens: The Tradition of Jewish Secular Thought*. Princeton: Princeton University Press, 2011, 176.
24 Jennings, Jerry L. "Engaging with the Unknown," *Journal of the History of the Behavioral Sciences* 60 (1), Winter 2024.
25 See the informative article by Joel Whitebook, "Jacob's Ambivalent Legacy," 139–155 *American Imago* 67 (2) (Summer 2010).
26 Slavet, Eliza. "Immaterial Materiality: The 'Special Case' of Freud's Theory of Jewishness," 353–382 *Jewish Studies Quarterly* 15 (4), 2008, 374.
27 Diller, Jerry Victor. *Freud's Jewish Identity: A Case Study in the Impact of his Ethnicity*. New Jersey: Farleigh Dickinson University Press, 1991. See, also, his edited collection, *The Jewish World of Sigmund Freud: Essays on Cultural Roots and the Problem of Religious Identity*. Jefferson, North Carolina: McFarland & Co., Inc., Publishers, 2010.
28 Reijzer, Hans. *A Dangerous Legacy: Judaism and the Psychoanalytic Movement*. Tr. Jeannette Ringold. London: Karnac, 2011, 10.
29 Leonard. Miriam. *Socrates and the Jews: Hellenism and Hebraism from Moses Mendelssohn to Sigmund Freud*. Chicago: The University of Chicago Press, 2012, 191.
30 Frieden, Ken. Freud's *Dream of Interpretation*. Albany: SUNY, 1990, 7. He adds, "Freud knew enough of Judaic traditions to be uneasy about his knowledge." If true, then, it is necessary to turn to some of these traditions and see, first, the extent of his knowledge and, second, the reason for the apparent uneasiness.

31 Goux, Jean-Joseph. "Freudian Unconscious and Secularization of Judaism," 217–225 *Disciplining Freud on Religion: Perspectives from the Humanities and Sciences*. Ed. Greg Kaplan and William Parsons. Lanham: Lexington Books, 2010, 220.
32 As presented by Mortimer Ostow in *Ultimate Intimacy: The Psychodynamics of Jewish Mysticism*. London: Routledge, 1995.
33 Bakan, David. *Sigmund Freud and the Jewish Mystical Tradition*. Boston: Beacon Press, 1958, xi. The contributions made since Bakan's publication have been consistent. See, among many examples, Seth Aronson's "The Problem of Desire: Psychoanalysis as a Jewish Wisdom Tradition," 313–326 *Answering a Question with a Question*. Ed. Lewis Aron and Libby Henik. Brighton, MA: Academic Studies Press, 2010.
34 Scholem, Gershom (Ed). *Zohar: The Book of Splendor*. New York: Schocken Books, 1963.
35 Huss, Boaz. *The Zohar: Reception and Impact*. Tr. Yudith Nave. London: The Littman Library of Jewish Civilization, 2008.
36 Idel, Moshe. *Kabbalah: New Perspectives*. New Haven: Yale University Press, 1988.
37 Thienhaus, Ole J. "Jewish Time: Ancient Practices, Hellenistic and Modern Habits, Freud's Reclaiming," 442–449 *Judaism* 48, 1999, 448.
38 Schneider, Stanley, and Joseph H. Berke. "The Oceanic Feeling, Mysticism and Kabbalah: Freud's Historical Roots," 131–156 *Psychoanalytic Review* 95 (1), Feb. 2008, 133.
39 Silverstein, Charles H. "Kabbalistic Influence on Alchemy, Psychoanalysis, and Analytic Psychology," 205–218 *Psychological Perspectives* 55, 2012, 205. The history of scholarship has not left one connection unexamined. See, among others, Shaul Magid and Edward Hoffman's article "The Way of Splendor: Jewish Mysticism and Modern Psychology," 445–447 *Association for Jewish Studies*, 32 (2), Nov. 2008. Space does not allow for a longer engagement with Tom Keve's *TRIAD: The Physicists, the Analysts, the Kabbalists*. London: Rosenberger and Krausz, 2000.
40 Beck, Mordechai. "The Secular Kabbalist," *The Jerusalem Report* Dec. 12, 2016, 4.
41 Frosh, Stephen. "Freud and Jewish Identity," 167–178 *Theory & Psychology* 18 (2), 2008, 169.
42 Eigen, Michael. *A Felt Sense: More Explorations of Psychoanalysis and the Kabbalah*. London: Karnac, 2013, 29.
43 Helperin, David J. "Methodological Reflections on Psychoanalysis and Judaic Studies: A Response to Mortimer Ostow," 183–199 in Mortimer Ostow' *Ultimate Intimacy: The Psychodynamics of Jewish Mysticism*. London: Karnac, 1995, 199.
44 Berke, Joseph H. *The Hidden Freud: His Hassidic Roots*. London: Karnac, 2015.
45 Eigen, Michael. *Kabbalah and Psychoanalysis*. London: Karnac, 2012, x.
46 Bakan, David, Dan Merkur, and David S. Weiss. *Maimonides' Cure of Souls: Medieval Precursor of Psychoanalysis*. Albany: SUNY Press, 2009, 137.
47 See, for an overview of the movement, George Y. Kohler's *Kabbalah Research in the Wissenschaft des Judentums (1820–1880): The Foundation of an Academic Discipline*. Munich: De Gruyter Oldenbourg, 2019.
48 Matley, David. "Philology as Kabbalah," 13–28 *Kabbalah and Modernity: Interpretations, Transformations, Adaptations*. Ed. Boaz Huss, Mario Pasi, Kocku von Stuckrad. Leiden: Brill, 2010, 19.
49 Bernstein, Richard J. *Freud and the Legacy of Moses*. Cambridge: Cambridge University Press, 1998, 2.
50 Schniedewind, William M. "The History of Classical Hebrew: From the Invention of the Alphabet to the Mishnah," *Religion Compass* 13 (4), 2019.
51 Atzmon, Leslie. "A Visual Analysis of Anthropomorphism in the Kabbalah: Dissecting the Hebrew Alphabet and Sephirotic Diagram," 97–115 *Visual Communication* 2 (1), Feb. 2003, 109.

52 Weiss, Tzahi. *Sefer Yesirah and Its Contexts: Other Jewish Voices*. Philadelphia: University of Pennsylvania Press, 2018.
53 Meghnagi, David. "A Cultural Event Within Judaism," 57–70 *Freud and Judaism*. Ed. David Meghnagi. London: Karnac, 1993.
54 Kradin, Richard. *The Parting of the Ways: How Esoteric Judaism and Christianity Influenced the Psychoanalytic Theories of Sigmund Freud and Carl Jung*. Brighton, MA: Academic Studies Press, 2016, 75.
55 Beller, Steven. "Solving Riddles: Freud, Vienna and the Historiography of Madness," 27–42 *Journeys into Madness: Mapping Mental Illness in the Austro-Hungarian Empire*. Ed. Gemma Blackshaw and Sabine Wieber. New York: Berghahn Books, 2012, 27.
56 Reitter, Paul. "Rereading Freud's Moses (Again)," 11–24 *The Germanic Review* 83 (1), 2008, 14.
57 Rolnik, Eran J. *Freud in Zion: Psychoanalysis and the Making of Modern Jewish Identity*. London: Karnac, 2012, 191.
58 Assman, Jan. *The Prince of Monotheism*. Stanford: Stanford University Press, 2009, 86.
59 Bar-Haim, Shaul. "The Mosaic Legacy of Sigmund Freud: How to Read Moses and Monotheism in the Twenty-First Century," 371–378 *Psychoanalysis and History* 22.3, 2020.
60 Zaretsky, Eli. *Political Freud: A History*. New York: Columbia University Press, 2015. A political interpretation will necessarily lead to the questions of a "racial unconscious," which, as I said earlier, requires a certain subtlety of thought – which a political consciousness may not be able to deal with. One of Zaretsky's chapters is called "In the Shadow of the Holocaust: Rereading Freud's Moses." It is, of course, our choice if we decide to take the shadow into account of Freud's arguments, both intellectual and personal ones. Since, for me, the identification with Moses is the most important direction, the political can (with an assumed risk) be set aside.
61 Chernillo, Daniel. "The Jews Killed Moses: Sigmund Freud and the Jewish Question," *Theory, Culture & Society* 41 (3), Oct. 2023.
62 The literature on the subject is extensive. See, for example, Emily A. Kuriloff's *Contemporary Psychoanalysis and the Legacy of the Third Reich: History, Memory, Tradition*. New York: Routledge, 2014. A study based on personal interviews gives us one perspective from a number of individuals. "Jewishness and Psychoanalysis – the Relationship to Identity, Trauma and Exile. An Interval Study" conducted by Per Magnus Johansson and Elizabeth Punzi, 140–152 *Jewish Culture and History* 20 (2), 2019.
63 Blumenberg, Hans. *Rigorism of Truth: "Moses the Egyptian" and Other Writings on Freud and Arendt*. Ed. Ahlrich Meyer, Tr. Joe Paul Kroll. Ithaca: Cornell University Press, 2017, 39.
64 Yerushalmi, Josef Hayim. *Freud's Moses, Judaism Terminable and Interminable*. New Haven: Yale University Press, 1991.
65 Indursky, Alexei Conte, and Daniel Boianorsky Kveller. "Freud and Judaism: Mourning, Trauma, and Transmission," 405–413 *PsicologiaUSP* 28 (3) (Dec. 2017), 409. They add: "the testimonial elements of the Freudian text is very clear," 410. The word testimony is more than appropriate in this case because Freud was surely aware of his approaching end and what this *first and last word* from him was going to leave an enduring legacy.
66 Gertel, Elliot B. "Fromm, Freud, and *Midrash*," 429–439 *Judaism* 48 (192), 199, 433. He adds: "the book today is regarded as an unorthodox, whimsical midrash," 436. Whimsical is altogether the wrong word.
67 "Great Men" is the title of one of Herman Westerink's chapters in *A Dark Trace: Sigmund Freud on the Sense of Guilt*. Leuven: Leuven University Press, 2013. This

work made me aware of a translation from "The Moses of Michelangelo" – "more than human" – as *übermensliches*. A necessary additional chapter suggests itself for the project at hand; but adding the connection between Nietzsche and Freud on the question of the *Übermensch* requires, at least, an additional chapter, and then likely a lot more.

68 Hundley, Michael B. "What is the Golden Calf?" 559–579 *The Catholic Biblical Quarterly* 79 (4), 2017, 560.
69 Sadger, Isidor. *Recollecting Freud*. Ed. Alan Dundes. Tr. Johanna Micaela Jacobsen and Alan Dundes. Madison: The University of Wisconsin Press, 2005, 99.
70 Gresser, Moshe. *Dual Allegiance: Freud as a Modern Jew*. Albany: SUNY, 1994, 5.
71 Fuks Bernardo, Betty. "Vocation of Exile: Psychoanalysis and Judaism," 7–12 *International Forum of Psychoanalysis* 8 (1), 1999, 8.
72 Biale, David. *Not in the Heavens: The Tradition of Jewish Secular Thought*. Princeton: Princeton University Press, 2011, 80.
73 Diamond, Sigmund. "Sigmund Freud, his Jewishness, and Scientific Method: The Seen and Unseen as Evidence," 613–634 *History of the Journal of Ideas* 43 (4), Oct.–Dec. 1982, 626. Diamond's idea of "the seen and unseen" will be made more explicit in the chapter to come and in relation not so much to a scientific method as to an experience that was fundamental for Freud's own development in perception as one criteria for determining the neurotic psyche and consciousness.
74 Richards, Arnold D. "Freud's Jewish Identity and Psychoanalysis as a Science," 987–1003 *Journal of the American Psychoanalytic Association* 62 (6), 2014, 1002.
75 Schäfer, Peter. "The Triumph of Pure Spirituality: Sigmund Freud's Moses and Monotheism," 381–406 *Jewish Studies Quarterly* 9 (4), 2002, 394.
76 Rubenstein, Richard L. "Freud and Judaism: A Review Article," 39–44 *The Journal of Religion* 47 (1), 1967, 44.
77 Gödde, Günter. "Freud and the Nineteenth-Century Sources on the Unconscious," 261–286 *Thinking the Unconscious: Nineteenth-Century German Thought*. Ed. Angus Nicholls and Martin Liebscher. Cambridge: Cambridge University Press, 2010, 266.
78 Kauders, Anthony D. "From Place to Race and Back Again: The Jewishness of Psychoanalysis Revisited," 72–87 *Space and Spatiality in Modern German-Jewish History*. Ed. Simone Lässig and Miriam Rürup. New York: Berghahn, 2017.

# Chapter 2
# Science, Medicine, and the Laboratory

### Freud's Idea of Wissenschaft

> The concept of the unconscious has long been knocking at the gates of psychology and asking to be let in. Philosophy and literature have often toyed with it, but science could find no use for it. Psycho-analysis has seized upon the concept, which it has taken seriously and has given it fresh content.
>
> (Some Elementary Lessons in Psycho-analysis)

The transition from Jewish origins and Freud's archaic heritage to the 19th-century scientific world-view calls for an attempt to examine his thinking at a time when two traditions were omnipresent in him as an individual and as someone who was on the way to beginning his university studies in 1873. Born during the period when Darwin published *On the Origin of Species* and essentially introduced a new interpretation of the world that created a chasm between religion and science, Freud's own life and experiences led him to a personal period of reflection and eventually of research and discovery. In addition to his cultural Judaism, according to our three main themes, one other development influenced him during his school days, as it did most everyone else who was not religiously minded and still moved by faith. The original sense of *scientia*, as a form of knowledge – objectively and according to the nature of the world – promised to be reflective of a state as opposed to metaphysical beliefs. He writes, "The theories of Darwin, which were then of topical interest, strongly attracted me, for they held out hopes of an extraordinary advance in our understanding of the world" (SE 20:8). *An advance*: the idea, in itself, will not be extraneous to our shift from the history of Judaism to the ideals of 19th-century science, above all in Germany and according to the precepts of *Naturwissenschaft*.

Our Introduction mentioned a number of studies whose self-described purpose had been to define the origins of psychoanalysis; prudence demanded that any return to origins would involve many different layers, historical and thematic; using the term overdetermination was preferable in order to suspend any presumption about being complete. For Freud's generation, Darwin was indispensable; and for reasons that were well beyond the discipline of biology or the new theory of evolution. And yet there were a number of other influences on Freud's thinking that led him to prepare for a course of university studies in medicine. Attending a lecture where Goethe's essay "On Nature" was read influenced him to choose the medical profession for his future. That first choice proved to be a fateful one, for many different reasons. As to the "awkward relationship of Freud and psychoanalysis vis-à-vis medicine and medical education,"[1] any such relationship, of an "awkward" kind, can be confirmed only when an initial period of study is addressed. Medicine was a beginning. His inherited Judaism, the culture of 19th-century science, and the practical aims of his university studies are now going to be thought as part of one process, each with its own sphere of importance for allowing Freud to see interdisciplinary connections as opposed to the limits of any one discipline.

A repetition will not be wasted. In his "Introduction" called "The Freudian Aftershock," Matt Fyytche writes, "There is ever a rationale to return to Freud, to tell his story and that of the history of psychoanalysis. Freud's story is not quite fixed, because we are still deciding what to do with him."[2] We should always add: he also makes us decide what to do with *ourselves* since we are never exempt from the obligation of a dual-analysis. No differently than the extent of his Jewish heritage, his place in the history of science is equally, if not more, debated. Reactions are not unexpected; and they are inseparable from our sense of him – and the differences in our various analyses. If we can make such a statement to remember the ongoing connection with Judaism, which should actually be embarrassing – "Freud's obsession with Moses can be traced back to his unresolved Oedipal issues"[3] – then our turn to his scientific interests might be as fraught with analytical temptations and all kinds of presumptions. How facile to invoke Freud's "Oedipal issues." How difficult to understand our own.

One study is instructive, especially as we follow several meanings for Freud's relationship, comprehensively, to the past and his progenitors. Opening with an introduction called "the father of psychoanalysis," the organization of the project as a whole is revealing: it begins with "where it was: Freud's biology of the mind" and leads to "where psychoanalysis has come to be: philosophy, science, society and ethics."[4] Complementing our interdisciplinary history, we can make one more comment on the idea of Freud's heritage or inheritance from co-editors. "It may seem odd to think that psychoanalysis and inheritance belong together, since inheritance, as such, rarely appears in discussions of psychoanalytic theory."[5] Although their idea of an inheritance is specifically one between the two individuals of the analytic situation (and so, for us, about another kind of transference and transmission) we remain closer to Freud and, now, his Jewish and scientific inheritance. Genealogies criss-crossed each other in his mind and engendered a new process of thinking.

The prejudice towards "Jewish science" was mentioned as a source of some concern for Freud, especially in the early years of psychoanalysis. The term should no longer cause any worry. Our interests are, rather, with Freud's inheritance of both Judaism and science and how philosophy, as a way of thinking, complemented both. At the same time, a reader can be cited for his arguments; they are, also, biographical. Alfred Tauber believes that Freud was more inclined to study philosophy than medicine, and only did so from practical considerations. "Freud expended a fair amount of intellectual (and psychic) energy in defining himself as an empirical scientist at the expense of a competing, seemingly repressed intellectual passion."[6] We are now involved in a number of different issues: medical and scientific and, according to Tauber, a "suppressed passion." The suggestion, not to be simply dismissed, despite the overstated *repression* – it was, quite the contrary, very conscious – can now be one of our starting points as we inquire into Freud's recollections about science and its meanings for him. There is, parenthetically, a significant difference between repression and decision. The latter can be both conflictual and conscious.

In "A Difficulty in the Path of Psycho-analysis," Freud singled out one community that, more so today in many cases, has become self-possessed by their physicalism: the apparent hard science of psychology and, by extension, neurobiology. "Psychology as it is taught academically gives us but very inadequate replies to questions concerning our mental life" (SE 17:137). *Academically*: in our time, the word and thing should make us extra aware. Is not the inadequacy in part evident by our particular definition of science and what is academic? And does not Freud expand the concept of science – *scientia,* as a form of knowledge that, for him, extended beyond the material and the physical – by making the force of the unconscious part of our reality? One emphasis was repeated time and again; he differentiated himself from the incomplete science of the day since they were limited by 19th-century aspirations (of objectivity) and so were fixated on the material and most especially on the idea of *heredity,* a biological concept quite different than a heritage. Heritage and heredity: for Freud, they were distinct and not collapsible into each other, above all when it came to the diagnosis of a patient.

In "A Short Account of Psychoanalysis," Freud presents with a suggestion that has been, if not overlooked, certainly underappreciated. The force should be striking today, in the 21st century, due to our own attitude to science and its meaning as a *narrowly restricted field.* Using the concept of *scientism* is a distinction to keep in mind.

> Psycho-analysis grew up in a narrowly-restricted field. At the outset, it had only a single aim – that of understanding something of the nature of what were known as the "functional" nervous diseases ... The neurologists of that period had been brought up to have a high respect for chemico-physical and pathological-anatomical facts ... They did not know what to make of the psychical factor and could not understand it. They left it to the philosophers, the mystics and – the quacks; and then considered it unscientific to have anything to do with it.
> (SE 19:191)

Our accounts will be consistent: according to Freud, there is something inherently incomplete about science – or, at least, in the concept of 19th-century science. It occurs to me, at the moment, that it might be in the best interest of psychoanalysis to worry much less about its supposed status as a science than to recognize how the various disciplines, for all their advances, are simply inadequate as a measure of a thinking and a therapy that demands a unique accounting. The moment is prolonged only because Freud himself thought it necessary to continue to make his case. Our early references here are intermixed for a reason. If Freud had been pressed to choose a side, it does seem as if the philosophers (and the mystics – those mentioned earlier as the practitioners of the Kabbalah) would be on his side more than the chemico-physicalists of his era who, in orientation, tended to be as orthodox as the beliefs they wanted to overcome. Scientism not only overestimated the value of science, it assumed its methods could exhaustively understand the nature of reality and, more importantly, human beings. Critics of scientism tend to highlight the faith, orthodoxy, authority, and exclusivity of the scientific project and its overconfident assumptions about itself and, of course, its practitioners.[7] The current state of physics, for example, is enough to make us prudent about all our inquiries, most especially when the dream of a "theory of everything" should be, in principle, and ontologically, well out of reach.

The adjective "Jewish" will be removed from science as Freud learnt and practiced it during his formative years while studying medicine at the University of Vienna and, later (in two highly significant periods) when he worked in Ernst Brücke's physiological laboratory and then at the Vienna General Hospital under the leadership of Theodor Meynert. Science, medicine, laboratory research, psychiatry: each of them had a decisive influence on his intellectual formation and on the nature of his interests during the period of his university studies. The manifest themes of Jewish culture and science are now going to be inter-related for the sake of understanding how Freud enhanced his ability to see – that is, to reason and think about the nature of consciousness and perception, both for the neurotics who would eventually be cared for psychotherapeutically and for anyone who believed it was possible to philosophically enhance one's perception. Doing so was intrinsic to Freud's idea of human intelligence and, therefore, being free from neurotic perception.

One problem, for Freud, stands out as being more universally conflictual than any prejudice of a Jewish science: how was psychoanalysis, as a practice and a theory, going to be accepted by the scientific and medical community? Science and medicine; they were related but not, precisely, synonymous. So how did Freud see psychoanalysis amidst both? Our first question is, strictly speaking, orientated to science, as a historical reality inherited from the ancient world and as one of the singular world-views that, in the 19th century, would transform the world. The problem can be stated at the outset as long as we keep in mind that, when Freud enters the university as a student, the future events are to be anticipated but kept in their proper place. One confrontation is not yet pressing. "If we accept the importance of the observation that Freud's psychoanalytic investigations were conducted while addressing a hostile scientific community, we should wish to make this our thematic concern."[8] For us, that is not the case because, between 1873 and 1876

– his first four years of study – one other origin of psychoanalysis is very much private and not yet known to Freud, not yet clear as to its meaning and implications. Nevertheless, the commitment to his early medical studies and then his turn towards research in a laboratory setting shows one aspect of his character. One argument is stated and suspended. "The most crucial gains of these years for Freud was his scientific development. He was always disposed to a materialistic worldview."[9] The first statement is partly correct; the second is less absolute since, as his many writings will show, his disposition was not only materialistic. His philosophy studies were not incidental; they showed his interest – to use a much-disparaged word – in metaphysics. The either/or does not sufficiently consider Freud's interests at the time. For all his sympathies to Darwin and biology, he recognized, early on, that the study of *bios* (life) could not proceed exclusively via the physical. How could it be? He revealed the unconscious to the modern mind and did so (with more precision than poets, novelists, and philosophers like Nietzsche) by arriving at the vision of the human psyche that was more than anything dynamic and not reducible to either nerves or, ultimately, the brain. If Freud can be called a "materialist," one origin places him in the proximity of, apparently, his favourite philosopher, Ludwig Feuerbach. How Freud interpreted and *understood* his materialism is another question. He was no reductionist.

In order for us to arrive at the time when he definitely turned away from physiology, which also meant contemporary ideas of heredity and "degeneration" and instead understood as form of psychical *regression*, science and its specifics for Freud can be followed more or less chronologically through the period ending in 1882 – which coincides with his collaboration with Josef Breuer and the cathartic psychotherapy of the patient initially named Anna O. Doing so from Freud's own recollections and theoretical formulations give us the broadest possible picture – as it did when, in the beginning, *Moses and Monotheism* was related to both the history of the Jewish people and of Freud's early life. At this point, in our time, we might wonder if any beliefs by the "scientific community" about psychoanalysis is at all relevant. For an analysand, the problem has been an irrelevant one since the distinction between theory and practice is, always, explicit.

> Psychoanalysis has suffered the ridicule of the scientific community for decades having been grouped with pseudo-sciences ... Even for those who recognize some form of scientific inquiry, psychoanalysis fails to live up to strict evidential standards we expect from scientific inquiry. Psychoanalysts, however, have been hardly perturbed by these critiques and have successfully carried on the discipline through the last century and into the new one.[10]

The "new one" is now the 21st. A commentator expressed a certain level of urgency in understanding the place of psychoanalysis for the present. Freud's own testimony remains, as it should, leading. In the entry he wrote for the *Encyclopedia Brittanica*, he introduces the invention of the term psychoanalysis by associating it with two meanings: "(1) a particular method of treating nervous disorders and (2) a science of unconscious mental processes" (SE 20:264). In short, psychoanalysis was, for Freud, a medical science committed to diagnosis and cure. At different times, his definitions were complemented and would extend into virtually all the disciplines of a civilization.

> In a letter written for the occasion of the Australasian Medical Congress, Freud outlines the meaning of purpose of psychoanalysis. He has no doubts as to its scientific status.
>
> Psycho-analysis is a remarkable combination, for it comprises not only a method of research into the neuroses but also a method of treatment based on the aetiology thus discovered. I may begin by saying that psycho-analysis is not a child of speculation, but the outcome of experience; and for that reason, like every new product of science, is unfinished. It is open to anyone to convince himself by his own investigations of the correctness of the theses embodied in it, and to help in the further development of the study.
>
> (SE 12:207)

Thisone statement, written in 1913, can be historically divided as a way to trace a certain self-conception of psychoanalysis as a therapeutic practice. Once we take the statement and separate it historically (prior to the psychotherapeutic purposes) we have Freud giving us a conception of his thinking, from his medical and laboratory studies, and of the reality of the scientific endeavour. It conforms to scientific principles by being a method of research, the outcome of repeated experience, unfinished, and then, like all sciences, ongoing in terms of investigations and development. For Freud, psychoanalysis methodically followed the principles inherent in all sciences and for good reason deserved its proper place as a *new science*. The occasional statements would be many and consistent. More examples can be chosen since, in the case of an encyclopedia article, he elaborates and gives us a pronounced sense of psychoanalysis.

All told, psychoanalysis was described, in the "Two Encyclopedia Articles" of 1923, as a procedure to investigate psychical phenomena, a method to treat psychological afflictions, and "a collection of psychological information obtained along those lines, which is gradually being accumulated into a new scientific discipline" (SE 18:235). *A new scientific discipline*. To reaffirm Freud's conviction it will be necessary to trace the three periods of his life while studying at the University of Vienna. Before doing so, and concentrating on his laboratory research above all because of his use of the microscope, the relationship to science will continue. In the *Introductory Lectures on Psychoanalysis*, to mention his preface to its Hebrew translation, Freud writes, "They gave," he begins,

> a fairly accurate account of the position of the young science at that period and they contained more than their title indicated ... Readers of Hebrew and especially young people eager for knowledge are presented in this volume with

psycho-analysis clothed in the ancient language which has been awakened to a new life by the will of the Jewish people.

(SE 15:11)

We should, before adding one more idea from the lectures, mention the references thus far; they have all been chosen for a reason: *new product of science, new scientific discipline, young science*. Whether Freud's aspiration should be shared by us today is no longer self-evident and, perhaps, should be turned around in such a way that psychoanalysis is no longer dependent on its shared principles. Psychoanalysis may in fact deserve to be considered as a unique invention, one based on principles not reducible to science and, indeed, transcendent of the age-old dreams of materialist objectivity. In a moment, the German term *Wissenschaft* (because it is not easily translatable) may be allowed to remain alone and independent and, perhaps strangely, unexpectedly, for its connection to Francis Bacon as an individual at the beginning of modernity. Life, and the life of the mind in particular, is too important to leave to the single-minded limits of science. "I can assure you," he writes in the Introduction to the lectures, "that the hypothesis of there being unconscious mental processes paves the way to a decisive new orientation in the world and in science" (SE 15:22). Have we missed what he was, in fact, saying? Did psychoanalysis fundamentally and irrevocably change science – enhancing human consciousness by the double-awareness of itself and of the world to be examined? (Is he not also asking us to consider how science may itself be, in part, neurotic, a question he asked for religion? One suspicion can be expressed again: has the university today produced a specific neurosis, one that has become a virtual pandemic since thinking otherwise than critically and morally is judged in the harshest way possible?)

"Clinical research and studies of other disciplines might expand the psychoanalytic model and contribute to the enhancement of the scientific status of psychoanalysis."[11] Without coming to a too-early conclusion, one question can be asked today: does psychoanalysis need such a status? Freud certainly worried about it; today the problem may have become senseless. Thus far, connections have been made according to Freud's own wishes. One piece of writing deserves closer attention since more than a few of its arguments (made in 1938) need to be revisited because of our context – thematically and due to our contemporary situation. One apparently incidental comment in the 1938 "An Outline of Psycho-Analysis" can act as a starting point for a specific interest in the phenomenology of the microscope and what Freud learnt above all about seeing, looking, and the latency of vision. So fundamental was the experience that he could still refer to it near the end of his life. Freud was a microscopist – which has two different meanings: as someone who worked, quite diligently, with acknowledged success for his scientific findings and publications well before the psychoanalytic ones, with a microscope in a laboratory; and metaphorically in his ability to create a new kind of perception in himself and so be able to eventually think about the nature of neurotic consciousness and how it distorted the image of the world. The microscope as a scientific instrument led him to a new understanding of perception; was it, in essence, scientific? The reference to the microscope is, for Freud, no mere analogy. He connects himself to two simultaneous traditions, both of which are soon to be another concern: one, the beginning of a new scientific sensibility as expressed by Francis Bacon in *Novum Organum* – in terms, for one, on the "idols of the mind" – and, two, how Freud's experience as a researcher in a laboratory looking under a microscope influenced his developing perception of an invisible world in the human psyche. The microscope led to what Catherine Wilson calls an "instrument-mediated perception."[12] But Freud understood his experience beyond himself as a subject who was mediated as soon as he made microscopic seeing allegorical.

At the beginning of the work and his description of "The Psychical Apparatus," he summarizes the knowledge of the psyche according to the nervous system and our consciousness. "Our two hypotheses start out from these ends or beginnings of our knowledge," he begins.

> The first is concerned with localization. We assume that mental life is the function of an apparatus to which we ascribe the characteristics of being extended in space and of being made up of several portions – which we imagine, that is, as resembling a telescope or microscope or something of the kind.
>
> (SE 23:145)

His illustration serves our purpose extraordinarily well since the following argument will be developed to emphasize just how much influence his six-year period in the laboratory had on him and on his views of human beings in terms of perception; for him personally, of course, the microscope (as an allegory more than the thing itself) was to have far-reaching influence on him – as, indeed, did the telescope since these two scientific instruments were invaluable for learning about the human location in the universe in the cosmos and the hidden world of microorganisms or other phenomena impossible to see with the naked eye. The figure of Galileo was an enduring one for all scientists since the 17th century. For Freud in particular, the connection between the telescope and the microscope could not be a better way to reflect on psychoanalysis; both scientific instruments – the latter one to be an intimate experience for him – were illustrations of the human attempt to both acknowledge the limitations of human perceptions and also the ingenuity to expand how we saw, as a physiological ability and as another, more developed one in terms of human consciousness. There were two orientations for Freud; one did not exclude the other.

Freud did not reach his insights philosophically; he did so by a combination of factors that, for one, revolved around the idea of *an idol* as an extra-Biblical problem. The Jewish prohibition against the worship of graven images was, for Freud, translated into the modern world as a universal distortion of reality by the vagaries of consciousness. His philosophical awareness of the problem would ultimately become a practical and psychotherapeutic one.

In "The Unconscious," he expressed one conclusion that had been developing, as explicitly as he states it, for a longer period of time extending into his university studies. Just as Kant warned us not to overlook the fact that our perceptions are:

> subjectively conditioned and must not be regarded as identical with what is perceived though unknowable, so psycho-analysis warns us not to equate perception by means of consciousness with the unconscious mental processes which are their object. Like the physical, the psychical is not necessarily in reality what it appears to us to be. We shall be glad to learn, however, that the correction of internal perception will turn out not to offer such great difficulties as the correction of external perception – that internal objects are less unknowable than the external world.
>
> (SE 14:171)

How did he come to his conclusion? The answer is less important than tracing the thinking and the experiences that led him towards a certain direction. It was not, like Kant, metaphysical – though we have no hesitation in affirming a positive transference between philosophy and psychoanalysis when it comes to understanding the complications of consciousness, perception, and reality. For the psychoanalyst, the inquiry is wholly practical and, more important than that, therapeutic and effective for neurotics who are always mixed up in their own defences and projections. In the second-to-last *Introductory Lectures on Psychoanalysis,* the process has to be conveyed. His suggestion, and its illustration, should be kept in mind for the rest of our sections on science. In the lecture on "Transference," he writes:

> If I say to you: "Look up at the sky! There's a balloon there!" you will discover it much more easily than if I simply tell you to look up and see if you can see anything. In the same way, a student who is looking through a microscope for the first time is instructed by his teacher as to what he will see; otherwise he does not see it at all, though it is there and visible.
>
> (SE 16:437)

The image appears to be merely an example. Freud, again, mentions the microscope and a way of seeing – a way he learnt about in a laboratory and by way of thinking about both the possible deceptions of reality and, at times, its inaccessibility.

One theme can be stressed again if we return to the posthumously published "An Outline of Psychoanalysis." The truth of the matter is not secondary to Freud or to psychoanalysis as the therapeutic capable practice of complementing the more arcane theories of phenomenology as the study of consciousness. There is no question of Freud's self-understanding as someone who was contributing to the enhancement of knowledge. "We may now feel tempted to make a survey of the increases in knowledge that we have achieved," he writes, "and to consider what paths we have opened for further advances" (SE 23:195). *Increase in knowledge*:

while one advancement should not be underestimated, most especially for therapists who are engaged with the responsibility of healing, there is a significant advancement that, for us today, may become equally consequential. One idea of *scientia* had been fulfiled. We are aware of Freud's lifelong relationship to the meaning of philosophy as a discipline. He may have made every effort to distance himself from philosophy as a theoretical disposition, and yet attentiveness to his expression and indeed the lifelong commitment he made to understanding and interpretation, can be witnessed in a distinction he makes. Instead of making an explicit connection between Freud as a thinker and a relationship to philosophy, academically understood or pursued as a separate study, his own sensibilities, as a researcher first and foremost, predisposed him to a relationship to the world as an inquirer (in terms of objective reality – as opposed to the projective fantasies of neurotics) and to a complete self-examination of our capacities to see, observe, perceive. Our focus on Freud take us to his writing and the belief he has maintained essentially since the beginning, which is "that the psychology of consciousness was no better capable of understanding the normal functioning of the mind than of understanding dreams" (SE 23:195–6). For the time being, and since the interpretation of dreams fall outside our historical focus, the particular creation of the interpretation of dreams will be postponed, looking instead at his sense in the inadequacy of a "psychology of consciousness" that does not taken into consideration how intuition, or the act of perception, cannot be located or have its origin in the self or, more precisely, the ego.

The far-reaching discovery of the tripartite structure of the psyche articulated in *The Ego and the Id*, though intimated in the earliest days of psychoanalysis with such concepts as *splitting*, is fully functional as a consideration before Freud goes to Paris and because of the factors we have outlined so far. One statement should prove to be suggestive and in no way simply accepted as a psychoanalytic truism. The implications of Freud's thought are still to be developed and according to *the vision* of the founder of psychoanalysis. "The data of conscious self-perception, which alone were at its [the study of consciousness] disposal, have proved in every respect inadequate to fathom the profusion and complexity of the processes of the mind" (SE 23:196). The terminology has been used before; there is, however, a nuanced addition that appears to be a kind of culmination of ideas he has been analyzing for most of his adult life. While a *humanist* emphasis can downplay the scientific, more or less modern categories that were irrelevant in the ancient world, we can read Freud with a different attitude and one not so constrained by the categories of the almost modern world.

> In our science as in the others the problem is the same: behind the attributes (qualities) of the object under examination which are *presented directly to our perception*, we have to discover something else which is more independent of the particular receptive capacity of our sense organs and which approximates more closely to what may be supposed to be the real state of affairs.
>
> (23:196, my emphasis)

Any phenomenological argument made for Freud's intelligence and the history of psychoanalysis has to pause, first, at this quite astounding statement as a prelude to our return to a period in Freud's life when the thought was already active and he was searching for an expressive language adequate not only to his observations – while looking under a microscope at the actions of a patient – but also for the advances he would eventually make in terms of our capacity to see. What is presented, directly, to our perception is only one of the several, possibly fragmented influences on what, eventually, will be understood and seen. The Hebrew prohibition against the idolatry of images and the temptation to represent a transcendent reality is equally applicable in science's self-understanding and precisely by recognizing how the telescope presented a view of the cosmos that was antithetical to seeing as a taken-for-granted and obvious act.

"We have to discover something else." The initial provocation marks, for us, another pause. At the moment, we are lacking in a form of awareness. The slow, methodical reading has its benefits. We must first come to the realization that a discovery has to be made; without it, conscious perception will be incomplete and, more seriously as we will learn with the concept of projection, vulnerable to the worst kind of distortions – indeed, hallucinations (which go unnoticed) that are never perceived as such and therefore never recognized for their pathology. One always has to keep one imperative in mind: Freud has no interest in phenomenology *as a philosophy* unless it can be explained for the psychological benefits of patients, or, more generally, for our knowledge and sense of self overall. The phenomenology Freud is developing is medical – even if, in Paris, he will recognize the implications of the vision of psychoanalysis for understanding the nature of being as such. In the quote above, he concentrates his efforts on "the receptive capacity of our organs." The emphasis on "reception" is, however, only one of, at least, two entirely different elements in the entire process. There is, he tells us, something "more independent" that the capacity to *receive*. The discoveries he made are, and should be, unsettling; for if there is indeed a fundamental and, in principle, always-present capacity of distortion in the act of perception, then we become extremely vulnerable to our unconscious interiority – which will have two different and competing impulses, from the id and the super-ego, as well as their antagonistic relationship. Freud comes to the realization that the reception of the field of vision, of reality, is not at all a relationship between the ego and the objective world, of things and people. Once the comprehensively unconscious is taken into consideration as influential in the act of perception – including in any self-awareness – then the self finds itself in the most precarious position and bereft of any support but itself and the intellectual work of something far more complete than "self-knowledge" but which includes the entire personality of the individual. We should not be surprised in the slightest at Freud's declarations in 1938.

The "Outline" is a testimony of a witness who saw, first, the complexities of the human and systematically presented it over a lifetime of work. One note sounds like resignation, but the conclusion would be misleading. "We have no hope of being able to reach the latter itself." Here he appears to confirm Kant's conclusion in the inaccessibility of the thing-in-itself. Is that the case? "It is evident that everything new that we have inferred must nevertheless be translated back into the language of our perceptions, from which it is simply impossible for us to free ourselves" (SE 23:196). The finality is deceptive; because, unlike the philosophical project of a reality independent of perception of experience, Freud has entirely different interests and ambitions. He has no interest in reality, in itself. The philosophical preoccupation is entirely irrelevant when the motive, for him, has to be therapeutic and therefore finding a way to assist the patient to transform himself and, as a consequence, his perception of reality. "In the meantime we try to increase the efficiency of our sense organs" (SE 23:196). The language may at times be offputting: sense organs does sound much too scientific and strictly physical. Some consolation is provided by the idea of "increase," which can bring together several of the arguments thus far and along lines that are much more humanistic than scientific. To "increase" we can also add, for example, a clarity of perception based on the psychoanalysis of our inner drives, (whether desires or compulsions, healthy or not) and towards not simply coming to the proper perception of reality but also, once Freud's vision is taken into consideration, for a certain enhancement in the possibility of perception. The conclusion to this one brief section of the "Outline" can assist us in the transference towards another section. The scientific and the philosophical, broadly understood, have been indispensable for Freud's early understanding of the psyche.

> The yield brought to light by scientific work from our primary sense perceptions will consist in an insight into connections and dependent relations which are present in the external world, which can somehow be reliably reproduced or reflected in the in the internal world of our thoughts and a knowledge which enables us to "understand" something in the external world, to foresee and possibly alter it.
>
> (SE 23:196)

The last point should not be minimized; for if the perception of psychoanalysis allowed us to better understand the nature of our sight (or better, our inability to see clearly because of the constant interference of our psyche) then it was possible to both become healthier, as an individual, and perhaps also to alter the nature of reality and its interpretation. In this sense, psychoanalysis is indeed a science, and one that merits ongoing analysis for its ability to present us with a view of reality that is part of our everyday experience. Physicists, for all their apparent sophistication, are nowhere near the ability to explain the experience or the real except in terms that are abstract in the extreme – like the picture of string theory.

One word in the vocabulary of psychoanalysis stands out, in general, prior to any other of a specifically analytical nature: *observation*, so closely aligned with the foundations of science, is so often repeated as one of Freud's self-conceptions as an inquirer. On many occasions he has been disappointed at the general reception of psychoanalysis as a science. The attitude has not substantially changed in light of the emphasis on the positivistic trend in psychiatry and, more recently, any advances made in the science of neurobiology. Freud has often made him feelings known on the matter.

> I have always felt it as a gross injustice that people have refused to treat psycho-analysis like any other science. This refusal found an expression in the raising of the most obstinate objections. Psycho- analysis was constantly reproached for its incompleteness and its insufficiencies; though it is plain that a science based upon observation has no alternative but to work out its findings piecemeal and to solve its problems step by step.
>
> (SE 20:58)

Any defence of psychoanalysis and its status as a science is not an urgent matter in a study on the psychoanalysis of perception – a concern best suited to a more attentive relationship between philosophy of consciousness and any contributions to therapy. Because, ultimately, if a psychoanalytic study is to remain at the theoretical level – however interesting such a work may be – it cannot accomplish the primary end of its purpose or its method. The belief is a matter of fidelity. The affirmation should by no means be contentious. For Freud, because psychoanalysis was "a science based upon observation" and, moreover, perpetually revisable due to new findings and therefore accepting its limitations as a science, his life-experience was transformative and cumulative. A reassessment of psychoanalysis as a science and following the remarkable admission in his autobiographical piece that he was deeply indebted to both the Bible "story" and Charles Darwin as an individual brings us to our next section and, without opposition at all, reconciled, quite easily, Biblical narrative and the science most associated with a proper name – indeed, the middle one between Copernicus and Freud himself.

One word in the vocabulary has been highlighted as foundational and prior to all the ones specifically related to the origins of psychoanalysis. One could present a number of consistent beliefs. A few should suffice to stress one scientific reality for Freud: the centrality of observation and the incompleteness of psychoanalysis as both a science and a practice – a position made enduring when he defined his invention as an interminable one – that is, as infinite as the universe, psyche and cosmos affirmed as inter-related, just as one of the earliest of scientific thinkers, Pythagoras, believed and taught. Science, for lack of a better word, remains *timely* and historical, which is one of its strengths and, also, one of its essential incompletions in terms of both itself and its subjects of study. Further reflection on Freud as a scientist does not make it at all difficult to recognize him as someone closely aligned with the scientific method, as can be expected from an individual who chose a medical profession, and who was furthermore motivated by deeper aspirations of the understanding of condition of human being – in the body, in the mind, and in society.

To begin, first, with Freud's lifelong preoccupation with the status of psychoanalysis as a science is in many aspects both a summing-up of his work and then the basis for a return to his origins as a student of anatomy and physiology at the University of Vienna. One cannot help but see how persistent the personal doubts were and how he could never (and never did) reach a point of total acceptance. Rereading the whole of Freud on this one outstanding question alone makes one realize how he could never reconcile himself to some members of the scientific community, to the point that he defined them as dogmatic as religious thinkers. In the *Introductory Lectures on Psychoanalysis*, he writes:

> It would be a mistake to suppose that a science consists entirely of strictly proved theories, and it would be unjust to require this. Only a disposition with a passion for authority will raise such a demand, someone with a craving to replace his religious catechism by another, though it is a scientific one ... It is actually a sign of a scientific mode of thought to find satisfaction in these approximations to certainty and to be able to pursue constructive work further in spite of the absence of final confirmation.
>
> (SE 15:51)

As we perhaps know better today, *any thought* that presumes to be both complete (or worse, ideal – like scientism or similar ideologies) needs a Freudian perspective. One of the parameters of his view of science has been set. A foundation was necessary in the transition from Judaism to science to show them as far more inter-connected if we allow ourselves to view each of these aspects of being. For just as we moved from the intricacies of the Hebrew language, the Torah, and Moses, a similar process will be attempted in Freud's self-understanding as a scientist who spent a considerable time looking under a microscope and to make the invisible both seen and understood – and more than in a microscopic specimen. When his own purely scientific achievements are taken into consideration as both an empirical accomplishment and an allegorical meaning extending beyond the scientific, then we can unify two of Freud's transferences (Judaism and science) as he prepares to travel to Paris and witness Charcot's theories and methods firsthand. Psychoanalysis has never been a "Jewish science." Its multidisciplinary reality has been, rather, on a number of significant relationships that shared similar insights.

One of the problems for the modern reader whose interest is to assess the relationship between psychoanalysis and science, in fact and according to Freud's hopes, is to see just how much overlap there was in his mind about the discipline he realized was new and a challenge for those whose preconceptions would not allow them to see the merit of psychoanalysis. For example, in the work that made his metapsychological theories of the psyche economic, topographical, and economic, he fully admitted that he has approached an aspect of a systematic philosophy as well as a hypothesis. In *Beyond the Pleasure Principle*, the theoretical negotiations are not without challenges. "We have arrived at these speculative assumptions in an attempt to describe and to account for the facts of daily observation in our field of study" (SE 18:7). By the end of the chapter on metapsychological questions, he finds himself (if not at an impasse) certainly with a sense of uncertainty. "On the other hand," he adds,

> it should be made quite clear that the uncertainty of our speculation has been greatly increased by the necessity of borrowing from the science of biology. Biology is truly a land of unlimited possibilities. We may expect it to give us the most surprising information and we cannot guess what answers it will return in a few dozen years to the questions we have put to it.
> 
> (SE 18:60)

We can only imagine what Freud would ultimately say to the advances made in psychiatric sciences and, to isolate one, the findings of neurobiology. One experiences no hesitation in saying that he would still maintain his individual course – one that was informed by science in general and biology in particular but that would have forced him to remain independent of the strictly materialistic conclusions that are so attractive (for some) today. Tracing only three of the influences on his early scientific thinking is therefore necessary.

In "The Claims of Science to Scientific Interest," Freud chose to concentrate on the discoveries he made in terms of dreams, parapraxes, and the analysis, for example, of obsessive actions. All the fundamental categories of psychoanalysis are not, however, merely theoretical, merely intellectual; they are ultimately aimed at the psychotherapeutic treatment of illness and, more generally, a more expansive understanding of life. "Psychoanalysis is a medical procedure," he writes, affirming its primary responsibility. More specifically, he makes the case that "for the first time in the history of medicine, psychoanalysis has made it possible to get some insight into the origin and mechanisms alike of neuroses and psychoses" (SE 13:165). Freud tirelessly promoted psychoanalysis as a related but separate medical science, no different than psychiatry and neurology, with the one caveat that materialists would always resist: its interest in consciousness made psychoanalysis unique and, therefore, suspicious in the eyes of practitioners who are focused on organic abnormalities and (more so today) on the neurobiological characteristics of human beings. The brain, as an object, would always be inadequate for Freud. The obstacles were numerous: psychoanalysis had to make room for itself as a medical science and as an alternative to psychiatry, a difference that has become even more contentious today. But if one wanted to supplement the diagnosis of something as disruptive to life as neuroses and psychoses, one would also have to say that psychoanalysis has allowed all of us to better understand that which is often most hidden from us and, therefore, dangerous.

"An Outline of Psychoanalysis" has served us to complete, in our short context, the place of science and psychoanalysis in Freud's thinking. One passage can be highlighted at the end since the *example*, easily passed over, presents us with an experience in Freud's life that was more important than has been, for the most part, realized. Two statements are to be connected, for their own intrinsic interest and then to know move, biographically, towards the period when he worked in a laboratory as a scientific researcher. "We have discovered technical methods of filling up the gaps in the phenomenon of our consciousness, as we make use of those methods just as a physicist makes use of an experiment" (SE 23:196–7). Freud would like the reader to accept the argument that psychoanalysis, in making our consciousness more complete, more known, more visible, is not different than a physicist conducting an experiment. Do we concede? Rather than a yes/no answer, the argument has to be followed until it reaches a decisive point; we can then move forward with a much more extensive analysis of a number of experiences. First: by attempting to make the unconscious more known, seen and perceived, "we infer a number of processes which are in themselves 'unknowable' and interpolate them in those that are conscious to us." Unknowable and previously invisible are, for Freud, synonymous. The final statement is the one that matters the most since it opens another inquiry. "If one looks through old text-books on the use of the microscope, one is astonished to find the extraordinary demands which were made on the personality of those who made observations with that instrument while its technique was still young – of all of which there is no question to-day." The statement, which is also an autobiographical one, brings us to another turning point – or, better, a number of inter-related ones. Science and psychoanalysis, as Freud understood their relation, can both be understood from the previous references from his writings while also leaving some room for us, today, to wonder if science can ever be complete when it comes to understanding the complexity of a human being. My objection is closer to: is science adequate to the complexity of psychoanalysis and might it not be disqualified, especially today in our often complacent age of scientism, for being too fixed on the age-old dreams of objectivity, proof, and verification – when we know, in more than one science, that theories are neither persuasive nor conclusive. One has only to mention the burdened sciences of physics and cosmology to realize how a world of fantasy (made up of multi-dimensional "strings," for example) has lost all connection to any kind of reality and, therefore, of any real significance to *anyone* except those who are protecting their academic status and credentials. Psychoanalysis, on the other hand, has always been precisely concerned with our everyday relationship to ourselves, others, and reality as experienced when conscious and asleep. The reference to the microscope is, for Freud, no mere analogy. He connects himself to two simultaneous traditions, both of which are now our concern: one, the beginning of a new scientific sensibility as expressed by Francis Bacon in *Novum Organum* – in terms, for one, of the "idols of the mind" – and, two, how Freud's experience as a researcher in a laboratory looking under a microscope influenced his developing perception of an invisible world in the human psyche. Robert Langs has presented "psychoanalysis as an Aristotelian science." He fulfils the intents of his project by "claiming that psychoanalysis is in principle and in large measure – though, of course, not entirely – an Aristotelian science."[13] By all means, any thorough study deserves attention. The following section, however, makes another, more modern choice and relates (in principle, as one aspect of the science as presented in Francis Bacon's *Novum Organum*) psychoanalysis to a form of thought that, in 1620, was both philosophical and scientific. Certain conclusions can be mentioned and then re-examined as we continue.[14]

## Francis Bacon and the Idols of the Mind

The question of the scientific status of psychoanalysis, so important for Freud throughout his life, personally and professionally, has been presented without any definitive answers, either way; if they are still pressing in the 21st century, any yes/no depends on the inquirer and the motivations. One certainty is, for me, beyond question: no analysand has ever been concerned with psychoanalysis as a *theory*. Our inquiry depends on a set of specific questions; they will be addressed in the ongoing project, including, now, on the multidisciplinary period of his university studies. Returning to Freud's scientific beginnings are both biographical and understandably found during, one, his university studies in medicine, two, the six years he spent in a scientific laboratory doing research and, three, working in his capacity as a doctor in the Vienna General Hospital at the same time as he was informed about the case of Anna O. Medical student, scientific researcher, intern, psychotherapist: the chronology of his studies appears to moving in one direction, at once based on necessities and on a personal disposition towards a certain kind of knowledge which is both highly regulated and, for him, incomplete since the one-dimensional view of mental illness was at the time almost universally determined by assumptions about biology and heredity. The intellectual heritage of Judaism was sufficient for him to understand the biology of heredity as reductionist; the how was not yet clear or worked out. The idea of an archaic heritage and biological heredity, however, were incommensurable. His university studies, which essentially lasted from 1873 to 1885, were to involve the gradual move away from the dominating scientific world-view of the day towards another, more nuanced, far less materialist explanation for our mental life. Was there one other element that later unified, for Freud, the scientific and the psychological? Before any such relationship could be developed (as he did), a historical precedent had been set; its influence has been largely ignored. A first intimation will begin another return to a magisterial beginning with Francis Bacon's *Novum Organum* in order to highlight but one writing, and then to trace only a few ideas from the work that, if read side by side with Freud, unfolds with a number of intriguing parallels. They inform each other in terms of the *spirit* of science. In lieu of a comparison of Bacon's ideal science and Freud's education, in medicine, laboratory research, hospital internship, and knowledge of the Anna O. case, we can start with his "Preface" to *The Great Instauration* and those who had "set up a virtual dictatorship in the sciences."[15] The language of the 1600's translates into our modern scientism and without, today, any of the benefits of philosophy. Freud was not as pessimistic as Bacon at the start of his studies. Did he come to the same conclusion and for many of the same reasons? Some of Bacon's most significant concepts in the *Novum Organum* can be selected in order to trace how a medical/philosophical attitude remained effective and then highly influential during a time, in the German-speaking world, when his ideas were again being discussed. To question, for one, "the omniscience of authority,"[16] the attitude was a general one and just as relevant for religion as it was for science. Bacon had made it necessary to again question norms and truism of thought. The term orthodoxy extended well beyond the religious. A selected few of Bacon's ideas – dealing with the "diseases of the mind," "self-analysis," "purgation" (this especially important for Breuer's cathartic method) can be examined, in order, and then set next to Freud's experiences as he moved towards the one experience in Paris that would begin a new period in his life as a psychotherapist. Silvia Manzo draws our attention to the kind of self-reflection essential to Freud and psychoanalysis and whose ideal was, also, evident in Bacon's relationship to the legitimacy of authority. His psychology is most important: "The psychological conditions of scientists are relevant in order to examine the extent of the scientific freedom."[17] Freedom: the problem was not one among others for neurotics and, if Bacon is taken seriously, for scientists who (may or may not) be effected by psychological conditions of their own. Our first preoccupation remains foundational. Thought cannot be separated from a psychological condition.

One of our questions can be posed again. "What is the situation of psychoanalysis with science nowadays?"[18] One answer, among others, needs a number of recollections; keeping them together is one obligation. The first is the one to take up some attention since medicine, broadly understood, and psychoanalysis will be inter-related for their role in diagnosis and in a cure. Diagnoses and remedies make for several overlaps. Before our present can be evaluated, Freud's own historical experience has to be traced. Doing so requires us to emphasize three strictly scientific influences in addition to Darwin, in general. If we are to identify "Freud's shift,"[19] from physiology to psychology, which is plural, a number of individuals have to recalled from the history of science and, more specifically, their relation to the physiology of sight and to the science of optics. Isaac Newton is prototypical. A history has to be accounted for, even if briefly and in passing. Mentioning Hermann von Helmholtz first, as a preeminent German scientist, is essential since he was responsible for turning "seeing into a scientific topic." His 1867 *Physiological Optics* was published during a period when he was lecturing on consciousness and perception and presenting a theory whereby the brain intercepted (or converted) signals sent by sensory organs via neural pathways.[20] How did Freud understand the relation between physical optics and psychical perception? His early intimations required him to experience several different periods of study; each of them would contribute to what we can call his vision. The eyes saw; the mind and psyche perceived and enhanced reality.

Turning to Goethe is one more opportunity to connect Freud's character, education, and self-formation. One has to again take note of his insistence on psychoanalysis as a "mental science." In his address when he received the Goethe Prize, he started by saying:

My life's work has been directed to a single aim. I have observed the more subtle disturbances of mental functioning in *healthy and sick people*, and have sought to infer – or, if you prefer it, to guess – from signs of this kind how the apparatus which serves these functions is constructed and mutually opposing forces are at work in it ... This path has seemed to us of importance for the construction of a mental science which makes it possible to understand both normal and pathological processes.

(SE 21:208)

My emphasis of healthy and sick people makes psychoanalysis a specifically medical science intended to both diagnose and cure psychological illness. We cannot, at the same time, neglect the importance of interpreting "signs," that is, symptoms whose appearance are a disguise and distortion of a deeper, underlying truth. The illness called hysteria had presented one enigma after another for clinicians. Abandoning physiological explanations would go a long way in making hysteria better understood and, therefore, at least possible to treat with more informed methods. Bacon's objectives were the same, and with a reminder of an additional benefit we will emphasize more than once. "Men's efforts have been expended quite pointlessly, it then follows that the difficulty arises, not in the things themselves, which we can do nothing about, but in human understanding and its use and application, for which there certainly is a remedy and a cure" (NO 105).

Freud's transition, from one study to the other, can be at least partially followed. Anyone who overlooks his training in medicine leaves out an origin to his studies and also one of his first choices. "It was hearing Goethe's beautiful essay on Nature read aloud at a popular lecture," Freud writes, "just before I left school that decided me to become a medical student" (SE 20:8). Perhaps his youth did not allow him to appreciate just how much Goethe's lyricism was not wholly compatible with the study of medicine and, ultimately, the human relation to the natural world. The same could be said of Darwin. "From a psychoanalytic perspective, Darwin can be considered Freud's intellectual father, a father whom Freud admired, emulated, and wished to supersede." Implied in the "father" figure is also the idea of superseding the past."[21] The relationship is undeniable; it cannot, however, be exclusive – for reasons already presented vis-à-vis Moses and others who will come on the scene, dead and living. Moses and Darwin are two monumental figures. Other, more biographical (and philosophical) experiences would follow. Beginning in 1873, Freud took a variety of courses at the university, in his general area of interest (i.e. physiology, anatomy, chemistry) as expected for a medical student and also a number of other subjects, such as philosophy courses by Franz Brentano. His influences are beginning to branch out – and from out of himself. A beginning is complicated by the history of science as experienced at the time when Freud was but seventeen years old.

A qualified affirmation comes to us, somewhat as a surprise, via Louis Althusser who began by stating his hypothesis.

> If it's true that Freud made a genuine scientific discovery, if then it's true that in psychoanalysis we're dealing with the rise of a new scientific discipline ... We're dealing with the rise of scientific discipline that presents itself as totally new with regard to a field that was constituted earlier.[22]

Whether the "field" can be regarded as singular is one question; calling it *earlier* is (historically true) and yet if we also taken into account its incompletion – which then Freud took into an entirely different direction by being both descriptive and diagnostic – the innovation is not in doubt. Our challenge remains to account for as many influences as were generated, creatively, from out of himself and as he internalized, as a transference, his perception of history and culture. Reducing Freud to a history is untenable. Understanding his self-formation requires much more than our complacent attitude to history as a defining category. Medicine, according to one established origin, begins with the name of Hippocrates and a place such as the Sanctuary of Asclepius and then proceeds all the way to Freud. Everything in between is both historical and individual; the latter is not strictly conditioned by the former.

It is important to recognize "his early training in medicine and of his interests and achievements before he entered into the investigation of the intricate, complex, and universal problems as envisages as psychiatry."[23] The interests were many and not always immediately known to us. Like the archaic heritage of a culture among others, his internalization of another (but intimately related) history can be added to his *Bildung* and in ways that extend far beyond disciplines of thought or the difference between the natural and the human sciences, a division that is not as apparent when the word *Wissenschaft* is introduced and whose context, at the time, was not limited to our 21st-century idea of "science." The origins of the word *scientia* were comprehensive and orientated to a kind of knowledge. Anyone educated in a Gymnasium and classically trained – for example, in philology, the art of reading (as Nietzsche was) – was unlikely to be narrow-minded about precedents, inheritances, and influences. Science, no less than education, are limited for us in the present unless we return to Freud's culture and recognize a pedagogical ideal that was not strictly defined by objective knowledge; the classical ideals of *paideia* and the German translation of *Bildung* into self-formation was but one aspect of his education and his chosen field. His entrance into university in 1873 initiates him into a culture and a period of study that, despite the pursuit of medicine, made it possible for him to attend lectures in other disciplines, including philosophy, a type of thinking Freud would remain in distant proximity to.

There are three distinct periods between 1876 and 1882: his education to become a physician, his physiological studies of specimens in Ernst Brücke's laboratory, and the time spent as a physician in the Vienna General Hospital. Each of these pursuits were, together, to complement a historical dimension with a strictly scientific one. His direct experiences can only be understood when, in time, they are all turned into a unity for him, and according to an originality of both thought and method. The return to the origins of Freud's scientific studies involves two distinct attitudes and periods: on the one hand, his relationship to *Wissenschaft* cannot be circumscribed by our idea of *science* (generally determined by empirical contours and methodology) since an entire tradition of thought, beginning with Francis Bacon – whose presence in Germany was formidable – straddled two different conceptions of science; on the other hand, once Freud graduates from medical school and he begins to work in a laboratory as a researcher, his interests are broadened despite the exacting work of the field. The scientist, then, is already determined by two equally compelling drives. One definition, *physicalist,* is too narrow, *materialist* equally so. His research, in terms of choices of subjects, shows him moving from strictly biological concerns to wider ones – from the reproductive systems of eels to the anatomy of the nervous system, a subject that would bring him close to neurological beginnings – which he would give up precisely because they might have explained *the mechanisms* of the nervous system but left their origins as obscure as ever for someone who could not rely on either ideas of heredity or strictly physiological processes. If we are to retain the internalization of Jewish sensibilities about the image, consciousness, and reality, the three-part process of his education and then the first experiences as a physician in a clinic are to be examined as part of one comprehensive experience. The work ahead will attempt to be more thorough in terms of his periods and developments. The studies to become a physician came first. Then, in time, and with the additional of other factors, like his studies with the philosopher Franz Brentano, "Freud began his career as a laboratory neuroscientist and yet, for a variety of reasons, later moved in the direction of clinical psychology and psychoanalysis."[24] One way to frame the movement is in terms of what Brendel calls the science/humanism divide – which, to stress again, was not divisive in the concept of *Wissenschaft* and even less for Freud's interests, both scientific and human.

For our purposes, and to connect the earlier discussion of Judaism with the beginning of a modern sensibility – in thought as such, scientific and comprehensive – we can turn to Francis Bacon and follow one trajectory among others and see how Freud's interdisciplinary interests (which were not simply intellectual or theoretical) led him from one origin to another. What Alexandre Koyré wrote about the many-sided developments of 17th-century thought can also be addressed to Freud himself who, in his mind, had to unify a number of different disciplines extending to the ancient world. "It is impossible to separate the philosophical from the purely scientific aspects of this process."[25] Freud's own process could be described equally well with the summary of the 17th century in terms of its "revolution." The transference between philosophy and science, which are inseparable in the ancient world and with the major figures of antiquity (with Epicurus being an essential chapter in the history of Hellenism and his study of *physiologia*) is perhaps one of the reasons that psychoanalysis has been so challenging for many to accept. Its internalizations of the philosophical, the scientific, the medical, and the psychotherapeutic – from Western history – made it interdisciplinary and not at all bothered by its open-ended ability to continue to develop in whatever direction was made possible, first and foremost, *by the lives of patients* and by a classical imperative of human well-being.

One origin can now be traced and for a reason that is explicit: if the Jewish prohibition on images and sensualism was intended to develop both human perception and the creation of a certain kind of reality, its ideal persisted and was transferred from religion to a way of seeing both an internal and external world. One of the reasons for Bacon's particular place in German *Wissenschaft* reflected how a tradition of thinking, which is also evident in Freud, combines two impulses at the same time, an idealist and a materialist sense of science. Despite Freud's avowed independence from his definition of philosophy, there is simply no way to separate psychoanalysis from its extensive, multi-dimensional historical roots, first in the ancient world and then in the advent of science as understood by Bacon – that is, as a philosopher and natural scientist who, as noted from his Preface, understood both disciplines to be founded on something more important than epistemology. Bacon revived an ancient principle of *physiologia* as practiced, for example, by Epicurus and in such a way that the pursuit of knowledge about the natural world was intended to "calm" the mind, in part because it could provide a view of the world different from superstition and the distortion of reality by assumptions and prejudices. Why did Epicurus name one of his most important principles the *Tetrapharmakon*? Philosophy was intended to be diagnostic and curative: a "four-part" cure was simultaneously philosophical and psychotherapeutic.

In the modern world, according to Bacon, thought had been compromised by a word and idea that is prominent in his *Novum Organum* and inseparable from the Jewish aversion to images and objects and as *idols of the mind*. Was there a transference between Judaism to one of the earliest expressions of a modern self-understanding? If so, one more connection can be established that now comes to us from two distinct periods, the classical and the modern. As a matter of the historical record, Bacon's influence was extensive particularly in Germany and was therefore an inescapable influence on the mind of any student going through the highly developed 19th-century Gymnasium education. "Bacon was already well established as a cultural icon in German-speaking Europe by the end of the eighteenth century."[26] Denise Phillips adds: "Bacon stood for something important in European cultural life and German authors defended Bacon as one of their own, a fellow laborer in the cosmopolitan history of Philosophie and Naturwissenschaft." The idea of a cosmopolitan history is introduced here, once again, to stress how the pejorative term of "assimilation" is much too narrow-minded to apply to Freud since his culture was expansive instead of reductionist; as it turns out, no differently than his view of science which, today, is so often forgotten, Freud did not narrow his self-conception and so did not suffer from the limitations others imposed on themselves out of a desire to reach the goal of objectivity and, in their mind, the truth. There will be more than a few opportunities in a section on science, medicine, physiology, and psychiatry, to present Freud's individuality and the disparate origins of his thinking; doing so will always be incomplete. But we can certainly agree with the fact that "there was a great gap between the knowledge of physiological function and that aspect of the total personality reflected by the limited mirror of consciousness. This gap was a challenge to Freud."[27] Our one beginning with medicine and Bacon's philosophy is one way to bridge this "gap" and trace Freud's interests during the earliest period of his studies. As a student of medicine, the empirical knowledge of anatomy, for example, was not learnt in isolation; his science was informed by *physiologia*, *scientia*, and *Wissenschaft*, each from their origins and as a history capable of being rearranged according to a new model of the self and the world.

Turning to Bacon's *Novum Organum* leads us to consider the philosophical themes of the "new tool" that was intended to overcome the "psychopathology of the intellect" and the "universal madness" that Bacon diagnosed. His language is not coincidental; the analysis he begins with is a psychological one. One of the arguments to follow involves the extension of the psychiatric diagnosis from a 17th-century thinker and how the use of his specific language was not at all different from the Biblical – such that the religious ideals of Judaism (and of the Bible more generally) were necessary to carry out an analysis of society. There is no question that, in history, there are signs of a "dysfunctional epistemic culture,"[28] as long as the ailments are understood to be, in origin and essence, psychological ones. Could science, then, be neurotic?

When Bacon alerts us to the idolatry of the mind, he has also inherited an archaic heritage which allows him to analyze the present in and through the wisdom of the Biblical past. The madness Bacon diagnosed at the level of knowledge and reason was inherited from a religious tradition that emphasized one human weakness: the temptation to turn an idea into an idol that would then be worshipped at the cost of human life. Each of his four idols could be discussed at length, each of them developed by Freud at one time or another and most especially in the publications of the 1920's when his concerns turned from the therapy of individuals (and the training of analysts) to a social and political analysis that began, not surprisingly, with the first in Bacon's list – the idols of the tribe or, in Freud's language, *group psychology*. Due to the danger of a general or a more insidious consensus, Bacon set out to "survey these regions in my mind," (NO 19) in other words, to carry out a *self-analysis* at the same time as any investigation into nature or others. All the idols of the mind as Bacon outlined them had to be examined one by one; the priority, however, could not be neglected. "Knowing as I do how much men's mental vision is distracted by experience and history, and how difficult it is at first ... I quite often add observations of my own, these being, as it were the first dealings and leanings and glances of history towards philosophy" (NO 27). Bacon's "mental vision," translated to the psychoanalysis of perception, leads us to the social realities most responsible for our "distraction" and to our inability to differentiate the source of our reality. "Only then, when he has begun to be his own master, let him (if he will) use his own judgment" (NO 41).

The tribe, cave, market-place, and theatre: The spirit of Bacon's arguments, as a whole and from the particular moment in the early 17th century, shows him to be committed to a number of inter-related ideas that are not easily limited by a narrow discipline – however broad the term *scientia* is to be understood; there are elements of the arguments as a whole that are both an archaic heritage from the classical world (that is to say, from the foundations of European thought) and ones that Bacon believes to be essential in the making of a new, modern world. We can, from his ending, retrace only a few of more important steps in his *Novum Organum*, emphasize how he considered the "new" to be established. His *instauration* was to be understood as a universal initiative. Turning to his summary allows us to recognize a philosophy and a *scientia* that is inspired by a psychotherapeutic goal and with a concept that, as both medical and aesthetic (used by Aristotle in his *Poetics*), allows us to anticipate Anna O.'s therapeutic care. Bacon's therapeutic philosophy of overcoming the idols of the mind end with their *purging*. "So much then for the several kinds of idols and their trappings, which must be steadily and sternly disowned and renounced, and the understanding entirely rid and purged of them" (SO 77). Did Freud recognize the themes in Bacon's *Novum Organum* and the way "the diseases of the mind" could be remedied, first with self-analysis, and then with a necessary purgation – which was essentially different than the problem of "anticipation" or, in Freud's language, projection?

At the end of the *Novum Organum*, Bacon writes of his principal ideas: "these either assist and cure the understanding and senses." Assist and cure. The work has outlined, precisely, a method to understand how we make ourselves ill and the ways we can also assist ourselves, and others, in achieving a sense of equanimity. His intent is much more than an intellectual one in the true interpretation of nature. The complement, which psychoanalysis would provide, involved moving from the intellect and the illness of ideas to the psychopathology of consciousness. Bacon stands out as an individual at the origin of modernity for advancing a perception of the world that was yet to be so drastically divided as if a form of property. One more of Bacon's insights, which coincided with a scientific instrument that would change the nature of research and our perception of the very small – as the telescope had done for the cosmic – led him to create one of his many facets of thinking: his *instances*. One is tempted to align one of Bacon's ideas with a 20th-century idea (on the *event*) and its significance in the history of culture, which for us began with the Sinai event and then extended down through history as a genealogy with more than theological meaning. Bacon had two distinct ways of discussing ways of perception – the first as an "*Instance of the Lamp*," with its allegory of illumination, and second with the long history of what he termed "revealing instances." In a work devoted to the enhancement of human understanding, he believed it was possible to come to the assistance of the senses. "It must of necessity be that the more plentiful and accurate are the representations or offerings of the senses themselves, the more everything will go forward easily and successfully." One of the achievements of science was to create an instrument that could "strengthen, enlarge and rectify the immediate actions of the senses; the second bring what cannot be perceived down to that which can" (NO 224). His language is leading; for his contemporary readers, his *object* was already evident to them. Freud himself will be fundamentally changed by his six years of working in a laboratory conducting research on aquatic specimens and enhancing how he looked and saw and began to have a vision beyond the material and the immediate. Bacon further added to his categories, in this case by naming one of his instances "the *Door* or *Gate*." Calling his initiative the door of perception is not anachronistic if we recall Aldous Huxley's thesis on psychedelic experience.

> Now among the senses, vision clearly holds the first place for providing information, so it is chiefly for this sense that we should seek out aids. And these aids appear to be three in number: they enable the sense to perceive things that are not seen, are a long way off, or to perceive them more precisely and distinctly.
> (NO 225)

One instrument made the sense of sight more acute than was available through human physiology. The one invention that made it possible to see "things that are not seen" is what he called "optic glasses," that is, scopes. For Bacon, a scientific invention had made it possible to see the invisible. How did the telescope become the scientific instrument that revolutionized not only the capacity in empirical seeing – seeing, in Bacon's language, the *latent* – but also one that Freud translated into another kind of perception that delved into the inner depths of a human being, there to "see" what others had only intimated in literature or philosophy?

Bacon's *Novum Organum*, as a foundational document for a new 17th-century philosophy (of life and of science) begins from an ancient suspicion in the reliability of the senses not simply at the level of epistemology, of knowledge as such, but in a reliable form of being and of life. Bacon's philosophical argument emulated the Jewish one insofar as it exposes the problem of sensualism and idolatry – the latter explicitly used by Bacon to discuss the idols most in need of being destroyed. His method, which he believes is hard to practise because it requires of every individual to be personally responsible for their own reason, judgement, and clarity of thought, can nevertheless become a matter of *existence*. Returning again to the Preface, he sets out both his method and his stated intentions. "I reject for the most part that mental process that follows the sense" (NO 38). Sense is not the only obstacle to the philosophical clarity Bacon would like to achieve for his readers. "But this remedy comes too late," he believes, if "to matter already lost, after the mind, through the daily intercourse of life, has become occupied with received and false doctrines, and is beset with the vainest *idols*" (NO 38). The language is explicit. First of all, the remedy is understood to be both a change and curative. To lead to both, every individual has to become aware of just how all received ideas – as a matter of tradition – are in many cases deceptive; the problem is not, simply, a matter of the true and the false. Bacon's language of idols, which he categorizes and whose effects are as true today as they were during his life, are universally applicable since their historical bind can be traced from the classical, to the modern, to the time when Freud was studying medicine and then began working in a laboratory in 1876. One is reminded, time and again, how much of the emergence of modern thought (even prior to Descartes) was focused on one preoccupation. Francis Bacon was not an academic. The independence of mind that allowed him to view history without prejudice led him – via the Bible and the Greeks – to the one realization and imperative. "There remains but one cure, one healthy course: the whole operation of the mind must be completely re-started." Cure and health: the words are medical and therapeutic, as they were for Jewish prophets and Greek philosophers. Bacon is, then, one more transference in the history of thought as it is internalized by Freud at a time when a number of inter-connected influences are all working in him. At the same time as Bacon is advancing a remarkable rethinking about the nature of philosophy in his time, he also mentions, as utmost necessities, the labour of the mind along with mechanical devices – like the microscope – to assist in our understanding. Once a human-made instrument is introduced into the discussion, we are at a transitional point for us that leads to the advancement of science. How so? Any number of examples could be chosen from the history of science, but since Freud himself occupied himself with a specific one (the microscope) we can briefly mention the importance of this one invention for a new of seeing objects and, ultimately, for making Freud extend his perception from the invisibility of the natural world to the signs of consciousness and the psyche as it projected itself into reality. The microscope did nothing less than provide him with an extra-sensory perception that could only be taken into account when the invisible traces of our psychology could be exposed to analysis, interpretation, and in a form of understanding that was not, simply, cognitive, but depth-psychological. Bacon writes as much as he moves from the problem of idols, a possible cure, and how our perception can be greatly improved. "Now (to pause for a while upon this example and look at it as under a [magnifying] glass)." The idea of magnification is only half-complete; the insight does not involve making the minutely small visible to the eye. That truth is merely a material one. Freud will extend magnification from space to time, from a sample of a specimen to a distant, past experience in the life of an individual and so to a depth of the psyche that, until him, could only be imagined (above all, by philosophers, novelists, and artists) and yet had never been formulated methodically.

A connection has been established: between the Jewish prohibition of idolizing images and the human concern with the enticement of sensualism, the same direction was adopted by Bacon as an imperative of reason. To complement Bacon's philosophical principles with a scientific invention – or rather, two (the telescope and the microscope), we should situate Freud's knowledge both as a thought and an objective instrument. Between Bacon's comprehensive philosophy and the empirically driven research as conducted in laboratories, through observation, Freud veered towards the human concerns that had inspired him from the beginning. At the end of his six-year period of research, on eels, fish, and crayfish, the next step was taken when he turned to human physiology. We have, when looking at this early period, a portrait of

> the young scientist Freud. It is a picture that has a striking likeness to that of the inventor of the psychoanalytic method. For Freud, as he has many times emphasized, psychoanalysis is first of all a new technique by which a whole realm of facts, inaccessible before, can be brought to light. It is a new instrument of observation, a new tool of research.[29]
>
> He makes an even more important affirmation for us since he emphasizes both science as a discipline and an instrument. I want to stress emphatically that Freud's persistent interest in the invention of methods, though due to the general trends of his mind, coincides with the basic ideas of the Brücke institute and with the logical structure of science. Science runs from a new instrument to a new body of facts. The invention of the microscope, for instance, preceded histology. And in the history of any limited scientific field, only new instruments and techniques can, in the long run, bring new facts. From there science proceeds to a new theory.

It was Freud's individual understanding of the meaning of the microscope beyond its function as an instrument that allowed him to abstract himself from any empirical observation and begin to reflect on the invisibility of human consciousness – which could only be recognized, in its complicated functions, according to signs and symptoms. While he reached a personal transition-point when he delivered a lecture in 1882 in front of the Psychiatric Society – "The Structure of the Elements of the Nervous System" – he soon moved in another direction, in part due to his own dissatisfaction with strictly empirical explanations and, as it turned out, coinciding with his friendship with Josef Breuer and their discussion of Anna O.

A substantial period of time can be revisited to see how Freud moved from one discipline to another, each of them cumulative in terms of his experiences as they would, comprehensively, determine him as an individual doctor, researcher, psychiatrist, and, finally, the inventor of psychoanalysis. Without adopting the completeness of a biography, the period between 1873 and 1885 demands an attention to a few of the more important experiences. Many others have to be omitted, due to space more than importance. However, given the emphasis of the period, we can isolate the more significant ones. We can add one more element that serves as an introduction to Freud's work as a scientific researcher in a laboratory and so related to a work published in the wake of Bacon's influence in Germany.

The situation in the 21st century has almost become fully determined (as a majority consensus, if not universally) when it comes to the decisive split between religion and science; and yet, once the discussion on Judaism earlier is examined impartially and without the burden of theology, then Freud's insights, in terms of the history and development of human perception, is no longer estranged from the history of science. In order for us to present a number of connections in a phenomenology of perception as handed down from Judaism to the history of science, a brief look at one origin of modern science can be mentioned. Since the interest here is specifically devoted to Freud, who studied medicine and is now a scientific researcher in a laboratory, we can return to a history and recognize how

> the significance of the microscope for the Royal Society lay in its promise of uncovering the hidden causes of things. Indeed, Hooke's title [*Micrographia*] alludes to hidden *writing*, recognizable as an endorsement of Bacon's concern to uncover an alphabet of forms explaining natural phenomena.[30]

The metaphors are instructive since they overlap with the earlier emphasis of the Hebrew alphabet, language, and the interpretation of writing as Freud understood them independently of theology. When we encounter him in a laboratory, looking under a microscope and conducting research on biological specimens, there are two simultaneous events occurring in his mind: on the one hand, no differently than Hooke when he was producing drawings of the microscopic world, examining an invisible world to the naked eye; on the other hand, the leap of the imagination and consequently in the realm of psychological knowledge, the microscope was a metaphor for the vision of the world beyond the empirical that could only be measured and evaluated with others. Freud was a natural scientist, in the tradition of Galileo, Bacon, and Hooke, since he was well aware of a sensualist temptation and, because of the fact, found it easy to move towards knowledge of invisible realities that could never be "seen" by any form of observation since one had to move towards the reality of reason and what it could deduce based on observation and thinking.

We can isolate Bacon's philosophy and Hooke's *Micrographia*, especially for the latter's "epistemology of sight,"[31] as long as when it comes to Freud we begin to think about an advance in scientific perception that exceeds even the microscopic at the material level and so delves into a different kind of invisibility that will culminate with the appearance of the perception of the unconscious and, as the "royal road" to its existence, the image of the dream. That particular foundation to psychoanalysis, its "royal road," remains in the future. At the outset of Freud's education as a scientist and thinker, he has also inherited another kind of archaic heritage, more recent, to be sure, but not disconnected from a culture adamant about the problems of sensualism and, to use Bacon's terms, idolatry. One of the developments of psychoanalysis in the history of science can be seen in Freud's allegiance but, also, a pronounced independence that made him unconvinced by any definitive materialism – or, to recall Hooke – a mechanistic philosophy of the world, which was only one aspect of the knowledge of reality at the time and not at all settled by either scientists, theologians, or philosophers who were not committed materialists.

The presence of the microscope, as a scientific instrument and, perhaps more importantly, as an allegory of perception, could not have been more significant for Freud's development as a thinker and for enhancing an intuitive form of epistemology; without being philosophically programmatic about human knowledge, the intersection between ancient Judaism and one origin of modernity in Bacon's thinking is inherited by Freud in way that was unique and original to the point of creating the conditions for a new way of thinking about the self, consciousness, and perception. Reminding ourselves, once more, of one name, gives us a sense of a dominant movement in culture. Hermann von Helmholtz's influence on 19th-century science was decisive; his direction towards physiology and mechanistic explanations was in part the will towards a detachment from previous, more "romantic" ideas about human beings, including the ephemeral idea of energy or, to be more traditional, spirit in the widest sense. One impression, of Freud as an individual, can be anticipated. "Freud was never really at home with physicalism, and he later abandoned its measuring and quantifying phenomena. He certainly did not accept its conflation of the physiological and the mental."[32] The conclusion is a correct one; the obligation to come involves laying out some of the more important experiences of his university studies and the movement from being trained as a physician. Medicine, as a subject of formal study, may have been first; many others were to follow.

We have accompanied Freud as a first-year student at the University of Vienna and laid out only a few of the more outstanding historical ideas and discoveries – the idols of the mind and the microscope. The latter now deserves more consideration since Freud's time in Ernst Brücke's laboratory – doing minute research on specimens using a microscope – should be seen, also, as an allegory of seeing. Our fascination with Bacon's unique subject of study – to expose our "cognitive" errors – is incomplete unless it adds the one he emphasizes with most concern: the medical-psychological consequences of our errors in thinking. His preoccupation is certainly not an epistemological one – as being factually correct or not.[33] *Medicina mentis*. His medical terminology, including "purging," not to be simply separated from Aristotle's dramatic term (for reasons to be examined in relation to Anna O.), shows him to be a classically inspired philosopher who recognized that all philosophy, all thought, unless it was dedicated to human well-being, could not hope to be complete. We should not be satisfied with Bacon's pejorative view of the widely accepted practices of astrology, alchemy, and "magic," however the latter term is understood. His motivation to expose idols was not in the most obvious examples, which can also be expressed with the idea of superstition. Overall, he was intent on demonstrating how our senses, our consciousness (mind) and our perception (of images and *idola*) were more than errors. They were detrimental to a mind that had to work, consciously, towards clarity and an awareness of how easy it was to be deceived, in oneself and then more comprehensively by others, individually and in society. Again, we could certainly discuss his suspicion of authority; and yet doing so would only make us aware of a social problem, outside ourselves, and so run the danger of a merely "objective" accounting of reality. The points of contact between Bacon and Freud could be expanded, for example, to include the translation of his "anticipation" into the psychoanalysis of projection.

In the context of a short section on science, laying one foundation for Freud as a thinker makes it then possible to turn to his scientific and neurological studies and experiences. Our earlier appreciation of the Jewish prohibition against the idols moves towards one of the origins of modern thinking in terms of the *eidolon* and its meaning as "false appearance."

Bacon inherits a classical awareness. "The concept of fallacy began to involve a psychological component."[34] This is the most important insight for us and for Freud as a thinker who, ultimately, was concerned with the illnesses caused by neurotic perception. The concept of "bias" is only one of the outcomes of a much graver problem. As long as a bias is understood as mere preference or reduced to epistemology (to a form of knowledge among others) then the significance of psychological perceptions and their distortions will not be understood either as a personal problem or, ultimately, a social one, which is effectively much worse since the perception can become a form of contagious reality. Bacon's definition of idols "offers a new account of human sensory cognition,"[35] so that the well-known connection between the Greek *eidolon* and an idea is understood as a distorted perception of reality. Did Freud share a sensibility that was ultimately Jewish, scientific, and philosophical, domains of thought that, in his mind, were not strictly separated and gave him sufficient resources to understand their relations as disciplines?

Freud never had the slightest doubt about his thinking as scientific. Others, foes and enemies – in his own lifetime and also in ours now in the third decade of the 21st century – have not been lacking. Only a few turns to the nature of science can be used as comparisons.

> Scientific appraisals should test hypotheses, weigh alternative views, revise conclusions in light of evidence, explain the outer (and innermost) reaches of human experience, and use methods appropriate to the nature of the subject. Although performing all these tasks admirably, Freud, who started as a neurologist (and is praised by enemies for being a talented one), rarely is given his due as a genuine scientist.[36]

*His due*: that one reality is now hopelessly divided. The contemporary and future reader has but one obligation: to look at the evidence and decide for themselves. There is only one way to approach this or any other serious question: "the lack of consensus on Freud's scientific achievements is an indicator that he should not be treated as a scientific revolutionary without a thorough analysis of his writings."[37] By all means, then, reading him should be the first requirement – along with a conscious understanding of one's motives and presuppositions. For the moment, Bacon's modern idea of the idol (which we do not interpret as a theological problem, despite its presence in the conflicts of his time) is presented as an overlap with Judaism and in a way associated with Freud's thinking. In lieu of a more complete comparison (of all four idols – including the tribe or the herd, so important for him in *Group Psychology and the Analysis of the Ego*) only one will be suggested here and to retain for a later time; for when we consider the "idol of the theatre" as a problem of a distorted perception and misrepresentation, subsequent experiences will confirm an analysis, first with Anna O.'s disturbance of vision and her private theatre and, second, Charcot's theatrical presentation of hysterical patients to a public audience in the Salpêtrière. Before examining later experiences, we now turn to Freud's scientific research in Ernst Brücke's laboratory and, more specifically, the investigation he carried out by looking under a microscope, a method of perception which he later transformed into an allegory by which to understand the invisible world of the psyche and its manifestation in displaced forms. Freud was, at the time, a young student. One has to imagine him, at the age of 20, in a laboratory and under the direction of a highly regarded individual in the scientific community and, more specifically, in an area defined by the discipline of experimentation, the laboratory. The specificity of his research, and the use of the microscope as an essential tool in collecting evidence, made him aware of an experience beyond himself as a subject who was mediated as soon as he made microscopic seeing allegorical. His interpretative ability (midrashic, exegetical, hermeneutic) allowed him to develop a particular relationship to the microscope and to a new way of thinking about the nature of seeing.

## The Microscope as an Allegory of Perception

During his talks at Clark University in 1909, Freud's "Third Lecture" introduces a topic that for us going forward will receive more attention as another supplement to our themes of consciousness and perception. He is telling his audience about one of the consequences of the theory and practice of psychoanalysis: enemies have not been lacking. One of his arguments, towards his "adversaries," can be cited – for a reason more important than for a response. As it turns out, his particular example has had a long and personal history, which his audience would have been unaware of, as is still mostly the case when it comes to Freud's medical studies, first, and then his extended period of scientific research in Ernst Brücke's laboratory.

> You will perhaps be surprised to hear that in Europe we have heard a large number of judgments on psychoanalysis ... and who go on to demand with apparent scorn that we shall prove to them the correctness of our findings. Among these adversaries there are no doubt some to whom a scientific mode of thought is not as a rule alien, who, for instance, would not reject the results of a microscopic examination because it could not be confirmed on the anatomical preparation with the naked eye, but who would first form a judgment on the matter themselves with the help of a microscope.
>
> (SE 11:39)

The microscope, as an instrument of perception, became for Freud a reality that allowed him to present arguments on the psychoanalytic ability to see phenomena that was not normally seen. "Psychoanalysis is seeking to bring to conscious recognition," he continues, what has been made unconscious. He ends the lecture with one more of the fundamental insights of psychoanalysis as a science of perception. "That is why it is so hard to convince people of the reality of the unconscious and to teach them to recognize something new which is in contradiction to their conscious knowledge." Psychoanalysis has proven to be a most difficult theory to be accepted since its premise, inevitably, makes everyone unsettled since it brings into question how rationality (so prized as an accomplishment of civilization) is continually vulnerable to the most serious kinds of misapprehension. If our conscious perception is constantly being effected by the unconscious, than any rigid, self-evident idea of our selves becomes highly vulnerable. The truth of psychoanalysis was being conveyed to his American audience who, in time, would highly value both its theory and its form of therapy, not to mention its place in general culture.

The reference to the microscope is no mere analogy or for the express purpose of an illustrations. Freud connects himself to two simultaneous traditions, an ancient and a modern one, both of which are now our concern as we continue to trace the consequences of the Jewish relationship to the image and perception, the second as expressed by Francis Bacon in *Novum Organum* – in terms, for one, on the "idols of the mind" – and, two, how Freud's experience as a researcher in a laboratory looking under a microscope influenced his developing perception of an invisible world in the human psyche. The microscope led to what Catherine Wilson calls an "instrument-mediated perception."[38] But Freud understood his experience beyond himself as a subject who was mediated as soon as he made microscopic seeing allegorical. The "mediation" was completely bypassed once Freud recognized how a form of visibility, in the context of science, and of looking at invisible objects, could be translated into a specific kind of perception for looking at human beings internally and, eventually, to understand the forms of their social life.

The observation of the inquirer, a word often repeated by Freud and much more than the idea of experimentation, is essential for him. The introductory statement may seem obvious; and yet the study of the principles of science as it developed did not emphasize observation as much as experimentation. Our attention on Freud, above all personally before seeing him as a scientific inquirer, gives us an opportunity to trace his own insights. The time spent in the laboratory added one element to his research beyond the focus on histology. The microscope, as an instrument, became metaphoric. While the experience of magnification allowed him to see the small particulars of the world (in one sense, seeing the invisible beyond the visible and therefore enhancing the "naked eye") the experience moved outside and well beyond the laboratory. The particular instrument of the microscope, distinguished since its invention by its possibility of significantly altering human perception, became for Freud an essential way of thinking about sight beyond its physiology and the limits of human visibility. There will be increasing reasons to see Freud not as an empiricist. The affirmation may strike us as inappropriate; but the sense one gets from his thinking is that he was fundamentally a *metaphysical* thinker, someone concerned with a comprehensive understanding of *human reality*. The empirical studies in the laboratory and his experience with a microscope were important preparations for his later reflections on human suffering, its causes, and its remedies. There is no disagreement with the argument that scientific observation as a development in the history of science and one that led to the "epistemic genre"[39] of observing and knowing. And yet for Freud, the abilities he developed in the laboratory and in the period of his exacting scientific research while looking under a microscope developed an acuity of perception that would become essential to the act of seeing and the more extensive perception of the world – ultimately from species to the invisible depth of human beings and towards the creation of a world. His original relationship to a scientific context had been, historically, well established since the earlier treatises on optics and the developments made by scientists, each with their own object of study. Freud was, of course, influenced by the director of his research laboratory, Ernst Brücke; but to appreciate his originality, one has to sense, first, the empirical directions of a scientific discipline and, then, Freud's own achievement once it was complemented by other experiences – principally, the case of Anna O.

The period of 1880–1882 can be highlighted for two different reasons as we continue to follow Freud's extended period of university education as a trained physician and scientist. One, which comes to us by the research carried out by Eugenio Frixione, can be mentioned first; keeping in mind, at the same time, how Breuer is about to discuss his therapy of Anna O. with Freud in terms of the "cathartic" method and what she called "the talking cure" is one more overlap to Freud's exacting work in the laboratory. In 1880, Freud can be described as a microscopist. He was, in another heritage, in a line with Marcello Malpighi (1628–1694) as the founder of microscopic anatomy,[40] continuing a certain kind of scientific research. His day-to-day work in a laboratory led him to a particular kind of thinking that became a way of seeing. How he arrived at a new perception (perhaps more than a new science) can be partly reconstructed. Helmholtz had invented the ophthalmoscope in order to observe the retina. Brücke had followed with a physiological theory of vision and by conducting experiments on the nature of sight. For example, he had discovered the principles of stereoscopic vision and the difference between sight with one eye as opposed to both.[41] If understood in terms of a particular relation and interpretation, Freud would be in a scientific lineage of the history of vision – with one important difference: the microscope became an allegory of perception and was one more step towards rethinking the nature of perception as a psychical (not physical) act. The microscope, to use a word from an 1856 publication, produced "revelations."[42] They were named so in contradistinction to their associations to religion. Scientific revelations had, if not supplanted the religious, certainly took precedence in the scientific community and among those who were intent on promoting one world-view (with its promises) as opposed to an ancient one that, in the 19th century, had been eclipsed.

In Brücke's laboratory, Freud's main area of study involves the minute examination of cells and fibres and the tissue of nerves. The scientific aspects are highly specific and challenging. Seeing through a microscope (with the resolutions available at the time) sometimes made the identification of the phenomenon not easily achieved. Partial visibility, complemented by the drawings and illustrations which were part of Freud's own publications, did not easily lead to exact and verifiable conclusions. Frixione's excellent and highly specialized article emphasizes how Freud's contributions to neurohistology have not been readily acknowledged. His scientific achievements in this particular area of study – there are others, including later publications on the cerebral palsy of children – are not often of any interest to the main scholarship on psychoanalysis. Our omission has led to areas of neglect and as a consequence our inability to fully appreciate Freud's many-dimensional interests and occupations while he was still, technically, a student. The purpose of this brief investigation of his scientific studies for quite an extended period of time is one more important background in our overall understanding of Freud as a thinker. His dedication to microscopic studies can be understood from the standpoint of a scientist and as someone who was diligently carrying out his duties – the ones assigned to him by Brücke as specific areas of research.

My interests are not, however, scientific per se. They are due to their allegorical significance – no differently than in the prohibition of images for pious Jews. The structure of cells was a direct area of study; but once we abstract ourselves from the specificity of his examination and imagine, instead, the significance of Freud's visibility (in the laboratory) as a question of *observation of magnitude* that can be altered, then we come halfway, as it were, to the development of Freud's intelligence. The Jewish sensibility and awareness of the possible "microscopic" study of the Hebrew alphabet and then its amplification in, one, the Torah and, two, the figure of Moses, once internalized and present for Freud as a scientist, creates an intelligence of relations. The scientific meaning of a *revelation* should not be the source of conflict for anyone. The *spirit* of a human endeavour is always commensurable, whatever the subject of study may be. Understood in their proximity and as reflections of the grounds of human intelligence, the religious and the scientific are, ultimately, expressions of one overall dynamic. The artistic, to continue with broad categories of understanding, all unified by an *aesthetic* sensibility, of all the senses and the perceptive one above all, will soon give us one more aspect to Freud's life and thought as he moves closer to the creation of psychoanalysis. One of Frixione's conclusions is another opportunity to make a connection that would be long-lasting for Freud in terms of the way he began to see. "Events leading the young scientist away from the microscopic aspects of the nervous system started in 1882."[43] His explanation is understandable, yet incomplete. Once we begin to think about Freud during this crucial period – for one, his graduation from medical school in 1881 – and the simultaneous laboratory studies and Breuer's therapy of Anna O., the convergences in Freud's mind were unparalleled.

The time between 1876 and 1882 was a decisive one for his experience in the laboratory and, more than his actual dissection of eels, how his perception changed during the time he looked through the microscope and understood the process to be much more than a technical one. The microscope gave him the intimation of being able to see beyond the apparent and so think about the concealed and the invisible.

When he was told by Brücke to leave laboratory research, Freud immediately turned to a direction he had been thinking about for a considerable period of time. The year 1882 marks a date of the utmost importance for him insofar as he began his research into the brain nerves and, at the same time, started his association with Breuer. The humanistic and the scientific are, for the moment, in a convergence. The following few years, until his stay in Paris, will move back and forth between two different kinds of orientation.

As an introduction to the significant statement regarding the invention of the microscope (as a consequence of the prior invention of the telescope) we can begin with the use of the microscope "to explore the nature of *veridical* perception."[44] The word can be emphasized – for two reasons. Jutta Schickore's study presents how the eye and vision were rethought because of the microscope. Human perception was altered as it investigated phenomena invisible to the naked eye. Veridical perception became substantive for the knowledge of scientific truth. How did Freud respond to this experience? While the first stage in the enhancement of perception led him to a veridical perception of phenomena invisible to the naked eye, the more original leap of the imagination led him from the external world of what is observable to the interpretation of external signs as inner conditions. The microscope and the symptom were inter-related concepts. The number of commentators who have been aware of the instruments in the history of science and Freud's relationship, above all, with the microscope, have been able to recognize parallels and influences. Robert Langs has coined an appropriate term: *psychoscopes*. "Both the telescope and the microscope ushered in new eras for physics and biology. Much the same may well prove to be true for the invention of a properly configured, working psychoscope."[45]

The microscope had a profound effect on Freud's thinking. If we read him with this all-important period in mind, we can trace its effects, also, in the examples he used to illustrate a point. Others also availed themselves of the idea. The significance of scientific instruments for the enhancement of human observation have been noted by some as analogies. "Like the microscope and the telescope, the analytic hour is an instrument that opens up a previously unseen world."[46] The analogy can be extended and for Freud be direct. The "unseen world" under the microscope and during the significant years of strictly scientific studies in Brücke's laboratory allowed Freud to develop an ability that would only be fully realized later and when thinking about the nature of his patient's illnesses that were (beyond the physical symptoms seen by physicians and displayed by Charcot) interior and disguised. It would be understandable for us to simply regard Freud's early studies at the University of Vienna since his entrance in the early 1870's as nothing more than his pre-psychoanalytic period. To do so would be to underappreciate the development of Freud's personality, and his non-scientific intellect, as he unknowingly matured into a thinker of the human and the complexity of its depths.

Paying attention to Freud during his time in the laboratory has made up for an omission and a defining feature of his character as an individual inquirer. The science of the microscope and the development of his own perception during the years of his study in Brücke's laboratory were not incidental. They were foundational to a certain sensibility that can be seen only when other issues apart from obvious ones are contemplated. That the microscope, as an instrument, appears as a *metaphor* (that is, as itself a transference of an idea) can set us towards the equally decisive experiences of Freud in Paris. "Freud's model of the psyche," Victor Schermer writes, "was based on the analytic 'microscope' applied to neurotic patients possessing the ability to verbalize in a representational and metaphorical manner."[47] One takes notice of the consistent, consensus argument on the transference between the visual and the linguistic. The transition is, of course, understandable and should not at all be controversial, and yet one can suspend the obvious certainty to insist on the phenomenological perception as primary and, therefore, not so easily neglected for its transformation into the verbalization of free-association. The microscope became for Freud an enduring symbol of a scientific invention that broadened the horizon of human knowledge and gave him access to the invisible – a category of philosophical thought that is not a matter of indifference to us even though we cannot build on the connection without an assessment, even a short one, of the history of phenomenology.

Neville Symington has distinguished himself with a number of writings which are marks of his vocation as a psychoanalyst and who also has no reluctance to discuss matters of the spirit. In one instance, his impressions of Freud can be used as a starting point.

> While the rest of his contemporaries were hurrying on with their medical training, Freud was behind a microscope, studying the gonadic structure of eels. He was involved in an atmosphere of research that was isolated in the extreme and quite cut off from the domain of human feeling.[48]

Symington seems to be implying that his "contemporaries" (he does not say his "peers") were doing what was expected of them and becoming physicians. He seems to be critical of Freud's dedication at the time. For me, the time spent in the laboratory presents no issues whatsoever. On the contrary, the image of the isolated thinker seems to be to be in keeping with his personality as well as his intense convictions. Being "cut off" is, of course, often necessary both because the work and thought demands absolute privacy and only with a certain kind of undivided concentration can one begin to achieve the intended goals. The following is as important as his *rabbinical* personality – specifically according to interpretation. Any remarks about "Jewish science" are to be rethought and without the limitations (above all, from enemies) who have formulated a conception of the meaning of such a relation. It is surely not reducible to the *ethnic*. The impulse, on my part (and one makes admissions as they are necessary), comes from a certain intellectual position on Freud personally and how two different cultural realities – the Jewish and the scientific – have to extend beyond the ethnic towards the *metaphysical*. Freud would, hopefully, not disagree with my assessment of him as a great metaphysician and due precisely to his unparalleled investigations of the complexities of our human *reality* – in ourselves and in the world. After his laborious studies of, precisely, elements of the *physis* of organisms, he was then prepared to extend beyond, towards what Aristotle categorically placed after matter – that is, *metaphysics*.

Symington believes Freud was cut off from human feelings. My argument is exactly the opposite: the time spent in the laboratory and the endless hours looking under a microscope began to give him an intuition that, prior to him, had only been imagined by the most creative of individuals in their respective fields, whether scientific or artistic, in a certain kind of consciousness of a relation and of the bind of *religio*. As we prepare to move ahead to Freud's relationship with Breuer and the first patient, Anna O., examined though the "cathartic" method, we cannot relinquish the arguments made thus far and on the intimacy of a certain kind of exalted human consciousness and perception.

The next decisive experience would be reached in Paris and while attending Jean-Marie Charcot's lectures and taking account of the methods he used (theatrical and photographic, above all) to represent his hysterical patients and the appearances of their bodies, facial gestures, and other outward signs of their conditions. One final comment from exceptional research done by Martin Wieser can further orientate us as we move from the laboratory and the microscope to the hospital and both the theatrical representation of hysterics and the photographs of their bodies and faces.

> There is an important connection between Freud's psychoanalysis and his early physiological research that has largely gone unnoticed: the connection is not one of physiological concepts and theories but one of scientific practice, which Freud became acquainted with at the laboratory of Ernst Brücke from 1876 to 1882. This practice was deeply concerned with *visuality* and, respectively, with techniques of making hidden (neuronal) structures and linkages observable.[49]

At this point we have reached the provisional end of one argument: the connection between Judaism in terms of a clarity of perception and microscopic observations as two complementary kinds of seeing, each of them intent on an awareness of our possible deception. One can hazard another concept if it is not immediately interpreted from its traditional context. Was Freud's own perception, now so conscious of how to look and see and find out for oneself, not *revelatory*? A statement in *An Autobiographical Study* provides one of *his* responses. The example stands out all the more for us.

During one of the many times Freud found it necessary to defend the science of psychoanalysis against sceptics and opponents, he did not turn to Judaism, but something more substantial to think about for his audience.

> It seemed to me that the main obstacle to agreement lay in the fact that my opponents regarded psycho-analysis as a product of my speculative imagination and were unwilling to believe in the long, patient and unbiased work which had gone

to its making. Since in their opinion analysis has nothing to do with observation or experience, they believed that they were justified in rejecting it without experience. Others again, who did not feel so strongly convinced of this, repeated in their resistance that classical manoeuvre of not looking through the microscope so as to avoid seeing what they had denied.

(SE 20:50).

Only someone who understood the significance of the microscope for the substance of his overall thinking could appreciate the argument. The analogy was perfect.

The transition to Freud's early experience with Josef Breuer from 1882 on does give us the opportunity to pose a question – perhaps, it will be understood rhetorically – and ask: "could psychoanalysis be a new kind of science?"[50] The scientifically minded and committed empiricists, like the neurobiologists of the day, for example, will have their own responses. As for us, when the most unlikely connection has been made between the Jewish sensibility to the alphabet, to language, and to the meaning of the Torah (as well as post-Jerusalem writings of the Mishnah and the Talmud) and how, for Freud, it was inseparable from an equally important kind of perception he learnt in the laboratory looking under a microscope, we can now turn to another of his fundamental experiences when he arrived in Paris and began to witness the theatrical presentation of hysterical patients as well as the photographs that were used to illustrate and confirm the diagnosis of hysteria. The always-present problem of the perception of idols, as Bacon thought about for an adequate science and an even more important way of seeing (so as to avoid pathologies of the mind) would remain one more decisive influence on his thinking.

Our own arguments, to be thorough, have not simply ignored other viewpoints. They should continue to be mentioned for what now appears to be an either/or emphasis. "Throughout his life, Freud continued to affiliate himself with the anatomical view, which still dominates neurobiology."[51] If only ambivalence was not so specific, it would not be difficult to admit that the desire for scientific legitimacy for psychoanalysis did continue to hold him, if not so firmly, tied to his early studies and the respect he maintained for science. At the same time, the momentous experience in Paris did accelerate the process he had already started to undergo in his relationship with Breuer and the discovery of strictly psychological explanation for mental disturbances of all kinds. The ones we examined (hypnoid states, somnambulism, *absences*) may today be explainable by neurobiological *theories*; their confirmation as anatomical anomalies are not, for all that, assured. Freud's long-lasting influence can also in part be evaluated by the persistence of a kind of *thinking*: all the proof and verification, from any science of the brain and with the most sophisticated instruments of *imaging*, will never overcome an inherent belief in the nature of the human.

It may very well be that, because of at least two sides of Freud's beliefs, the matter will never be settled. All one can do, in the end, is go back to the writings themselves and sustain one's preference with more than enough evidence while not forgetting, out of laziness or convenience, that there are competing perspectives that do not render the whole *relative* (which could lead to nonsense and meaninglessness) and that ask us to be perpetually committed to reading and interpretation.

Without difficulty, simply from rereading the *Standard Edition* with one motive in mind, a compendium could be presented on Freud's attitude to his readers as he talked about psychoanalysis. In the *Introductory Lectures on Psychoanalysis*, he says:

> I do not wish to arouse convictions; I wish to stimulate thought and to upset prejudices ... You should not for a moment suppose that what I put before you as the psycho-analytic view is a speculative system. It is on the contrary empirical – either a direct expression of observations or the outcome of a process of working them over.
>
> (SE 16:243–244)

The speculative and the empirical will continue to be divided; the reasons are not external to psychoanalysis. All we can do is present the evidence as Freud himself did.

The conflict has not been settled; the demands have eluded resolution. In the end, one alternative has been chosen because only by defying pre-established structures of thought could it be possible to reach a different set of principles. They were not going to be held hostage by one dominant view of the world. For all of Freud's expectations, from himself and from psychoanalysis, to achieve legitimacy by being proclaimed scientific would not have settled the indecisiveness from a community. How strange, at this point, that we can call upon someone who was no friend of psychoanalysis and take counsel from him. Wittgenstein writes: "we feel even when all possible scientific questions have been answered, the problem of life remains completely untouched."[52] *The problem of life* was never going to be answered (it has not yet and won't) by biology or any other science except according to the limits and principles of its own self-identification and objects. To state, unequivocally, its incompletion is not intended as a critique. It only signals the need to shift the conditions of our thinking. One statement – "psychoanalysis is in need of no theoretical underpinnings, least of all scientific one"[53] – is not by any means a conclusion and a definitive turning away from a problem. To continue to make it relevant in the ongoing theme, one other primary influence on Freud's life and thinking is necessary both to prepare us for an examination of the Anna O. case and the invention of catharsis – which is both a medical term, otherwise known as purgation, and an affective-aesthetic one from Aristotle's *Poetics* – and Freud's singular experience in Paris.

Attaching ourselves to philosophical statements is one way to conclude a section where we have gone with Freud from the experience of the microscope in the laboratory to questions of importance for him in the creation and understanding of psychoanalysis at a later time. One transition in the work as a whole leads to one date in particular and in the relationship between Josef Breuer and Freud in 1882 while the former was treating Anna O., a young woman of outstanding intelligence who was also enduring a number of painful psychological and physical symptoms of hysteria associated with the contemporary idea of *conversion*. The concept, as introduced, will present us with a number of avenues for examination and how the psychological could be so intrusive into life that it could transform the condition of the body. To prepare for a focus on Anna O.'s symptoms as they are indicative of many others associated with the knowledge of hysteria at the time, one requires our attention.

The most recent contributions from the scientifically minded have not been at all preoccupied with the status of psychoanalysis as a science; instead, their research has been more fruitful, most especially for those of us trained in the human sciences and therefore not as informed (as we should be) on the advancements of specific sciences or their history. Our appreciation of Freud has been enriched by individuals who have been willing to set aside the limits of disciplines and their empirical self-understanding to think, as Freud did, along metaphoric lines – that is, as transferences of meaning. Taking us in one more direction than the ones already presented, each of them of interest separately and as a synthesis, one observation on "the relationship between Freud's core of being and the microscopically perceivable cell nucleus"[54] brings together all three themes of the investigation of the chapter, on the nature of science, Freud's laboratory work on histology, and the metaphorical meaning of the microscope. When the cell nucleus as an object of study was displaced from the laboratory and the microscope to a human interiority, the cross-references multiplied our knowledge of the beginning of psychoanalysis.

Approaching the end of the chapter and, thus far, laying out three instances of Freud's interest in science and its specific practice, in the laboratory, we can better be prepared for the next two sections, related as they are but also separated by an irreconcilable difference that will establish one uniqueness of the privacy of individual therapy instead of the publicness of the institution. "To the end of his life, Freud continued to believe that psychoanalysis is at once a science *and* an ethics – a method of self-understanding *and* a technique for living well."[55] His humanism, properly understood and without our contemporary prejudices, is inseparable from him as an individual and, then, necessarily, his studies. While it may be *practically* true that "Freud became a medical practitioner because it was impossible to pursue the desired career of a microscopist researcher,"[56] the experience as a whole was internalized along with all the other influences and interests of his life. The circumstances of Viennese society sums up one of the episodes in the history of one abandoned science (a well-established one) and the eventual creation of psychoanalysis. The necessity of abandoning a professional career, however, did not interfere with his ability to adopt everything he had learnt and seen in the laboratory. From the time he left the laboratory in 1882 to the time he went to Paris, he was able to enhance everything he had learnt from the perspective of scientific observation and apply it, in his own inestimable way, to the awareness of the psychiatric experience – which he was able to do during his time, in 1885, at the Oberstein psychiatric hospital.

A reminder is in order for anyone who, self-possessed about the certainties of science, does not sufficiently think about what Frederick Schauer calls the "motivated production" of scientific facts. There is no reason to discredit the demands that science makes on itself, for its objective rigour, exacting standards, and how evidence and proof are enduring criteria. "Although most of the factual world successfully resists adapting to our preferences, often, and perhaps surprisingly, our *perception* of that factual world does conform to our preferences."[57] To the idea of perception, we may also add the necessity of judgement. The biblical tradition of divine revelation and the history of scientific observation were latent realities for Freud – with one slight difference when it came to the inventions of instruments, which, in themselves, were to be invaluable when the microscope was progressively refined and allowed Freud to see the cross-sections of cells and then translate his perception into the quite surprising drawings that he made accompanying his publications. The detail of his drawings does more than tell us about his artistic competence or the marvellous capacities of the microscope to make the naked eye more perceptive. One of the developments in the history of microscopy can be witnessed in "the shift from the *virtue of mechanical objectivity* to the *virtue of trained judgment*."[58] Trained judgement: in Freud's case, something more was on the way to being created and from out of several difference cultural histories and individual abilities.

Although Ian Hacking's discussion of the microscope includes technological advancements well beyond Freud's time, doubts (first) and then his conclusion can be questioned in terms of its specific *context*. "Microscope do not work in the way most untutored people suppose. But why it may be asked, should a philosopher care about how they work? Because a correct understanding is necessary to elucidate problems of scientific realism."[59] He twice uses the word "work," as in a technical function. The problem, as Hacking sees it, was irrelevant for Freud. He was not ultimately preoccupied with a philosophical problem vis-à-vis his scientific research. We better understand Freud's thinking when the "scientific realism" of his research (into eels, for example) is set aside as a mere empirical pursuit and then advanced towards a much more expansive way to think and see. The stride is made due to "the extension of our senses since the advent of the original telescope and microscope,"[60] as long as we also consider how the limits of our senses – presented by Judaism, Bacon, and the microscope – are then applied to our understanding of the invisible depths of human beings.

The early period in his life can be mentioned at the end when, in writing the incomplete and posthumously published "An Outline of Psychoanalysis," Freud once again turned to a summary of psychoanalysis. In Part III, on the psyche and the external world, Freud anticipated his statements to be among the last, so when he writes of a final "survey of the increases in knowledge that we have achieved by work such as this and to consider what paths we have opened for further advances" (SE 23:195) he was writing in the spirit of a science that was, infinitely, open to further changes in the future. The chronology of psychoanalysis was, for him personally, reaching an end; and because of it, he did not waver from some indications on the future and:

the assertion that the psychology of consciousness was no better capable of understanding the normal functioning of the mind than of understanding dreams. The data of conscious self-perception, which alone were at its disposal, have proved in every respect inadequate to fathom the profusion and complexity of the process of the mind, to reveal their interconnections and so to recognize the determinants of their disturbances.

The commitment to aligning psychoanalysis with the method and spirit of scientific inquiry has never been given up; if anything, this one last testimony is another indication of just how much psychoanalysis was, by its very nature, scientific. As far as the one certainty (and mystery) of human consciousness, its particularity in terms of the different aspects of the psyche,

> this hypothesis has put us in a position to establish psychology on foundations similar to those of any other science, such, for instance, as physics. In our science as in the others the problem is the same: behind the attributes (qualities) of the object under examination which are presented directly to our perception, we have to discover something else which is more independent of the particular receptive capacity of our sense organs and which approximates more closely to what may be supposed to be the real state of affairs.
> 
> (SE 23:196)

Freud is doing nothing less than defining the very problem of human consciousness and perception vis-à-vis the external world and how our image, what we see as real, is often distorted by our very capacity to see. The problem of science is, in essence, constitutive of our ability to see and the always easy reliance on the obvious, the taken-for-granted, the consensus view. The section deserves a line-by-line reading. Our needs are not as exacting as that. We can, briefly, continue with the association Freud makes between the real world and our conscious perception of it. One analogy remains. How remarkable that one experience has become permanent, conceptually and as an illustration. The perception of the self, others, and reality may be compromised by all kinds of obstacles. And yet the encounter of the psyche and the external world can nevertheless be clarified – as the cosmos was illuminated in its order by the telescope and by the instrument so familiar to him.

> If one looks through old text-books on the use of the microscope, one is astonished to find the extraordinary demands which were made on the personality of those who made observations with that instrument while its technique was still young – of all of which there is no question today.
> 
> (SE 23:197)

At the at the end of the second chapter and on the connection, in Freud's consciousness, between his Jewish and scientific inheritance, we can pause for a moment before moving with Freud to his collaboration with Breuer and then his stay in

Paris and the period of studying hysteria with Charcot. A Jewish sensibility to the Hebrew alphabet, the Torah, and Moses the individual has taken us to Freud's observations and the centrality of the microscope as an allegory of seeing. By so doing, we can be reminded by Bruno Latour's sociology of science of an impression we often neglect.

> It was obvious that the key for insuring the objectivity of science was entirely different from the mode of insuring the faithfulness of the religious spirit, but this difference does not mean that there was direct certainty in one case and pure invention on the other.[61]

Latour's categories are not chosen at random. The *religious spirit* is neither theology imagined by the orthodox or the atheists – both of whose certainties make some of us highly sceptical. Latour's term, "network of translation," is a productive metaphor; our reference point, today, might be technological and inseparable, for example, from a router. Understood in both ways as a complex set of inter-related ideas and the need to translate them into a common, shared language (spirit is, then, surely applicable to religion and to science) we therefore find ourselves in one more transition and by unifying, in a relationship, religion and science; we can proceed on to Freud's sojourn in Paris for a few brief months in 1885–1886 and see how a certain kind of exposure to the theatrical exhibitions of hysterics and the diagnosis of their symptoms became one more experience that, together, set him towards the commitment to psychotherapy. Before doing so, however, and examining one of the most formative periods of Freud's early life as a researcher, the relationship with Breuer and, more specifically, the cathartic therapy of Anna O. adds one more phenomenological element to Freud's insights.

One fundamental reorientation of thought, psychoanalytically speaking, will eventually take place when the archaic heritage of a civilization, in its specificity and more generally, will begin anew from the single psychical world of an individual. The connections have been made often enough for the insight not be repeated in any detail; but if Descartes is the one turning point towards a new era of modernity, bringing Bacon's philosophy to one culmination, then we can also acknowledge Freud as one incomparable heir who began not from his thinking (his ego) but rather from a relationship with the totality of an individual as the ground of any lasting depth-psychology. Anna O. has rightfully taken her place as the foundational individual patient of a cathartic method that would soon be transformed and be more exactly defined. The initial theme shared by Judaism and science are, comprehensively, brought forward in order to understand Anna O.'s particular afflictions and how they were inseparable from a distorted perception and the consequence of a number of internal conflicts. How Freud's discussion of the case of Anna O. at the same time as he was moving from laboratory research to his psychiatric residency is one more decisive step in the process he called a "new science" and which can now be analyzed at the most personal level possible.

## Notes

1 Lipsitt, Don R. "In Freud's Pocket: A Totem of Medical Ambivalence?," 738–751 *American Imago* 77, No. 4, Winter 2020, 746.
2 Fyytche, Matt. *Sigmund Freud*. London: Reaktion Books Limited, 2020. He adds an important note that will figure in the whole of the discussion to come. "There is no other science that has spawned quite Freud's method, and quite this acute perspective on mental life." Science and mental life. The word "mental," here, makes all the difference since this form of life cannot be reduced to *bios*, the *biology* of life.
3 Appelbaum, Jerome. "Father and Son: Freud Revisits His Oedipus Complex in Moses and Monotheism," 166–184 *American Journal of Psychoanalysis* 72 (2), Jun. 2012, 167.
4 Sharpe, Matthew, and Joanne Faulkner. *Understanding Psychoanalysis*. London: Routledge, 2008. There are as many genealogies as there are histories of psychoanalysis. In this case, whether there was any beginning such as the "biology of the mind" is, for me, not at all certain. Without addressing the question of society and ethics, there is only one way to look at the disciplines of philosophy and science. For someone taught in the German Gymnasium system, philosophy was less a discipline with a long history than it was, also, a way of thinking. The philosophical, always implicit, remains a deciding factor in the connection between Judaism and science.
5 Goldbach, Joel, and James A. Godley (Eds). *Inheritance in Psychoanalysis*. Albany: SUNY, 2018, 1.
6 Tauber, Alfred I. "Freud's Philosophical Path: From a Science of the Mind to a Philosophy of Human Being," 32–43 *The Scandinavian Psychoanalytic Review* 32, 2009, 32. See, more comprehensively, *The Reluctant Philosopher*. Princeton: Princeton University Press, 2010.
7 The literature on the subject is now well established. A few works can be mentioned. See, for example, Tom Sorell's *Scientism: Philosophy and the Infatuations with Science*. London: Routledge, 1991, and Frederick A. Olafson's *Naturalism and the Human Condition: Against Scientism*. London: Routledge, 2001. See, also, a number of co-edited collections, the first one by Richard N. Williams and Daniel N. Robinson, *Scientism: The New Orthodoxy*. London: Bloomsbury, 2015, and the second by Jeroen de Ridder et al, *Scientism: Prospects and Problems*. Oxford: Oxford University Press, 2018.
8 Axelrod, Charles D. "Freud and Science," 273–293 *Theory and Society* 4 (2), 1977, 275. If the hostility of the scientific community against Freud and psychoanalysis is still in the future, the only issue to focus on during this early period is on Freud's relationship to *himself* as a scientist and researcher.
9 Yilmaz Anil, Yunus. "Ernst Brücke and Sigmund Freud: Physiological Roots of Psychoanalysis," 568–591 *Journal of the History of the Neurosciences* 31 (4), 2022, 571.
10 Hunt, Roger. *Freud: A Mosaic*. Newcastle upon Tyne: Cambridge Scholars Publishing, 2012, 49.
11 Fonagy, Peter and Mary Target. "What Can Developmental Psychopathology Tell Psychoanalysis About the Mind?," 307–322 *Who Owns Psychoanalysis?* Ed. Ann Casement. London: Routledge, 2004.
12 Wilson, Catherine. *The Invisible World: Early Modern Philosophy and the Invention of the Microscope*. Princeton: Princeton University Press, 1995.
13 Langs, Robert. *Science, Systems and Psychoanalysis*. London: Routledge, 1992, 172.
14 Parisi, Thomas and Leonard D. Goodstein. "Why Freud Failed: Some Implications for Neurophysiology and Sociobiology," 235–245 *The American Psychologist* 42 (3), 1987.

15 Bacon, Francis. *Novum Organum*. Tr. and Ed. Peter Urbach and John Gibson. Chicago and LaSalle: Open Court, 1994, 10.
16 Anonymous. "The Influence of Francis Bacon on Medical Science," 134–135 *The New Zealand Medical Journal* 133 (1519), Jul. 31, 2020, 134.
17 Manzo, Silvia. "Francis Bacon: Freedom, Authority, Science," 245–273 *British Journal for the History of Philosophy* 14 (2), 2006, 246.
18 Dos Reis Biaza, Rafel, and Carlos Henrique Kessler. "Psychoanalysis and Science," 414–423 *Psicologia USP* 28 (3), Dec. 2017, 421.
19 Drouin, Emmanuel, Marion Hendrickx, and Patrick Hautecoeur. "Freud's Shift," 553 *Lancet Neurology* 22 (7), 2023. One shift is not enough: for us to take note of only the most important, we would have to mention, one, the figure of Helmholtz in German science and, following him, more personally, Ernst Brücke and Theodor Meynert. They will all be mentioned at the right time. One more comment is, at the outset, important: Helmholtz was interested in the optical mechanism of the eye as a way to understand consciousness and perception. Freud would come to uniquely understand how physiology could not possibly explain the act of perception and its origin in the psyche, both the unconscious and the super-ego.
20 Schuler, Romana Karla. *Seeing Motion: A History of Visual Perception in Art and Science*. Berlin: De Gruyter, 2015. Helmholtz later published *The New Development in Visual Theory*.
21 Meiring, Henry James. "Darwin of the Mind: Freud's Darwinian Image," 171–187 *Imagining the Darwinian Revolution: Historical Narratives of Evolution from the Nineteenth Century to the Present*. Ed. Ian Hesketh. Pittsburgh: University of Pittsburgh Press, 2022, 173.
22 Althusser, Louis. *Psychoanalysis and the Human Sciences*. T. Steven Rendall. New York: Columbia University Press, 2016, 47–8.
23 Jelliffe, Smith Ellie. "Freud and Psychiatry: A Partial Appraisal," 326–340 *The American Journal of Sociology* 45 (3), 1939, 326. She adds. "Obviously it would be a task of great difficulty to attempt to bring together all the influences that started Freud on his psychiatric odyssey and that carried him along the path he has so brilliantly illuminated." All the influences is impossible; however, in this case, one that has not received any attention (as far as I'm aware) has less to do with either medicine and psychiatry and is a philosophical "instauration" that owes something to both Judaism and science.
24 Brendel, David H. *Healing Psychiatry: Bridging the Science/Humanism Divide*. Cambridge, Mass.: The MIT Press, 2006.
25 Koyré, Alexandre. *From the Closed World to the Infinite Universe*. Baltimore: The Johns Hopkins University Press, 1957, 2.
26 Phillips, Denise. "Francis Bacon and the Germans: Stories from When Science Meant Wissenschaft," 378–394 *History of Science* 53 (4), Dec. 2015, 383.
27 Chapman, Ross M. and Edith Wigert. "Freud and Psychiatry," 855–857 *American Journal of Orthopsychiatry* 10 (4), 1940, 855.
28 Weeks, S.V. "Francis Bacon's Doctrine of Idols: A Diagnosis of 'Universal Madness'," 1–39 *British Journal for the History of Science* 52 (1) (Mar. 2019).
29 Bernfeld, Siegfried. "Freud's Scientific Beginnings," 163–196 *American Imago* 6 (3), 1949.
30 Lynch, William T. *Solomon's Child: Method in the Early Royal Society of London*. Stanford: Stanford University Press, 2001, 70.
31 Jordynn, Jack. "A Pedagogy of Sight: Microscopic Vision in Robert Hooke's *Micrographia*," 192–209 *Quarterly Journal of Speech* 95 (3), May 1999.
32 Dalzell, Thomas. *Freud's Schreber Between Psychiatry and Psychoanalysis: On Subjective Disposition to Psychosis*. London: Karnac, 2011, 152.

33  Corneanu, Sorana and Koen Vermeir. "Idols of the Imagination: Francis Bacon on the Imagination and the Medicine of the Mind," 183–205 *Perspectives on Science* 20 (2), 2012.
34  Walton, Douglas. "Francis Bacon: Human Bias and the Four Idols," 385–389 *Argumentation* 13 (4), Nov, 1999, 387.
35  Cooper, Amy. "Francis Bacon's Idols and the Reformed Science," 328–350 *Studies in Philology* 116 (2), Spring 2019, 340.
36  Jacobsen, Kurt. *Freud's Foes: Psychoanalysis, Science, and Resistance*. Lanham: Rowman & Littlefield Publishers, Inc., 2009, 11.
37  Weinert, Friedel. *Copernicus, Darwin, and Freud: Revolutions in History and Philosophy of Science*. Oxford: Wiley-Blackwell, 2008, 187.
38  Wilson, Catherine. *The Invisible World: Early Modern Philosophy and the Invention of the Microscope*. Princeton: Princeton University Press, 1995.
39  Pomata, Gianni. "Observation Rising: The Birth of an Epistemic Genre, 1500–1650," 45–80 *Histories of Scientific Observation*. Chicago: The University of Chicago Press, 2011.
40  Vogel, Wolfgang H. and Berke, Andreas. *Brief History of Vision and Ocular Medicine*. Amsterdam: Kugler Publications, 2009.
41  Wade, Nicholas J. "Ernst Brücke on Stereoscopic Vision," 159–164 *Strabismus* 30 (3), 2022.
42  Carpenter, William B. *The Microscope and Its Revelations*. Seventh Edition edited by W.H. Dallinger. London: J & A Churchill, 1891.
43  Frixione, Eugenio. "Sigmund Freud's Contribution to the History of the Neuronal Cytoskeleton," 12–24 *Journal of the History of the Neurosciences* 12 (1), Mar. 1, 2003, 20. The literature on Freud's early scientific is extensive. All of it can be consulted for giving us a more detailed knowledge of Freud's scientific studies and the many ways they influenced his many discoveries of psychoanalysis. Other examples are John E. Gedo's "The Enduring Scientific Contributions of Sigmund Freud," 200–211 *Perspectives in Biology and Medicine*, 45 (2) (Spring 2002).
44  Schickore, Jutta. *The Microscope and the Eye: A History of Reflections, 1740–1870*. Chicago: The University of Chicago Press, 2007, 84, my emphasis.
45  Langs, Robert. *Science, Systems and Psychoanalysis*. London: Karnac, 1992, 47. One of his introductory statements can be adopted since I'm not entirely sure if the debate on psychoanalysis as a science is either necessary or productive. Is it, to use a metaphor, a red herring? Langs writes: "the absence of a definable science of psychoanalysis is also of no great cause for concern," 4. It may very well be for individuals who are academics; but I doubt very much if psychoanalysts, in their daily practice – which is appreciated, by an analysand, for being extremely demanding on many levels – even worry about the scientific status of their therapy. Don't we have all the evidence we need for psychoanalysis as therapeutic and medical?
46  Schwarts, Joseph. *Cassandra's Daughter: A History of Psychoanalysis*. London: Karnac, 2003, 12.
47  Schermer, Victor. *Meaning, Mind, and Self-Transformation: Psychoanalytic Interpretation and the Interpretation of Psychoanalysis*. London: Karnac, 2014, 191.
48  Symington, Neville. *The Blind Man Sees: Freud's Awakening and Other Essays*. London: Karnac, 2004, 14.
49  Wieser, Martin. "From the Eel to the Ego: Psychoanalysis and the Remnants of Freud's early scientific practice," 259–280 *Journal of the History of the Behavioural Sciences* 49 (3), Summer 2013, 259–260, my emphasis. Space makes it impossible to adequately acknowledge the informative and perceptive work done by Wieser. One other article, co-written with Thomas Slunecko, should also be consulted. "Images of the Invisible:

An Account of Iconic Media in the History of Psychology," 435–457 *Theory & Psychology* 23 (4), 2013.
50  Gomez, Lavinia. *The Freud Wars: An Introduction to the Philosophy of Psychoanalysis.* London: Routledge, 2005, 34.
51  Yovell, Yoran. "From Mechanics to Metaphor – On Freud's Struggle with the Biology of the Mind," 513–524 *Journal of the American Academy of Psychoanalysis* 25 (3) (Sep. 1997), 515.
52  Wittgenstein, Ludwig. *Tractatus Logico-Philosophicus.* 6.52.
53  Appelbaum, Jerome, "Should Psychoanalysis Become a Science?," 1–15 *American Journal of Psychoanalysis* 71 (1) (Mar. 2011).
54  Bock von Wülfingen, Bettina. "Freud's 'Core of Our Being' Between Cytology and Psychoanalysis," 226–244 *Berichte zur Wissenschaftgeschichte* 36 (3), 2013, 230.
55  Kronman, Anthony T. *Confessions of a Born-Again Pagan.* New Haven: Yale University Press, 2016, 108.
56  Vogel, Ladislaus Z. "Freud's Early Clinical Work," 94–101 *American Journal of Psychotherapy* 48 (1) (Winter 1994), 98.
57  Schauer, Frederick. *The Proof: Uses of Evidence in Law, Politics, and Everything Else.* Cambridge, Mass. Harvard University Press, 2022, 227. The quote comes from the chapter "Seeing What We Want to See."
58  Weiss, Dieter G., Günther Jirikowski, and Stefanie Reichelt. "Microscopic Imaging: Interference, Intervention, Objectivity," 35–54 *Traces: Generating What Was There.* Ed. Bettina Bock von Wülfingen. Berlin: De Gruyter, 2017, 54.
59  Hacking, Ian. "Do We See Through a Microscope?," 305–322 *Pacific Philosophical Quarterly* 62 (4), Oct. 1981.
60  McCarthy, John A. *Remapping Reality: Chaos and Creativity in Science and Literature: Goethe – Nietzsche – Grass.* Amsterdam: Rodopi, 2006, 13.
61  Latour, Bruno. "Coming Out as a Philosopher," 599–608 *Social Studies of Science* 40 (4), 2010, 601.

# Chapter 3

# Anna O.'s "Private Theatre"

## The Splitting of Consciousness

> The synthetic function of the ego, though it is of such extraordinary importance, is subject to particular conditions and is liable to a whole number of disturbances.
> (Splitting of the Ego in the Process of Defense)

Freud's internalization of both a Jewish sensibility to perception and the equally important method of scientific observation – which he developed phenomenologically during his laboratory research and his experience with the microscope – has brought us to the period of 1880–1882 when he was nearing the end of his scientific studies on aquatic specimens and starting his tenure as a physician at the Vienna General Hospital headed by Theodor Meynert. Freud's professional experience would again be complemented by Meynert's anatomical methods and by his concentration on the pathogenesis of mental illness and its localization in the brain.[1] The strictly scientific relationship to the anatomy of the brain was, however, only one aspect of a new equation for Freud to analyze, just as his dissection of eels, for example, had turned him for a time to the function of the nervous system. Anyone working, today, on the connection between neurobiology and psychoanalysis have their own "return" to Freud, so much so that, without the slightest controversy, he "can also be seen as an early neuroscientist and physiologist."[2] The connection, though significant for a completely different kind of study, a strictly physicalist one, is here set aside in order to concentrate on Freud's experience between two seemingly antithetical orientations – one he participated in as a physician in a psychiatric clinic, the other during this discussions with Josef Breuer on the case of Anna O. One article that makes Freud's later "rhetoric" dependent on his scientific studies also makes a comment that is, for us, essential and for the same reasons as the previous allegory of perception. Laying out a relationship and a transition is necessary in order to see how Freud's experiences were both cumulative and discerning.

Before Freud began his career as a therapist, he spent over a decade working as a medical biologist. First in the laboratory of Ernst Wilhelm von Brücke, in the orbit of Hermann von Helmholtz's thought, and later in neurologist Theodor Meynert's laboratory, Freud focussed principally on the visualisation of (primarily neuronal) cells.[3]

Freud's "visualization," given our previous arguments, as Biblical, philosophical, and scientific, was not about neuronal cells or any other empirical phenomena – except as indicators, phenomena as signs to be interpreted for a new way of thinking. A number of impressions were, for Freud, examined one by one and then incorporated into a system of thought he had yet to systematically create.

The many-sided influences on his thinking reach one more decisive moment when his relationship with Josef Breuer, and the manner of dealing with one psychologically ill patient in particular, gives him one more impetus away from the physicalism of his time and towards an inquiry into human consciousness, both for the healthy and the ill. The ur-patient of psychoanalysis has been recognized as the anonymously named Anna O., her identity later revealed as Bertha Pappenheim in Ernest Jones's biography of Freud. All the commentaries on her, as a patient, and as a person during her treatment by Josef Breuer, are now included in a virtual library – which, historically, may say more about *our* thinking about the phenomena of 19th-century hysteria and our political motivations, than on the case itself. "The specific etiology of her breakdown and, perhaps more interesting, of her eventual recovery and productive later life, must depend heavily on the investigator's general assumptions and theoretical bent."[4] No assumptions need be made on her breakdown. The "etiology" has never been satisfactorily presented; all we have (all Freud dealt with) were her symptoms and what they meant for him in terms of his interest, beyond this one individual, in the consciousness of the mentally ill. The all-important sense of a "split consciousness," which was preliminary and not quite exact, was the first sense of Anna O.'s condition, more of a many-dimensional fragmentation than a neat division. A sharp division is also evident in the scholarship on the case. Anna O., along with the illness called hysteria, has been the rationale for a deep-rooted denunciation of history.

We are always "reopening a closed case."[5] What we read, again and again, is in the *Studies on Hysteria*; the case, as written, is by no means complete when we consider Freud's evaluation of her symptoms. Our interpretation is, always, a personal matter. No question: hysteria has been, historically, an enigma[6] and at the origin of so many of our contemporary conflicts on a number of problems, especially social and political ones. Enigma: there will be many more; and still we have no other choice but to return to Breuer's account and, after, what the case study meant for Freud in the immediate years following, and as they culminated with his time in Paris. We can claim, hope, and desire all we want about "hysteria beyond Freud."[7] No "beyond" can be achieved unless we are first quite sure about our understanding of Freud's relationship to the first case and many others after. Reading the co-written "Preliminary Communication," if we concentrate on the discussion of symptoms before all other considerations introduces us to the concept of hysteria at the time and how Freud, in particular, began to understand its phenomenology. Discussing the case of Anna O. with Breuer was an altogether different experience than his observations of the mentally ill as they were treated in a general hospital by an anatomical physiologist.

During the transition from the university laboratory to the clinic – and with a now enhanced perception, a historical and scientific one – Freud moved from the *objects* of science such as biological specimens to the one irreducible subject of being and the patient who was more than a problem for general medicine. He was motivated by the understanding the individual person, not the mechanism of their body and brain. The following few years were highly influential due to his gradual transition from a doctor, scientist, and psychiatrist towards a new way of representing classical and modern ideals of psychotherapy. For him to *become* the inventor of psychoanalysis, he had to first of all bring himself into being by both internalizing a classical, modern, and contemporary reality and rearrange their meaning in himself, first of all, and then in a new practice. How he did so can be outlined from his own recollection as he presented it in writing. One fact stands out for us. If we consult his writings on the origins of psychoanalysis, we find him starting from one place.

Turning to his many autobiographical writings is necessary as a foundation and for tracing a certain consistency in his recollections. Many examples could be chosen; attending to each of them and recognizing nuances of difference, here and there, would not substantially alter all the events as they were understood for his experiences. A few of them are, however, indispensable for the portrait they give us of a time and, eventually (not an insignificant amount of time later), the decision to publish the *Studies on Hysteria* and, more specifically for us now, the jointly written "Preliminary Communication." We are, here, at quite a distance from the attempt to write "a new historiography of psychoanalysis" and, in particular, with any concern with the belief that "psychoanalysis seeks to assert its scientific bona fides."[8] The "Preliminary Communication" suspends any such ambitions. Here, we also have to take the opportunity to reflect on the disciplinary (and/or) personal responses to a historical period and Freud's life. A contributor from "the Royal Society of Medicine" does not change our expectations. "It is an irony that psychoanalysis should rest on such dubious disease entity as hysteria."[9] One is hard-pressed to find the irony; and if hysteria, as a *category*, is "dubious," there is nothing uncertain about Anna O.'s experiences of her life. She experienced, for example, her *absences* and a number of other ideations, perceptions, and hallucinations; trying to understand them, today, remains an obligation if Freud's thinking is to be also understood. We might have all the "factual information that is available about Anna's illness,"[10] and yet we are no closer to bridging the gap between her life and Freud's emerging theories. Finding a few of their cross-sections can be done in part. Starting out from Freud's historical recollections, in a few chosen writings, gives us one portrait; the "Preliminary Communication" will give us another. Both will add something to our understanding of Freud's place in his life prior to the momentous time in Paris.

In "On the History of the Psychoanalytic Movement," Freud makes an admission that might too easily be ignored as nothing but a sign of his self-understanding. "No one need be surprised at the subjective character of the contribution I propose to make here to the history of the psychoanalytic movement, nor need anyone wonder at the part I play in it. For psychoanalysis is my creation" (SE 14:7). *Subjective character*. Another term might simply be personal, the latter without self-consciousness or undue prejudice. Freud takes as much credit as he assumes responsibility. In any case, there will be no disavowal. Leaving aside the recent events, in 1914, of the change in the editorial board of the psychoanalytic *Jahrbuch*, due to the falling-out with Carl Jung, and returning instead to his reconstruction of the origin of psychoanalysis, there is one period that is, for him, definitive. The preceding influence of Judaism and science and their shared views on perception might have been neglected for Freud as he takes the reader to the time when he developed a relationship with Josef Breuer "when I was still a student engaged in passing my examinations (1880–2)." The period has been presented earlier as a transitional one. As for Breuer, Freud acknowledges him for his early experiments with hypnotism and the cathartic method; but unlike, for example, the 1909 lectures in America, when he had given Breuer perhaps too much credit for the beginning of psychoanalysis, he is now more accurate. The history, in many ways, speaks for itself; as it will when we turn to the later account of the period in question and the postponed publication of *Studies on Hysteria*. In the account of the history of psychoanalysis in 1914, he makes a statement that should be stressed. All his critics, then and now, have never so much as acknowledged Freud for this one sensibility. "I myself had only unwillingly taken up the profession of medicine; but I had at that time a strong motive for helping people suffering from nervous affections or at least for wishing to understand something about their states." To our detriment, and so often misunderstanding the purpose of psychoanalysis (which an analysand never forgets), Freud is now no longer a physician in the traditional sense, a scientist working on specimens under a microscope, or a would-be psychiatrist examining patients in a clinic. He has devoted himself to easing human suffering by understanding the causes of psychological maladies and searching for an individual cure for every patient. The theoretical presentation as outlined in *Studies on Hysteria* and the case of Anna O. in particular will take up our attention in due time; for the moment, there is more to outline in terms of Freud's own beginning as he has defined it. Only one fact is now emphasized: his association with Breuer proved to be more important than any other experience. The determination is as important for us as it is for Freud when he tells us about a difference. His language is no less important than his own originality.

The first difference between Breuer and myself came to light on a question concerning the finer psychical mechanism of hysteria. He gave preference to a theory which was still to some extent physiological, as one might say; he tried to explain the mental splitting in hysterical patients by the absence of communication between various mental states ('states of consciousness', as we called them at that time) ... I had taken the matter less scientifically; everywhere I seemed to discern motives and tendencies analogous to those of everyday life, and I looked upon psychical splitting itself.

(SE 14:11)

The groundbreaking idea of a patient's split consciousness was so important that Freud would return to it near the end of his life, as if something previously omitted had to be addressed – if only to lay greater stress on this one discovery in the nature of the psyche and, in one particularity, splitting as a psychical defence.

The "splitting" itself, whose reality was perceived through the analysis of Anna O.'s absences – the state of her consciousness *temporally* – was not for Freud a physical phenomenon.

The physicalism of his medical, scientific, and psychiatric period was no longer predominant. The remnants would remain with him for a significant period of time as he continued his own theoretical splitting between the biological and the phenomenological, the brain and the psyche – as our own contemporary splitting has been defined by our historical as opposed to symptomatic realities. There would be quite a few more episodes, starts and stops, postponements and hesitations, on the way to his definition of psychoanalysis – which turned out just as he had imagined, interminable because the original findings of psychoanalysis were capable of generating more and more complexities, both for the internal dynamics of human beings and their experiences. Subsequent articles on the history of psychoanalysis all turned to this one period in Freud's life as the beginning of psychoanalysis. The historical truth of his account serves to remind his readers of a time and, equally important, the accumulation of life-experiences that could be in principle underestimated but certainly not forgotten. When we then return to other examples of Freud's history, which is never separated from an autobiography, we find ourselves in one place.

In the section of "Psycho-analysis" called "Prehistory," Freud begins with the years (1880–1882) when Breuer was treating Anna O., a period, moreover, "before the investigations of Charcot and Pierre Janet into the origin of hysterical symptoms" (SE 20:263). Consulting any other historical and biographical piece of writing confirms Freud's recollection of the origin of the method that, ultimately, led to the foundation of psychoanalysis. In *An Autobiographical Study*, he again makes the same observation. "Even before I went to Paris, Breuer had told me about a case of hysteria which, between 1880 and 1882, he had treated in a peculiar manner which had allowed him to penetrate deeply into the causation and significance of hysterical symptoms" (SE 23:19). Freud did not hesitate to always attribute the initial direction of a certain kind of awareness to Breuer. The instances of his acknowledgement are repeated. For example, in the *Introductory Lectures on Psychoanalysis* in "The Sense of Symptoms," he writes, "The sense of neurotic symptoms was first discovered by Josef Breuer from his study and successful cure (in 1880 and 1882) of a case of hysteria which has since become famous"

(SE 16:257). The claim of a "successful cure" turned out to be too optimistic. The initial "failure," on Breuer's part, can be understood to be one of incompletion. The doctor-patient relationship was not, at the time, completely understood. Recognizing a transference – one as affective as in reading and so internalizing an aspect of the past was no less a reality in the psychotherapeutic situation, one of the many realities to be understood and incorporated into psychoanalysis as a theory and a therapeutic practice. To be sure, one of Freud's achievements – rarely acknowledged? – turned out to be a sort of psychical splitting in the doctor himself. The strict boundary between doctor and patient, easily maintained between the healthy and the organically ill, could not be assumed so easily when it came to the psyche. The transference, for all its importance, was not at first noticed; there were other, more pressing symptoms. Other details of the Anna O. case and the others in *Studies on Hysteria* came to light at the time they did on Freud's insistence. Breuer, apparently, did not strongly favour publication, for a number of reasons. Robert Kaplan believes that "Freud's rush to get *Studies on Hysteria* into print in 1895 was to ensure that Pierre Janet did not get credit for discovering the psychological treatment of hysteria."[11] The "rush" was understandable and intrinsic to the nature of scientific discoveries. Charles Darwin was under the same kind of duress to publish *On the Origin of Species* – though with a mutual respect shared by another individual who had come to the same conclusion on the theory of evolution. In any event, any pressing reasons for the publication are incidental to our immediate concerns with its meaning. They are matters of publications and irrelevant to Freud's understanding of Anna O. and the material Breuer presented to him. At this point, and later when her symptoms are analyzed as a whole, especially in terms of her disturbances of vision and her "private theatre," Anna O. remains a crucial reference.

What can we learn from the jointly written "Preliminary Communication" of 1893, more than a decade after the end of Anna O.'s initial treatment by Breuer, and how can we isolate Freud's own analysis as it develops later? The publication, originally separate from the *Studies on Hysteria* and despite its date, attests to a number of insights that would be essential to the development of psychoanalysis once Freud continued on his own. "With *Studies on Hysteria*, Freud embarks on a new kind of science."[12] If the word "science" is to be retained, after all, though without any commitments one way or the other, we do so only because of Freud's own self-demand and less for the status of psychoanalysis today. We are just as likely to affirm that Freud embarked on a multi-dimensional initiative that was inseparable from the ancients, the early modern, and his own contemporary situation. While a majority of scholars are fixated on his immediate historical context, and the 19th-century category of hysteria, Freud's thinking is much more expansive. The "new science" did not, however, begin with the writing of the case studies. An entire chain of other factors were involved in Freud's development. A few indications can be singled out. They are intimations of a process that is, also, medical insofar as it depends on recognizing a symptom and then tracing it to a cause. In itself, the symptom – what can be *seen* in an action or a thought of the patient – does not reveal the cause. On the contrary, hysteria, or any neurosis, depends on showing a sign as a way to hide its origin. Although they open the introduction with "a chance observation has led us, over a number of years, to investigate a great variety of different forms and symptoms of hysteria" (SE 2:3), the scientific, medical, and phenomenological procedure is a classical one: symptoms are observed and then traced to an origin that, in every case, has been consciously forgotten by the patients themselves and only revived, unintentionally, in the process of speaking and, therefore, of translating an experience into a form capable of being interpreted according to various nuances of meaning. One kind of interpretation, historically[13] understandable but perhaps, today, less and less convincing especially when we turn to Freud's experience in Paris, has made the attempt to single her out as *a woman*, with all the consequences whose motives are social and political.[14] To take another example from others that will be mentioned: can we really think about Anna O. and "her use of her body as a signifier?"[15] The theoretically minded and gender conscious might be satisfied; but, surely, Anna O. cannot be given any intentionality and certainly nothing as conscious as the "use" of her own body and precisely because the *conversion* of psychical dynamics and bodily expression was entirely unconscious. Or, to use an example from a completely different discipline, are we to diagnose her illness as, perhaps, meningitis or tuberculous encephalitis or, more cryptically, "slowly evolving brain lesions?"[16] How does one begin to reconcile feminist theory with neurobiology? Mentioning two extremes, a political and strictly scientific one, leaves Anna O.'s experiences (as symptoms) *entirely unexamined* insofar as they are psychical. Freud was coming closer to a sense of the unconscious dynamics of the mentally ill and how their internal "split" was complicated by a number of factors that would be individual to the patient and so developed over the history of psychoanalysis.[17] The differences, in our perception, are becoming more distinct and more incommensurable. Feminism, brain lesions, unconscious dynamics: how we situate ourselves amidst these competing ideas reveals more about us than a psychological state of mind. If *we are Freudian*, and really concerned with Anna O. as an individual, her case matters for showing what the case meant for Freud at the beginning and according to his own individuality. One decision is today paramount. How we relate to her case does not hide our motivations. Are we ultimately concerned with Anna O.'s life-experience or with a definition and one of the drives of academic thought today, critical theory?[18] Is feminist theory relevant?

In the "Preliminary Communication," there are many statements that stand out; to a casual reader, they may be entirely missed, as was most probably the case at the time. We are in a better position to take notice of the arguments, however subtly they are presented. One notices some restraint, a note of scientific prudence since the revelations are far-reaching. They will all become explicit when Freud sets himself to writing a number of essays at a time when psychoanalysis was on its way to being formed self-consciously. Many of his ideas are implicit. The first: "external events determine the pathology of hysteria to an extent far greater than is known and recognized" (SE 2:4). The affirmation is a startling one since it puts forward a unique argument that is relevant for anyone's psychological state – including theorists: the "external events" are experiences and are not to be traced to physiology or, more importantly, biological heredity. The mechanism is, precisely, psychical and so depends on a relation between an experience and its long-term effect. One has to appreciate just how innovative the psychology was at the time. This one beginning defied virtually the whole tradition of a science intent on being traceable to the materialism of the body. Many symptoms were, of course, already known and included in the general analysis of hysteria. They should be more than obvious to us since some forms of hysterical illness persists into our present – with a different kind of 21st-century hysteria, which too often is interpreted *politically* and ideologically and so risks misdiagnosing the individual. A *political* theory of hysteria, however, runs the risk of making the details fit a ready-made explanation and so end up in an endless and self-confirming rationalization. We are beginning to sense, with Freud, that theory can also be highly neurotic.

Out of all the symptoms mentioned, one is the most important since it highlights Freud's awareness of the most important issue. He takes note of the physical symptoms of hysteria – attacks, convulsions, tics – but one will here be emphasized because it is the first indication of the nature of neurotic perception: "various forms of disturbance of vision, constantly recurring visual hallucination." By the latter, Freud is not primarily describing one of the most serious effects of psychosis, that is, actual hallucinations, visible forms. The psychoanalysis of perception is already one of his main preoccupations; and because there are no physical origins to the way the neurotic *sees*, the one explanation remaining is the one that will set him towards understanding the real power of the psyche and its capacity to alter the very nature of reality in and through psychical projections. The "disturbance of vision" is not to be traced to some defect in the eyes themselves, nor to some organic illness. No eye examination will ever be able to discover the meaning of the perception of the patient. Freud comes upon one of the most far-reaching of the insights that will be foundational for psychoanalysis: the psyche can distort the nature of reality repeatedly and consistently due to one experience of either a real or imagined trauma from the past. The consequential prism is then absolute. Time may be intrusive and disruptive for the present. The distinction, to be made later, will also be original to Freud. In terms of vision and hallucinations, that is, the misrecognition of an experience, his example is clearly his own. That it overlaps with both the idea of an image and perception is an anticipation of the classic work that is, in 1892, only a few years in the future. The connection between the symptom and the cause, Freud tells us, "consists only in what might be called a 'symbolic' relation between the precipitating cause and the pathological phenomenon – a relation such as healthy people from in dreams" (SE 2:5). He is already on the way towards recognizing how a healthy and pathological psyche is only separated by degrees. As for a dream, as an image and its perception, there is an unmistakable internal mechanism that creates the image as well as the possibility of it being seen when the ego is passively in a state of sleep or, as in Anna O.'s case – and in a condition that is a perennial, as real today as in the 19th century – a *somnambulism* that renders the ego weak and vulnerable.

Equally important, the same psychical projection capable of creating images in dreams has a similar function, in terms of ideation, during an everyday experience. The later theory of drives can be traced to the power of the psyche to intrude into everyday reality and produce a consistent psychopathology. Did Freud already see the state of the hysteric in terms of a kind of hypnosis and somnambulism that was not recognized as such? The year 1892 may be too early for Freud to have started his interpretation of dreams; nevertheless, the beginning of the work that will be defining for psychoanalysis has been prepared in a distinction that is historically classical. The visible and the invisible: Judaism, science, and the beginnings of psychoanalysis are each dependent on a particular kind of perception that extends beyond the assumptions on what constitutes the apparent. Freud already understands that any pathological phenomena, when specifically related to perception, originates in the psyche and in such a way as to distort what is seen. Neurosis is a kind of idolatry. The hysteric, or, more generally, the neurotic, is someone who has been deceived by a perception that they themselves have psychically created and then, perversely, confirmed. Without making the case for an equation, it does seem as if *academics* (especially those who have made a career of promoting a view of Freud and psychoanalysis) are vulnerable to the exact same process. One has innumerable examples to judge the merits of the arguments – indeed, for and against, which excuses no one of doing their own work. We can mention one title. The centuries-old "mystification" of the Anna O. case can be read; and then one has the obligation, so often ignored, of doing the reading oneself to see how the perspective appears.[19] Refutations, intellectually speaking, are irrelevant. The more one concentrates on the "Preliminary Communication" as another defining announcement in the history of the knowledge of depth-psychology, the more one recognizes all the connections as they have been inherited and transformed for the sake of a new of thinking and, ultimately, a new way of treating human suffering and the failed lives as experienced by all kinds of neurotics. (One has to make an argument over and over again – as did Freud: neuroses cannot be cured by fixing all the apparent and supposed problems of a society. That attempt has been made too many times, and almost always with disastrous results).

The justly famous statement *"hysterics suffer mainly from reminiscences"* can only be understood in its full effect when the memories are *watched*, over and over again, and so keep the patient in a state of dependence on the past. Freud's early impressions will all be developed. For the patient to become free of the past, the return has to be one where the recollection of the image (in a kind of self-hypnosis and compulsive perception of an event, specific or vague depending on its reality) is no longer simply watched; the perception passively enjoyed, as a symptom, has to be turned into a reasoned description in words. In other words, the perception of the immediate image has to be turned into *meaning* and in such a way that the earlier confirmation, of reality, becomes something other than its hardened sense. The hysteric is always passive in relation to the images being conjured up from the past and the working-over of the images in the imagination; the act of speaking, which interrupts the insistence of the image, transforms the experience and sufficiently for it to no longer be affective. The one who speaks is removed from the past into the present of the psychotherapeutic situation. Breuer used the Aristotelian term "catharsis" to describe the process; one wonders how much he truly understood from the classical description, originally used in the interpretation of Greek tragedy – that is, from the experience of a spectator who was watching a play unfold on stage, no differently than the hysteric who was both actor and spectator, both identities locked into a form of reciprocity that could not end until there was an interpretative intervention. Aristotle's concept, catharsis as a kind of "purgation" and therefore therapeutic, will demand our attention in due time and for making a theory of tragedy – a theatrical form, in terms of a scene and in acting out the part of a character – explanatory also for the hysterics who will be put on display at the Salpêtrière in Paris. As a spectator of the hysterics in an institution, Freud will not be passive and a mere onlooker or satisfied with the explanation of their conditions. The entirety of his past and the three events of our project – Judaism, science, Anna O. – will be unified once the time in Paris is placed in a comprehensive context, one that will be partially complete with a turn to Aristotle's analysis of Greek tragedy.

One could very well turn to the "Preliminary Communication" and the whole of the *Studies on Hysteria* and see, in their first suggestive form (like the previous example of the meaning of dreams), Freud's subsequent ideas. For example, in the same paragraph when the concept of repression is first introduced, another fundamental human experience is mentioned for the first time. There are cases "in which the patients have not reacted to a psychical trauma because the nature of the trauma excluded a reaction, as in the case of the apparently irreparable loss of a loved person" (SE 2:10). The association of mourning and melancholia is in the future and his development of a metapsychology; keeping in mind the relation of memories and forgetting, the case of mourning for the dead can be the cause of the most mortifying kind of recollections. Indeed, the relationship, whatever its former state, cannot be altered – except in the present, by the individual, and alone. One is therefore open to an either/or situation: the permanent recollection of the memory of the dead, with its possible guilt, for instance, or the process later to be called the "working-through" and done only when the fixation to the past is no longer a psychical imposition. We should remind ourselves that Anna O.'s illness started at the time when her father became seriously ill and she took care of him. Of course she suffered from a "depressive illness," which is less important for us at the physical level than for Anna O.'s perceptual state or the theory of her later "upswing into energetic social and intellectual behaviour, characteristic of cyclothymic personality."[20] But these are nothing but categories; they tell us almost nothing about the specifics of her illness or, more importantly for us, how Freud understood the relation of her symptoms as a cluster he will figure out as the splitting and fragmentation of consciousness and so bring him closer to the dynamic elements of the psyche.

There are other symptoms mentioned in the communication that, again, are specifically related to perception. These, for the moment, are not developed. They are origins to an entire way of thinking that will take years of observation. Mentioning them in the context of a first statement on a psychotherapeutic method is again done to stress just how important it was for Freud to recognize what the psyche was capable of producing. When, for example, there is the mention of "positively abnormal psychical states," one wonders if Freud thought so when "semi-hypnotic twilight states of day-dreaming" and "autohypnosis" are both mentioned. As another sentence that could be read too quickly and without sufficient attention, the idea of autohypnosis alerts the reader to the nature of consciousness and in the power of the psyche to put the individual in such a passive state that all recollections, or perceptions in the present, are internalized without the ability to reflect and put the experience into words. The opening of "Mourning and Melancholia" is suggestive for the discussion at the moment, especially if we recall Freud's (then) passing reference to dreams and their meaning. "Dreams having served us as the prototype in normal life of narcissistic mental disorders, we will now try to throw light on the nature of melancholia by comparing it with the normal effect of mourning" (SE 14:243). Without advancing this one line of interpretation, Anna O.'s mourning and depression – due to her father's death – we can instead return to an original observation, a "splitting" that makes a neurotic susceptible to internal and unconscious dynamics. The types of splitting, as they were developed later, need not be applied to Anna O.[21] Only the initial recognition should matter to us at the moment.

> Hysterical reminiscences and autohypnosis are simultaneous products of the unconscious, what is soon termed *"the splitting of consciousness."* Freud recognized something essential about the psychical mechanism of hypnosis. It was a universal condition. Of course it was much worse with neurotics since they could, literally, hypnotize themselves without the slightest idea of the process – in which the unconscious overwhelmed the ego and reduced it to a mere passive capacity to perceive, like a spectator.

We have already been obliged to speak of abnormal states of consciousness in which these pathogenic ideas arise, and to emphasize the fact that the recollection of the operative psychical trauma is not to be found in the patient's normal memory but in his memory when he is hypnotized. The longer we have become occupied with these phenomena the more we have become convinced that *the splitting of consciousness which is so striking in the well-known classical cases of under the form of* 'double- conscience' *is present in a rudimentary degree in every hysteria.* (SE 2:12)

Hypnosis is, therefore, not simply an early psychotherapeutic procedure; self-hypnosis has already been recognized in the many forms of neurotic life (indeed, in everyday life) and most particularly in the knowledge of human beings and their vulnerability to a "split consciousness" and in the "*double-conscience*" discussed by French psychologists such as Pierre Janet.

Reading the "Preliminary Communication" towards the time of the first discussions between Breuer and Freud – and then with the addition of Freud's experience in Paris, which we will turn to shortly – an array of ideas come together that make an understanding of the whole more accessible. Isolating some of the more evident concepts, the French "double-conscience," which has the added benefit of being both consciousness and the later conscience of the super-ego, as well as the "splitting of consciousness," makes one insight unavoidable: the analysis of neurotic symptoms was, in the beginning, inseparable from the realization that the ego was not at all whole and could be fragmented. The idea of a divided consciousness was, in itself, preliminary. Freud would later make the psyche much more complex, first by identifying three inter-related processes (id, ego, super-ego) and in defining their respective characteristics at the topographical, dynamic, and economic level. In 1893, these are not for Freud conceptually explicit; their characteristics have, however, already been traced as to their origins and effects. How much of the communication is Freud's need to be specifically defined. In any case, Breuer's contribution from this point forward ends. He was satisfied with his popular practice and his reputation as a physician in Vienna. Freud, on the other hand, was in the uncertain period between being a student and working in a profession which he had not yet chosen. He had gone from a medical school, a laboratory, and a psychiatric clinic without being at all certain of his future. The time of his association with Breuer, from 1882 on, was highly mixed and uncertain. One has to appreciate just how difficult his situation was at the time. The *Studies on Hysteria* can be appreciated both for its intrinsic value and for our own relationship to Freud as we try to account for a period in his life that is more than, and different from, chronology.

"The basis and *sine qua non* of hysteria is the existence of hypnoid states" (SE 2:12). A state of hypnosis was therefore a description of consciousness as it was both "split," or, more accurately, fragmented by the nature of unconscious psychical mechanisms and its effects on perception of the self, others, and the world. While the too-specific term of hysteria is used in 1892, in a matter of time it would no longer be customary. Freud would substitute one form of psychological illness for a number of more specific neuroses. The outstanding feature of all forms of neuroses would involve hypnosis since the individual in question was only partly self-aware, if at all during the more intense moments when the unconscious overwhelmed the capacity of the ego to recognize its own perceptions. Consciousness was reduced and the capacity of the ego greatly diminished. A hypnoid state, Freud realizes, cuts off communication within the ego and alienates awareness; in other words, any possibility for self-reflection is rendered impossible by the dynamic and force of the particular kind of hypnotic consciousness. Because these states are highly variable, they must also be psychically organized in a particular way – a problem Freud would set himself to solving over the long history of psychoanalysis as he first created it. The hypnoid states are the precondition for an illness to develop into a heightened form. *Everyone*, in other words, lives in and out of hypnoid states – in day-dreaming, for example, or fantasies and ideation; the difference between the everyday and the neurotic occurs when the hypnoid state becomes overbearing and makes it less and less likely to be able to know, consciously, when it occurs and why. The images of the ideation, for example, are compulsive, and to use a word and concept, "enjoyable," a source of pleasure, whether masochistic or not. Freud has come upon a reality of consciousness so pervasive that it will take a significant amount of time, and the observation of many patients, to detail, in its origin, effect, and consequence. The nature of consciousness predisposes everyone to its variations; the neurotic, however, has been determined to such an extent by the projective power of the unconscious that interfering with the image of an ideation, or a memory, takes self-reflective effort and a consistent reminder of being vulnerable to internal drives. It is easier to simply be passive in the face of the constant assault on the perceptual senses. The present literally disappears, a phenomenon described as an "absence," an experience that is hypnotic most especially in terms of time, the past of the memory now taking the place of the present with such force that the immediate appears only as incomplete, disturbed, and distorted. The French term *"absence,"* when applied to Anna O., will allow Freud to see one more aspect of the divided psyche in terms of time and personal history. The defensive withdrawal from reality, as a measure of intended self-protection, only exacerbates the symptoms and makes any consciousness of the condition impossible – until such time as it leads to the "talking cure" Anna O. herself named. The levels of meaning have to be recognized; they are, in time, revealed in the painstaking process of free association.

Although Freud is not without an interest in "attacks," as he will witness in Paris, his interest is less in the *event* of an illness than in its constitution as a whole. An attack, in itself, can be distracting because the focus will be, as it was in Charcot's clinic, on the aspect of its performance and theatrics, its acting-out. The spectacle of the hysteric will be too immediate. The body, especially when witnessed for its contortions, became a psychiatric spectacle and doubly so since it was viewed in the context of an institution. Thinking ahead, from this deliberate point, we can see how Breuer's private practice was retained and made essential for psychoanalysis since the patient would no longer be in a public institution and would be asked to remain still while lying on a comfortable couch and without seeing an observer. The ego had to first of all be able to control the body. Freud would do it as a psychotherapist who would treat patients privately and, after a number of different procedures, settle on the talking cure that Anna O. had identified. In Section IV of the "Preliminary Communication," Freud recalls both Charcot's definitions and, at the same time, the spectacle that had made it possible to identify them. The *"grande attaque,"* for all its relevance for anyone observing the hysterical episode, was not to be a concern for Freud since psychoanalysis made the analytic time the only essential starting point for treatment of any kind. The body, lying down tranquilly, was antithetical to the interest in the acting-out of the hysteric and any outward physical display.

Freud, at this time, continues to depends on an inherited language, which is one of the reasons he continues to use French terms, such as "*condition seconde.*" Deferring to the acknowledged experts in the field was understandable at the time. The attitude did not hurt him in the end since he ultimately created his own vocabulary; any reliance on innovative terms was in any case more fully developed, such that something like a "*condition seconde*" moved from the psychical to a "somatic innervation," a compulsion that forced the body to move according to the force of the psyche. Freud makes a connection that was not recognized before him. "When the attack makes its first appearance, it indicates a moment at which this hypnoid consciousness has obtained control of the subject's whole existence" (SE 2:14). Freud moves from the attack as it manifested in the body to an understanding that is complete. He could not be more unequivocal: *control of the subject's whole existence*. The awareness of a whole existence has reached one more culmination; whereas Charcot, as we will soon see, became fixated on the mechanism of hysteria, in the body, internally and externally, Freud found himself taking an original direction. He could not be swayed from the insight. Once he saw its meaning, and what its consequences could be both for a diagnosis and a treatment, there was no returning to all the prior experts and their tradition. He would continue, for a time, to refer to the history of psychical diagnosis and treatment. There was also a profound sense that he had found something uniquely his own. Everyone was aware of a type of "hypnoid consciousness." Freud took every single one of the descriptions of the conditions of the neurotic and recognized something common in all of them. Once he began to analyze his own patients, it was only a matter of time before he came to define a universal characteristic of human consciousness. Poets, novelists, and philosophers had given expression to the unconscious; for the first time the intimation of its reality would be analyzed in a patient, given a diagnosis and, more importantly, made it possible to provide a cure – the same word used by Plato, Epicurus, Bacon, and Nietzsche, to name but four thinkers who did not separate philosophy from psychotherapy. By now examining the ur-case of psychoanalysis, Anna O., and then concentrating on the patients Freud began to analyze, we can then see just how central his preoccupation with perception would become. For the time being, we can postpone the reasons for the break in the personal and professional relationship between Freud and Breuer. We can retain the one version on the nature of the transference – that is, between Breuer and his patient. We should also keep in mind the nature of any transference between individuals and wonder to what extent the end of a collaboration was not complicated by age, ambition, and personality. Others have recognized the impact of his strictly scientific work and publications. "Freud's work is understood to have made a considerable contribution in its own right to the evolutionary theory of the nervous system."[22] Be that as it may, for the immediate concerns, with Anna O., the "evolution" of the nervous system would be much better interpreted according to her experiences and how the development of a young person into an adult can suffer all kinds of obstacles and impediments, many of them serious enough for the individual to regress to such a previous state of being – due to absences and a double-conscience – that healthy maturity is postponed and achieved, if at all, only after a prolonged struggle to become healthy. How does the case of Anna O. began the long process whereby Freud will confirm his phenomenology of mental illness at the same time as his access to the unconscious and, more completely, the psyche? The history of the concept of a "split consciousness" had led to all kinds of deliberations. Freud's first awareness of this one characteristic of the fragmented psyche proved to be one more element in forming a sufficient theory to understand the phenomenon and, ultimately, treat it. Thus far, the "Preliminary Communication" has served as one origin to the understanding of hysteria. Breuer's case history, and some of its particulars, will be retained by Freud as elements that, later, will be incorporated into a more detailed assessment of the neurotic.

Commentators who generally favour the biological emphasis of the origins of psychoanalysis come to one conclusion – which is, in fact, based on a first assumption.

> Considering the latent biologism of Freud's lifelong thought and the influence of Meynert on Freud prior to the psychoanalytic turn, might it be the case that, while neurology helped introduce Freud to the mind, the Freudian conception of mind was conceptually grounded in the work done under the supervision of Meynert?[23]

Since Perkins-McVey frames his thinking in the form of a question, we can answer: no. The immediate response will be have to be detailed and unequivocal. First of all, there was nothing "latent" about Freud's interest in biology. The period of study was pursued with utmost diligence, and with several important results[24] but in no way did these strictly neurological findings contribute to psychoanalysis, except as an important comparison and divergence. When the experience of the cathartic method came into contact with neurology, Freud moved in one direction without hesitation – as will become, finally, evident after his stay in Paris. Despite the research carried out in Meynert's clinic, Freud would never be satisfied with a physiological explanation of mental disturbance and certainly not with a theory of anatomical pathology. While it would be straightforward to refer to Freud's situation within the so-called mind-body problem, the next years in the development of his psychological intuition in many ways redefined the intellectual problem since "the mind" ultimately becomes a dynamic psyche. Once a topography is understood to be, for all practical senses, impossible to determine (even so – what does it matter if we know where the nerve signals of anxiety *are*?) then the more important relationship between the economy of a drive and its dynamism gets to the essential for a human experience. Freud is, at the time, within a scientific paradigm; and yet, because his own mind is capable to internalizing a number of different traditions, he can never remain content with a purely mechanistic understanding of human beings. While the contributions of scientifically minded scholars are always beneficial since they give us additional information on Freud's *practical* studies at the time, they cannot always acknowledge Freud's thinking as it would be later revealed.[25] Readers who are, by disposition or intellectual commitment, historicists, are going to inevitably situate Freud within his milieu and time. Doing so limits both our understanding of Freud's development as a thinker and his originality when he was, quite literally, in the middle of two culturally determined realities. How he worked his way through both to reach his own individual conclusions and, consequently, the invention of psychoanalysis, will occupy the remaining of the project, first with attention to Breuer's cathartic method and their association together as pioneers in *therapeutic psychology*. One affirmation can be repeated again and again. Günter Gödde writes, "In order to establish the scientific nature of his new path for psychology, Freud went beyond clinical psychology and began to focus on a more general theory of the psyche."[26] The sense of "scientific nature" can be retained for the purpose of the discussion. An addition might be a *specific* theory and then, equally if not more importantly, its relevance for the treatment of neuroses.

## Phenomenology of an Illness Called Hysteria

Rereading Breuer's account of Anna O. gives us an impression of the many complicated experiences at the time called hysterical and how Freud began to interpret the meaning of its symptoms, initially, and then later when he was able to fit them into a greater and more comprehensive whole. Her symptoms can be outlined, in general and then specifically, according to a diagnosis and then given more precise explanations when Freud understood their relations. There is, unfortunately, little room for a separate discussion of Josef Breuer as a physician and for his own life. His documentation of the Anna O. case, despite any reservations we may have about later insights, provided by Freud himself on the transference or by other scholars, nevertheless deserves a certain appreciation.[27] In one of Freud's accounts, he informs us that the case of Anna O. was written "in a much abbreviated form, censored, too, from consideration of medical discretion" (SE 19:279). We should not make any ready assumptions about, precisely, what was abbreviated and censored. Enough has been written about the discovery of the transference. The abbreviation, for Freud, was more a matter of thinking all the way through the nature of her symptoms and, first of all, the sense of what splitting actually meant.

According to Breuer's account, his descriptions were quite general (say, as Anna O.'s "broodings") but also much more specific and closer to a diagnosis that Freud would develop from an initial "pathological splitting of consciousness" (SE 2:42) to an understanding of the psyche's dynamics. The diagnosis depends on the medical knowledge at the time and, more importantly, the differences Freud notices and continues to reflect on, both during the time of his clinical work at Meynert's clinic and, eventually, at the Salpêtrière with Charcot. However, if we take into consideration not so much the account as reported by Breuer to Freud but on the myriad of symptoms that he evaluated over a significant period of time, we can make the attempt to identify a process of thought. How did Freud respond to the case of Anna O., and how did he evaluate her symptoms in a way that, soon (when in Paris and then for the decade after until the publication of *Studies on Hysteria*) they would be one reason among others for turning in his own direction and definitively away from any physiological account much less a mechanistic explanation? And that was part of the problem: what good could a diagnosis be if, in the end, it was powerless to intervene except in ways that was, at best, useless, or worse, even more injurious? The moment Freud began withdrawing from the materialistic vision of a psychologically ill human being and complemented the cathartic method with a term that would summarize psychoanalysis as a human science (free association and interpretation), it was then possible to unify all the disparate origins of the diagnosis and invent an entirely new vocabulary to better reflect both the experience of the patient and a new way to conceive of the psyche. A novel way of seeing a patient, and the human psyche, had to be devised if a deeper understanding of mental illness could be reached. One contrast can be reflective for us – as previously mentioned, between her inner life and her society, the specifics of her illness and the nature of the 19th century. Whether a "feminist reinterpretation" can help us to understand Anna O. is an outstanding question.[28] Henri Ellenberger has called for, perhaps, an impossible task. "The time has come for a complete and truly objective appraisal of Anna O.'s story."[29] Is this possible? If so, it would take a number of characteristics that are, in any one individual, unlikely. Too many competing interests are still too obvious for anyone to provide an "objective appraisal" of her illness. Many of our motivations have nothing to do with psychotherapy. A feminist reinterpretation is unlikely to give us anything more from that one perspective. The "objective" will continue to be elusive. The *subjective*, in this case not a compliment at all, can be seen when Daniel Boyarin calls Bertha Pappenheim "my hero."[30] There are no shortages of ideological indulgences when it comes to women and hysteria; ignoring Anna O.'s actual experiences and opting for the socially heavy interpretation has its consequences. Have any of them actually clarified the nature of neuroses? Have they really been concerned with Anna O. as an individual; or has she served instrumental reasons and arguments? Finally, are fanciful hypotheses, for example, about her drinking aversion as symbolic of sexual disgust, warranted at all by the case history?[31] Freud has often been accused of being a pan-sexualist; *pan-genderism* might be a beginning category to look back at one theory among others from the 20th century.

Interpreting her life according to some pre-established theory about social estrangement (as a human being or, more specifically, as a woman) might be more indicative of a late 20th-century fixation than on her actual state. One note in particular will have consequences for the beginnings of psychoanalysis.

Throughout the entire illness her two states of consciousness persisted side by side: the primary one in which she was quite normal psychically, and the secondary one which may well be likened to a dream in view of its wealth of imaginative products and hallucinations, in large gaps of memory and the lack of inhibition and control in its associations.

(SE 2:45)

The apparently offhand comment, on the dream as a particular state of consciousness, will be developed by Freud into one of the foundations of psychoanalysis. The insight, we should emphasize, applied equally to the neurotic and the more or less normal.

The innumerable descriptions of her malady are overwhelming when the attempt is made to include then into a diagnostic whole. Modern reinterpretations may be rationalizations and justifications of a certain way of seeing the world; they do not, however, tell us anything about her very personal experiences as they are diagnosed according to the most revealing concepts – first, as a medical perception of her *absences*, somnambulism, hypnoid states, *condition seconde* (to mention four prominent ones) and then her own self-descriptions of a *private theatre*, an intuition of her part that was profound when considered next to Breuer's cathartic method. A tragic form was, indeed, being re-enacted. Freud would eventually realize just how meaningful Greek tragedy would be for the understanding of a human predicament within families; at the time, between 1880 and 1882, a process had begun. Whether we can agree with Joel Whitebook that we should not accept "the psychoanalytic profession's retreat into purely clinical issues,"[32] we should also not allow academics to determine the interpretation and understanding of the history of psychoanalysis and completely neglect the psychotherapeutic, especially if done in the name of feminism and "critical theory." There are different kinds of "dual inheritances" as Whitebook sees them. Social theory is one half of his equation. Our own has been more than an either/or and has made every effort to trace relations and sympathies, especially as they influenced Freud's thinking during an original time in the period of our concern. Anna O.'s symptoms are, in any case, specific. Does social theory make them any clearer for us?

For the purpose of this particular section on Breuer's case study of Anna O., three pairs of concepts will be chosen. Each of them have their own affiliation and pertinence. There are the related French psychological terms of *absence* and *condition seconde* and their close relation to a state of somnambulism and a hypnoid state; there are the medical terms *macropsia* and *disploplia,* both with decidedly physiological explanations; and there are the more general terms, *disturbances of vision* as well as the previously mentioned "private theatre." Each of them has a different origin and relevance: neurological, medical, and depth-psychological. Freud has yet to exclude any interpretation as long as it proves useful, both for his understanding and for any individual treatment. As definitions, they are different. How Freud recognized their ultimate relationship was one more contributing factor to the emergence and development of the thought and practice to be named psychoanalysis. Breuer, as mentioned above, had access to many contemporary concepts – first and foremost as a physician. Others were used to understand the complications of the hysterical mind; and we should not forget that Anna O. was no ordinary young woman, both because of her personality in 1880 and the productive life she went on to lead – a life of service and dedication to her community, running a shelter for Jewish unwed mothers, for example, a vocation many women from "well-to-do" families could never undertake.[33] The disapproval, of course, would have been significant. Breuer described her as "markedly intelligent, with an astonishing quick grasp of things and penetrating intuition. She possessed a powerful intellect" (SE 2:21). No one today is likely to overlook the comment. Freud has not always been acknowledged for this therapeutic objectives; as he so often emphasized, one of the purposes of psychoanalytic therapy was to restore a measure of independence to a patient and to enlarge their ego, that is, increase their intelligence and ability to perceive beyond the limits of their neuroses. Intelligent, intuitive, intellectual: these are noticeable capacities, more so when contrasted with the severity of her illness. Some evaluations of the case are, to say the least, surprising. One goes very far – to the personal. "This first case of psychoanalysis serves as a cautionary tale about the unconscious use of destructive aggression by a well intentioned physician."[34] One would like to know how anyone comes to this kind of conclusion. "Destructive aggression." Where, from the case history, does anyone notice anything as severe?

Our inquiry is now focused on one issue: if Freud is now in a situation of being able to analyze *the symptoms* of this one patient specifically in terms of her perceptual experiences, can we make a third connection between Jewish phenomenology and the allegorical significance of the microscope? Do Anna O.'s specific symptoms allow Freud to add one more element to his reflection on human psychology that, finally, will reach a first culmination in Paris? To follow his life and writings towards an answer requires us to move forward to the much-postponed publication of *Studies on Hysteria*. Freud's own writing, as well as the case history, are informative for making it easier to continue to build on many connections as they were all unified towards the creation of psychoanalysis. Although the origin of psychoanalysis has two foundational aspects, the Jewish and the scientific as presented here, the third was necessary if the knowledge of consciousness, in the healthy and ill alike, had to be more precisely defined in terms of symptoms and psychical origins. We know, as Freud emphasizes, that *one* breakthrough came, in one way, with the discovery of the specifically erotic transference between patient and practitioner. However, the transference, as such, was only one manifestation (in the therapeutic situation) that was universally observable in human relationships. Turning to Anna O. is therefore necessary in order to see how Freud responded to the case history and doing so, first with the introduction to *Studies on Hysteria* and, after, the conclusion. How did Anna O.'s phenomenological symptoms convince Freud of the *direction* to be taken *prior to his trip to Paris*? In order for us to try to imagine Freud's thinking over a few years' time, her experiences have to be highlighted and her symptoms made prominent; doing so will lead us, in the next section, to the relationship between Breuer's concept of catharsis and how Freud specifically understood its therapeutic relation to Aristotle's *Poetics* and, later, the significance of Oedipus and the unconscious dynamic within families.

At the time Josef Breuer began treating one of the patients with the method called "cathartic" while Freud was continuing to work towards his graduation and so become licensed as a medical doctor, their relationship and their discussions about this one case were going to profoundly change their futures and, for a time, develop a working relationship that would include the publication of *Studies in Hysteria* in 1895. Breuer told Freud about Anna O. late in 1882 – when her period of being treated by him had ended. Her illness, as severe as it was, was certainly not "cured." Returning to the case history, as Breuer wrote it, can be read from an individual perspective: how did Freud think about the case, when he first heard it, and what did he begin to think about given the information he had about Anna O. at the time?

Freud did not hesitate to always attribute the initial direction of a psychological treatment to Breuer. The decision to begin a practice of listening to a young patient, who was intelligent and perceptive enough to recall the specifics of her experience, was a joint effort that began without intentions – certainly none at the level of a worked-out method. The doctor-patient relationship started in a conventional manner and then developed over a two-year period, with all its upheavals, and then was terminated for reasons we can reconstruct, if always with an awareness of still missing some of the pieces. The transference, for all its importance, need not be analyzed for our purposes. The facts are a matter to be interpreted from the case history as we have it and, so too, from Freud's reflections. My disagreement on the following could not be stronger. Edgar Levenson believes that "we cannot *see* the hysterical young girl through Freud eyes."[35] If we conceded, then we also have to add: then *no one can see her*; and that conclusion is unacceptable.

The instances of Freud's acknowledgement of Breuer's originality are repeated. For example, in the *Introductory Lectures on Psychoanalysis* in "The Sense of Symptoms," he writes, "The sense of neurotic symptoms was first discovered by Josef Breuer from his study and successful cure (in 1880 and 1882) of a case of hysteria which has since become famous" (SE 16:257). The finality of a "successful cure," if portrayed as such by Breuer, turned out to be much too optimistic. The period after the appearance of that one work and a number of other related writings would result in Freud's determined, and singular, reflection on outstanding questions. In *An Autobiographical Study*, he makes mention of a pre-Paris period.

> Even before I went to Paris, Breuer told me about a case of hysteria which, between 1880 and 1882, he had treated in a peculiar manner which had allowed him to penetrate deeply into the causation and significance of hysterical symptoms.
>
> (SE 20:19)

At this moment when returning to the history of the events and their consequence, it becomes ever more necessary to remind the reader of the two previous sets of arguments and, however divergent they may be, how their confluence are enhanced during the time when Breuer is reading the notes of the case to Freud. His recollection acknowledges his first impression. He was struck by an original perception on the part of Breuer. "I had the impression that it accomplished more towards understanding of neuroses than any previous observation" (SE 20:19). It strikes the reader with some surprise that he could acknowledge the case and not find objections or, at the very least, responses based on what he later discovered when the cathartic method was transformed into psychoanalysis. The next sentence, written with extreme brevity, is telling, in more ways than one. "I determined to inform Charcot of the discoveries when I reached Paris, and I actually did so. But the great man showed no interest in my first outline of the subject, so that I never returned to it and allowed it to pass from my mind" (SE 20:19–20). These connecting events have much more significance and perhaps merited a longer discussion. If Freud allowed it no more thought while he was in Paris, Anna O. would be a singular figure whose experience, and therapy, would remain foundational for him in the years to follow and when the time in Paris had been included with all his other studies.

Since a study of Freud's mind and ideas is making the attempt to intersect several different possibilities at once – his Judaism, the science of the laboratory and the perception of the microscopist, the practitioner in a psychiatric clinic – an order in the presentation is necessary. Therefore, keeping in the mind the order of the next several sections and the work as a whole, the orientation now has to both keep in mind the connection between the particulars of Jewish and scientific perception and then take up Breuer's case study of Anna O. and see if there was something in her *consciousness* and *perception* that was repeatedly mentioned as essential and yet never discussed with the attention it deserved. That Bertha Pappenheim went on to live such a productive life, not what one would expect from a typical 19th-century woman, is a testament to her intelligence and strength of character (which Breuer does not fail to mention, nor did Freud) as well as how she was able to overcome many of her most difficult symptoms. What were they more precisely? And do they give us any reason to believe that the case had a profound effect on Freud's treatment of future neurotics and due, specifically, to a number of observations that were inseparable from an acute sensibility and an awareness of the meaning of certain states of consciousness? Did a culturally inherited midrash and a scientifically developed set of observations based on his years of looking under a microscope give him the foundations of an enhanced kind of perception and the ability to probe beyond the apparent? One argument is repeated. If an answer is forthcoming, we can keep one fact in mind. How did Freud respond to the case study of Anna O., and did he carry the observations to Paris with him such that the experiences there – which were by consensus theatrical – make Freud attuned to the phenomenon of mental illness in a new way? The following set of arguments is based on the unity of four fundamental experiences: midrash interpretation of texts, microscopic analysis of specimens, his analysis of the Anna O. case, and the few months of witnessing the diagnosis of hysterics at the Salpêtrière. How did Freud respond to Breuer's case? Are there any symptoms, taken together (though they are presented separately and often in a noticeable list of differences) that alert Freud to one of the theories of the psyche which will have the most impact in the long-term development of psychoanalysis? By embodying, intuitively and programmatically, Jewish and scientific sensibilities, how did he assess Anna O. as an individual case and as a representative of the dynamics of the psyche? Our organization of the history is not chronological, for reasons that are question marks and based on the initial experience, not its written form many years later. Doing so makes the case of Anna O. necessary prior to Freud's time in Paris and so acts as a preparation to his reflections while observing patients at the Salpêtrière and considering Charcot's theories – as well as the displays of the hysterics who became theatrical and made their attendants spectators to a psychodrama that was not at all easy to diagnose and difficult to treat. We have many accounts of their conditions as well as their acts; their symptoms are catalogued and scrutinized. In due time, Freud's experience in Paris would be one more to add to the others that contributed to his reflections.

For us to read the account and to concentrate on our continuing issue – that is, how the dynamics of the psyche determine the consciousness and perception of the ego – requires a specific and necessary limit to seeing the case. The numerous times her neuroses are identified specifically in terms of her perceptions have not been as emphasized as they should be. The causes are, for Breuer and Freud, more important because, at the time, so arresting. And yet, setting aside the thesis to come on their part and on the arguments made by Freud in the following few years, a number of ailments can be emphasized for drawing our attention to how her symptoms are being experienced. Some of them can be mentioned. Anna O. suffers from "an enormous number of hallucinations." The *forms* (not the content) of these hallucinations are mentioned in a peculiar way. As hallucinations, they do *not* have the force of a prolonged psychotic experience. The word hallucination may, in fact, be misleading. The language has yet been created to describe how the power of the psyche can overwhelm the consciousness of an individual to the extent of making them passive spectators to their own *thinking* – "hallucinations" that are not in the perceptual field, as such, but only active, recurring, and compulsive in the imagination. Anna O. will, at times, literally *see* a distorted reality. Freud's ultimate discovery involved being able to trace the particular dynamic when a thought is turned into a figment of the imagination and then made real as an ideation.

There are much clearer ways of representing her consciousness; and Anna O. cannot be seen as a psychotic when we are told about her "systematic day-dreaming" and, more particularly, and in her own words, the creation of her "private theatre." She is perfectly aware of her day-dreaming and, perhaps because of the strength or, more likely, their enticement, she cannot forego *the pleasure and pain* of being a spectator to the ideations created in her mind. By adopting Freud's term – *endopsychic perception* – we can begin to think about one of the fundamental acts of human consciousness and when it can (almost passively) watch a fantasy or a recurrent scene, again and again, to the point of obsession and of being unable to be free from its imagistic and affective compulsion. Anna O.'s consciousness of her private drama does nothing to alleviate any distress during the experience. Simply coming up with the proper language for the experience is proving to be a challenge. The various ways her case is presented does give us enough of a sense of her condition: "she was living through fairy tales in her imagination" (SE 2:22). Leaving aside the one theme of the temporality of consciousness, Anna O. is clearly capable of being in two "places" at once. That one ability has certainly been necessary for life to be, at times, bearable; the extent of the imagination, when the unconscious exercises its considerable power, can so easily overwhelm the conscious decision of the ego.

Our ability to understand and interpret her specific situation is not a consolation. There are more than enough "objective" conditions one can imagine for her to be physically present just enough for her to be responsible in the eyes of others. Her "real life," however, is not the issue. Anna O. becomes an individual who, for Freud, presents a number of difficulties that have to be solved. They are not, simply, in the realm of a cure. Understanding her condition is a serious challenge. What struck Freud with enough force to remain unresolved is in the very nature of the human psyche and what it can activate, in life, when certain pressures are felt to be intolerable. The external circumstances of her life are not of any interest except insofar as she may be exemplary in showing us how the psyche can project an alternative reality, in the form of ideations, images, and scenes for the sake of perception. In her case, an alternate reality was preferable than the one foremost in her mind; but are we so sure, as some interpreters tend to be, that the fundamental problem is a social one and attributable to a historical reality?[36] Freud's objection for us, theoretically, to any such wishful thinking will become unequivocal: simply put, an ideal reality would not prevent neuroses. The psyche and the real are, in essence, related: *how* is still the outstanding question.

Breuer called his method of treating Anna O. "cathartic." There is no way to avoid the obvious connection between the concept as it was discussed in Aristotle's *Poetics* and Anna O.'s "private theatre" – with one addition that is not at all like the situation of a drama unfolding on a stage and the spectator who is watching. Anna O. is both the creator of the drama and the spectator, with one important element that is no different that the dream-work: the drama of her theatre is not intentional and is intricately mixed with her day-dreams and fantasies – whose content is now elusive except for the brief intimations given to us in the case study. There is no will in the acts; Anna O. has a split consciousness, an unconscious creating the dream, an ego passively looking on and then trying to understand its significance by talking about it to her doctor. According to Aristotle, the catharsis is supposed to be experienced by the spectator to a Greek tragedy and thereby being relieved of certain emotions – fear and pity. For Anna O., however, no such relief is possible since she has not yet recognized how to create a distance between herself as a patient and as someone capable to interpreting the meaning of her perceptions. Anna O.'s perceptions, once they are made central to her case, become more captivating for giving us a picture of her interior condition. The way her case is presented leaves us with ongoing questions because the descriptions of her "severe disturbances of vision" (SE 2:22) are much too vague for us to properly understand. There are many other physical symptoms she suffers from; her body, as a whole, exhibits a wide range of ailments that are *limiting*. The psychosomatic condition, today described as a form of "conversion," cannot be neglected. Her body stiffens and is rendered paralytic. These are the signs of what, at the time, would be the classical signs of hysteria. But again, since my interests are always going to tend to the psychical first and foremost, one other symptom – not separate from her day-dreaming and her theatre – is what is described as a "persisting somnambulism." This has been overlooked as a condition for Anna O. as it has been, potentially, misdiagnosed *today* with an assortment of 21st-century maladies that have all been defined – whether successfully, or accurately, is open to debate. The traditional understanding of this state of being semi-awake is incorrect. Rather, the condition is much more ubiquitous than has been diagnosed. To be speculative and to make a case for the continuity of hysteria from one century to the next and into our own, the state of being somnambulistic would have to be rethought as the condition of being withdrawn from a certain awareness and *unconsciously* so, creating an acceptable split in character as one of the manifestations of a *defence*. Are *some forms* of autism inseparable from an infantile defence prolonged indefinitely?

We know, also, that Anna O.'s father died halfway through her illness. There was no way at the time for Freud to think of the effects of mourning on her already serious illness. It was no doubt another contributing factor. The fact of his death does not figure in the analysis. Once again we have the condition of "disturbances of vision" which Breuer admits "was hard to analyse" (SE 2:23). Again, they make no effort in sharing any of these possible disturbances, hallucinations, and dramatic ideations. They are, however, part of a comprehensive and elaborate system of defence which Freud will later analyze more completely. Give the information on the case and despite the reticence in conveying the precise nature of her perceptions, we can be confident enough in moving forward with the thesis and of now making the case of Anna O. one more phase in Freud's mind as he moved closer to the few months' stay in Paris and working with Charcot. The diagnosis of a "split consciousness," for all its relevance as a first diagnosis of a psychical condition (and conflict) leaves too much unanswered as to its specific mechanism – at the time.

The diagnosis has been made, the effects of her condition recognized. "Two entirely distinct states of consciousness were present which alternated very frequently and without warning" (SE 2:24). *Two states of consciousness*: the identification of how consciousness can be split will be only one of the many consequences to follow from Anna O.'s case. The one most pressing will be to undertake a more depth-psychological interpretation of her consciousness and identify the psyche and its partial independence from ego – indeed, to such an extent that the split, made easier by somnambulism which acts, in effect, like a censor to awareness, is no longer regarded as alien. The split, as a kind of division, is only accurate up to a point. The supplement to her case with the symptom of the French term "*absences*" is one more clinical finding that, in time, will become all-important in the way we attempt to further portray the psyche. Furthermore, her "disturbances invaded even her moments of relatively clear consciousness." Her neuroses were becoming aggravated. The split in her consciousness was becoming more uneven and unbalanced and the moments of *presence* were fewer and, for periods, non-existent. Even in the first few pages of the case history, there are a number of symptoms that are described but not analyzed. Breuer gives us no meaning in any of them individually or on the whole. For psychoanalysis to be invented as both an explanation of symptoms and a treatment, Freud had to piece together all the details of her illness and find a commonality that could be unified and so present a coherent picture of the manifestation of hysteria as only minimally understood at the time.

There is a quite remarkable transition, as there should be, when Breuer and Freud turn to Anna O. and begin to notice how, in addition to her perceptive difficulties, there are also linguistic problems. These have been amply studied and, in my context, are not going to be pursued despite their inherent interest. To analyze the connection between the linguistic and the perceptive would add considerably to the thesis and make the work branch out in too many directions – on the literary and the aesthetic in addition to the obvious one related to the psychoanalysis of Anna O.'s definition of the "talking cure." For my purposes, the concentration has to remain on her fragmented consciousness and the characteristics of her perception. The omission will be explained more fully later. If my main argument is correct and the nature of a split consciousness is constitutive and not accidental (it does not have a cause independent of the post-natal life of the human) then one of the conclusions can take us to the affirmation of an ontological condition irrespective of experience and make the self/reality connection a matter of perceptual degrees. Anna O., in her time, may have been a severe case, with its own individual suffering; she does not, however, appear in any way anomalous for us in the present and as a reflection of all our possible experiences. Rethinking the case of Anna O. leads us to one unavoidable conclusion: none of her symptoms are, specifically, historical or a reflection of *her time*. Despite all the social and political arguments about the case, every single one of her symptoms are modern. The argument, for me, is more immediate and returns us, first, to a human condition and, second, to the specific characteristics that are as prevalent now as in the 1880's. To historicize Anna O. to some restrictive view necessarily fails to address the nature of human consciousness and its vulnerability, at any time, to be (to use one diagnosis) somnambulistic. Although the term refers to a state of being semi-awake, there is a better, more complete description once we recall some of the symptoms mentioned in the "Preliminary Communication" and that are now supplemented with others that all contribute to a more developed understanding of the relationship between the fragmented psyche and consciousness.

Without arguing for its primacy and in no way minimizing the linguistic aspect of her illness, the focus remains on her perception: "there was a high degree of restriction in the field of vision" (SE 2:26). Let's remind ourselves, at the risk of a repetition, how Freud's exacting laboratory work and his continual preparation of the microscope for observation gave him a sensibility he was unlikely to ever forget and that, by 1882, had become synonymous with his work as a researcher and a scientist. The transition soon to be made from the dissection of specimens to the witnessing of hysterical patients in Paris was made possible by the Anna O. case and how he began to view her particular signs and symptoms. The "restriction" of her vision was, described in a different way, split according to the two main ways of recognizing her condition and life: at once susceptible to the most serious kinds of ideations and with a sometimes accompanying "somnolent state" (SE 2:27), its closeness to a dream-state not incidental since it gives us an intimation of a weakened and passive ego susceptible to unconscious forces. Sensing Anna O.'s consciousness as a "hallucinatory absence" (SE 2:42) does bring it close to the state of the ego during a dream. How systems within the psyche can influence the self is underway as a consideration of a diagnosis.

Despite, then, the psychical impairment of her speech, including its specifics – being only able to speak English – the focus remains on her perception, her field of vision, and its connection to a state that is described as "somnolence." Thinking about a form of unconscious self-hypnosis and its somnambulistic effect would explain how absences were created. Overall, we get a sense of withdrawal from reality in all kinds of forms. One is not enough. Listing them all we see an emerging pattern, one that will be summarized with the French concept of *absence*. Or, to be symmetrical, Anna O. is not present. Her psyche, which has less to do with repression than a defence (they are active simultaneously, in different degrees) has forced her to withdraw her attention on the present and instead either become fixated on her internal images, her "theatre," alternating with minimal perception of the present. The dynamics are complex, for just as she can become somnambulistic and absent, she was also capable of generating another reality – a process we can describe, again, as a defence as long as we keep in mind that her defence was only one of a number of virtually simultaneous processes.

There are many different ways to define Anna O.'s states. Arguments made previously and to be expanded in later sections are going to be specifically *neurotic* ailments; so when we talk about drowsiness or lethargy (another way to put this is the obvious *weakness of the ego*) the reasons cannot be, for us, based on the reality, for example, of overwork or lack of sleep as objective reasons for *fatigue*. There are more serious incapacities that are not due from objective conditions – which can often disguise the ailment of being "overtired" or "exhausted" – but from the ego being continually exposed to unconscious dynamics. Elaine Showalter coined her own neologism, *hystories*, to analyze some of the more neurotic characteristic of society. "Hysteria not only survives in the 1990's, it is more contagious than in the past." Our time has become even worse, as she realized, in part due to the "cultural narratives" and their proliferation in an era of instant communication and social media.[37] "Canonical hysterics" refers to individual like Anna O. It appears we have a number of our own modern hysterics, each with new symptoms and lives. The historical reality has changed; the interior dynamics of the individual remain as they always have, highly dynamic and so making conscious perception susceptible to all kinds of disturbances.

A psychical impulse is not always easy to present without being supported by inadequate metaphors. *Anaesthesia* is another, as is the sense of a "dissociation" (SE 2:41). What does it mean to be both tired and numb and to recognize the condition as one originating in the conflict of the psyche – of a split consciousness, with the unconscious being forceful – instead of the necessities of daily life? Needless to say, our modern conditions of life does make it seem as if many of us (overworked, overtired, sleep deprived) are suffering because of the way we live day to day. The objective conditions are one factor. Freud offers us a number of responsibilities that are not going to be given any rationalization or excuse. No one can argue against the fact that objective conditions can indeed make us ill; the problem comes down to emphasis and then analyzing the effects as to their origins and consequences. Individual afflictions are always specific and defy any generalizations, which is one reason to avoid arguments on the social conditions of Anna O. Turning her into a victim of society does no one any good. Understanding Freud's concerns, overall, is the focus, as it has been from the beginning. The various cluster of symptoms and experiences have been mentioned; how he understood their relation was one of his preoccupations. A systematic understanding was simply not possible at the time, in part because of the difference between one patient of the cathartic method and, after 1882, the patients he saw in Meynert's clinic. Once again, we find Freud between two diverse orientations. Emphasizing one of his responsibilities, scientific research (for example, into nerve cells and "neurons"[38]) fails to consider his private thinking on the nature of neuroses and how best to treat them therapeutically and according to each individual case. The science of such research is too specific for our concerns and outside the scope of our project. His professional responsibilities are acknowledged in part to show a necessity in terms of his livelihood as opposed to his real interests. There is no question that Freud continued with scientific research. The publication of many articles on strictly anatomical subjects shows him to be diligent and conscientious – perhaps, to a fault, if one can frame his life in this way, as a kind of compromise since he was still professionally unsettled. The nature of his scientific work had been ongoing. We become more intimate with his life at the time in terms of a personal struggle and conflict; the experience was not to be wasted. Freud was disciplined enough to carry out work despite his interest being, at best, secondary. He may have been interested in "sensory-motor physiology,"[39] more so in connection with the kinds of paralysis common in some forms of hysteria and therefore to continue to develop his own understanding of the psyche-soma relation. One mentions the scientific scholarship to, again, try to sense how Freud dealt with two competing and in many ways irreconcilable interests: the anatomical and the psychical and how they were related and, also, distinct and separate. However we trace the chronology of his ideas, even before they were expressed in writing, it should be not at all controversial to affirm that Freud had never been persuaded by the ambitions of the "brain" scientists to explain psychology and, as he experienced it, its *depth* – a metaphor, parenthetically, that requires us to think of the vertical and, also, the transcendent. How Freud tended more and more towards a different, unique, and original interpretation of psychological disturbances was ongoing.

The diagnoses are often described according to already-existing models (exclusively French) that, for the time being, are retained since they are an indication of medical authority and a tradition of thought. The innovation of the cathartic method could not be portrayed as singular and without any relationship to previous medical history. Protocol had to be followed in terms of scientific acknowledgement. Be that as it may, in due time Freud will no longer rely on such concepts as *condition seconde* or *absence* since psychoanalysis will create its own distinctive vocabulary. For someone as cultured as Freud was, he knew that the creation of a language was to do nothing less than create a world, of both meaning and reality. Breuer availed himself of the language of hysteria at the time. Freud would not be so indebted since, over time, he would literally invent a dictionary of terms that would become the exclusive language of psychoanalysis. In the case of Anna O., Breuer's language relies either on terms borrowed from other individuals working in the fields or, like somnambulism, rely on taken-for-granted meanings. So far, a few of the symptoms have been mentioned in order to get a sense of Anna O.'s complicated condition. There are also specific symptoms that, together, make for a more comprehensive sense of the way her particular form of hysteria determined her perception. "The alternation between two states of consciousness" is one of Breuer's descriptions. *Two states* is, in itself, not enough. One involved an absence from her present; she could be so compelled by another scene – in fantasy or memory, we don't know – that she was literally no longer present, except physically to a person next to her. To call them "hallucinations" is, perhaps, an approximation of its real sense. The term *absence* is, despite its own ambiguity, closer to the real experience: the withdrawal from reality was so complete that she could lose herself in an internal image, its force strong and complete enough to remove her, essentially, from herself. As for the term *"condition seconde,"* which supplemented *absence*, Breuer adds to the array of unusual experiences when he discusses Anna O.'s "transfer into the past," as if the present could be effaced and substituted by an apparently reproduced memory, in all its detail, of a previous time, real or imagined. Whether this return to the past was a deep-seated desire in order to change an occurrence, or a state of being, Breuer does not speculate. We can, however, imagine how Freud would have reacted to all these reports and the manner in which they became part of his knowledge of a hysterical *form of being*. Although there were distinct episodes and innumerable changes in her temperament, and in her symptoms, we have to wonder – based on later theories and practices – how they all fit into growing list of symptoms. How the case of Anna O. was incorporated into Freud's knowledge and emerging speculations can only be imagined and then retraced from later, post-Paris psychotherapeutics – which can be seen in his own patients in the *Studies on Hysteria*. The one insight that is most important for Freud and his gradual but certain turn away from physiological effects and mechanistic explanations can be understood, for example, in the interpretation of another of Anna O.'s symptoms – that of *macropsia*.

Although the particular form of this illness can be explained physiologically – for example, during effects of drugs, such as morphine, which Anna O. took – there is another explanation that views the perception itself as a psychical one. A person suffering from macropsia has the sense that all the objects that are visible – say, the size of a room and its contents – are in fact much larger than they are, with the effect that the person feels much smaller. In this case, one has to ask if the distortion of one's size is a physical manifestation of an unconscious process. In terms of her consciousness, such a perception would be overwhelming since the range of sizes and shapes would have increased in proportion to her own *diminution* – a concept most especially relevant for the ego. Generally speaking, she was *less than*. Or, described in another way, she was overwhelmed by her surroundings without recognizing how a room, for example, represented an inner state of being. In her communication to Breuer, she seems to be aware, in one way, of her condition. The ability to see, however, is itself skewed and its communicated is in distorted form. "Another time she told me there was something the matter with her eyes; she was seeing colours wrong. She knew she was wearing a brown dress but saw it as a blue one" (SE 2:33). Although Breuer does not seem to have the ability to understand her perception as meaningful at the level of allegory, Freud's hermeneutic sensibility made him aware of another layer to the communication. Anna O. is talking; but the therapist who hears her has not yet understood the levels of meaning in her speech, something Freud will develop as a condition for psychoanalysis to be invented. The problem is not – as Anna O. "knows" unconsciously – bout misrecognizing colours, a relatively benign misapprehension. Colours, hue, shade: these are metaphors for another kind of appearance, which she suspects but cannot yet identify. The conclusion Breuer himself draws from this particular perception may or may not be accurate. It was, perhaps, related to her father; but the reader does not have sufficient information to be able to come to an idea, never mind a conclusion. We are left, as was Freud, with many details and just as many questions and unsolved possibilities. When Breuer then adds yet another diagnosis specifically relevant to the state of her perception (a convergent squint with disploplia) we are again confronted with so many symptoms that, together, they all accumulate towards one consistent illness. Calling her various states "disorders of vision" is, as a description in general, adequate; yet when we add all the ones together, as they have been outlined here only very briefly and so to see her condition in general, we come to a provisional conclusion as to Freud's reflections on the case and as they would be understood later. We can misdiagnose a disploplia if we are content with the idea of "double vision." For Anna O. the secondary perception, which is always more indistinct, hazy, and displaced, explains her split consciousness and the time of her perception. Without adding any possible definitions of her perceptions, such as dis-alignment – a condition in which she herself and the world are unmatched and estranged from each other – every single one of Freud's diagnoses, whether based on a pre-existing medical vocabulary or pieced together from his impressions, all converge into a recognition of the dynamism of the unconscious more than the diagnosis of a single patient. Analyzing Anna O. *as a woman* has its partial relevance; one feminist truth, however, is not free from being an impediment to understand a human condition and a universal affliction.

One of her symptoms, mentioned only once, had to be of particular interest to Freud. She suffered both from a "macropsia and convergent squint." (SE 2:40) Although Breuer did not spend much time on this one form of disturbed perception, for Freud it had to have taken up some thought. The condition of *macropsia*, characterized by the enlargement of objects of perception (things seen are bigger, the subject seeing feels smaller) was for Freud no passing impression and one of the more remarkable aspect of this one case. For just as he had been looking under a microscope to expand his own perception and then the knowledge of science, a hysterical reaction could involve precisely its opposite. The object became larger and commensurable with the consequence of Anna O. feeling smaller in the world of objects. The reactive squint was nothing more than a futile attempt to alter her perception by narrowing her eyelids. The claim of a "final cure" need not be evaluated, either from Breuer's conclusion to the case study or, more importantly, the life of Bertha Pappenheim as we know it. The finality of any kind of remedy as made possible by Breuer's method, and as a forerunner to Freud's more complete and transformed psychoanalysis, is less relevant for us at the moment as we come to a summary and a continuation. Breuer writes:

> I had a very strong impression that the numerous products of her secondary state which had been quiescent were now forcing their way into consciousness; and though in the first instance they were being remembered only her secondary state, they were nevertheless burdening and disturbing her normal one.
> (SE 2:47)

Keeping in mind that Freud had been privy to the case history, we have to wonder about his interpretation as he has received it and the original thoughts he may have later had. There must have been a great number of observations made by Breuer in the write-up of the case to have been a lingering problem for Freud before his trip to Paris and a long time after. Any possible contribution by Freud to the writing of the case study can be, for some, speculative, while for others it does show signs of some involvement. Whatever our personal preference on the matter, it is dependent on a decision; one cannot overlook the implications of the still embryonic language and the strong sense of the active presence of the unconscious. The word "products" might be vague; the dynamic is perfectly clear when we understand how *something* is forcing its way into her "consciousness" to the point of overpowering her perception. All the various diagnoses – say, from the tradition of French studies, on *absences* and *condition seconde* – leave no doubt as to the nature of her illness and, on top of it all, how her symptoms show her to be oscillating between two different experiences, the present of her body and the past of her psyche. That is certainly one way to think about the modern description of a *conversion disorder*. The case study, as discussed with Freud and then written for the *Studies on Hysteria*, would continue to demand his attention since so much of her illness was, for a time, beyond explanation. Her many symptoms, however, were beginning to make sense as a whole. How Anna O. never quite left Freud's memory can be traced for its effects and for the memories they left with him. The Clark lectures of 1909 can again be consulted for telling us about Freud's history on the way to creating psychoanalysis.

In my estimate, this is the most consequential discovery made by Breuer and Freud – not the certain knowledge of *the unconscious* (which has been known intuitively by philosophers such as Epicurus and writers after him) but how it could so powerfully interfere with normal, everyday perception and distort human life to a remarkable degree. Although we can agree with the Breuer/Freud discussion on the case and recognize Anna O. as suffering from the illness at the time called hysteria, the nature of her illness overall required all of Freud's attention and thinking. A coming experience would be decisive for giving him the ability to see how the particulars of any neurotic illness could be better understood and, therefore, treatable in ways that were to prove more beneficial, and certainly more humane, than in an institution.

The examination of the jointly written "Preliminary Communication" established the boundaries of the diagnosis as Breuer and Freud discussed in terms of three chosen pairs, each of them chosen specifically for their phenomenological importance. A final inquiry will now be added as it pertains to Anna O., and we will try to do so, as much as possible, within the continuity of earlier Jewish discussion on the malady of being infatuated with images (idols), the psychopathology of the mind according to Francis Bacon, and, finally, Anna O.'s neurotic symptoms. A final association can be made that advances a historical problem from the classical to the modern to Freud's contemporary situation in terms of the hysterical imagination and the method of catharsis as first presented by Aristotle in his *Poetics*. If the associations can be sustained and carried forward, then we are prepared to accompany Freud to Paris and examine the relatively short experience between 1885 and 1886 while he was a "student" at the Salpêtrière. Idolatrous images, idols of the mind, the private theatre of a neurotic: how are they manifested in Aristotle's interpretation of the experience of the spectator (while watching a dramatic re-enactment) and how are his categories, interpreted from the perspective of the present, able to clarify Freud's growing intimations?

## Memories of Anna O.

One significant period in Freud's development in terms of his direction towards a depth-psychology independently of the historical certainties and assumptions of his time can be traced, first, in the "Preliminary Communication, second, the many inter-related symptoms of Anna O.'s neuroses – the ones most significant to us as experiences of "absences," her disturbances of vision, and the acting-out and spectatorship of her own private theatre. Her state of consciousness, somnambulistic and self-hypnotic, was for Freud one indication of the force (later to be called *drives*) of the unconscious. One experience, overall, can be mentioned now and then retained as essential for Freud's experience in Paris: the theatrical display of the patients deemed hysterical, Freud's recollection of catharsis as a possible cure and its all-important connection to Aristotle's *Poetics* and his conception of tragedy as a theory of understanding neurotic life. The early chronology will lead us, soon, to Freud's period in Paris. The period can be anticipated in a roundabout way when we turn to Freud's many recollections of the time and the importance of Anna O. as a first patient, for him indirectly. His recollections are many; drawing from them makes it possible to connect an entire life in the development of psychoanalysis – however one defines it, as medical, a science, a form of psychotherapy, or something more. By this point in the project, the categories, however they are understood, are far less significant for us than the attempt to understand the particulars of an illness without, simply, or reductively, defining it according to a historical context, either of an era or in the development of a science of mental illness. Any social analysis has been deemed reductive. The designation of hysteria should now be less significant; the concern, with Anna O., has been twofold: first, the experiences of her illness and, second, how each manifestation of a particular psychological difficulty was understood by Freud over a significant period of time. His recollections were also an examination of his own life and the transitions of his studies and his personal thinking.

Freud returned to the case history of Anna O. during the lectures he delivered at Clark University in 1909. The formal presentation of a period in his life also takes us, the reader, to a more complete picture of the times, certainly much more informed than his listeners. His recollection, during a time when his fame was now established, can be examined for the ideas so far emphasized and for being fundamental in the creation of a new analysis of psychological illness. Since the psychoanalysis of consciousness and perception has been central to the foundation of a form of understanding psychological illness and how to treat it, there can be no better terms to re-examine than the original one, catharsis, and then the phenomenon that Freud discovers as, first, a dynamic between Anna O. and Breuer and, later, as a universal condition of all relationships. The *transference*, for all its importance, does not have to be emphasized in our case since other preoccupations are chosen to be more significant for this one patient and how her illness's symptoms projected her interior life in a particularly dramatic way. Whether "in analysis transference emerges as *the most powerful resistance* to the treatment" (SE 12:101) is not, for Anna O. and our relationship to her, relevant. The issue of her transference, or the fantasy of a phantom childbirth, are ancillary issues to the one guiding focus, as is Breuer's decision to terminate his treatment of his patient. Should we now bring our attention to the one element of Breuer's experience with Anna O.

that he intuitively understood and then more or less consciously repressed? Can we refer to "the true story of Anna O." and specifically discuss what John Forrester has called the "sexual transference" and, more specifically, the "sexuality which implicated the doctor?"[40]

There has certainly been more gossipy kind of research around Freud and psychoanalysis than any other significant thinker; due to the intimacy of the theory and therapy of private lives, psychoanalysis has been naturally exposed to a particular kind of interest and curiosity. Reactions can tend to the extreme. Introducing one of the outstanding features of the case (a particularly strong transference, which left Breuer at a loss and in no small measure worried about his wife's jealousy) is only one. The retrospective account on the erotic aspect of her case and its implications for her treatment, by Freud and all those who followed, is not going to be of any concern for us. Transferences are to be understood as comprehensive; the emotional element may or not be present in the form we assume. Ronald Britton writes, "The story as it was known to Freud is not fully told in Breuer's case study of Anna O. ... I want to emphasize that the details that are not included in Breuer's account was known to Freud at the time."[41] What remains to be determined is the exact content of the details. Are they, as some would like to suggest, sexual and erotic – in the psychical sense of a transference between patient and doctor? Perhaps. To make proposals about the details, as Freud interpreted them, asks us to be speculative and to believe, unequivocally, in the interpretation Freud gives us in subsequent writings at a much later time. There is no reason to dispute his claims; and yet one is drawn to the particulars of the case that are not specifically transferential and that confirm how a therapeutic practice is also revealing of human interiority in such a way as to be of service for us today and in ways that exceed the sexual. Britton therefore asks researchers to be attentive to Breuer's account, as he wrote it, and then see how Freud's own thinking about the case led him to a more dynamic analysis of one case and then a deeper intimation of psychical complexities. The period, unfortunate in some ways, is detailed theoretically much later. There are, then, decisions to be made as to its examination. The postponement of a decade is not insurmountable, although it does make it necessary to anticipate how Freud himself made connections that would contribute to the origins of psychoanalysis. The case of Anna O. is, in Freud's mind, revealed much more when he arrives in Paris and begins an analysis of a diagnosis by an expert and, then, reaches his own conclusions. One has to wonder about Freud's own transference as he thought about the life and illness of a young woman who was not, personally, known to him. His knowledge, though indirect, nevertheless had an impact on him. Anna O. changed him.

The case of Anna O., more so because of its status as the first, left with Freud with information he had to selectively analyze and then come to his own conclusions, which were not at all immediate. Her medications were, in addition to everything else, one more feature of the case. *Prescriptions* of choral hydrate and morphine should not be neglected. There is now more than ample evidence that

Anna O., during her therapy with Breuer and well after (including intermittent stays at a mental hospital in Switzerland that began in October 1882 and lasted until 1885) was addicted to powerful narcotics.[42] Does that partially explain some of her various states that could be understood as periods of withdrawal? Perhaps, though we have no sense at all that she was ever without narcotics and did not have them handy. Did she self-administer morphine? These are, again, tangential issues. And there are others that can be mentioned as essential to her life-experience and the particular kind of grief she felt – like the death of a sibling and then her father's passing. In his own biography and on Breuer and Freud's discussion of the case in the summer of 1883, Peter Gay writes from his reading of a correspondence. "The scene, as Freud reconstructed it for his fiancée, displays the unforced intimacy of the two friends and the high level of their professional gossip."[43] Has Gay mistaken the conversation between two friends and doctors and the "gossip" of Freud's letter to Martha? Needless to say, Freud's intimate letters to his fiancée can be expected to be personal in a completely different way than two colleagues discussing a highly problematic case. Surely, there is considerable difference between what is revealed to a fiancé and to a colleague who is working on a sensitive case.

Following the trail of Freud's numerous writings and his recollection both of the 1880–1882 period as well as the working relationship he had with Breuer for several years after is an important aspect of the origin of psychoanalysis; outside of the purely historical events, which have been reconstructed with some thoroughness, there are nevertheless outstanding interpretations from Freud on specifics that are essential for us as we continue to build upon the main examination of neurotic consciousness and perception. When he looks back at the case of Anna O. during lectures he delivered at Clark University Lectures of 1909, does he offer us anything new to the case? One of Freud's intentions was to present the origins and history of psychoanalysis, what he called "a new method of examination and treatment" (SE 11:9). Is it relevant that, on this occasion, he does not use the word science? Perhaps; in any case, the language is explicitly medical. As he would, consistently, throughout his life, he always acknowledged Breuer's contribution to one version of a beginning – despite knowing that "earliest beginnings" extended beyond an individual and included an entire history that had yet to be consciously incorporated into the whole. "I had no share in its earliest beginnings. I was a student and working for my final examinations." That one belief is, for us, no longer possible to uphold. The specific date, the autumn of 1882, fixes Freud in a context. He was, from our account, at one more crucial period. Looking back at the time and with everything he knows about how psychoanalysis and his own private practice has changed, the case of Anna O. and the many symptoms of her illness have been catalogued numerous times. Despite its ambiguity – between, on the one hand, psychoanalysts and, on the other, academics whose stakes in the matter have other motives and objectives – our own attitude remains on Freud himself and the states of his thinking. Not all of Anna O.'s symptoms have been given equal importance. Given my argument, one stands out above all the others; this one "disturbance of vision," which is a neurotic symptom different in quality from others of a *physical* nature, represent in many ways the quintessential example of one form of ideation. Perceptions of reality, when they are transmitted unconsciously, can be readily understood in an original explanation, the splitting of consciousness. Splitting, we concluded, was not entirely accurate. Keeping in mind the interpretation, of Breuer's writing and of Freud's response (at the time), we can now see what remained foremost in his mind. The lecture presents his audience with information they were not all aware of; one is unsure about how much they could have been informed about Freud's development as a thinker over a substantial period of time. His details of Anna O. are less about her or Breuer's treatment than the impression *Freud* later developed. Only in Paris does he piece together a number of remarkable associations, including an obvious one that has remained, for the most part, unexamined. One more way to describe the original sense of psychical splitting is given another interpretation when projection is included. In the Clark Lectures, Freud says:

> I would like to make a preliminary remark. It is not without satisfaction that I have learnt that the majority of my audience members are not members of the medical profession. You have no need to be afraid that any special medical knowledge will be required for following what I have to say. It is true that we shall go along with the doctors on the first stage of our journey, but we shall be required to soon part company with them and, with Dr. Breuer, shall pursue a quite individual path.
>
> (SE 11:9–10)

*A quite individual path*, from the medical to something other. Freud's direction is inseparable from his own *positive transference* of the case and, also, the cultural (Jewish), intellectual, (scientific) and personal relationships he enjoyed with his supervisors as a student, as a research assistant, and as an intern. By this time, Freud has recognized just how far his individual initiatives had taken him. Beginnings could be easily acknowledged; the nature of his interpretations, on several different levels, had brought him to a new relation to being – which was more comprehensive than anything of a scientific or medical nature. Or, if we are to recall the argument in the Introduction and Kuhn's definition of a "scientific revolution," it does seem as if Freud is presenting his American audience with such a definition. Psychoanalysis was a revolutionary theory and practice; if they heard him with one kind of acuity, he was informing them about the aims of psychoanalysis as one of freeing neurotic individuals *from themselves*. The splitting was, in effect, temporal.

His return to the case of Anna O. gives him the opportunity to tell the audience – one stresses: they were not aware of the full implications of his talk – of a personal direction. The symptoms he now chooses to discuss are numerous, both somatic and psychical. One stands out. "Her eye movements were disturbed and her power of vision was subject to numerous restrictions" (SE 11:10). Psychoanalytically interpreted (at a later time, and with more knowledge) the enigma of neurotic illness has been identified as an endopsychic perceptual one. The insight, which he soon discusses, is not about the psychical transference between patient and therapist. Rather, we begin to see how Freud saw the various pieces of her ailments and unified them into a more specific picture of the psyche. Anna O. did not have any physical damage to her eyes – or, for that matter, her brain; nevertheless, a psychical problem of unknown cause had the ability to restrict her eyesight and, more significantly, her perception of not being able to properly recognize reality. The reactions, now recognized as forms of defence, included her fairy tales and her private theatre.

The concept of *"absences,"* adopted and used from French research, makes the reduction of perception more inclusive. Anna O. has problems seeing things, in focus, according to their size. These are objective obstacles. There are others that are not about seeing the objective world accurately – as everyone else does – but about how the world, of meaning and intentions, is seen by Anna O. in a distorted way. The *reduction* of sight is one symptom; the *distortion* of perception is quite another. These have been previously identified with precise medical terms; and yet, as Freud continued to treat patients and saw similarities, the power of the psyche to alter perception (and the personality itself) became dominant. The early intimations have been concretized theoretically and, equally as important, in the treatment of neurosis, which did not change since Anna O.'s initial talking cure and served as the knowledge of a particular kind of translation that demanded a reflective awareness of the difference between the immediacy of an impression and its interpretation. Although the term "symbolization" can, in principle, be used, a preferable one is hermeneutic and interpretative. "It may seem paradoxical that psychoanalysts write about the irrepresentable, so much is analytic theory determined by the notion of representation and, in particular, by the sense it has of unconscious representation."[44] The problem is not, in fact, on the notion of the "unrepresentable." Our concern is not nearly as abstract and, on the contrary, could not be more practical for our everyday life, pathologically and normally speaking. Freud offers a comment.

> In one discussion from *Instincts and Their Vicissitudes*, Freud turns to a *philosophical* problem as presented by Kant. We need not refer to the metaphysical fantasy of knowing the thing-in-itself – which Freud has no interest in. However, the analogy is an effective one.

Just as Kant warned us not to overlook the fact that our perceptions are subjectively conditioned and must not be regarded as identical with what is perceived through unknowable, so psycho-analysis warns us not to equate perception by means of consciousness with the unconscious mental processes which are their object.

The idea of the "subjectively conditioned" has to be more precisely, more psychically, defined. When perceptions, of oneself, others, or the reality of the world, originate in unconscious processes, then we have the making of a double-crisis, the distortion of self and reality simultaneously and hence the binding condition of neuroses. Anna O. is the ur-patient of psychoanalysis not for being historically first; more than any other early patient – where her symptoms would be confirmed in Paris – she represented the phenomenology of neuroses as a whole.

> Like the physical, the psychical is not necessarily in reality what it appears to be. We shall be glad to learn, however, that the correction of internal perception will turn out not to offer such great difficulty as the correction of external perception – that internal objects are less unknowable than the external world.
> (SE 14:171)

Psychoanalysis, therefore, does not suffer from a philosophical and most surely not a metaphysical problem. Internal perception, once it is recognized as at the origin of the external real, can be analyzed for its distortions and all the machinations of which the psyche is capable. The discovery Freud makes is, arguably, much more significant than a philosophical one (if we understand the discipline merely in an academic way) because he made himself familiar with a psychical process in a patient, a process he would ultimately turn on himself in the form of a self-analysis and in the interpretation of dreams, the project that confirmed his intuition about the unconscious and the images it was capable of producing, during sleep and during somnambulistic states of consciousness.

When Freud began to treat his own patients after returning from Paris and doing so by using Breuer's method, he had come upon a problem that was not going to be easily resolved, not without a larger number of patients and the work of verifying their associations. As far as Anna O.'s case was concerned, findings were not going to be easily dismissed. On top of the *absences*, which were indication of her split consciousness in terms of a disjunction between the self and time, there were fragmentary psychical realities. The equally incomplete "*double-conscience*" goes some way in representing her consciousness; there are many more dynamics than two. "They were profoundly melancholy fantasies – 'day-dreams' we should call them – sometimes characterized by poetic beauty" (SE 11:13). The aesthetic has to be also emphasized since, independent of any relation to art, it implies the senses – as the Greek *aisthesis* invites us to do. The "beauty" of her day-dreams, and of her private theatre, can now be examined with more completeness since, until this time, the Aristotelian concept of catharsis has been mentioned without any interpretation. One piece of information is not without its cultural relevance – and, to use a colloquialism, close to home. In 1880, the uncle of Martha Bernays (Freud's future wife) published a book on Aristotle's concept of catharsis. The term, in whatever way it was understood at the time, was influenced by the popularity of Jacob Bernay's book. He was a philologist by training. One of his teachers, Friedrich Wilhelm Ritschl, was also the single most-important professor related to Nietzsche's studies and appointment to the University of Basel. To make the connection between Breuer's adoption of the term *catharsis* and one, non-medical, origin in Aristotle's *Poetics* makes it necessary to turn to Freud's interpretation of Anna O.'s experiences as, precisely, tragic. The term (tragedy), however, has a specific meaning and cannot be reduced to a blanket-term for one event, or a series of them. Freud realized how the structure of tragedy was reproduced in psychical ailments. The patient's life, conduct, and words were all intended to recall an experience or a fantasy in the past; as symptoms, however, they were ultimately a futile acting-out that made memory virtually impossible. Breuer sensed, still without precision, what Anna O.'s psyche could produce. Breuer writes:

> I had a very strong impression that the numerous products of her secondary state which had been quiescent were now forcing their way into consciousness; and though in the first instance they were being remembered only her secondary state, they were nevertheless burdening and disturbing her normal one.
>
> (SE 2:47)

The idea of a *condition seconde* had already been recognized for its complications. The force, from one place in the psyche to another, could be detected and yet be vague as to its origin and consequences. Only Freud, in time, found his way (from an early thinking-through and self-analysis) towards the enigma not of hysteria, per se, but to a universal process. We can see Freud's own beginnings in terms of their individual particularities. "A broad range of chance events often has a role in the preparatory stage of the creative process of individuals with prepared minds."[45] Preparatory, prepared mind; these are crucial and have been established for Freud personally. The tragic and the neurotic is one more connection that he makes; it will, for obvious reasons, continue and lead to one of the foundations of psychoanalytic theory in terms of familial conflict and illness.

As the 1909 lecture goes on, Freud divulges a theoretical discovery; how the audience responded to it and its relation to the earlier example of fantasies and aesthetic "day-dreams" is hard to imagine. Readers today are left with a problem to contemplate. "*Our hysterical patients suffer from reminiscences.* Their symptoms are residues and mnemic symbols of particular (traumatic) experiences" (SE 11:16). Without simply turning both observations into a contradiction, Freud leaves us with an enduring problem that, for him and for us, will soon become much more serious. Before looking at the time when the problem becomes most acute, Freud anticipated one important objective: "we are on the point of arriving at a purely psychological theory of hysteria" (SE 11:18). Freud admits that, for the time being, he has not yet arrived. He had been on the way for a considerable period of time, and he was willing to admit that the process was ongoing. Would it be "interminable," as he wrote in one of his last papers on technique? For us, it has been so. The return, from our standpoint, leaves us with just as much work to do in our engagement with Freud's writing as for the future – especially for analysands who, post-termination, can find themselves in familiar places both theoretically, with Freud, and very personally. The examination of Aristotle's theory of catharsis has been one return, to the classical world, as significant as the earlier interpretation of the meaning of Moses for Freud personally and for an understanding of modern thought, from Bacon, to psychoanalysis. How do we move from Aristotle's catharsis and, in Freud's concluding section of *Studies on Hysteria*, provide the transition towards Paris and so anticipate how the way towards a period of study was also a turn towards himself?

As has already been mentioned, the many autobiographical recollections from the whole of Freud writings are to be read together and so make it more accessible for us to see a complete portrait. In "The Resistances to Psycho-Analysis," a singular writing with its own set of ideas, Freud tells us that "a particularly bad reception was accorded psychoanalysis, which the present writer began to develop nearly thirty years ago from the discoveries of Josef Breuer (of Vienna) on the origin of neurotic symptoms." *Bad reception*. The phrase makes it difficult not to rely on the idea of transmission – which is to say, the received. As for Freud's entire comment,

> Its original significance was purely therapeutic: it aimed at creating a new and efficient method for treating neurotic illness. But connections which not be foreseen in the beginning caused psycho- analysis to reach out far beyond its original aim. It ended by claiming to be of importance for every field of knowledge that is founded on psychology.
>
> (SE 19:124)

The argument, again recalling the ongoing discussion of science, implies that there was one inescapable ground to all knowledge. There was simply no way to avoid the reality of the psyche in everything human.

One possibility has been ignored; true enough, the term *catharsis* was used by Breuer as a specifically medical term and to convey the idea of a cure and what was also called "abreaction." The medical process of a catharsis or "purgation" was understood to be a relief and as a release of a built-up pressure due to the pain of a persistent memory. Two points can be added. They have not been prominent in any discussion of the origin of Breuer's use of catharsis and its derivation from Aristotle's *Poetics*. Any connection would have to turn to the experience of the spectator in terms of a catharsis of pity and fear for the suffering of the character on stage. In Breuer's cathartic method, however, the experience would have to be shared, as a transference, between Anna O. and himself. Leaving aside what we know about the actual "love-transference" in the therapeutic situation or, more personally, Breuer's decision to end his treatment of Anna O., my point here is to concentrate on our therapeutic understanding of catharsis and on another term, a classical one again from Aristotle, that begins to give us an indication of how to better understand what Anna O. experienced in terms of her relationship to time. Continuing with our allusion to phenomenology and the consciousness of time, introducing the concept of *hysteron* may give us an opportunity to consider what may have been a cultural unconscious influence on Breuer and, on Freud, indicative of further thought. The temptation of etymological tracing is hard to resist; it will be kept to a minimum and suggestive enough to be at least considered. If the Greek term for hysteria and the word *hysteron* are considered in their inter-relationship, we are not far from the recognition of the temporality of an experience that, relying on the fact of the uterus, giving us an indication of time and *a period*. The materialism of the 19th century made it impossible to recognize an altogether different connection: the uterus, or anything related to it physiologically, was irrelevant. A period had to be understood allegorically. Although we could, at this point, involve ourselves in an extensive discussion on the perception of the menstrual cycle in culture or the physiological experience of women during that particular time of the month, both would be, in essence, a diversion from the origins of psychoanalysis as Freud began to conceive it when hysteria was no longer a physiological condition but a dislocation of the psyche in time. Reading the account of Anna O.'s symptoms is now making it much more likely to view her experiences from two Greek terms and as they relate to Aristotle's view, precisely, of *tragedy*. *Catharsis* and *hysteron* both have their origin in Aristotle's *Poetics* and serve as the transference of a cultural reality in the Greek world.

Martha Nussbaum interprets the word *catharsis* as it applies to the Greek theatre in terms of "clarification."[46] Her interpretation allows us to apply the sense of clarifying to the therapeutic situation insofar as the patient, Anna O., had no idea of either the sense of her symptoms or their causes. Clarification seems to be an opportune phenomenological and not merely cognitive idea that can be viewed as one of the ways to assist the patient to understand the nature of her experiences. (We will see how the theatrical theories are even more relevant when, in the next chapter, we follow Freud to Paris and witness firsthand his role as a spectator in Charcot's theatre of hysteria – one augmented by the new-found use of medical photography as another mode of representation which had the added feature of immobilizing the patient in order to view them, ad nauseam, from the point of view of the doctor and as part of the instrumentalization of the patient within an institution).

The psychotherapeutic method tried and tested by Breuer and called "cathartic" returns us to Aristotle's *Poetics* and the concept of "catharsis," which was expressed in one way as a kind of purgation. Aristotle opens with a definition that we can retain and expand upon. "Concerning poetics, both itself and its species, let us speak about (a) the effect which each of them has."[47] His specifics, in terms of a literary work – its plot, for example – is not of any concern to us. Rather, the sole preoccupation of *the effects* has to be the first point of reflection for the spectator and the drama on stage. Since, in all representations on stage, there is an imitation, of a character and a scene, a personality and a life-situation, two dramatic elements are occurring at the same time – as a spectacle to be perceived by the spectator and an internal feeling that is experienced as an emotion. Again, Aristotle's exacting categories – like harmonic modes and rhythm – are of no importance when we concentrate on the relationship of the imitation and the effects. However, one of his distinctions is crucial for an understanding of Anna O. and then Freud's psychotherapy of hysteria. In her acts, Anna O. can certainly be described, without the term being pejorative, as *histrionic*. Throughout her illness, she was expressing, within her possibilities, states of mind. Given the language used to describe her condition, and her relationship to many of its effects, she was attempting to first present her fantasies, hallucinations, stories, and most especially her "private theatre," as an incomplete interpretation. Can we present Anna O., and forms of extreme hysteria, as a *tragic character*? We can if we keep in mind the model of tragedy as presented by Sophocles in *Oedipus the King*. Just as he precipitated the events leading to the fulfilment of his fate by trying, precisely, to avoid it with heroic determination, all of Anna O.'s symptoms are an attempt to get to the origin of her profound conflicts, only to be intertwined in their meanings and effects to the point of being in a permanent state of entanglement – as both the actor and the spectator. Between one and the other, she cannot find a place for a reflecting, unlike the spectator of a tragedy who, sitting in the audience, experiences a necessary physical separation (a kind of buffer) between an internal world and the unfolding drama on stage. How did Breuer, and then Freud, explain the process of catharsis as one of speech, recollection, and affect? How, then, was Anna O. an interpreter of her own drama – unfolding in the present – as a distorted imitation of other, forgotten and repressed, scenes from the past? Did she, in fact, interpret the meaning of her condition? Or was that necessary step only understood and then carried out by Freud? Breuer's optimism of Anna O.'s "cure" was misguided. She was never cured. The failure, however, was necessary in order for Freud to recognize how the cathartic method was insufficient. Its premise was correct; its method, as a whole, was incomplete. How did he ultimately move from catharsis to psychoanalysis? The question, because of our specific historical period, 1873–1885, cannot be completely answered. Our period is only the condition of the possibility of an answer that occurs, slowly, methodically, from the post-Paris period until the opening of the 20th century with *The Interpretation of Dreams*. The case of Anna O. demands more attention because of its unfolding just a few years before Freud goes to Paris and takes with him a number of insights. The immediate problem is: what does he see, beyond appearances, beyond the image, beyond the scenes of a life? If, as Jean-Michel Yves argues, "the real object of the theatre is not so much identification and illusion as the experience of the unconscious itself," one other necessity remains. The experience is not enough, and we know that one limitation since, for Anna O.'s theatre, the unconscious was fully visible and yet remained outside the range of perception. Despite her speech and the attempt to interpret and understand her condition, she never did so – not in terms of self-reflection and certainly not towards an improvement in her condition. The interpretative work to be done was carried out by Freud because of the limitations of the cathartic method, despite all its promise, and the particularities of Anna O.'s case as a histrionic one and as a tragic character who was not on stage but, more seriously, in life where the actor and the spectator were one and the same. For Freud, the moment he placed himself in the role of a spectator and began to think about the nature of the psychical drama being enacted by a patient, he became more and more able to see beyond the superficial drama, the symptoms, and lead himself to their origins. The origins were not, simply, to be found in a forgotten and repressed past. They were omnipresent in distorted form, in the very private theatre she had devised as an imitation of her internal world. She was never capable of understanding their meaning. That work became the obligation of the therapist who, eventually, became a psychoanalyst and recognized the elements of "the architecture of the soul."[48] The chronology towards a highly complex edifice is, for all intents and purposes, ongoing. Anna O. remains the ur-case of a process that could only reach a breakthrough once Freud returned to the case again and again and so confirmed the limitation of a catharsis that would never be complete only with the sense of a "release" – which could only ever be temporary. If we return, from 1909, to the actual chronology of events as they were experienced by Freud, another essential one takes us to the end of our stipulated period (between 1873 and 1885) and so to the formative period he spent in Paris.

Our question, psychotherapeutically speaking and with Anna O. as the individual of most concern to us at the moment, involves both speech and imitation – but not as Aristotle presented them. Rather, how does a patient achieve catharsis by speech? Speech is only one of the necessary efforts: the other is the recollection of a scene, one or more, that is in some way at the origin of the present forms of the histrionic acts. Freud's insight, only intuitive at first, more of a suspicion than a concrete and certain realization, involves the difference between the patient's distorted mimesis (the act in the present) and its model. Recalling the original scene is not enough; the retelling of one or more incidents must be accompanied by the affect. The emotions are crucial; without the affect, the first stage of understanding and so the alleviation of the pain will not be achieved. We now know that the cathartic method, for Anna O., did not provide her with a lasting remedy. There are many more factors to her illness. Identifying them all, from our limited knowledge of her life, and virtually nothing of her childhood, makes that task impossible. So we are left with Freud's own relationship to the case and his understanding of her private theatre. Aristotle, due to his understanding of the experience of the spectator, did provide Freud with a psychotherapeutic perspective. If tragedy "moves the soul," Aristotle writes, "by peripeties and recognitions," (P 639) then, once the therapist places himself in the analogic position of the spectator, the *peripety* is not due to a sudden transformation or turnaround in the patient; rather, both the peripety and the recognition are his own as he finds himself with a clearer understanding of the symptoms as they appear in disguised form. The patient can experience moments of a catharsis, as Anna O. did. However, only when Freud began to understand the dynamic of the patient's consciousness, their psyche, could he move to the next stage in the understanding and treatment. The peripety, as a "change in fortune," occurs for the psychotherapist. He sees differently, and does so based on the complicated move from the appearance of the symptoms to their reasons. Why does the patient, for example, create a specific "plot" to experience? What is it intended to achieve? In a later, pivotal paper, Freud will make the distinction between acting-out and working-through. The repetition of a scene, intended as a form of recollection, is destined to remain divided from its origin and so inaccessible. The act is an imitation of a memory (or a fantasy) that remains unconscious for the patient. The interpretative responsibility of the analyst is then to recognize its origin and nature. Clearly, taking only these reflections into consideration as Freud thought about them in the early 1880's, we can see his own private peripety as he turned, more and more self-assuredly, from a physiological consideration of psychological illness to a psychical interpretation. Anna O.'s private theatre and Breuer's cathartic method were necessary to move from Aristotle's literary theory to an analysis of a particular kind of psychological mimesis.

As Freud writes in "The Psychotherapy of Hysteria," "I must confess that that during the years which have since passed – in which I have been unceasingly concerned with the problems trounced upon it – fresh points of view have formed themselves on my mind" (SE 2:255). We are, at this juncture, at an end; or rather, at another turn towards the past. For during this year of writing the last section of *Studies on Hysteria*, in 1895, the following years until the last month before the turn of the century require the analysis of too many publications. They have to be postponed. Before we can turn to Freud's many "fresh points of view," one final period has to be discussed. Anna O. has been pivotal. The problems Freud addressed because of the case reported to him were many and intricate. Only a few have been discussed; others are postponed for another time and occasion when they can be included in other lines of inquiry. These developments, Freud writes,

> have led to what is in part at least a different grouping and interpretation of the factual material known to me at the time. It would be unfair if I were to try to lay too much of the responsibility for this development upon my honoured friend Dr. Josef Breuer. For this reason the considerations which follow stand principally under my own name.
>
> (SE 2:255)

*Under my own name.*

The extreme difficulty of her everyday life was, for Freud as he thought about the case, an immediate one. Her symptoms were individual. History, however, has often turned from her individual experiences to their *social* meanings. The literature on the subject, from those in the Humanities and who are not, necessarily, either interested or knowledgeable about psychoanalysis, can be divided into two concerns: her treatment, first, and then her significant life later. One tradition has been extremely critical. All the sympathy is given to the patient. So we have one kind of decision: one the one hand, with the language of late, 20th-century theory, Jenn Cole emphasizes *her morality* by saying that "I open myself to the other," and on the other, writes that "my work ... is an act of theory off yet another patriarch."[49] The either/or can be perpetuated. But doing so will make it impossible to understand Anna O. as an individual and without relying on theory much less any references (whatever they are supposed to "mean," to a "patriarch.") Another direction in the scholarship has followed her from her experiences as a young woman with severe psychological anguish to someone who, literally, invented herself.[50] Her case, *as a social worker*, is highly revealing psychologically. However we relate to the case of Anna O. or to Freud and psychoanalysis, the obligation to interpret ourselves (before our analyses or projections) had better be as thorough as possible, otherwise we always run the risk of presenting ourselves with a little too much virtue and not much intelligence, a little too much theory and not enough reflection. Being "good," today, is often a catch-all substitute. The debates, and recriminations, will no doubt continue for the foreseeable future, at least until such time as the obsession with the critical theory of the late-20th century becomes something more expansive, more nuanced, and not driven by the attempt to impose guilt on the past and on history as a whole.[51] It may be realized, perhaps soon, how academic attempts to understand the past have been compromised by initial conditions of thought and, so, at the end, in need of being rethought just as much as the distortions of neurotic perception. Julia Segal writes, "Phantasies make up the background to everything we do, think or feel: they determine our perceptions and in a sense *are* our perceptions."[52] An admission will soon have to be made: academic phantasies have been responsible for some of the most conspicuous acts of neurotic life. How the realization will change institutions of higher learning, and us, remains an open question. Segal's call to *understand ourselves* cannot be an academic exercise. When academic phantasies and projections become one form of knowledge, a 19th-century problem for neurotics has become, in our time, an individual and an institutional reality.

## Notes

1 Whitehouse, P.J. "Meynert, Theodore Hermann," 1117, *Encyclopedia of the Neurological Sciences, Second Edition*, 2014.
2 Arminjon, Mathieu, François Ansermet, and Pierre Magistretti. "The Homeostatic Psyche: Freudian Theory and Somatic Markers," 272–278 *Journal of Physiology – Paris* 104 (5), 2010.
3 Bock von Wülfingen, Bettina. "Freud's "Core of Our Being" Between Cytology and Psychoanalysis," 226–244 *Berichte zur Wissenschaftsgeschichte* 36 (3), 9/2013.
4 Schonbar, Rosalea A., and Helena R. Beatus. "The Mysterious Metamorphoses of Bertha Pappenheim: Anna O. Revisited," 59–78 *Psychoanalytic Psychology* 7 (1), 1990, 61.
5 Skues, Richard A. *Sigmund Freud and the History of Anna O.: Reopening a Closed Case*. New York: Palgrave, 2006. The case, of course, has never been closed; and can never be since our ongoing interpretations of the case (if it depends on us more than the words we read) will effect the phenomenon in question. We can, to the best of our abilities and, one hopes, with sufficient awareness of our interests, motivations, and convictions, not let our own biases interfere with the *descriptions*. Now that we have

moved from Freud's experiences to the detail of the symptoms of a neurotic patient, how will we respond? My objectives have been clear and prepared: how does Freud understand the complications of neurotic perception once he becomes familiar with her case and, equally as important, how do his insights carry him forward to Paris?

6  Bogousslavsky, J. *Hysteria: The Rise of an Enigma*. Basel: Karger, 2014.
7  Sander, Gilman. (Ed). *Hysteria Beyond Freud*. Berkeley: University of California Press, 1993.
8  Cotti, Patricia. "Towards a New Historiography of Psychoanalysis: In Defense of Psychoanalysis as a Science – An Essay on George Makari's *Revolution in Mind*," 133–146 *Psychoanalysis and History* 14 (1), 2012, 136.
9  Hurst, Linda C. "What Was Wrong with Anna O.?," 129–131 *Journal of the Royal Society of Medicine* 75 (2), 1982. One of the more intriguing responses from physicians, neurobiologists, and scientists in general has been their diagnosis of the case of Anna O. based on the case written by Josef Breuer. They seem, from the perspective of an analysand, highly speculative and conjectural. One, of course, admits to having not the slightest knowledge in medicine, but when someone confidently asserts (or "postulates") an organic causation to Anna O.'s illness, scepticism follows since an entire way of thinking, psychoanalytically, would have to be abandoned.
10  Castelnuovo-Tedesco, Pietro. "On Rereading the Case of Anna O.: More About Questions That Are Unanswerable," 57–71 *The Journal of the American Academy of Psychoanalysis and Dynamic Psychiatry* 22 (1), 1994, 60.
11  Kaplan, Robert. "O Anna: Being Bertha Pappenheim – Historiography and Biography," 62–68 *Australasian Psychiatry* 12 (1), 2004, 63.
12  Bowman, Marcus. *The Last Resistance: The Concept of Science as a Defense against Psychoanalysis*. Albany: SUNY, 2002, 87.
13  La Berge, Ann, and Mordechai Feingold. *French Medical Culture in the Nineteenth Century*. Leiden: Brill, 1994.
14  As in the topic by Cecilia Tasca et al. of "Women and Hysteria in the History of Mental Health," 110–119 *Clinical Practice and Epidemiology in Mental Health* 8 (1), 2012.
15  Hunter, Dianne. "Hysteria, Psychoanalysis, and Feminism: The Case of Anna O.," 465–488 *Feminist Studies* 9 (3), 1983, 467.
16  Charlier, Philippe, and Saudamini Deo. "The Anna O. Mystery: Hysteria or Neuro-Tuberculosis?," 14 *Journal of Neurological Sciences* 381, 15 Oct. 2017.
17  Jiraskova, Terezie. "Splitting of the Mind and Unconscious Dynamics," 24–27 *Activas Nervosa Superior* 56 (1/2), 2014.
18  See Sanz Giancola, A., and C. Alvarez Garcia. "Hysteria: A History of Conceptual and Clinical Pathomorphosis," 545–546 *European Psychiatry* 65 (1), 2022.
19  See Mikkel Borch-Jacobsen's *Remembering Anna O.: A Century of Mystification*. London: Routledge, 1996. The question can be asked: *whose* mystification?
20  Merskey, Harold. "Anna O. Had a Severe Depressive Illness," 185–194 *The British Journal of Psychiatry* 161 (2), Aug. 1992, 185.
21  Blass, Rachel B. "Conceptualizing Splitting: On the Different Meanings of Splitting and Their Implications for the Understanding of the Person and the Analytic Process," 123–139 *International Journal of Psychoanalysis* 96 (1), 2015.
22  Schabert, Gerhard. "Freud and Evolution," 295–312 *History and Philosophy of the Life Sciences* 31 (2), 2009, 298.
23  Perkins-McVey, Matthew. "Critical Localization and the Nerve Cell: Freud's Work in Meynert's Psychiatry Clinic," *History of Psychology* 2024, 13.
24  For a sense of the overall concentration of his early scientific studies, see Mark Solm's "An Introduction to the Neuroscientific Works of Sigmund Freud," 1–35 *The Pre-Psychoanalytic Writings of Sigmund Freud*. Ed. Barford, Duncan, Filip Geerardyn, and Gertrudis van de Vijer. London: Karnac, 2002. A more specific one can seen in

the research carried out by Gerhard Hildebrandt, Christina Ruppert, Martin N. Stienen, and Werner Surbeck. "Georg Büchner, Sigmund Freud and the 'Schädelnerven' (cranial nerves) – Research on the Brain and Soul in the 19th Century," 1999–2014 *Acta Neurochirurgica* 156, 2014.

25 Amacher, Peter. *Freud's Neurological Education and Its Influence on Psycho-analytic Theory*, 5–93, *Psychological Issues*, IV (4), Monograph 16. New York: International Universities Press, Inc., 1965.

26 Gödde, Günter. "Freud and the Nineteenth-Century Sources on the Unconscious," 261–286 *Thinking the Unconscious: Nineteenth-Century German Thought*. Ed. Angus Nicholls and Martin Liebscher. Cambridge: Cambridge University Press, 2010.

27 Hirschmüller, Albrecht. *The Life and Work of Josef Breuer: Physiology and Psychoanalysis*. New York: New York University Press, 1989.

28 Such "reinterpretations" are now legion. A first one is mentioned; others will follow, each with their own concentration. See, for one, Jennifer L. Pierce's "The Relation Between Emotion Work and Hysteria: A Feminist Reinterpretation of Freud's *Studies on Hysteria*," 255–270 *Women's Studies* 16 (3–4), 1989.

29 Ellenberger, Henri F. "The Story of 'Anna O.': A Critical Review with New Data," 254–272 in *Beyond the Unconscious: Essays of Henri F. Ellenberger in the History of Psychiatry*. Ed. Mark S. Micale. Princeton: Princeton University Press, 2014, 270.

30 Boyarin, Daniel. *Unheroic Conduct: The Rise of Heterosexuality and the Invention of the Jewish Man*. Berkeley: University of California Press, 1989. The context is the chapter called "Retelling the Story of Anna O. Or, Bertha Pappenheim, My Hero."

31 Marchese, Frank J. "An Overlooked Sexual Element in the Breuer-Anna O. Case," 261–276 *North American Journal of Psychology* 20 (2), 2018.

32 Whitebook, Joel. "Our Dual Inheritance: On Psychoanalytic Social Theory Today," 1–14 *American Imago* 76 (1) (Spring 2019), 3.

33 For an intimate portrait of Bertha Pappenheim, see Mark J. Blechner's "The Three Cures of Bertha Pappenheim (Anna O): The Talking Cure, the Writing Cure, and the Social Cure," 3–25 *Contemporary Psychoanalysis* 58 (1), 2022.

34 Gilhooley, Dan. "Misrepresentation and Misreading in the Case of Anna O.," 75–100 *Modern Psychoanalysis* 27 (1), 2002, 77.

35 Levenson, Edgar A. *The Fallacy of Understanding and the Ambiguity of Change*. Hillsdale N.J.: Routledge, 2005, 8.

36 The question can be answered by the reader and according to their own objectives – especially if they are not professionally therapeutic but based on other, more academic considerations. A few research papers will be mentioned in due time, especially in relation to her later vocation in life, which can broadly be described as a form of social work, indeed, as one origin of social work specifically devoted to women's issues. Her later, very productive life can of course always be read back to her condition. See, to start, Carol Swenson's "Freud's Anna O.: Social Work's Bertha Pappenheim," 149–163 *Clinical Social Work Journal* 22 (2), 1994. Those who trace her illness as a young woman to her productive later life have substantive arguments. One possibility has, perhaps, not been sufficiently raised: did Bertha Pappenheim become devoted to others because of her early experiences as a patient with Breuer? Or did her care, specifically for women, give us a different sense of the way she understood her life?

37 Showalter, Elaine. *Hystories: Hysterical Epidemics and Modern Media*. New York: Columbia University Press, 1997.

38 Perkins-McVey, Matthew. "Cortical Localization and the Nerve Cell: Freud's Work in Meynert's Psychiatry Clinic," 333–349 *History of Psychology* 24 (4), 2024.

39 Guenther, Katja. "The Disappearing Lesion: Sigmund Freud, Sensory-Motor Physiology, and the Beginnings of Psychoanalysis," 569–601 *Modern Intellectual History* 10 (3), 2013.

40 Forrester, John. "The True Story of Anna O.," 327–347 *Social Research* 53 (2), 1986, 330.
41 Britton, Ronald. *Sex, Death, and the Superego: Experience in Psychoanalysis*. London: Karnac, 2003, 7.
42 See, for example, Sergio de Paula Ramos's "Revisiting Anna O.: A Case of Chemical Dependence," 239–250 *History of Psychology* 6 (3), 2003.
43 Gay, Peter. *Freud: A Life of Our Time*. New York: Doubleday, 1989, 63.
44 Botella, Cesar, and Sara Botella. "A Psychoanalytic Approach to Perception," 83–106 *Symbolization: Representation and Communication*. Ed. James Rose. London: Routledge, 2007, 88.
45 Dìaz Chumaceiro, Cora L. "Serendipity in Freud's Career: Before Paris," 79–81 *Creativity Research Journal*, 11 (1), 1998, 81.
46 Nussbaum, Martha. *The Fragility of Goodness*. Chicago: The University of Chicago Press, 1986.
47 Yvens, Jean-Michel. "Catharsis: Psychoanalysis and its Theatre." Tr. Andreas Weller. 1009–1027 *International Journal of Psychoanalysis* 92 (4), Aug. 2011, 1017.
48 Smith, David L. *Approaching Psychoanalysis: An Introductory Course*. London: Karnac, 1999.
49 Cole. Jenn. *Hysteria in Performance*. Montreal and Kingston: McGill-Queen's University Press, 2021, 183.
50 Mark J. Blechner has divided her life into three phases and so showed how she lived through "The Three Cures of Bertha Pappenheim (Anna O.): The Talking Cure, the Writing Cure, and the Social Cure," 3–25 *Contemporary Psychoanalysis* 58 (1), 2022. Others that can be consulted are Meredith M. Kimball's "From 'Anna O.' to Bertha Pappenheim: Transforming Private Pain into Public Action," 20–43 *History of Psychology* 3 (1), 2000, Elizabeth Lorentz's "Jewish Women and Intersectional Feminism: The Case of Bertha Pappenheim," 24–50 *Feminist German Studies* 29 (1), 2023.
51 Titles, as always, are suggestive. See Deborah Elise White's "Studies on Hysteria: Case Histories and the Case Against History," 1035–1049 *MLN* 104 (5), 1989. We are not yet in a position (culturally) to be able to look back at the last half-century and more of "critical theory" – in whatever form one chooses to analyze the academic phenomenon in institutions of higher learning, but one images the time is drawing near when the previously inviolable ideas will be scrutinized. The assessment will, I think, be much worse than previous anxiety about a "backlash." The self-possession of an age will receive little sympathy; very little will be deserved.
52 Segal, Julia. *Phantasy in Everyday Life: A Psychoanalytic Approach to Understanding Ourselves*. London: Karnac, 1995, 22.

# Chapter 4

# Jean-Martin Charcot's Neurology

One could see how, to begin with, he [Charcot] would stand undecided in the face of some new manifestation which was hard to interpret, one could follow the path along which he endeavoured to arrive at an understanding of it, one could study the way in which he took stock of difficulties and overcame them, and one could observe with surprise that he never grew tired of looking at the same phenomenon.

(Report on My Studies in Paris and Berlin)

## Freud's Obituary of Charcot

Freud's obituary of Charcot after his death on August 16, 1893, recalled a number of memories from his experience of working with him during his short stay in Paris and the observations he made at the Salpêtrière hospital among a majority of anatomically trained clinicians; the tribute to the man, scientist, and world-renowned neurologist who had been so important for Freud's early experience of the illness called hysteria as well as other pathologies of the brain also gives us intimations of a particular kind of thinking that was, in the early history of depth-psychology, moving towards significant changes. A consensus would not dissuade Freud from the direction of his thinking. Ultimately, the physicalist emphasis of the medical culture at the time proved to be unshakeable for the clinicians in Paris; considering Freud's experiences as they have been presented thus far, he was not persuaded by the commonplace theory of heredity or by the exclusive focus on biology. The *inheritance* of nervous disorders – recognized as the "Salpêtrière doctrine"[1] – was, for Freud, far less certain than for his peers; his background, including the standout case history of Anna O., had left him with too many variables as to the causes of mental illness. The *symptoms* he had discussed with Breuer were too complicated to be caused by an organic illness. Anna O.'s symptoms in terms of her consciousness and perception had a still-undiscovered etiology. The *force* of the unconscious as the origin of endopsychic perception was coming to light.

When our first theme (an archaic heritage as Freud understood it, within a family and culturally) is placed side by side with heredity, a virtual chasm opens up between one and the other. Biology and culture are, historically, incommensurable – *more so* despite the fact, to be discussed later by Freud, of the phylogenetic and ontogenetic relationship. There are no arguments in acknowledging the facts as they are maintained by historians of science; the assessments are superlative. Charcot has been described as "the first professor of diseases of the nervous system in the world."[2] "One of the most influential physicians in the history of modern medicine."[3] "Charcot was one of the great organizers and systematizers of nineteenth-century medical science."[4] He did so – in particular, regarding hysteria – with a method that, shortly, we can analyze in terms of its demonstrations and *theatre*, a method Freud will compare with the cathartic method of psychotherapy and its origins in Aristotle's *Poetics*. Tragedy will turn out to be existential as well as dramatic. Before turning to Charcot's clinical pedagogy at the Salpêtrière, however, a more personal assessment can be presented, first by Freud himself in an obituary and, at the same time, his place in the history of the understanding and treatment of nervous disorders as they were understood in 1885 when Freud arrived in Paris. Charcot's neurological accomplishments were remarkable. Still, for Freud, a personal inclination kept him independent and capable of evaluating the knowledge of the times. His individuality was essential; as was the sense of the reality around him. What he *thought* about Charcot was not, strictly speaking, medical. Freud's relationship was more intimate – not so much between them, professionally, as in understanding of a direction in thinking, which was independent from the beginning. He was no doubt professionally interested, for example, in the *paralysis agitans* of someone suffering from Parkinson's disease;[5] but this one neuro-degenerative disease, for the most part a geriatric illness, could not determine his interest in other, more psychical forms of paralysis.

The world-renowned neurologist had first been trained in an altogether different milieu. His ability in one sphere was transferred to another. Charcot's early interest and practice of art remained with him. "His penetration of disease required the ability to comprehend, in a single glance, an essential image of the inner disorder from a variety of superficial appearances, a skill that he had honed during his earlier years as an aspiring artist."[6] While we are rightly sceptical of any immediate experience at a "single glance," his power of observation is well-attested, as were his many innovations in the diagnosis of illness and in the care of others, including the particular illnesses of the elderly. He also "founded geriatry."[7] The preceding sentence can be read with a certain acuity; doing so allows us to isolate a phenomenology, even if as an exaggeration (a "single glance") and the idea of an essential image, first, and then an inner cause that could only be uncovered if the superficial appearance was not taken for granted and seen, in many cases, as a kind of cover-up. In the obituary, Freud is acknowledging Charcot's abilities, as well as his own; for he took one extra, difficult step and found the appearance not to be material at all. Freud too had a highly developed aesthetic sense, for the plastic arts and literature if not for music. The one step he took that went the farthest involved the deep division between anatomy and the psyche. His main preoccupation had been one of consciousness. Freud's own ability to observe went beyond looking at patients. He saw Charcot as someone whose artistic background, when he was young and not yet persuaded by his father to take up the profession of medicine, effected his methods and findings.

Near the end of his life, and in a posthumous publication mentioned first in the Introduction ("An Outline of Psychoanalysis") Freud summed up an original problem. For the purpose of a contrast, we can highlight a difference in definition and, therefore, of reality. He was, since he turned towards the interest in human subjects, puzzled by one mystery as it had been reflected on by both philosophy and science. "The starting-point for this investigation is provided by a fact without parallel, which defies all explanations and descriptions – the fact of consciousness" (SE 23:157). *Without parallel*: the words are not to be passed over without a measure of awareness. While an entire community had been fixated on a materialist understanding of mental illness, Freud had already considered too many factors for him to be convinced of a strictly physiological explanation for the reality of a designated hysteric. He represents a singular transition from both the individual experts at the time and the institutions of psychiatry. Charcot had been the most important – after Breuer; others had played their part in Freud's ability to separate all the current theories and adopt or discard them as he saw necessary, according to patients as he observed them and as he tried to understand their particular relation to life. Some attention to the vocabulary of a scientist and as someone intimately familiar with the ambience of the laboratory – where observation and verification are, for the certainty of knowledge, essential – can also be seen in another related, though somewhat different, disposition: while *observation* is one description of the scientifically minded, Freud complemented the ability with even more acute awareness of the nature of human perception – which was relevant in the direct relationship between the world and the viewer. The clinician was not exempt.

Did he learn to be even more "visual," indirectly from Charcot and from his time at the Salpêtrière, both in himself and in the way any form of psychological treatment would have to deal with the perception of patients as they lived out their particular form of illness? If we follow Freud to Paris as someone who has been intuitively aware of the Jewish relation to the image as such, his experience in the laboratory looking under a microscope, and Anna O.'s disturbances of vision and her private theatre, the following few months in Paris will be a final set of impressions that will lead him to a unique view of patients and the uniqueness of human consciousness. Their treatment, not yet started by him personally, was only a few months' away. (When read with particular attention to Freud's repeated themes, something more than a general impression comes about). Given his view of patients in the Salpêtrière for a few short months – their presence and their role in being exhibited – Freud would make the direction already sensed more definitive. The relatively short experience, from October 1885 to February 1886, introduced Freud to a specific context for the examination of patients generally diagnosed as hysteric. The basis for one diagnosis was dependent on another; and there lay the problem for Freud as someone who was on a threshold and did not quite know how to move beyond it. If there were any doubts and hesitations, in Paris he overcame them and committed himself to another way of thinking and, then, back in Vienna, to a new psychotherapeutic practice. Heritage and heredity: in Paris, Freud placed himself between them. He was not, like Charcot, "a prisoner of empirical evidence," nor was he "focused in particular on his patients' family history"[8] in terms of inherited illnesses. Here is the fundamental difference: the family "history" would indeed be crucial, but not through biological heredity. Rather, the factor was one of experience; or, to use a familiar word, internal "image" as used by Katrin Shultheiss between the mind and the brain, experience or biology.[9]

The obituary has been chosen as a starting point and to see one of Freud's many memories; the combination of the personal and the professional places us in a context from which to then be more specific both about Charcot and Freud, their professional relationship, and then both similarities and divergences. Before the obituary, a short note included in Freud's 1906 Preface to his collection of shorter writings on the theory of the neuroses from the years 1893–1906 is a personal one. The passing of time since his short period in Paris, the death of Charcot, as well as the considerable work accomplished by Freud in what seemed to him a defining period of more than 20 years in the development of psychoanalysis, gave him the opportunity to make one more acknowledgement. All his autobiographical writings would be equally conscientious. In the Preface, he wrote:

> The fact that I have put my Obituary of J.-M. Charcot at the head of this collection of my short papers should be regarded not only as the repayment of a debt of gratitude, but also as an indication of the point at which my own work branches off from the master's.
>
> (SE 3:5)

A distinction could be made: there is a difference between personal gratitude and a professional debt. The occasion to revisit Freud's numerous comments on his Paris experience with Charcot will give us a deeper, more complete sense of the development of his ideas on the neuroses. Bringing them together, consciously and methodically, adds one more element to our knowledge of Freud. Charcot's methods of treating the psychologically ill, leaving aside the moral judgements today quite common whenever hysteria is discussed, leave us with the obligation to examine them and, more importantly, see how Freud interpreted and understood them. How he did so, from the unified perspective of the possible illusion of the image, the allegory of the microscope, and Anna O.'s perception of her private theatre completes one period of his *Bildung* – a self-formation to be incorporated into the practice of psychoanalysis for the purpose of his patients' education. The obituary has been chosen as a starting point from which to then return to one of the most important period of Freud's life. Consciousness had been a formidable philosophical problem; transposed to the field of psychology (as he began to understand its complexity) any assumption about its unity had been shattered – as was obvious from the acts of the patients he saw in Paris. Our uncertainties, or personal directions, continue to this day. They are not exempt from analysis. How do we think back to 1885 with relevant observations? For Freud, there was no way for him to set aside all he had learnt from discussing the case of Anna O. and moving in his own direction. One symptom, disassociation, was for him already an aspect of the split consciousness. "Freud and Breuer consider the crisis as a dissociation of the content of consciousness, reflecting the return of an unconscious traumatic memory."[10] The hysterical "crises" witnessed at the Salpêtrière were not the same as a quite-different epileptic seizure, for example, and so understood without relying on some abnormality in the function of the brain. The "disassociation," like the previous sense of a psychical split, occurred as a dislocation between one period and another.

The historical reality is now well known. There is no controversy in stating the obvious – as long as we always keep Freud in mind as someone who was highly sceptical of any relation between heredity and mental illness. "The 1880's marked the heyday of hereditarianism in France."[11] The consensus could be confirmed, even if we also acknowledge the debates taking place at the société medico-psychologique and the particular viewpoints of other authorities beside Charcot – like Valentin Magnan at the Sainte-Anne asylum who, according to Dowbiggin, were working on their own individual theories with a measure of independence. Freud had moved beyond that connection prior to 1885 and so arrived in Paris as a researcher but in no way unprepared to question the professional assumption of the authorities of the times. Charcot's school of neuropathology was the most well known; the field was filled with a number of individuals who were essentially pursuing the same kind of research, each with their own subtleties and orientations under the guidance of Charcot. How Freud diverged can be recollected from history and experience. He did "branch off," in a direction in which the metaphor, of tree and branch, may not be accurate enough. As always, turning to his writings gives us an access to both him and the times. The obituary he wrote for Charcot leaves us with personal memories; taking note of what he chose to include does not relieve us of the responsibility of being more thorough and of returning, postmortem, to the influence of an individual who, in 1885, was recognized as a world-leader in his field.

Since we have followed Freud and his transition from the scientific laboratory to the clinic and the examination of human beings who were suffering from various maladies of the mind, we can note, first of all, the unity of a certain kind of method with the development of Freud's depth-psychology in one of its formative stages. When we notice the repetition of words such as examination and investigation as they relate to a scientific method of observation, we can also take note of the beginning of not so much as a transformation in his conduct as a man of science and/or medicine, but rather a necessary supplement we can rightly call aesthetic as long as the word does not mislead us into thinking about the sensibility in strictly artistic ways. Or, to be less determined in terms of a conclusion at this point, Charcot's entire relationship to patients and the clinic was inseparable from a number of disciplines: the scientific, the medical, and then artistic forms that were all incorporated, each in their own way, at the Salpêtrière. To be *cultured,* at the time, required one to be interdisciplinary in one's knowledge and profession. Did Freud *see* patients without immediately imposing an explanation *on* them? Did he realize how the life and acts and emotions of a person in an institution was not at all conducive to learning about them (as human beings) with a long and complex life-history? His personal practice, started in only a few months' time, is an adoption of Breuer's personal treatment of a patient; it also marks the strongest possible contrast with a patient in an institution as large as the Salpêtrière.[12]

How does Freud represent both himself as an individual thinker and as someone who would go on to revolutionize our understanding of the psyche as well as the nature of perception, itself determined by the conscious ego and other, more concealed dynamics of the psyche? Although Freud is talking about Charcot, he has (by 1893) understood his own development as a scientist, a doctor, and a clinician.

> He exposed himself to all the chances of an examination, all the errors of a first investigation; he would put aside his authority on occasion and admit – in one case that he could arrive at no diagnosis and in another than had been deceived by appearances.
>
> (SE 3:18)

*Deceived by appearances.* The remarks are as autobiographical as they are a eulogy. All the concepts are there for us to witness with clarity; one has to notice the cluster of themes. They are all of a kind. Freud's own developing analysis is made possible by the consistency of a method involving examination, investigation, and finally a diagnosis of signs requiring subtle interpretations. Theory, among doctors and, as a fact, among anyone who is motivated by a certain discipline, has the capacity to distort and deceive. In other words, we can deceive ourselves, especially when it comes to signs, on the body or as expressed by the patient in many forms of acting-out. Can we not immediately recognize one of the most far-reaching of psychoanalytic insights when the unconscious is recognized for its effect in distorting perception – that is, seeing a convincing reality when Freud realized it could also be delusion and, soon identified, as a projection for defence or any number of other self-protecting measures by the neurotic?

Freud's respect for his teacher is also a sign of an independence of mind and (as we saw with the "Preliminary Communication" in the *Studies on Hysteria*) how far he had developed his own thinking and practice. Before he arrived in Paris, Freud had already come to a suspicion, if not yet a conclusion, about the difference between biology and the mind or, stated differently, between heredity and acquisition. Freud concentrated on one difference: if heredity could not be adequate as an explanation for psychological illness, he had only one place to go – towards consciousness and, ultimately, the nature of the psyche as a complex dynamic. "So greatly did Charcot overestimate heredity as a causative agent that he left no room for the acquisition of nervous illness" (SE 3:23). *Heredity and acquisition*: the distinction Freud makes during the obituary was already a position he was struggling with prior to arriving in Paris and leaning, against consensus, to a less positivistic explanation.

That one difference, already intuited early on, would be repeated and accentuated, as he did in one of the introductory statements of "The Aetiology of Hysteria." Freud says,

> As you known, in the view of the influential school of Charcot heredity alone deserves to be recognized as the true cause of hysteria, while all the other noxae of the most various nature and intensity only play the part of incidental causes, of 'agents provocateurs.'
>
> (SE 3:191)

What he saw – both from clinicians and patients, in the nature of a transference later to become central to psychoanalysis and to the understanding of any relationship – allowed Freud to take one more step from biology to the psyche. The sentence alone can set us now towards the final section of our study on Freud's development of psychoanalytic perception and how the once-traditional view of physiological heredity as the most readily accepted theory for the origin of nervous illness was finally transformed into the psychical and experiential account of neuroses. The neuroses could indeed be inherited from one's family. The inheritance, however, did not occur at the level of biology – in our modern language, genetically – but through the accumulation of day-to-day experiences within the dynamics of *any* family. Freud already knew too much about one individual, Anna O., and her family experiences – taking care of an ill and dying father, for example – to believe that biology, heredity, could account for the many intricate aspects of her mental illness.

The characteristics he emphasizes for Charcot were equally true for Freud himself insofar as he was able to unify reflection and perception. A *culture* (that is, an entire Western history) was a foundation with innumerable levels, some of them specifically individual. Freud recognized such a culture in Charcot.

> He had the nature of an artist – he was, as he himself said, a 'visuel,' a man who sees. Here is what he himself told us about his method of working. He used to look again and again at the things he did not understand, to deepen his impression of them day by day, till suddenly an understanding of them dawned on him.
>
> (SE 3:12)

These "things," one imagines, are the patients' appearances and expressions, physical and verbal. How much understanding was achieved is, for us, less a mystery to uncover than to wonder at his public method – which was, first, highly theatrical and based, in part, on displaying patients to an audience.

Given the previous section on Freud's training as a physician and scientist, it is hard not to regard him in the same way and of also taking about himself at the same time as writing a eulogy about Charcot. The additional comment should lead us much further into Freud's unique abilities. "In his mind's eye the apparent chaos presented by the continual repetition of the same symptoms then gave way to order." According to the method he had developed in the examination of his difficult patients, Freud could identify and share a certain affinity with a procedure: "the eye could travel over a long series of ill-defined cases." In this particular section of the obituary, we see Freud giving his teacher and mentor a tribute while also recognizing some of the same developments in himself and due to his experiences long before his student days and his chosen medical profession. We should not forget, as is essential to psychoanalysis, that a connection is tethered by many different and sometimes unnoticed ties. "He might be heard to say," Freud stresses again, "that the greatest satisfaction a man could have was to see something new – that is, to recognize it as new; and he remarked again and again on the difficulty and value of this kind of 'seeing'" (SE 3:12). This quintessential language, as humanistic as it is scientific, would be infinitely repeated; aligning this with our first discussion to a revelation should present no difficulties. Should we now bring our attention to the one element of Breuer's experience with Anna O. that he intuitively understood and then more or less consciously repressed? Over and over again, the obituary presents Charcot less as a scientist than as an aesthetically sensitive individual whose ultimate interest, as a doctor, was a perceptual one. In the *New Introductory Lectures on Psychoanalysis*, during a period when Freud's focus was on ego-psychology – that is, therapeutically striving to making the ego strong against its three opponents (the id, super-ego, and the external world) – Freud wrote that "in ego-psychology it will be difficult to escape what is universally known; it will rather be a question of *new ways of looking* at things and new ways of arranging them than a new direction" (SE 22:60). Freud nevertheless tells us something essential about himself and how psychoanalysis was created in the first place. *A new way of seeing*: such had been essential for *all* innovations – in religion, science, and art. One human characteristic was fundamental.

In retrospect, and during a time when Freud had embarked on the ever-more distinct method of psychoanalysis, the writing serves as a transition towards his own self-analysis and disclosure of others – all in the context of a medical procedure, and a therapy, that would forever be aligned with a scientific method that expanded the horizons of analysis. He continues the obituary:

> He would ask why it was that in medicine people only see what they have already *learned to see*. He would say that it was wonderful how one was suddenly able to see new things – new states of illnesses – which must be probably as old as the human race; and that he had to confess to himself that he now *saw a number of things* which he had overlooked for thirty years in his hospital wards.

The italics are mine. One comment can be here emphasized and as one more supplement to the all-important faculty of perception, most especially for a doctor who was attempting to find causes and origins to mysterious afflictions. There were no "signs," as such, on the body; and yet a patient *acted out* a whole variation of physical movements, facial features, and enigmatic forms of communication in order to express something indirectly. Did Freud have a particular understanding of the comment that, for the time being, was kept to himself? Did he not ultimately realize that the analysis of patients who were confined to a psychiatric institution were already determined by a place and historical set of procedures by which to recognize certain symptoms and not others – like the origin of hysteria? Just as he had learnt to look in a certain way by reading the Bible "story," he at one point had come to the realization that in order to understand the often mysterious nature of mental illness, it was best to do so under quite different conditions than the ones found in the environment of a hospital and, more seriously, within one of the institutions associated with severe stigma and ostracism. How fitting, then, for Freud: by calling the Salpêtrière "that museum of clinical facts," he gave himself one other metaphor by which to explain the personal experience during his time in Paris. A first crucial distinction could not be more all-important. Breuer, the physician, visited patients in their homes. Freud was only a few months away from creating a new atmosphere for patients in his own home. In the "Future Prospects of Psycho-analytic Therapy," Freud mentioned the beginning of his treatment of neuroses in what he called "my modest abode" (SE 11:146). The care of a patient in a room that had not the slightest appearance to a doctor's office and was the farthest thing in appearance from a psychiatric institution is one of Freud's innovations that should be much more emphasized. A Hippocratic oath, when considered in the light of 19th-century psychiatry, could only lead from a massive institution to the privacy of a home where the ambience was personal – and, not to minimize one important factor, the design of its décor, including the comfortable sofa.

By the end of the obituary, we begin to glimpse Freud more and more; and though, from everything we know about him, there was never a time when he felt to be "under a shadow," his own self-possession comes to the fore when he writes, "Among the circle of young men whom he [Charcot] thus gathered round him and made into participants in his researches, a few eventually rose to a consciousness of their own individuality and made a brilliant name for themselves" (SE 3:15). Is there any reason that Freud does not mention any of these "brilliant" individuals by name? We could, without fail, mention Pierre Janet, an individual who deserves his own unique credit in the history of treating mental illness. Doing so does increase a certain responsibility that, here, cannot be met since he would be a lengthy digression. There are many virtues that Freud personally had and that became essential to psychoanalysis – for therapy and for contributions in writing: at a time when he was beginning to think more deeply about groups and the nature of society, the virtues of originality, creativity, and independence cannot but fail to impress a reader who senses the nature of Freud's character and intelligence. The metaphor of "rising" to consciousness is one of a few choices. Elevation is one. Just as he would uncover the mystery of dream interpretation first and foremost in a personal way, so too did his knowledge of consciousness increase in Paris – first in himself and then in the way he understood the interior life of the patients he saw.

There are so many inter-relationships, of interests, scientific and psychological, that are almost too numerous to keep in mind and to account for: in all his biographical accounts, as well as their correspondence and, finally, the obituary, Freud clearly portrays the experience in Paris with a particular language. One cannot but fail to notice the one repeated characteristic that struck Freud the most; the reason may be an intimate one, in other words, the perceptive ability that he discusses, more than once, was also one of his own most valued characteristics. The insight, to put it one way, could only have been recognized by someone who, over and above the scientific and the psychological, was philosophically sensitive to the mystery of human consciousness and its concealed reality. Ultimately, Freud had been preoccupied by one fundamental problem: if consciousness could never be accessed by any of the sciences, despite their promise in making new discoveries based on tried-and-tested accomplishments, then how could psychology be developed enough, enhanced enough, to reach a still hazy human reality? Darwin had called his investigations into the origin and evolution of life his "mystery of mysteries." Freud had his own; and no science known to him was capable of being illuminating enough to his satisfaction. Only because of his conscious situation, between science and psychology, could he maintain the tension and the difference between one and the other without making a hasty judgement and reaching a conclusion that might satisfy others and yet would always leave him far from confident. One belief can be repeated again and again. In the context of a preface to a work by Theodor Reik, Freud writes, "Psychoanalysis was born out of medical necessity. It sprang from the need for bringing help to neurotic patients" (SE 17:259). He continues and again stresses his divergence from the certainties of the times: "Its further course led it away from the study of somatic determinants of nervous disease to an extent that was bewildering to physicians." The obituary was one more recollection for Freud to see just how far he had come from a time when a "split consciousness," in patients, was consciously and rationally understood to be an intellectual process as well. The achievement of a consciousness determined by the ego was a momentous event.

> When human beings began to think, they were, as is well known, forced to explain the external world anthropomorphically by means of a multitude of personalities *in their own image*; chance events, which they interpreted superstitiously, were thus actions and manifestations of persons. They behaved, therefore, like paranoics, who draw conclusions from insignificant signs.
> (SE 6:259)

In *The Psychopathology of Everyday Life*, Freud chose a specific term to explain how reality was formed "in their own image," (my emphasis in the quote) and that perfectly illustrated the psychical process of projection and what it can create – without any awareness at all since the process was unconscious. What Freud called "endopsychic perception" was one of his great discoveries; because if certain realities were *"nothing but psychology projected into the external world,"* then psychoanalysis had both made a discovery and way to alter both internal and external life. Philosophers (like Kant) had only interpreted consciousness and the world. Freud proposed how both could be changed one individual at a time. Not to be forgotten as an equally important innovation, the doctor was now fully implicated in both diagnosis and cure.[13]

Given the attempt to more specifically define a Freudian phenomenology, we can turn briefly to a specifically medical concept as it relates to *nosography*. Although the subsequent description and classification of a general neurosis or hysteria in particular follows an original diagnosis (by looking at symptoms) there may be a unique kind of observation already evident for Freud prior to going to Paris. If the first part of our study has correctly identified three of the fundamental influences of Freud's life and thinking – Judaism, the microscope, Anna O. – can we now begin to complement his experiences while working with Charcot and his reflections on a cultural reality obvious to him because of his stay in Paris? The general idea of diagnosis and, more particularly, an individual discernment was part of the daily practice of the examination of patients at the Salpêtrière; the experience of living in Paris and his appreciation of the culture was adding something to his clinical situation. One question can be asked: *"what exactly was Freud's complex position toward diagnostic issues?"*[14] We are, with this question, at the point of Freud's originality insofar as all the knowledge available at the time and as taught by the recognized authorities in the field was, for him, felt to be incomplete. There was, in any *objective* diagnosis of the symptoms of a patient, something missing; an essential experience, recognized by Freud in the very foundation of psychoanalysis, was not at all taken into account and precisely because medical science required a certain objectivity. Clinicians were focused on a medical/scientific explanation and so looked past, and beyond, the individual patient. Researchers who have focused on Freud (and not historical conditions) are drawn to his individuality as he came upon insights and discoveries. They eventually became explicit and systematic. "His theories no longer cohered with the ideas of treating the mind as a mere epiphenomenon of the brain."[15] He had found an even more exacting discovery. The appearance of the conscious mind itself was an epiphenomena of a dynamic unconscious that required all his attention to reveal. He was now a long way from the specific research in Ernst Brücke's laboratory – but not at all distant from a thinking he was beginning to unify and, in many ways, according to the dynamics of his own unconscious and the intimacy between a certain Jewish understanding and the perceptions of microscopic seeing. The one important divergence, for Freud, proved to be Charcot's conviction in the hereditary aetiology of neuroses. A fact can be repeated for emphasis: "For Charcot, as for his psychiatric colleagues, this position had the attributes of scientific respectability and at the same time kept the methodology of experimental science subordinate to conventional clinical and anatomical modes of investigation."[16] There were other "modes" that can be more closely examined.

Charcot's famous and well-attended lectures were characterized by a dramatic self-presentation as well as the use of images and illustrations. Freud might not have been as captivated by the images used to substantiate a point; nor was he much impressed by the showcase of patients in a public setting and with Charcot talking about then in their presence and, as can be imagined, with very personal discussions of their conditions. The theatricality of Charcot's lectures and public examinations were methods that were quite alien for someone who had personal and individual relationship with his patients in the early days of the cathartic method employed by Breuer, not to mention the later decision to adopt the very private, very discreet situation of psychoanalysis on the couch. If we can reconstruct Freud's attendance both in and out of the clinic, for the doctors working in the hospital setting of the Salpêtrière or the wider public attending the lectures, more than a few "methods" must have struck him with a sense of incompleteness. One affirmation can be made – and in part as an introduction to his developing perception: while Charcot predicated his analysis on the *physical manifestations* of one psychological illness or another – hence his use of drawings and photographs to confirm his diagnoses – Freud was already moving in entirely different directions.[17]

In light of Freud's *testimony*, and the occasion of an obituary that did not leave him unaffected in terms of memory, we can see how the experience in Paris was a fundamental one and a definitive turning point. Although, as his autobiography has shown on numerous occasions, Freud's evaluation for the origin of psychoanalysis was traced to Breuer, the period of Freud's personal relationship with the scientist and physician who treated Anna O. with the cathartic method was, according the several inter-connected arguments so far, one of a few (chosen though by no means exhaustive) that comprehensively led Freud from one stage of thinking to another: his originality was, in the end, revealed in the ability to unify a number of different impressions, in history and in himself. Testimony and autobiography: both have been emphasized for being parts of a whole, reflectively for himself and in relation to others. Our relationships, which is to say our transferences, with others in life or in history, go a long way to providing us with a more complete portrait of any individual and in ways that extend far beyond any narrowly conceived ideas of history. The psychical can exceed the actual in ways that psychoanalysis has informed us about.

Presenting, for a final time, a defence of Freud's scientific credentials may be necessary for some readers. They are not the least bit in doubt when one becomes familiar with his early studies, in the laboratory, in the clinic, and the publications coming out of his research. The transition to Paris and this relatively short stay can be given a widely different cultural context. If anyone is hesitant about recognizing Freud as a scientist, then the state of neurology and psychiatry (in the Greek sense of a *psyche-iatros*, a doctor of the soul) is put to the test at the Salpêtrière.

There are several cultural realities in evidence at the same time. There has been sufficient knowledge about the tortured history of mental illness and its treatment in and out of institutions. Hysteria: the word alone is, today, the cause of just as much fantasy as reality. An introduction to Freud's travel has been introduced as a desire to be free of a rigid context of study and assessment; the circumstances of his study grant are, one hopes, also an indication of how others, superiors in the bureaucratic sense, viewed him and his abilities. What he saw in Paris is, for us, a last chapter in the early development of Freud's phenomenology of perception as it was enhanced by an entire history in culture and in himself: the Jewish attitude towards the image and an associated sensualism, Bacon's writing on the idols of the age and the experience of the microscope, and Anna O.'s disturbances of vision and the private theatre she fantasized to relieve herself, tragically, of her anguished condition. In Paris, both the life of the patients at the Salpêtrière and the ways clinicians diagnosed, analyzed, and then represented will become one more experience that adds to the others and leads Freud, in 1886, to establishing his own individual experiments with a proper treatment.

One of the concluding statements in the obituary should be kept in mind not for the sections to come, but rather for the third and final part and the one concentrating on a few of the most significant clinical experiences. Freud's noticeable and respectful adulation for his teacher is also a sign of an independence of mind and how far his own clinical practice had changed. We should by no means overlook this momentous change in the method of treating psychological afflictions and more specifically how important the immediate surroundings for a patient actually were. "So greatly did Charcot overestimate heredity as a causative agent that he left no room for the acquisition of nervous illness" (SE 3:23). The sentence alone can set us now towards the next section of our study on Freud's development of psychoanalytic perception and how the once-traditional view of physiological heredity as the most readily accepted theory for the origin of nervous illness was finally transformed into the psychical and experiential origins of neuroses.[18]

In the "Report on My Studies in Paris and Berlin," Freud again stressed how Charcot's method was "led by the favourable character of his material to the study of the chronic nervous diseases and their pathological anatomical basis" (SE 1:7). One word, for Freud, changed everything; for he would come to see the problem of chronic nervous diseases according to pathological psychical basis. That one "turnaround" would have a number of origins. One other article, in part on sensory-motor physiology, is not going to be easily accessible. There are, nonetheless, conclusions by the author that reaffirms one foundational argument even though we might not be able to fully understand just how scientific Freud's studies were. One more conclusion can be read and to begin to look ahead both to his association with Breuer and to the period of study in Paris with Charcot – someone who continued to believe in "lesions" even though autopsies of hysterics did not reveal any observable damage to the brain. "Freud's analysis in his earlier work on hysteria had shown that pathology could arise not only because areas had been damaged, or connections cut, but due to a pathological *organization* of nervous elements."[19] He did not need to see any kind of anatomical investigation – either from a corpse or the signs on a body; instead, the theatrical display of patients made him sharpen his vision, just as he had done in Vienna in a laboratory.

## Hysterics at the Salpêtrière

Freud's obituary of Charcot has left us with the memories of an individual who, as a scientist, neurologist, and the administrator of a clinic housing thousands of patients, relied on his powers of observation and on the discernment of his perception to see what, before him, had mostly eluded others. Freud's recollections all emphasized Charcot as a *visuel*. Still, he had seen with a perspective that then allowed Freud to extend it. His diagnostic abilities as a physician and scientist are beyond question when it comes to such as diseases as Amyotrophic lateral sclerosis (ALS), which in France is still called Charcot's disease. His personal characteristics, as a medical practitioner treating nervous disorders, were the ones Freud recalled with the most ease. The memory he repeats more than once recalls Charcot's perceptive ability – which Freud shared to the point of a positive transference, and perhaps something more demanding when physiology and heredity were no longer essential to his diagnoses. One shared commonality diverged. Psychology and pathological anatomy were to remain, for Freud, connected at a distance. The difference would only increase over the years. Understandably, Charcot's achievements convinced him of the efficacy of his own clinical-anatomical method. He had, after all, made a number of important discoveries in the field of medicine. The diagnosis of physiological diseases was impressive and, in a moment, will be mentioned for the historical record and then to see how today's medical professionals (neurologists and neuro-psychiatrists) differ so strikingly from academics in the human sciences. Charcot's perceptive ability – aided by his prodigious memory as well as his aesthetic sensibilities – can be more specifically defined and set in a broad context, first from his childhood and then from his interest in the visual arts, in themselves and in the lecture hall where he used visual demonstrations for his pedagogy. However, once we move from one kind of recollection, the obituary, to another, one difference has to be noted. Freud's experience will be contrasted, shortly, with an array of modern assessments of both Charcot and the illness called hysteria. The idea of "the dramaturgy of Dr. Jean-Martin Charcot" and his "famous (infamous) treatment of hysteria"[20] will be mentioned so as to, also, provide a portrait of our modern academic culture. The history of hysteria, as *perceived from the present*, tells us more about academics than about the 19th century. All the critical theory in the world will not make our knowledge of Freud any more informed or his interest in the actual experience, and suffering, of individual patients better understood. Our historical inquiries, if motivated by exposing hysteria as a *category*, will not be able to understand the nature of an experience, or its meanings. We can judge "Charcot and the infamous Lecons du Mardi"[21] as much as we care to; nothing will come of this kind of historical condemnation, certainly no understanding. Easy judgements will be perpetuated and moral comfort extended to those who need it most, for themselves and to be recognized for their feelings.

The passing of time since his short period in Paris, the death of Charcot, as well as the considerable work accomplished by Freud in what no doubt seemed to him a defining period of 20 years, gave him the opportunity to reveal one more of his intellectual origins. The occasion to revisit Freud's numerous comments on his Paris experience with Charcot will give us a deeper, more complete sense of the development of his ideas of neurotic illness. Bringing them together, consciously and methodically, adds one more element to our knowledge of Freud and the origins of psychoanalysis. In *An Autobiographical Study*, Freud tells us about two facts. They can again be emphasized.

> Even before I went to Paris, Breuer told me about a case of hysteria which, between 1880 and 1882, he had had treated in a peculiar manner which had allowed him to penetrate deeply into the causation and significance of hysterical symptoms ... He repeatedly read me pieces of the case history, and I had an impression that it accomplished more towards an understanding of neuroses than any previous observation.
>
> (SE 20:19)

Freud's preparation for his stay in Paris has to be specifically recalled beyond one more memory. "I determined to inform Charcot of these discoveries when I reached Paris, and I actually did so. But the great man showed no interest in my first outline of the subject, so I never returned to it and allowed it to pass from my mind." In fact, Anna O.'s case history did not pass from his mind; and never would. It served him as one of the most important transitions in Freud's thinking about neurotic illness as a whole and the way his contemporary world viewed psychological afflictions. If only a material basis could be discovered, an enigma could be solved. An entire culture, in terms of the medical-psychiatric establishment, had to be questioned before the truth of the psyche could be uncovered. A few brief elements can be mentioned; they are disparate and tied irreducibly to history and the perception (and reality) of distinct eras. As we anticipate what Freud learnt in Paris and then the period from 1886 to the publication of *The Interpretation of Dreams*, one sense of him, as an individual, can now be hazarded. Neville Symington writes: "a piece of knowledge may not be understood and its significance allowed to startle the mind unless it is within a pattern of understanding to which it is related."[22] As we follow Freud during his Paris sojourn, it seems more and more evident that the knowledge of the times was, for him, incomplete; if a "pattern of understanding" is to be mentioned, then Freud became capable (because of the themes outlined thus far since his archaic heritage and the meaning of a trans-historical transference) of seeing something that proved to be impossible for others. In Paris, Freud traced a history and, at the end, found himself with his own original creativity when everything he had discovered was properly included in a systematic way for going forward.

Several researchers have traced an extended history and made a connection that strikes one for its *medieval* references. Nicole Edelman writes that "the major hysterical seizures of La Salpêtrière that Charcot demonstrated in the amphitheatre of his hospital recalled the days of demonic possession."[23] Needless to say, the presentation of hysterics in a public setting was, in a specially built amphitheatre, a curious mixture of the medical and the theatrical. Although nurses (especially those who were nuns) were most susceptible to fantasy interpretations, one imagines the scientifically trained doctors had moved beyond the perceptive limits of the theological past. One observation has been made by a number of commentators who have called into question the medical institution of treating mental illness and at the Salpêtrière in particular. Charcot's classification of hysteria "feeds off well-established visual iconography developed in conjunction with notions of demonic possession and exorcisms."[24] It is hard to imagine, however, that Charcot, or anyone working with him, had any such "notions." The reference to visual iconography is important; but perhaps not for the reasons imagined by Bronfen and the many critics who, like her, have made academic interpretations about the historical subject of hysteria. When we keep in mind, as we now should with special care, Freud's knowledge of Anna O.'s symptoms as we have presented them, we should attempt to understand Freud's perceptions before our historical critiques. The presuppositions of late 20th-century academic culture are more obvious and unconvincing than ever. A psychoanalytic assessment, which will be inevitable later despite being urgent now, will be instructive about one development in liberal culture.

The various forms of Anna O.'s acting out in her private theatre, presents us with a much different view of the internal drives of an illness. The connection between "possession" and mental illness has the most ancient of roots. When we combine Christian theology, the principles of the theatre, and the introduction of photography into the imaginary perceptions of mental illness, our research in the present takes on all kinds of intricate characteristics. The facts about the history of psychiatry in Paris in 1885 are well known; the various disciplines alongside the scientific have also been identified. One does wonder how an entire medical community dealt with the theology and theatrics of hysterics and then, to add to the already complicated mix, photographed their faces and bodily postures and classified each of them according to theories that were unlikely to do anything more than describe what everyone could see. "When Charcot began his work, possession was no longer believed in but all of the other causes were still clamouring for attention."[25] One era had been, in one way, overcome; a historical fantasy of possession was replaced by another world-view – scientific, in its own way and perhaps overly optimistic about the power of its physicalism. Our era, on the other hand (believing itself to be academically sophisticated and, in its own way, self-possessed) has led itself towards a distortion of the human due to the most abstract of theoretical principles.

How was Freud's perception developing at the time? Can we, with some degree of confidence, speculate about his *thinking* as he witnessed both the procedures of examination and the identification of hysterical acting-out? Did he, as an independently minded observer, notice a strange reciprocity between medical professionals and their patients, a transference that was mutually binding? Theological fantasies had been dispelled by the exacting work and thinking of scientists. The modern substitutes were not, however, free of their own presuppositions. They were not superstitious as such; and yet a certain kind of conviction did make for lapses in perception and judgement. Are academics today no less vulnerable to the easy diagnoses of a *social problem* as the cause of hysteria? And was it not Freud who, in his own way, had a message for us today? In "Hysteria," he opens with a historical assessment; academics today are not free from it, in their own way and according to their own certainties. "The name 'hysteria' originates from the earliest times of medicine and is a precipitate of the prejudice, overcome only in our own days, which links neuroses with diseases of the female sexual apparatus" (SE 1:41). Our modern theories have merely inverted the disease: where the uterus was, society now is. In the meantime, the individual is theoretically sacrificed for the sake of one category – like "patriarchy," one concept intended to be, also, psychiatric.

Hysteria: today the word conjures up all kinds of fantasies of our own. Our view of the 19th century has certainly been influenced by one outstanding phenomenon, which can be surveyed, in part, when we are not so eager to judge.[26] Krohn's word, *elusive*, may be the best one to adopt.[27] There are others, including enigma. The enigma is, also, our own; our perceptions of history have been skewed by a worldview that has become definitive if not, quite, monolithic. Exceptions remain for anyone who does not follow an academic party line. The concept of hysteria does serve many of our ideological commitments, to the detriment of understanding the experience of the mentally ill and, more importantly for us, Freud's experiences.

Georges Didi-Huberman's *The Invention of Hysteria* has summarized one attitude towards the history of hysteria and recognized unquestionable aspects of the treatment of the illness in the 19th century. And, despite this and many other works, we would have more information on the institution of psychiatry and yet be no better aware of Freud's specific experiences at the time of his visit to the Salpêtrière. Didi-Huberman points out how the clinic operated according to "spectacular evidence," the former a word that forces us to more closely analyze the relationship between the theatre and the spectator in a way that defies simple scientific observation and catalogue – a procedure that would be supplemented by photography.[28] Snippets from reviews are informative since they reveal one or two impressions. In the context of one review, Sander Gilman writes about "the world of the Parisian psychiatric clinic and its most important disciple, Sigmund Freud."[29] The word "disciple" is more than overstated. We have Freud's testimony and his work for such a relationship (Freud as a disciple) to be mythology. Gentlemanly deference, as one expects from a cultured 19th-century individual, is quite different than being a "disciple." In any event, the Greek *mathesis,* usually translated as disciple, is more commonly a student. Any such belief misunderstands Freud's professional relationship with Charcot. The definitions of hysteria inevitably leave us with uncertainty. "A wide variety of somatic (perceptual and motor) and psychic disturbances may appear in the absence of any known organic pathology, or may accompany organic illness and grossly exaggerate its effects."[30] May appear, may accompany; nothing is excluded, and so we are left with a possible and/and that ultimately demands a choice to be made. The psyche-soma relation is unavoidable. How we choose to think about their relation comes down to a human interest. One impression has been adopted by many commentators. All the sociological observations, such as "the medical *victims* of the Salpêtrière,"[31] brings us no closer to understanding Freud at the time and how his thinking was becoming more and more independent – as can be appreciated more at this point now that all our themes can be brought together as one culmination. Summing them up, more than once, serves to highlight the arguments so far: the Jewish relationship to the image, the allegorical significance of the microscope, Anna's O.'s private theatre, and Charcot as a *visuel* and the theatrical presentation of hysterics. Anyone who has focused on the limits of a medical society, as a sociologist or social critic, will be unable to reflect, with any kind of impartiality or insight, into Freud's thinking at the time.

We can, with the information available to us, proceed with a critique of the historical conditions of the mentally ill in the late 19th century; but that has been well known for quite some time and in ways that are pertinent at the cultural level beyond the medical/therapeutic. Mary Gluck, for example, has drawn much wider connections: "hysteria was also an integral part of popular culture,"[32] incorporated into one of the many forms of representational entertainment, theatrical and otherwise, and inseparable from Charcot's *Leçons du Mardi* and his highly popular Friday evening lectures.[33] As for Charcot, he was not so close-minded that he rejected ideas based on assumptions. He even wrote an essay on "faith-healing" (*la foi qui guérit*) in 1892, a late-enough date to show us that, despite his broad scientific training, mysterious phenomena could be examined with some objectivity. The assumptions of his audience, however, were as disparate as their private beliefs, cultural or religious. The people in attendance, as a whole, are not in question. Our sole focus is on Freud's experience and what he ultimately took away from Paris – and what he left behind. His time in Paris separates a before and after in the foundations of psychoanalysis.

The 19th century may have viewed itself as free from the superstitions of the past; the remnants, especially in terms of psychological illness and the bizarre displays of patients, could become active again. In a world where the metaphysical and the medical were not so divided from each other – in the popular imagination if not by doctors – one can understand how the hysteric was also seen as otherworldly. Physical contortions could be so extreme as to seem nearly impossible. The miraculous and the demonic, as signs beyond the real, had their own powers of persuasion. Charcot's evolutions in the diagnosis of hysteria did not completely free him from a prior history of physiognomic speculations and how the various changes in the bodily postures, physical gestures, and facial expressions of the ill could be interpreted and classified. There was, in addition, an equally intrusive *metaphysical* set of fantasies and religious pathologies as they imagined the ill and their "possessed" bodies; the presence of a demonological influence, despite the scientific attitude of clinicians and their commitments to hard empiricism, was not insignificant. Two different sensibilities of cultural realities (the physiognomic and the demonological) made itself felt in the wards of the Salpêtrière as modernity became prominent through the recognition of fundamental differences.

The reconstruction of the 19th-century treatment of the mentally ill can begin from one extreme at a time when the superstitions of the past had not been fully overcome by the advancements in reason and science. As far as the idea of demonic possession, the association was only possible because of religious belief and due to the bizarre nature of all kinds of illnesses, some organic, others psychological, on occasion a combination of both that made diagnosis extremely challenging. Concentrating, for example, on the tendency of the hysteric to be histrionic, physically, in words, utterances, and sounds, Charcot's pedagogical method included putting patients on display. While the fantastical could turn to the demonic for an explanation, Charcot's science was also informed by an aesthetics made rational for the purpose of demonstration and observation. There are overlapping interests. For us, he is secondary to Freud's experience – which is to say, his knowledge of Charcot's medical discoveries, for one, and then the presuppositions of his methods. They were complicated by different influences. Aesthetic, first, from his childhood prior to his studies, and then informed by a medical and scientific focus.

Charcot cannot be neglected for his place in the history of medicine. Since he has been named "the father of neurology" and for his discoveries of several well-known afflictions – multiple sclerosis, ALS, Tourette's syndrome, and Parkinson's disease, to name but the ones generally known by everyone today – we can note the considerable difference between these degenerative diseases and the illness called, too broadly, hysteria. Narrowing down its specifics, Charcot had to recognize the difference, for example, between the physical effects of hysteria, such as convulsions, and epileptic seizures. As his "student," Freud was able to see firsthand how a large number of patients were diagnosed. The strictly neurological association, for Charcot, was not adopted by Freud since his own already emerging psychological ideas were incompatible with a mechanistic explanation of the effects as they were *displayed* physically. The hysteric was presented to a large audience during Charcot's public lectures. How Freud responded to the individuals he witnessed publicly, and during the rounds at the clinic, are nowhere on record; his impressions can be deduced from his own direction, which was already well on its way prior to arriving in Paris. The Anna O. case was omnipresent for him. The reasons have been outlined earlier. How the young Viennese woman under Breuer's care became the ur-patient of psychoanalysis can be reconstructed from the historical record. Freud made a connection that allowed him to recall Anna O.'s disturbances of vision with her private theatre. How so?

Jean-Martin Charcot incorporated visual art into his normal day-to-day practice of neurology. His innate artistic talents were due to his visual perception and remarkable memory. His drawings first started as a hobby and then later became scientific. His drawings correlated to his anatomo-clinical method and portrayed his patients' postures and clinical neurological signs.[34]

Owing to his early interests in art and his own artistic practice, we can now turn to, first, the displays of the hysterics of the Salpêtrière before an audience of public onlookers.

"In the classroom, Charcot presented a multi-media display of patients, anatomical diagrams, specimens for examination, and projection slides."[35] Comprehensively, this has been defined as a "medical scenography."[36] We have, then, quite divergent views of Charcot presented to us, which range from the demonological, the strictly scientific, the artistic and, today, the critical. At the outset, and placing them in the context of Freud's own testimony, we can follow most especially the relation between the generally medical and the artistic. There are other elements of the institution that we can also bring to our attention. Choosing the theatrical has two purposes. Freud was in an ideal and singular position to understand the patients that were displayed to a large audience during Charcot's lectures. We have to imagine him, as an onlooker, who can make the connection between the lesson as Charcot presents it and his interpretation – one based on his knowledge of the Anna O. case and, above all, both her disturbances of vision and her private theatre. How *we interpret* the scene depends on our interests and sensibilities. The theatrical and the scenic were all visual and exposed to perception. If the metaphor, or reality, of the theatre is to be retained, one form of perception and interpretation has to be added to others – including the post-mortem examination of the body (above all, the spine and brain), all with their own kinds of representation. Demonic possessions, autopsies, the theatre of hysterics: these were all part of the clinical picture at the time. The viewpoints are numerous and often contradictory; scholars, in their respective fields – especially when contrasted by the medical and the academic – provide us with decisions. We should need no reminder, from science, that a hypothesis, an experiment, and an observation cannot ever exclude the human subject who will inevitably be at the origin of a theory no less than its conclusion. Science, despite its excessive confidence in objectivity, never fails to remind us of ourselves and our conscious, and unconscious, contributions to our own knowledge.

Andrew Scull begins one chapter of his *Hysteria: The Disturbing History* with a description of the Salpêtriere and Charcot's methods of displaying his patients as a "spectacle and a circus." There were two kinds of spectacles, both of them dependent on a specific act of perception. Although Scull does not develop this one connection, he nevertheless mentions it as an essential part of the clinic as a whole. The appearances of the living and the dead, on the one hand as a living spectacle on stage, on the other hand as a corpse who would reveal, during an autopsy, any organic lesions on the brain or the spine and so confirm an anatomical theory. "Of necessity, this new hospital medicine required a constant supply of patients who would soon turn into corpses, for it was this never-failing availability of previously examined bodies that allowed the comparison of the living and the dead."[37] The "juxtaposition of clinical notes and autopsy reports is the foundation of the anatomo-clinical method, which connected clinical signs with anatomical lesions, championed in the second half of the twentieth century by neurologist Jean-Martin Charcot at the Salpêtrière hospital in Paris."[38] There are three interconnected kinds of examinations taking place in Charcot's hospital: one, the living body as it exhibits all the theatrical movements of the hysteric and for the attention of the audience; two, the photography of the hysteric in all its physical manifestation and, three, the post-mortem dissection in which the clinician will be allowed to, literally, see from himself – *autos-ipse*. Theatre, photography, post-mortem perception: the three are combined in such a way as to make visible the life and death of the hysteric. Whether we agree or not with the name of the Salpêtrière as a "Temple of Science," the 19th century had no doubts about its own productivity in advancing medical science and the diagnosis of previously unknown diseases. The difference between the post-mortem dissection of someone who had suffered from a degenerative disease that could be observed, say, in the brain or in the spine, and the autopsy of a hysteric confirmed, for Freud, an irreducible difference. Did he come to such a conclusion during his attendance of autopsies which, as he tells us in his "Paris Report," "I rarely missed" (SE 1:8).

We are, in 1886, at a turning point; for if Freud in Paris gives us a glimpse of the most "advanced" psychiatry at the time and the neurological emphasis by Charcot, the fundamental difference between one "hard" science and Freud's subtlety leads him away from anatomy (and certainly the anatomy of the dead body) to the psyche and its elusive nature from any purely physical analysis. Freud had been educated in the tradition of German *Bildung*. If he had developed, as a *humanist*, according to Jewish attitudes to perception, his microscopic analysis, and the reflection on Anna O.'s disturbances of vision, he was perhaps the only individual who, in Paris, could make the widest possible distinction between the exacting science of neurology as practiced at the time and his own inclinations – which were forcing him to turn in an almost opposite direction, away from physiology, anatomy, and ultimately the materialist emphasis on the understanding of a human being. The inquiry as a whole reaches this one point since, for Freud, the experience in Paris was to be a lasting one, and with a number of comparisons that would establish his individuality over and above all the experts in various fields at the time, including Charcot. Their relationship would continue, productively, until 1893. As Charcot's German translator, Freud would benefit from this association – in terms of a professional reputation and for his own legitimacy. "That Freud was in the company of such eminent scientists as Charcot goes a long way to explaining his need to have psychoanalysis accepted as a science."[39] And to be accepted as a scientist who could rely on the well-known work of the famous neurologist – as least in the eyes of others who, for their own reasons, could associate Freud with the science as conducted in Paris. The decade after Freud's Paris experience was to be one of a gradual distance from Charcot's expertise and reputation.

While Charcot was displaying his patients and inducing them to act out their own private conditions, Freud observed an impossible situation – for both patient and doctor; neither one nor the other could make real, in the form of conscious understanding, the origin and causes of the particular ailments being seen. Catharsis, for Freud, was both a form of therapy and a method by which to understand how the illness was created in the first place. Catharsis, for all its promise of a cure – which, as we know, was not a reality for Anna O. – nevertheless allowed Freud to make an all-important connection between the disturbances of vision and the ideational theatre. The perception in the present was filled with both actual (or fantasy) memories as well as unconscious projections. The medical observations as created by Charcot were effective when diagnosing, for example, the physical characteristics of neurological diseases such as Parkinson's; he could not, however, make the same connection when it came to the kind of hysteria that Freud suspected was psychical in nature, not at all organic. Did Freud recognize just how revolutionary his insights were – even if uncertain and incomplete? The entire breadth of science in the aftermath of Darwin's great discoveries turned out to be limited when it came to the understanding of a human element that was not connected to biology or, more precisely, to the brain. All of Charcot's considerable discoveries of his own had been neurological; hysteria or, more generally, the various forms of neuroses, had no biological basis and had all been caused by one or a number of experiences that were, in fact, or in fantasy, traumatic. While we can acknowledge the numerous instances of the critical theory of hysteria as an illness or the institution of the asylum as a whole, we would (by being fixated on historical conditions) fail to understand Freud's thinking at the time. Our interests are, in any case, always obvious. Amy Koerber is one of innumerable examples.

> The rhetoric of speculation such as Charcot was aimed at audiences of their fellow experts, whose expectations of scientific evidence underwent a steady increase between the seventeenth and the twentieth centuries. In response to the increasing demand for scientific evidence, the experts sought innovative empirical approaches to understanding and treating conditions such as hysteria.[40]

And yet, Charcot's methods of examination were far less about "scientific evidence" than, first of all, trying to understand the figure of the hysteric. More importantly, our historical interests are themselves responsible for drawing us away from Freud, in our case, and concentrating on larger social questions, of history and society and, unavoidably, the situation of women as the great majority of hysterics.

The return to Freud's recollection and the history of the period makes us aware of the complexity of the elements all coming together in a way that was not, at the time, fully understood. Freud needed much more time to come to an understanding of both the wide discrepancy in the medical fields and, more importantly, in himself. Our questions are endless; not all of them can be answered. Demonic possession, autopsies, theatrical displays of patients: every element leaves us with an array of possibilities. all of which were reflected on by Freud based on all his prior experiences. *Any* assessment of the history of psychiatry or its 19th-century specifics leaves little to the imagination as far as the methods of the care of patients is concerned. The impressions at the Salpêtriere were not, by much earlier standards, inhumane – which may not be saying very much to the moral historian. The assessments vary; and with good reason. Sander Gilman gives us one portrait. The opening, on science and perception, confirms my leading argument: observers, in the present, are one-sidedly preoccupied with themselves more than the condition of patients. The argument for a certain kind of *mistreatment* is hardly far-fetched. The perceptions by the doctor making the diagnosis was paramount. It does seem remarkable when reading the literature that the clinical picture appears to be far more important than any sense of a cure. One historical remnant can be repeated.

> Hysteria was a disease which, according to nineteenth century science, had to be seen to be understood. This Lineannean means of describing illnesses through the visible signs and symptoms (to use Jean Martin Charcot's terms, taken from the witch-hunting manuals of the Inquisition, the *stigmata* of the illness, for the stigmata diaboli which marked the bodies of the witch) dominated nineteenth-century European, but especially French, psychiatry.[41]

The situation was even worse once we take into consideration the use of photography in the clinic. The images of women, when looked at beyond their manifest appearance (of the grimaces of faces, open mouths, and protruding tongues) along with the peculiar postures, no longer can be looked at as medical or scientific. The conjunction of the demonic and the pornographic is not far apart when photographs are examined specifically according to the postures of the body.[42] The evidence asks for discretion; modern-day theoretical haste determines the extent of our perception.

There have been sufficient studies of the predicament of patients in psychiatric hospitals. For our purposes, a glance is sufficient and in particular when Charcot's methods are reviewed. Everything we know about him, including his youthful artistic interests and talents, gives us a sense of him as a doctor. The purpose is not ultimately to critique him personally or the state of the care for the neurotic and the hysteric in the late 19th century. Tracing Freud's development is much more important for us since we see him being both independent of mind and capable of making important decisions for his own therapeutic endeavours especially in the next decade leading up to *Studies on Hysteria*. "Charcot, the scientist, used his artistic perception to enhance his diagnostic abilities." At least, he believed (and so did others) that he was doing so. His personal life and the celebrated parties at his home, which included the artistic celebrities of the day, did nothing to alter his sense of self or his conscious appreciation of the aesthetic life. "Charcot's descriptions emphasized the visual and the kinetic rather than the unseen and purely psychological."[43] The distinction was ultimately made by Freud as he came to two early and inter-related decisions: the scepticism about heredity as an explanation for the aetiology of hysteria proved to be consequential. But so was the suspension of belief when it came to the presentation of individual hysterics for exhibition and examination. Freud was not so taken by the physical debilities of the hysteric (like, for example, the symptom of neurasthenia). As Justice-Malloy points out, Freud was more interested in the "unseen," that is, the psyche of the hysteric. Is there, for us, a defining moment from Freud's Paris experience that, now taking everything into account, can prepare us for the creation of psychoanalysis proper once he opens his private practice in Vienna?

The history of psychiatry is not for the faint-hearted or those who are susceptible to excessive empathy; our judgements and all the recriminations that are possible do nothing, today, to inform us about Freud's experiences between 1885 and 1886 and everything he then took back with him to Vienna. Taking note of only some of the literature on 19th-century psychiatry and that all-too-enticing subject of hysteria would be a long task in itself. A few more can be mentioned; doing so brings us into contact with a late 20th-century phenomenon. The conjunction of the hysterical and the sexual, in its actuality and possible exploitation, needs no imagination. Indeed, all the photographs now available from the Charcot period at the Salpêtrière are enough to give us a glimpse into the situation both for the patients and all the people involved in their inclusion in a photographic catalogue. Patients were shown in terms of "muscles, nerves, and sex." A critical sociology is a discipline in itself; there will come a time, eventually, when an entire literature will be examined and, according to historical distance (say, in the next century), will look back on the critical imagination as it functioned specifically, first, in institutions of higher learning, and then as it became more widespread in society as a whole. One can only imagine what *their evaluations of us* will be. There will certainly be, one hopes, no self-glorification and moral indulgences. Our own theoretical archive will be scrutinized; the impression will not be a favourable one. Statements such as the following are legion. "Within the context of the prevailing ideology of degeneration, hysteria, chorea, and neurasthenia appear as medical 'constructions' which physicians exploited for their own ends."[44] This has now become the legitimate cynicism of theory. The ailment, whatever it was, could simply be included in a social "construction" and so become devoid of all reality. Physicians were cynical and exploitative. Our contemporary judgements are too self-assured, as only morality can be.

As we prepare to leave Paris with Freud and return to Vienna and the beginning of his private practice, the few months spent at the Salpêtrière left him with a distinct relationship, above all, to *himself*. If we could single out one indelible experience, and one that would be retained from 1885 until the end, it would be his perceptual relationship with his patients. The perception would not be one-sided and certainly not captured in the still image of a photograph that was, for some, the confirmation of a diagnosis. The momentous shift from the one-sided diagnosis by the neurologist to the subjectivity of the patient made for an entirely new situation in the treatment of neurotic disorders. When we then take into consideration the speech of the patient, what Anna O. would call the "talking cure," then we are in a position to now turn to the early psychoanalytic writings and then the *Studies on Hysteria* to see how much progress Freud had made in the diagnosis and treatment of neuroses. A question has been asked: was one experience more definitive than all the others? A hypothesis can be hazarded once we take into account the importance of Greek tragedy for Freud and its leading him to establish one foundation of psychoanalytic theory. Once we unify Anna O.'s private theatre, Charcot's demonstrations of hysterics to the public, and Freud's intuitive sense of the meaning of acting-out, we come to his realization of Breuer's unrecognized meaning of catharsis and its origin in Aristotle's *Poetics*. A theory of tragedy (not for a spectator at the theatre, but for a therapist reflecting on his patient) led Freud to far-reaching insights into the dynamics of the psyche.

## Before Freud's Return to Vienna

The period between 1873 and 1886 has been described according to four overlapping themes in Freud's life, culture, education and, through a process of observation and selection, leading to an increasingly individual path forward in the analysis, understanding, and treatment of nervous illnesses. Our sense of the hysterics of the Salpêtrière as "medical muses"[45] seems, when related to Greek mythology, both unusual and contextually skewed. The Greek reference does, however, lead us to a final consideration of Freud's overall thinking in the winter of 1886 as his period in Paris comes to a close. The post-1886 period is a new beginning in Freud's life and professional practice. The years ahead require a thorough investigation because of the development of one psychoanalytic sensibility that has been, if not ignored, at least underappreciated. Naming Freud's innovation a psychoanalysis of perception takes us to the unity of his experiences over a substantial period of time. How it moves forward is the subject of this last section – both to end the project and to imagine a necessary follow-up when Freud opens his private practice in Vienna and the treatment of patients we will come to know, individually, in the *Studies on Hysteria*. The relatively short stay in Paris was significant insofar as the whole of his previous history reached one culmination – none more important than in first seeing how Anna O.'s symptoms were reconfirmed with the patients at the Salpêtrière both in terms of their experiences and as they were presented, theatrically, for others to observe and for how they acted out a number of symptoms. The historical scholarship, in this undertaken by three collaborative researchers, can be profitably consulted for more information on the way Charcot "constructed"[46] neurology and for our knowledge of one individual who, for a time, was important for Freud. There were to be others, especially in France, who continued with their individual work and perspectives and made contributions to our knowledge of the neuroses as the century reached its conclusion.[47] The practice of hypnosis, which has been omitted for reasons for space more than subject matter, was important and remained so – including for Freud who did not give it up until he realized there was a more effective relationship between doctor and patient. More important than the practice of treating a patient, Freud was on the verge of seeing how the whole of his past experience brought him to one more aspect of the ancient world that, inevitably, would be complementary to the Jewish relationship to the image and to the possible distortions of perception.

We have reached one conclusion; or, more accurately, a transition from which it will be necessary to take our themes on Freud's understanding of perception forward towards the elaboration of psychoanalysis. At this turning point, one experience (latent for Freud until now) becomes more explicit in terms of his thinking about the nature of neuroses; for if Breuer had, rightly, called his psychotherapeutic method "catharsis," both due to its medical idea of "purgation" and, for Freud, intimately related to Aristotle's conception of being a spectator at a theatrical presentation, one inquiry had yet to be undertaken. The origins of the concept of catharsis were both, at their origins, medical and aesthetic, in the practice of healing and in Aristotle's *Poetics*. Did Freud complete one more aspect of his interdisciplinary thinking by turning to the interpretation of tragedy and recognizing how its *structure* revealed something essential about neurotic experience? How Freud understood an aspect of Greek tragedy – for the "actor" (the neurotic) no less than the "spectator" (the analyst) – put him in a position to see the affects of the transference and, ultimately, a foundation in the Oedipus Complex. The year 1886 is our endpoint because of Freud's sense of the future as he reflected on it by way of drama and neurosis. The "acting-out" of the patients had not been understood by the clinicians at the Salpêtrière deeply enough. *One* connection can now be better understood by turning, first, to Aristotle's *Poetics* and then one of the most important papers on the "technique" of psychoanalysis. Freud's awareness of Anna O. private theatre as well as the theatrical display of the hysterics of the Salpêtrière had become connected; how so led Freud from one aspect of the ancient world, the creation of tragedy as an aesthetic form, to its deeper understanding both for the individual patient and as a condition of family life. The Oedipus Complex was still, explicitly, more than a decade in the future. Freud already had intimations of the significance of tragedy and its role in the psyche and for the everyday life of neurotics. A later comment, one of many, takes us in several historical directions at once.

In one of his histories of the psychoanalytic movement, he mentions "other new factors which were added to the cathartic procedure as a result of my work which transformed it into psycho-analysis" (SE 14:15). The "other" factors have been, in part, outlined. Defining the four principal ones as scientific, medical, cultural, and therapeutic – to choose categories – is acceptable in terms of a description. There is much more to be gained when we allow ourselves some freedom from any self-imposed limits, of disciplines or ways of thinking, and see Freud as an individual who was capable of internalizing disparate elements and retain them in himself, intellectually and, then, practically. Someone who was so aware of the propensity of human consciousness to split was no doubt insistent on his self-awareness, as time would prove with his own self-analysis and interpretation of dreams. One instance out of innumerable others:

> In my young days I had more of a taste for reading philosophical works. In later years I have denied myself the *very great pleasure* of reading the works of Nietzsche, with the deliberate object of not being hampered in working out the impressions received in psycho-analysis by any sort of anticipatory ideas. I had therefore to be prepared – and I am so, gladly – to forego all claims to priority in the many instances in which laborious psycho-analytic investigation can merely confirm the truths which the philosopher recognized by intuition.
>
> (SE 14:16)

The emphasis of "very great pleasure" is mine. The reason is not explained; it may be inferred and beginning from Nietzsche's *The Birth of Tragedy*. Despite a few efforts, no one has made an attempt at an intellectual lineage from one unparalleled philosopher to an equally unparalleled psychologist.

Returning to the lecture as one final turning point leads again to the affirmation that, for all of the acknowledgement of Charcot's influence on his thinking, there were simply too many diverse ideas all converging in Freud's mind on the way to creating psychoanalysis. Freud is saying one thing and most definitely thinking another; he will soon reveal how *his* advances are more significant and are soon going to transform previous knowledge of the psychical origins of hysteria. The *construction* of the lecture is precise as it is methodical. "It may safely be said that everything new that has been learnt about hysteria in recent times goes back directly or indirectly to his [Charcot's] suggestions" (SE 3:27). Whether *anything* can be safely said at the end of Freud's lecture about hysteria – in terms of traumatic paralysis or anything else – is one of his intentions as he presents some of the most important, though by no means exhaustive, ideas on hysteria as he now understands it. His expository exactness has often been noted, as a thinker and writer who had significant rhetorical facility. To tell his audience that the lecture is based on Charcot is done for the sake of acknowledgement as well as legitimacy. Although he will also reveal some of his own findings, for the time being he relies on a professional association of a scientist and medical practitioner who had an international reputation.[48] For someone who was also responsible for creating rehabilitation clinics dealing with physiotherapy, speech therapy, and hydrotherapy, a relatively new physician who was now practicing psychotherapy would benefit from their personal relationship. In "My Studies in Paris and Berlin," Freud again stressed how Charcot's method was "led by the favourable character of his material to the study of the chronic nervous diseases and their pathological anatomical basis" (SE 1:7). One word, for Freud, changed everything; for he would come to see the problem of chronic nervous diseases according to a pathological psychical basis. That one "turnaround" would have a number of origins. Calling it a *peripeteia*, borrowing one of Aristotle's concepts, is appropriate since Freud had become self-reflexive and was now certain of a direction.

One memory deserves special mention, for its content and timing. As he wrote years later in *An Autobiographical Study*, one of his ideas, suggested to Charcot, did not make any difference. The lack of enthusiasm, or genuine corroboration, did nothing to dissuade Freud from a path he was to pursue virtually alone.

> Before leaving Paris I discussed with the great man a plan for the comparative study of hysterical and organic paralyses. I wished to establish the thesis that in hysteria paralyses and anaesthesias of the various parts of the body are demarcated according to the popular idea of their limits and not according to anatomical facts. He agreed with this view, but it was easy to see that in reality he took no interest in penetrating more deeply into the psychology of the neuroses. When all is said and done, it was from pathological anatomy that his work had started.
>
> (SE 20:13–14)

Anatomy and psychology: the difference, years later, remains the one that separates Freud from Charcot. We can emphasize two of his insights: one, the symptoms suffered by neurotics and the "idea of their limits" and the sense of going well beyond the facts of physiology and anatomy and, therefore, *more deeply*. The metaphor sums up a certain vision of human beings insofar as, psychologically, they are deep and complex and in ways dynamically different than the anatomical perception of the scientist, doctor, or neurologist. The autopsy had been one ultimate depth. Freud had discovered another. The explanation for Freud's ongoing commitment to both science and psychology was complicated by more factors than the first, obvious one; because, upon his return to Vienna and the opening of his private practice, his wide-ranging interests kept him tied to science. The later, non-psychoanalytic publications, are evidence of his continuing scientific interests in demanding and still unclear illnesses, some of which he would contribute to better understanding, like children's cerebral palsy and aphasia, illnesses which were part of Charcot's history of discoveries.

We have another reason for complimenting Freud on his honesty and acknowledgement of Breuer who, as a family physician, treated patients like Anna O. *in her home*. In Paris, the difference could not have been more evident for him. There are two reasons to concentrate on; and they are not disconnected to Anna O.'s private theatre and the nature of her symptoms. First, the hysterics of the Salpêtrière were regularly exhibited to a large audience of medical practitioners and the merely curious from different strands of society. The fascination can be analyzed from a number of perspectives. Tragedy, spectacle, drama: all our concepts can be recalled to give us a sense of the exhibition. The display of patients was only one. Another one became one more "technique" in the whole dramatic enactment of these individuals and how they were first presented to an audience and, ultimately, photographed. Drama and photography; or, stated otherwise, the idolatry of the hysteric was more or less complete.

Coming to the end of Freud's stay in Paris is a transition whose consequences will be felt for a long time and, due to its complexity, require another analysis. We can return to one of the periods already outlined, in part, and then think ahead to the history Freud himself will emphasize as foundational. In an encyclopedia article he wrote, one of many where a theme will be repeated, he gives the reader a task.

> The best way of understanding psycho-analysis is still by tracing its origins and development. In 1880 and 1881 Dr. Josef Breuer of Vienna, a well-known physician and experimental physiologist, was occupied in the treatment of a girl who had fallen ill of a severe hysteria.
>
> (SE 18:235)

This one beginning, out of others, can be chosen for the long period of time to follow. The case of Anna O. has been examined, in context if not in its full analytic content. Unfortunately, we have no other details from Breuer's *experience* – that is, his own, not his patient's. "Breuer," moreover,

> refrained from following up his discovery or from publishing anything about the case until some ten years later, when the personal influence of the present writer (Freud, who had returned to Vienna in 1886 after studying in the school of Charcot) prevailed on him to take up the subject afresh and embark upon a joint study of it.

We are, then, at the beginning of a period in Freud's life that can be revisited and followed, in some detail, until the creation of psychoanalysis and, with *The Interpretation of Dreams*, a new century. As he comes to the end of his Paris period, however, one more connection has been made.

The academic motive of a critical reassessment of the history of hysteria has been one necessary addition to our knowledge; and yet one fears that the *critique* of both the doctors and the institution as the Salpêtrière can lead to an unintended omission. "The images in the *Iconographie* riveted the French public, and were prolifically reproduced in many popular novels, etchings, caricatures, and in both café-concerts and avant-garde performances."[49] Once we think more about the representation of hysterics – in the form of a theatrical display or photography – then we can easily forget the women some scholars believe they are standing up for and making us aware of. If the patients themselves are going to be made real and not only *objects* of scientific and medical attention, then it seems to me that it is precisely Freud who began to think deeply about them and their *condition of life* and then how to, first, more accurately diagnosing their pain and, second, finding a more adequate method of treating them. By following Freud from his Paris period, which is pivotal and personally transformative, and prepare for his return to Vienna and the beginning of his private practice in 1886, we can advance beyond the limits of hysteria as it was observed and treated before Freud. We can, again, make an often-repeated observation both for the patients at the Salpêtrière and asylums in general.

"One result in practice," Gauchet and Swain write, "is that patients are neglected or were simply forgotten, in a process engendered and maintained by the machine designed to comprehend them."[50] The poignancy of their work as a whole is not lost on anyone who has spent some time reflecting on the history of institutions for the mentally ill and, more particularly, the actual conditions at the time in the Paris hospital where Freud spent formative months as an observer. The scientist in him was restrained; he showed no inclination (directly, that is) to evaluate the nature of the hospital and the care of the patients by doctors who were – as far as one can tell from the reports, which are not exhaustive – not immune from Charcot's theories or methods. His evaluation of the clinic has not been the subject of any investigation. We have no sense if, even privately, in his own mind, he recognized the hospital to be an inappropriate place for the treatment of individuals who were gathered together, en masse, and identifying with each other or, worse still, emulating the conditions hoped-for by their attending doctors. A critique of the psychiatric hospital will bring us no closer to identifying Freud's experience at the time and how he managed to leave Paris with a certain sense of a better way to conduct a therapy for ill individuals. Gauchet and Swain make the important affirmation of "the founding reversal of Freud," which for me involves several interconnected impressions that need to be more specifically described as they pertain to the emergence of psychoanalysis as in many ways an antithetical practice to the large-scale institution. Gauchet and Swain are worthy of emphasis because they rightly make us again aware of the conditions of a patient in an asylum; they also separate Freud as an observer and for the individual conclusions he is beginning to reach. How he does so requires one analysis that has not received enough attention. By way of a beginning, we can turn to someone who has written on the meaning of the theatre, for it brings us closer to one of Freud's thought processes as he saw the image, Anna's theatre, the display of neurotics, and a classical interpretation.

At the beginning of Jacques Rancière's *The Emancipated Spectator*, he set out with a series of proposals on rethinking the reality of the theatre, performance, and the spectator. Although his was an aesthetic problem (and a political one) the argument can be shifted in order to make it crucial for Freud in 1886 and as he witnessed the "performances" of hysterical patients. Rancière uses the term spectacle to refer to "bodies in action before an assembled audience," which makes the clinic a different kind of spectacle and, indeed, a specifically medical/psychological one. His political observations are more relevant for Freud when they are considered only from the individual case and without reflecting on the admittedly important aspect of the social – and the difference, for example, between the normal and the pathological. The ancillary questions are many, varied, and impossible to examine; accepting certain limits is necessary if the specific questions are going to be addressed as they influenced Freud. The spectacle of hysterics is what Freud witnessed; how they will be crucial in the testimonies (that is, the case histories of the future) will have its origins in Paris and during the time when Freud, at one of the many culminations of his life as a thinker and therapist, found an original direction for his future. Rancière adds: "More than any other art, theatre has been associated with the Romantic idea of an aesthetic revolution, changing not the mechanics of the state and laws, but the sensible forms of human experience."[51] Understood from the perspective of Freud's personal experience and as foundational for psychoanalysis, the statement above is most meaningful when we omit the political emphasis and, instead, focus on the one subject who has been denigrated in so much of late 20th-century thought. In Paris, it is Freud himself who becomes not only an "emancipated spectator" of the theatricality of human suffering; he transfers himself into the experience of the hysteric in order to realize the reality of a disjointed interiority and then the possibility of a new medical/therapeutic dedication. What does he accomplish? Or, stated as a long-term project, what does he hope to achieve? The aesthetic revolution will involve the ability to recognize the consciousness and perception of the mentally suffering and then add, through diagnosis and a remedy, the possibility of a new and enhanced kind of treatment. There can be no real conclusion to Freud's development at the time; ending the project in the spring of 1886 is simply a decision to separate a before and after. Although the idea of an "emancipated spectator," as Rancière presents it, deals specifically with theatre as an art form, we find ourselves at an appropriate place for an end, and a transition, by bringing together a final set of relationships. Freud changed a sensible form of human experience by understanding images, looking, disturbances of vision and, finally, a connection that he had been thinking about since his discussions with Breuer, that is, the origin of the term *catharsis* in Aristotle's *Poetics*. While Aristotle, as always, created a number of *categories* to explain tragedy, Freud's interpretation turned out to be as far from any aesthetic formalism as can be imagined.

Now that the conditions have been set for Freud's arrival in Paris in the autumn of 1885 and for a few months' of observation of Charcot's methods of diagnosis and treatment of hysterics at the Salpêtrière, we can add one more crucial element in Freud's cultural thinking as we presented it in terms of Judaism, science, and the first patient of the "cathartic" method. The term, *catharsis*, has thus far been used without drawing attention to its meaning beyond the medical one attributed to it, as a physician, by Breuer. One relation, however, will prove to be unavoidable (for Freud's thinking as a 19th-century culturalist) once the medical and the category of ancient Greek aesthetics are joined together. How are 19th-century neurology and Greek ideas on tragedy, and, more specifically, those in Aristotle's *Poetics* on Greek tragedy, inter-related?

Admittedly, the connection is hypothetical. To make the theory a possibility, and verifiable as a characteristic of Freud's thinking, a few different explanations will have to be presented. His recent collaboration with Breuer and his intimate knowledge of the case of Anna O. had left Freud with impressions that would be long-lasting and become foundational for the beginnings of psychoanalysis. The theory of "catharsis" had proven to be effective – at least in the observable time-frame. How did the medical sense of the term, in Paris, take on an entirely different meaning, one that would have long-term consequences for Freud's study of hysteria? To answer the first question, we have to turn to the Salpêtrière and one of the methods used by Charcot to present the patients to an audience of doctors and a whole array of spectators who were titillated by the gestures and grimaces of hysterics. Attention to the culture of the world-famous Parisian hospital and its illustrious master was, in part, due to a certain notoriety and fame associated with the exhibition of hysterics. They were, to use a precise word, spectacles. The spectacle of a medical examination, during Charcot's *Leçons du Mardi* and the use of individuals for the observation of others, allowed Freud to witness a reality that was not, simply, the manifest. How the medical and the "entertaining" was unified in a hospital circumstance remains one of the defining features of the mental hospital in Paris and one at a time when Freud, as a member of the audience, as a *spectator*, viewed the events with an original understanding. Once the medical catharsis used by Breuer was considered from the perspective of Aristotle's theory of tragedy (for the spectator, and for Freud in particular) an entire and original meaning was impossible to ignore. At the same time as he had already transformed the diagnosis of hysteria from a physiological and anatomical one to a strictly psychical one, Freud also transcended the supposedly objective conditions of observation by Paris psychiatrists and began to see the patients from the consciousness and perception of the patients themselves and with the forms noticed as recurring in Anna O. – the hypnoid states, somnambulism, and most especially the *absences* in relation to her lived experience of time. Any knowledge of what Allegra Fryxell has called "research into pathological temporalities"[52] in the 20th century may have to be moved to an earlier history and one inseparable from the case of Anna O., the hysterics witnessed in Paris, and the connection Freud began to make with tragedy.

The argument, here, does not depend on Freud's direct knowledge of Aristotle's *Poetics*; his familiarity with Greek tragedy, which he would have studied as part of the curriculum of the 19th-century Gymnasium, is sufficient for us to look deeper into both its form and content and the intimate relationship between the characters on stage and the audience. If we abstract ourselves from one historical event (say, the festival of the Dionysia in Athens) and the exhibition of hysterical individuals as *tragic*, Freud's perceptions at the time can be reconstructed with a hypothetical conviction. Our thinking on the relation is the issue. Many have sought to find a definitive "turning point" when Freud and psychoanalysis emerged from the limits of 19th-century medicine and neurology. How did Freud make the connection once he understood himself as a conscious spectator in front of a dramatic hysteric? Charcot's lessons were theatrical; and yet Freud was no mere spectator who passively looked on and perceived the acts in their immediacy. One reason has to be imagined from his knowledge of Anna O.'s private theatre and the name given to the treatment by Breuer. Catharsis was no by-chance definition. Its connection to Aristotle and his theory of tragedy was purposeful. We have to return to the Salpêtrière and see Freud as one of the spectators and the connection he makes between the hysterics' drama, catharsis, and Aristotle's *Poetics*. More specifically, even a brief examination of some of Aristotle's concepts, as a theory of tragedy (as a dramatic form), are applicable and illuminating for understanding a psychical process by a patient and an analyst. Highlighting, then, the relation of the Aristotelian *peripeteia* and recognition, and then the aspect of suffering (witnessed by the spectator – by the analyst) and its relation to "houses," that is, everyday families as opposed to dynastic monarchies, we see an entire process that can be translated from one philosophical exposition to another. "The traditional interpretation of catharsis attributes to tragedy a therapeutic effectiveness."[53] We could present an entire history of scholarship on Aristotle's theory of tragedy in terms of the theatre or literary theory. Doing so would not bring us any closer to Freud's own *peripeteia*, a "turning around" that was much closer to a philosophical understanding than on the structure of a play. Freud accomplished his own turnaround when he reinterpreted catharsis and tragedy for the life and experiences and perceptions of a neurotic who, in their life, were acting out a number of symptoms in order to remember; but the very attempt to do so only consigned them all the more readily, all the more tragically, to the form of their illness – as Anna O. had done with her private theatre. Catharsis, for Freud, was not achieved by watching the spectacle of hysterics at the Salpêtrière.

In the *Poetics*, Aristotle writes, "Recognition, as the name itself signifies, is a change from ignorance to knowledge" (1452a). The recognition was not, however, achieved by the patient since their very act, which was intended to remember an origin, only served to conceal it all the more readily. Freud already suspects that the case of Anna O., and her split consciousness, requires an act of repression. Only the spectator, aware of the split consciousness of the actor (patient) can find an access to the origin, requiring a thorough interpretation of the actor's body and speech. Aristotle continues. "But the kind of recognition most [proper] to the plot and to the action is the one first mentioned, for such a recognition, along with peripety, will arouse either pity or fear" (1452b). Freud now creates, in himself, a fundamental difference. As a spectator, he does not *feel* anything; to feel would be to unconsciously mimic the patient and so experience something morally beneficial but therapeutically useless. Freud alters the Aristotelian relationship between actor and spectator, patient and doctor, by recognizing how the feelings are expressed, as it were, on stage, while he must be the individual capable of turning the physicality of the drama around and recognizing their psychical origins. "For tragedy, as an imitation, has been posited as being of *actions* which arouse pity or fear." Freud recognizes that the patients displayed in Charcot's hysterical theatre are imitating, tragically, a distorted memory of the past. Whatever the actions produced in terms of feelings was, for Freud, an obstacle to understanding their purposes. Once again, the past of his entire cultural *Bildung* had prepared him to see the patients at the Salpêtrière as tragic actors on stage who were, literally, being directed by two forces, an interior and exterior one, one psychical and unconscious, the other medical and neurological. Only Freud's individuality was capable of recognizing how the entirety of the theatrical displays conducted by Charcot were tragic in the precise sense of the term, both for the patients and the doctors. The patients were acting out in order to remember and also demonstrate, to a perceptive observer, what they had suffered and endured. The neurologist could only respond by focusing on the body and its movements and so be always at a second-order perception of an unconscious reality. Charcot was deceived by the hysterical body. Its image proved to be too enticing and, because of it, capable of concealing other, more hidden affects. What Aristotle writes about *two characters on stage* is the situation between the patient and the doctor as Freud witnessed it. "Since recognition occurs between persons, (a) in some cases only one of them is recognized by the other, and this occurs whenever *the identity* of only one of them is clear, (b) in other cases both have to recognize each other." For Freud, the problem of recognition is no longer between two characters on stage. In the *psychoanalytic situation*, the two steps will eventually occur between the analyst and the analysand: my italics of the word identity means there will be a recognition of the identity of the analysand by two people in a transferential relationship. A transference, when consciously understood, is the opposite of imitation. Aristotle's theoretical discussion of Greek tragedy, before any catharsis can take place, takes us back to the beginning. "Two parts of the plot, then, are concerned with peripety and recognition; a third part is concerned with suffering." A turnaround, a recognition of suffering, and an explanation of its cause: for Freud, as for anyone even before they become a patient, there is human suffering and in a way that had motivated him from some of his earliest memories of his purpose. Suffering leads the patient to a doctor or a clinic, depending on circumstance or severity of the illness; the responsibility of the analyst, then, is to understand the suffering in terms of the patient's experiences and then, first, recognize the cause and, finally, lead them to a peripety that will be compelling enough for them to alter themselves and their life.

We can argue about the epiphany or the more drawn-out period when Freud came to his own conclusions about the relationship between Anna O.'s private theatre, the displays of hysterical patients by Charcot, and the interpretation of the actor/spectator relationship as theorized by Aristotle. One other experience was to move him further along this one unique path of *thinking*. Before turning to the one "technique" that was added to the theatrical (the photography of hysterics), Freud can tells us, in a short part of the second lecture of 1909, about the changes in himself.

> The great French observer [Charcot], whose pupil I became in 1885–6, was not himself inclined to adopt a psychological outlook. It was his pupil, Pierre Janet, who first attempted a deeper approach to the peculiar psychical process present in hysteria, and we followed his example when we took the splitting of the mind and disassociation of the personality as the centre of our position.
>
> (SE 11:21)

In what way was Janet led to this "deeper approach" since, as Freud tells us, he was also thinking about patients in terms of their nervous system? He was still considering heredity and degeneracy. In 1909, Freud had advanced so far that he can rethink Janet's process, acknowledging the idea of depth and complexity while setting aside the 19th-century assumptions about the individual's biology. Freud goes on. "Hysterical patients, he believes, are inherently incapable of holding together the multiplicity of mental processes into a unity, and hence arises the tendency to mental disassociation." Freud's language presupposes an understanding of the whole of his developments after more than 20 years. In Paris, however clear his perceptions were, how much they were already worked out, he had intimations of both the depth and the split in their individuality, their identity, their psyche. The suffering alluded to earlier is now precise. It often involves "mental weakness" and "diminished capacity." In the lecture, Freud unfortunately does not develop this one important point. His writings are filled with a discussion of the neurotic and the limits they place on themselves and on the fulfilment of their life, as a person and in relationship with others. In the lecture, he is more intent, for the time being, to show his own recognition and peripety.

> When, later on, I set about continuing on my own account the investigations that had been begun by Breuer, I soon arrived at another view of the origin of hysterical dissociation (the splitting of consciousness). A divergence of this kind, which was to be decisive for everything that followed, was inevitable, since I did not start out, like Janet, from laboratory experiments, but with therapeutic aims in mind.
>
> (SE 11:22)

The arguments have taken us to one moment. There were many more along the way. But if we emphasize Freud's concern from the time he himself was working in a psychiatric clinic, and when Breuer had concluded his treatment of Anna O., we can appreciate how the scientifically trained physician and scientist, who at one time completed hundreds of dissections, now had to face the one human reality of psychological suffering. An analogy is not out of place: Freud becomes an ever more original thinker in the same way as, in the ancient world, some one individual saw the theatrical displays of violence and death in a religious temple and found himself disassociating himself from history and tradition – to become "secular" or, like a philosopher, create a new way of thinking and life.

Finally, one more Aristotelian observation can highlight the 19th-century problem between organic heredity and psychology. Freud was well on his way to abandoning one of the truisms of science at the time and finding a particular attitude to the individual and the family. Aristotle writes, "The best tragedies are composed about a few houses ... and any others who do or suffer terrible things" (1453a). One might want to add, exceeding Aristotle's distinction of "houses," by which he means *families,* that all of them more or less *suffer terrible things* in fact or in fantasy. And it is, usually, one individual from a family who somehow best represents an entire history and experience, in one household, or in a drawn-out genealogy that brings us to a form of inheritance well known to Freud and then transferred to us, in his writing, in analysis, or both. The drama unfolding on Charcot's medical stage was experienced by Freud as an epiphany. His understanding of human perception (of Anna O. and of his own) led him to understand the entire relationship of the patient to the psychiatric institution in a way only he could unify. Only Freud, with knowledge of the image, the sights of the microscope, the disturbances of vision of the neurotic, could then see all the various methods by which the neurologist examined the visible patient. Freud's discoveries are soon to become momentous because of his ability to unify disparate parts of history, culture, and experience. Needless to say, the connection to Sophocles's *Oedipus the King* will become yet another cornerstone in the edifice of psychoanalysis. The intimations are innumerable and constant; recognizing them (to use Aristotle's term) simply hints at the resources at Freud's disposal, in himself, as a thinker. What he leaves to us, as his own heritage and, more importantly, transference, is part of our ongoing interest in Freud as the founder of psychoanalysis from out of a range of historical and cultural sources. The return to Vienna in 1886 and the opening of his private practice begins another period for Freud as a cosmopolitan who would, in the next two decades, revolutionize our knowledge of the neuroses and their psychotherapeutic care. He had his own turnaround; his own experiences, from now on, would become even more essential to his relationship to his patients and to his ability not only to understand the force of a transference, but to also ensure each patient became conscious of their own inner resources.

"One becomes an analyst because one believes in the power of openings, of reversals and revelations, of breaks in a system that can create new sensualities."[54] One, first of all, becomes an analysand and a reader of Freud because of the intimations of how any possible future revelations will be made possible. Sensualities: translated into our language of phenomenology, an analyst (or a former analysand who writes on Freud) is both committed to the revelations that, once experienced, will make all former perceptions of oneself, others, and the world impossible to prolong. The history of the origin of psychoanalysis has been written numerous times. Any further contribution to phases of the early period, if they are to be in any way meaningful, have the obligation to re-examine outstanding questions in Freud's mind as he understood them and to present them today with the relevance owed to them. Taking a last look at *An Autobiographical Study* and stopping at a particular place in Freud's narrative, one of the many declarations about the importance of periods as he saw them are made.

> If the preliminary cathartic period is left on one side, the history of psychoanalysis falls from my point of view into two phases. In the first of these I stood alone and had to do all the work myself: this was from 1895–6.
>
> (SE 20:55)

The beginning has been set. But not definitively so; because if we take into consideration different dates and different phases, then curtailing one period is perhaps not enough to extend our own inquiry and to wonder how many other factors were involved in a period that, for us, has to be considerably different and longer and actually begin outside of any date he would acknowledge and with cultural factors he only sometimes divulges. There is no simple way to outline all the phases of Freud's life and the personal transformations he went through to arrive at the date stated above. We can only approximate, incompletely, the complexity of Freud's thinking.

The brief analysis of only a few of Aristotle's concepts from his *Poetics* have been suggestive enough for us to see how much of Freud's thinking had developed over the period of our concern, 1873 to the spring of 1886, and how it was now prepared to once more complement a prior knowledge of the ancient world, his Jewish heritage, with an equally influential Greek one, most especially when it came to the creation of tragedy. Concluding remarks by Stanley Cavell, a thinker whose familiarity with cinema has broadened the scope of his understanding of psychoanalysis, writes:

> In Freud's practice, one human being represents to another all that the other has conceived of humanity in his or her own life, and moves that other toward an experience of the conditions which condition that utterly specific life. It is a vision and an achievement quite worthy of the most heroic attributes Freud assigned to himself.[55]

The word *vision*, perhaps more modern and acceptable to us (as opposed to the theologically heavy revelation) is appropriate insofar as the psychoanalysis of perception was created by Freud to alert us to the psyche and its power to effect reality itself.

A number of concluding remarks are left; they summarize, for me, a certain relationship to psychoanalysis and, also, a fidelity to Freud. Harry Guntrip takes us to one of our first themes (psychoanalysis and science) and expresses his conviction. "To state concisely the incontrovertible hard core of psychic fact discovered by Freud, an achievement which will place him for all time among the immortals of scientific discovery."[56] Omitting the adjective and, simply, affirming Freud's discoveries, is enough for us at the end of a period that has taken us from his Jewish heritage, scientific research in the laboratory, knowledge of Anna O., and the formative period in Paris as all contributing to the creation of psychoanalysis. The year 1886 can be anticipated, beginning with Freud opening his private practice on Easter Sunday and, for us, looking ahead to another formative period that will end at the turn of the century with the publication of *The Interpretation of Dreams*.

## Notes

1 Koehler, Peter. "About Medicine and the Arts: Charcot and French Literature at the fin-de-siècle," 27–40 *Journal of the History of Neuroscience* 10 (1), 2001.
2 Ferreira Camargo, Carlos Henrique. "Jean-Martin Charcot: The Polymath," 1098–1111 *Arquivos de Neuro-Psiquiatra* 81 (12), 2023.

3 Waraich, Manny, and Shailesh Shah. "The Life and Work of Jean-Martin Charcot (1825–1893): 'The Napoleon of Neuroses'," 48–49 *Journal of the Intensive Care Society* 19 (1), 2018.
4 Wilson Smith, Matthew. *The Nervous Stage: Nineteenth-Century Neuroscience and the Birth of the Modern Theatre*. Oxford: Oxford University Press, 2018.
5 As he witnessed when attending Charcot's lectures. See Olivier Walusinki's "Jean-Martin Charcot's Lesson on Parkinson's Disease," 604–605 *Revue Neurologique* 173 (10), Dec. 2017.
6 Cambor, Kate. "Freud in Paris," 177–189 *New England Review* 30 (2), 2009.
7 Clanet, M. "Jean-Martin Charcot: 1825–1893," *The International MS Journal* 15 (2), Jun. 2008.
8 Walusinski, Olivier. "The Concept of Heredity and Degeneration in the Work of Jean-Martin Charcot," 299–324 *Journal of the History of Neuroscience* 29 (3), 2020, 314.
9 Schultheiss, Katrin. "The Internal Image: Mind and Brain in the Age of Charcot," 23–46 *Modern Intellectual History*, 18 (1), 2021. There are no shortages of similar discussions. See, for example, Ståle Gundersen's "Freud and the Mind-Brain Problem," 4–12 *The Scandinavian Psychoanalytic Review* 46 (1–2), 2023.
10 Bruno, J., J. Machado, and Y. Auxéméry. "From Epileptic Hysteria to Psychogenic Non Epileptic Seizure: Continuity or Discontinuity for Contemporary Psychiatry?," *European Journal of Trauma and Dissociation* 5, 2021.
11 Dowbiggin, Ian. *Inheriting Madness: Professionalization and Psychiatric Knowledge in Nineteenth-Century France*. Berkeley: University of California Press, 1991, 121.
12 For its origin and early history, see Ivan Berlin's "The Salpêtrière Hospital: Confining the Poor to Freeing the Insane," 1579 *American Journal of Psychiatry* 160 (9).
13 Diamond, Michael J. "The Impact of the Mind of the Analyst: From Unconscious Processes to Intrapsychic Change," 205–236 *The Second Century of Psychoanalysis: Evolving Perspectives on Therapeutic Action*. Ed. Christopher Christian and Michael J. Diamond. London: Routledge, 2011.
14 Lepoutre, Thomas, and François Villa. "Freud and Charcot: Freud's Discovery and the Question of Diagnosis," 345–368 *International Journal of Psychoanalysis* 90 (2) (2015), 347.
15 Brendel, David H. *Healing Psychiatry: Bridging the Science/Humanistic Divide*. Boston: The MIT Press, 2006, 97.
16 Gelfand, Toby. "Charcot's Response to Freud's Rebellion," 293–308 *Journal of the History of Ideas* 50 (2) (Apr.–Jun. 1989), 299.
17 For an essay on Charcot and the medical culture of the times (irrespective of Freud's presence) see "Charcot and the Salpêtrière School," in *Beyond the Unconscious: Essays of Henry F. Ellenberger in the History of Psychiatry*. Ed. Mark S. Micale. Princeton: Princeton University Press, 2014.
18 The introduction to Freud's arrival in Paris can be postponed for a moment in order to make one presentation of the kind of "critical theory" that is now so common and, at the same time, misguided. This from Marie Lathers's *The Aesthetics of Artifice: Villiers's L'Ève Future*. Chapel Hill: The University of North Carolina Press, 1996.

> The walls of Freud's consulting room at Berggasse 19 displayed the bibelots, decorative symptoms, or icons of the psychoanalytic movement. They included a copy of Andre Brouillet's painting La Leçon clinique du Dr. Charcot ... Brouillet's canvas depicts one of Charcot's theatrical demonstrations of hysteria at the Salpetriere Hospital – it represents, therefore, a possible origin of psychoanalysis, its primitive scene: hysteria staged before the male medical gaze as a bona fide disease. (p. 111)

Spurious and, unfortunately, convincing for those who are uninformed. For what could be more antithetical than the public display of a patient at the Salpêtrière and

Freud's invention of a private analytic setting? The ubiquitous word ("gaze"), so fashionable among a certain group of critical theorists sums up, precisely, what they cannot and have never been able to themselves see. The myopia of the mid-1990's, like other eras, including our own, now seems much more visible.

19  Guenther, Katja. "The Disappearing Lesion: Sigmund Freud, Sensory-Motor Physiology, and the Beginnings of Psychoanalysis," 569–601 *Modern Intellectual History* 10 (3) (Nov. 2013), 597.
20  Tait, Peta. "Performing Neurology: The Dramaturgy of Dr. Jean-Martin Charcot," 217–239 *Australasian Dram Studies* (71), Oct. 2017.
21  Duggan, Patrick. *Trauma-Tragedy: Symptoms of Contemporary Performance.* Manchester: Manchester University Press, 2017, 19.
22  Symington, Neville. *A Healing Conversation: How Healing Happens.* London: Routledge, 2006, 12.
23  Edelman, Nicole. "Gustave Boissarie, Jean-Martin Charcot and Sigmund Freud, Three Doctors' Responses to Some Unusual Bodily Phenomena: Convergences and Divergences (in the Late Nineteenth and Twentieth Centuries)," *Sign or Symptom?: Exceptional Corporeal Phenomena in Religion and Medicine in the 19th and 20th Centuries.* Ed. Tine Van Osselaer, Henk de Smaele, Kaat Wils. Leuven: Leuven University Press, 2017, 44.
24  Bronfen, Elisabeth. *The Knotted Subject: Hysteria and Its Discontents.* Princeton: Princeton University Press, 1998, 174.
25  MacMillan, Malcolm. *Freud Evaluated: The Completed Arc.* Cambridge, Mass.: The MIT Press, 1997, 49.
26  Gutman, Stephen R. "Hysteria as a Concept: A Survey of Its History in the Psychoanalytic Literature," 182–228 *Modern Psychoanalysis* 31 (2), 2006.
27  Krohn, A. *Hysteria: The Elusive Neurosis.* New York: International Universities Press, 1978.
28  Didi-Huberman, Georges. *The Invention of Hysteria: Charcot and the Photographic Iconography of the Salpêtrière.* Tr. Alisa Hartz. Cambridge, Mass.: The MIT Press, 2003.
29  Gilman, Sander L. "Review," 716–717 *Isis* 95 (4), 2004.
30  D. Abse, Alfred. "Hysteria," *The Freud Encyclopedia: Theory, Therapy, and Culture.* Ed. Edward Erwin. New York: Routledge, 2002, 235. We could cite one definition after another; the clinical picture would be enhanced. Our knowledge of history would increase; and yet we would remain oblivious to Freud's interpretation of his own experiences and how, cumulatively, they led to the writings that were postponed until the time came to make them public.
31  Sirotkina, Irina. "Review," 303–305 *British Journal for the History of Science* 39 (141), Jun. 2006. Victims is in my italics.
32  Gluck, Mary. *Popular Bohemia: Modernism and Urban Culture in Nineteenth-Century Paris.* Cambridge, Mass.: Harvard University Press, 2005, 132.
33  These can be read for the purpose of research and to decide if any direct influence can be traced between Charcot's lectures and Freud's professional commitments over a significant period of time. Brief references have been made, which does not relieve us of another responsibility. At some time in the future, a comparison of Charcot's writings as a whole with Freud's emerging theories may fill in some gaps in our current knowledge. See, as a start, "Jean-Martin Charcot (1825–1893): A Tuesday Lesson: Hysteroepilepsy (1888)," 193–199 *From Madness to Mental Health: Psychiatric Disorder and Its Treatment in Western Civilization.* Ed. Greg Eghigian. New Brunswick, NJ: Rutgers University Press, 2010.
34  Renish, N, et al. "Jean-Martin Charcot: Pioneer of Neurology," 1–6 *Cureus* 16 (8), 2024, 4.

35 Goetz, Christopher G. "Jean-Martin Charcot (1825–1893)," 374–5 *Journal of Neurology* 252 (3) (Mar. 2005), 375.
36 Marshall, Jonathan. "Dynamic Medicine and Theatrical Form at the Fin de Siècle: A Formal Analysis of Jean-Martin Charcot's Pedagogy, 1862–1893," 131–153 *Modernism/Modernity* 15 (1), 2008.
37 Scull, Andrew. *Hysteria: The Disturbing History*. Oxford: Oxford University Press, 2009. 106.
38 Garrigou-Kempton, Émilie. "Dying at the Salpêtrière: Autopsies and the Afterlife of the Hysteric," 123–136 *Esprit Créateur* 61 (1), Spring 2021, 125.
39 Clifford, Vicki. *Freud's Converts*. London: Karnac, 2008, 11.
40 Koerber, Amy. *From Hysteria to Hormones: A Rhetorical History*. Philadelphia: Penn State University Press, 2008, 47.
41 Gilman, Sander. *The Jew's Body*. New York: Routledge, 1991, 61.
42 Pichel, Beatriz. "From Facial Expressions to Bodily Gestures: Passions, Photography and Movement in French 19th Century Sciences," 27–48 *History of the Human Sciences* 29 (1), 2016.
43 Justice-Malloy, Rhona. "Charcot and the Theatre of Hysteria," 133–139 *Journal of Popular Culture*, 28 (4) (Spring 1995), 134.
44 Quin, Grégory, and Anaïs Bohuon. "Muscles, Nerves and Sex: The Contradictions of the Medical Approach to Female Bodies in Movement in France, 1874–1914.," 172–186 *Gender and History* 24 (1), 2012, 183.
45 Hustvedt, Hasti. *Medical Muses: Hysteria in 19th Century Paris*. London: Bloomsbury, 2011.
46 Goetz, Christopher G., Michel Bonduelle, and Toby Gelfand. *Charcot: Constructing Neurology*. Oxford: Oxford University Press, 1995.
47 Mayer, Andreas. *Sites of the Unconscious: Hypnosis and the Emergence of the Psychoanalytic Setting*. Chicago: The University of Chicago Press, 2013.
48 Brigo, Francesco et al. "'Spreading the Word of the Master': The Contribution of Italian Physicians in the Early Dissemination of Jean-Martin Charcot's Theories," 3787–3794 *Neurological Sciences* 41 (2), 2020.
49 Cole, Jenn. *Hysteria in Performance*. Kingston/Montreal: Queens/McGill University Press, 2021, 5.
50 Gauchet, Marcel, and Gladys Swain. *Madness and Democracy: The Modern Psychiatric Universe*. Tr. Catherine Porter. Princeton: Princeton University Press, 1999, 93.
51 Rancière, Jacques. *The Emancipated Spectator*. Tr. Gregory Elliott. London: Verso, 2009, 6.
52 Fryxell, Allegra R.P. "Psychopathologies of Time: Defining Mental Illness in Early 20th Century Psychiatry," 3–31 *History of the Human Sciences* 32 (2), Apr. 2019.
53 Schaper, Eva. "Aristotle's Catharsis and Aesthetic Pleasure," 131–143 *The Philosophical Quarterly* 18 (71) (Apr., 1968), 135.
54 Webster, Jamieson. *Conversion Disorder*. New York: Columbia University Press, 2018, 17.
55 Cavell, Stanley. "Freud and Philosophy: A Fragment," 386–393 *Critical Inquiry* 13 (2), 1987, 393.
56 Guntrip, Harry Y. *Personality Structure and Human Interaction: The Developing Synthesis of Psychodynamic Theory*. London: Karnac, 1995, 56.

# Works Cited

All references are from the *Standard Edition of the Complete Psychological Works of Sigmund Freud*. Ed. James Strachey. London: Vintage Books.

"A Difficulty in the Path of Psychoanalysis," SE 17:135–144.
"Analysis Terminable and Interminable," SE 23:209–253.
*An Autobiographical Study*, SE 20:1–74.
"An Outline of Psychoanalysis," SE 23:139–207.
"Address to the Society of B'Nai Brith," SE 20:271–274
"Beyond the Pleasure Principle," SE 14: 1–64.
*Civilization and its Discontents*, SE 21:57–145.
"The Claims of Psychoanalysis to Scientific Interest," SE 13:163–190.
*The Future of an Illusion*, SE 21:5:56.
"The Future Prospects of Psychoanalytic Theory," SE 11:139–151.
"The Goethe Prize," SE 21:205–212.
*Group Psychology and the Analysis of the Ego*, SE 18:69–143.
"Hysteria," SE 17:41–57.
*Inhibitions, Symptoms and Anxiety*, SE 20:87–172.
*Introductory Lectures on Psychoanalysis*, SE 15.
"Josef Breuer," SE 19:277–280.
"Lines of Advances in Psychoanalytic Therapy," SE 17:157–168.
"Mourning and Melancholia," SE 14:237–258.
*Moses and Monotheism*, SE 23:1–137.
"The Moses of Michelangelo," SE 13:209–238.
*New Introductory Lectures on Psychoanalysis*, SE 22:1:182.
"On Narcissism," SE 14: 67–102.
"On the History of the Psychoanalytic Movement," SE 1–66.
"On the Teaching of Psychoanalysis in the Universities," SE 17:169–174.
"Preface and Footnotes to Charcot's *Tuesday Lectures*," SE 1:133–143.
"Preface to the Translation of Charcot's *Lectures on the Diseases of the Nervous System*," SE 17:21–22.

"Psychical or (Mental) Treatment, SE 7:283–302.
"Psychoanalysis," SE 20:259–269.
"The Question of Lay Analysis," SE 20:177–258.
"Remembering, Repeating, and Working-Through: Further Recommendations on the Technique of Psychoanalysis (II)," SE 12:145–156.
"Report on My Studies in Paris and Berlin," SE 1:1–15.
"Some Elementary Lessons in Psychoanalysis," SE 23:279–286.
"Splitting of the Ego in the Process of Defense," SE 23:271–278.
*Totem and Taboo*, SE 13:1–162.
"Two Encyclopedia Articles," SE 18:233–259.
"The Uncanny," SE 17:217–256.

# Bibliography

Anonymous. "The Influence of Francis Bacon on Medical Science," 134–135 *The New Zealand Medical Journal*, 133(1519), July 31, 2020.
Aaron, Lewis and Henik, Libby. "Introduction" to their co-edited *Answering a Question with a Question: Contemporary Psychoanalysis and Jewish Thought*. Brighton: Academic Studies Press, 2010.
Althusser, Louis. *Psychoanalysis and the Human Sciences*. T. Steven Rendall. New York: Columbia University Press, 2016.
Amacher, Peter. *Freud's Neurological Education and Its Influence on Psycho-analytic Theory*, 5–93, *Psychological Issues*, IV(4), Monograph 16. New York: International Universities Press, Inc, 1965.
Appelbaum, Jerome. "Father and Son: Freud Revisits His Oedipus Complex in Moses and Monotheism," 166–184 *American Journal of Psychoanalysis*, 72(2), June 2012.
Appelbaum, Jerome. "Should Psychoanalysis Become a Science?," 1–15 *American Journal of Psychoanalysis*, 71(1), March 2011.
Arminjon, Mathieu, Ansermet, François, Magistretti, Pierre. "The Homeostatic Psyche: Freudian Theory and Somatic Markers," 272–278 *Journal of Physiology – Paris*, 104(5), 2010.
Armstrong, Richard H. *A Compulsion for Antiquity: Freud and the Ancient World*. Ithaca: Cornell University Press, 2005.
Aronson, Seth. "The Problem of Desire: Psychoanalysis as a Jewish Wisdom Tradition," 313–326 *Answering a Question with a Question*. Ed. Lewis Aron and Libby Henik. Brighton: Academic Studies Press, 2010.
Assman, Jan. *The Prince of Monotheism*. Stanford: Stanford University Press, 2009.
Atzmon, Leslie. "A Visual Analysis of Anthropomorphism in the Kabbalah: Dissecting the Hebrew Alphabet and Sephirotic Diagram," 97–115 *Visual Communication*, 2(1), February 2003.
Axelrod, Charles D. "Freud and Science," 273–293 *Theory and Society*, 4(2), 1977.
Bacon, Francis. *Novum Organum*. Tr. and Ed. Peter Urbach and John Gibson. Chicago and LaSalle: Open Court, 1994.
Bakan, David. *Sigmund Freud and the Jewish Mystical Tradition*. Boston: Beacon Press, 1958.
Bakan, David, Merkur, Dan, Weiss, David S. *Maimonides' Cure of Souls: Medieval Precursor of Psychoanalysis*. Albany: SUNY Press, 2009.

Bar-Haim, Shaul. "The Mosaic Legacy of Sigmund Freud: How to Read Moses and Monotheism in the Twenty-First Century," 371–378 *Psychoanalysis and History*, 22(3), 2020.
Beck, Mordechai. "The Secular Kabbalist," *The Jerusalem Report*, 12, 2016.
Beller, Steven. "Solving Riddles: Freud, Vienna and the Historiography of Madness," 27–42 *Journeys into Madness: Mapping Mental Illness in the Austro-Hungarian Empire*. Ed. Gemma Blackshaw and Sabine Wieber. New York: Berghahn Books, 2012.
Berke, Joseph H. *The Hidden Freud: His Hassidic Roots*. London: Karnac, 2015.
Berlin, Ivan. "The Salpêtrière Hospital: Confining the Poor to Freeing the Insane," 1579 *American Journal of Psychiatry*, 160, Number 9.
Bernfeld, Siegfried. "Freud's Scientific Beginnings," 163–196 *American Imago*, 6(3), 1949.
Bernstein, Richard J. *Freud and the Legacy of Moses*. Cambridge: Cambridge University Press, 1998.
Biale, David. *Not in the Heavens: The Tradition of Jewish Secular Thought*. Princeton: Princeton University Press, 2011.
Bielik-Robson, Agata. "Psychoanalysis as Tovat Hayim: In Promise Salvation," 55–70 *European Judaism*, 55(1), March 2022.
Bogousslavsky, J. *Hysteria: The Rise of an Enigma*. Basel: Karger, 2014.
Boyarin, Daniel. *Unheroic Conduct: The rise of heterosexuality and the invention of the Jewish man*. Berkeley: University of California Press, 1989.
Blass, Rachel B. "Conceptualizing splitting: On the different meanings of splitting and their implications for the understanding of the person and the analytic process," 123–139 *International Journal of Psychoanalysis*, 96(1), 2015.
Borch-Jacobsen, Mikkel. *Remembering Anna O.: A Century of Mystification*. London: Routledge, 1996.
Blechner, Mark J. "The Three Cures of Bertha Pappenheim (Anna O): The Talking Cure, the Writing Cure, and the Social Cure," 3–25 *Contemporary Psychoanalysis*, 58(1), 2022.
Bloom, Harold. "Freud: Frontier Concepts, Jewishness, and interpretation," 135–152 *American Imago*, 48(1), Spring 1991.
Blumenberg, Hans. *Rigorism of Truth: "Moses the Egyptian" and Other Writings on Freud and Arendt*. Ed. Ahlrich Meyer, Tr. Joe Paul Kroll. Ithaca: Cornell University Press, 2017.
Bock von Wülfingen, Bettina. "Freud's "Core of Our Being" Between Cytology and Psychoanalysis," 226–244 *Berichte zur Wissenschaftgeschichte*, 36(3), 2013.
Botella, Cesar and Botella, Sara. "A Psychoanalytic Approach to Perception," 83–106 *Symbolization: Representation and Communication*. Ed. James Rose. London: Routledge, 2007.
Bowman, Marcus. *The Last Resistance: The Concept of Science as a Defense Against Psychoanalysis*. Albany: SUNY, 2002.
Brendel, David H. *Healing Psychiatry: Bridging the Science/Humanism Divide*. Cambridge: The MIT Press, 2006.
Brenner, Ian. *Dark Matters: Exploring the Reality of Psychic Destitution*. London: Karnac, 2014.
Brigo, Francesco, et al. "Spreading the Word of the Master": The Contribution of Italian Physicians in the Early Dissemination of Jean-Martin Charcot's Theories, 3787–3794 *Neurological Sciences*, 41(2), 2020.
Britton, Ronald. *Sex, Death, and the Superego: Experience in Psychoanalysis*. London: Karnac, 2003.

Bronfen, Elisabeth. *The Knotted Subject: Hysteria and Its Discontents*. Princeton: Princeton University Press, 1998.
Brottman, Mikita. *Phantoms of the Clinic: Thought-Transference to Projective Identification*. London: Routledge, 2011.
Cambor, Kate. "Freud in Paris," 177–189 *New England Review*, 30(2), 2009.
Carpenter, William B. *The Microscope and Its Revelations*. Seventh Edition edited by W.H. Dallinger. London: J & A Churchill, 1891.
Carroll, Michael P. "'Moses and Monotheism' Revisited – Freud's 'Personal Myth?'" 15–35 *American Imago*, 44(1), Spring 1987.
Castelnuovo-Tedesco, Pietro. "On Rereading the Case of Anna O.: More About Questions That Are Unanswerable," 57–71 *The Journal of the American Academy of Psychoanalysis and Dynamic Psychiatry*, 22(1), 1994.
Cavell, Stanley. "Freud and Philosophy: A Fragment," 386–393 *Critical Inquiry*, 13(2), 1987.
Chapman, Ross M. and Wigert, Edith. "Freud and Psychiatry," 855–857 *American Journal of Orthopsychiatry*, 10(4), 1940.
Charlier, Philippe and Deo, Saudamini. "The Anna O. Mystery: Hysteria or Neuro-Tuberculosis?," 14 *Journal of Neurological Sciences*, 381, 15 October 2017.
Chasseguet-Smirgel, Janine. *The Ego Ideal: A Psychoanalytic Study on the Malady of the Ideal*. Tr. Paul Burrows. New York: W.W. Norton, 1985.
Chasseguet-Smirgel, Janine. "Some thoughts on Freud's Attitude During the Nazi Period," in *Freud and Judaism*. Ed. David Meghnagi. London: Karnac, 1993.
Chernillo, Daniel. "The Jews Killed Moses: Sigmund Freud and the Jewish Question," *Theory, Culture & Society*, 41(3), October 2023.
Chessick, Richard D. *The Future of Psychoanalysis*. Albany: SUNY Press, 2007.
Clanet, M. "Jean-Martin Charcot: 1825:1893," *The International MS Journal*, 15(2), June 2008.
Clifford, Vicki. *Freud's Converts*. London: Karnac, 2008.
Cole. Jenn. *Hysteria in Performance*. Montreal and Kingston: McGill-Queen's University Press, 2021.
Cooper, Amy. "Francis Bacon's Idols and the Reformed Science," 328–350 *Studies in Philology*, 116(2), Spring 2019.
Corneanu, Sorana and Vermeir, Koen. "Idols of the Imagination: Francis Bacon on the Imagination and the Medicine of the Mind," 183–205 *Perspectives on Science*, 20(2), 2012.
Cotti, Patrica. "Towards a New Historiography of Psychoanalysis: In Defense of Psychoanalysis as a Science – An Essay on George Makari's *Revolution in Mind*," 133–146 *Psychoanalysis and History*, 14(1), 2012.
D. Abse, Alfred. "Hysteria," *The Freud Encyclopedia: Theory, Therapy, and Culture*. Ed. Edward Erwin. New York: Routledge, 2002.
Dalzell, Thomas. *Freud's Schreber Between Psychiatry and Psychoanalysis: On Subjective Disposition to Psychosis*. London: Karnac, 2011.
De Mendelssohn, Felix. "The Jewish Tradition in Sigmund Freud's Work," 31–47 *Psychoanalysis, Monotheism, and Morality: The Sigmund Freud Symposia 2009–2011*. Ed. Wolfgang Müller, et al. Leuven: Leuven University Press, 2013.
de Paula Ramos, Sergio. "Revisiting Anna O.: A Case of Chemical Dependence," 239–250 *History of Psychology*, 6(3), 2003.
de Ridder, Jeroen, et al. (Eds). *Scientism: Prospects and Problems*. Oxford: Oxford University Press, 2018.

Diamond, Michael J. "The Impact of the Mind of the Analyst: From Unconscious Processes to Intrapsychic Change," 205–236 *The Second Century of Psychoanalysis: Evolving Perspectives on Therapeutic Action*. Ed. Christopher Christian and Michael J. Diamond. London: Routledge, 2011.

Diamond, Sigmund. "Sigmund Freud, His Jewishness, and Scientific Method: The Seen and Unseen as Evidence," 613–634 *History of the Journal of Ideas*, 43(4), October–December, 1982.

Dìaz Chumaceiro, Cora L. "Serendipity in Freud's Career: Before Paris," 79–81 *Creativity Research Journal*, 11(1), 1998.

Didi-Huberman, Georges. *The Invention of Hysteria: Charcot and the Photographic Iconography of the Salpêtrière*. Tr. Alisa Hartz. Cambridge: The MIT Press, 2003.

Diller, Jerry Victor. *Freud's Jewish Identity: A Case Study in the Impact of his Ethnicity*. New Jersey: Farleigh Dickinson University Press, 1991.

Diller, Jerry Victor. Ed. *The Jewish World of Sigmund Freud: Essays on Cultural Roots and the Problem of Religious Identity*. Jefferson: McFarland & Co, Inc, 2010.

Donner, Michael P. "Is Psychoanalysis a Jewish Science? Why Do You Ask?" *Psycritiques*, 55(40), 2010.

Dos Reis Biaza, Rafel and Kessler, Carlos Henrique. "Psychoanalysis and Science," 414–423 *Psicologia USP*, 28(3), December 2017.

Dowbiggin, Ian. *Inheriting Madness: Professionalization and Psychiatric Knowledge in Nineteenth-Century France*. Berkeley: University of California Press, 1991.

Drouin, Emmanuel, Hendrickx, Marion, and Hautecoeur, Patrick. "Freud's Shift," 553 *Lancet Neurology*, 22(7), 2023.

Duggan, Patrick. *Trauma-Tragedy: Symptoms of Contemporary Performance*. Manchester: Manchester University Press, 2017.

Edelman, Nicole. "Gustave Boissarie, Jean-Martin Charcot and Sigmund Freud, Three Doctors' Responses to Some Unusual Bodily Phenomena: Convergences and Divergences (in the late Nineteenth and Twentieth Centuries)," *Sign or Symptom?: Exceptional Corporeal Phenomena in Religion and Medicine in the 19th and 20th Centuries*. Ed. Tine Van Osselaer, Henk de Smaele, Kaat Wils. Leuven: Leuven University Press, 2017.

Eghigian, Greg. (Ed). "Jean-Martin Charcot (1825–1893): A Tuesday Lesson: Hysteroepilepsy (1888)," 193–199 *From Madness to Mental Health: Psychiatric Disorder and Its treatment in Western Civilization*. New Brunswick: Rutgers University Press, 2010.

Eigen, Michael. *A Felt Sense: More Explorations of Psychoanalysis and the Kabbalah*. London: Karnac, 2013.

Eigen, Michael. *Kabbalah and Psychoanalysis*. London: Karnac, 2012.

Ellenberger, Henri F. *The Discovery of the Unconscious: The History and Evolution of Dynamic Psychiatry*. New York: Basic Books, 1970.

Ferreira Camargo, Carlos Henrique. "Jean-Martin Charcot: The Polymath," 1098–1111 *Arquivos de Neuro-Psiquiatra*, 81(12), 2023.

Ffytche, Matt. *The Foundation of the Unconscious: Schelling, Freud, and the Birth of the Modern Psyche*. Cambridge: Cambridge University Press, 2011.

Ffytche, Matt. *Sigmund Freud*. London: Reaktion Books Limited, 2020.

Fine, Reuben. *The Development of Freud's Thought*. New York: Jason Aronson, Inc., 1973.

Fonagy, Peter and Target, Mary. "What Can Developmental Psychopathology Tell Psychoanalysis About the Mind," 307–322 *Who Owns Psychoanalysis?* Ed. Ann Casement. London: Routledge, 2004.

Forrester, John. "The True Story of Anna O.," 327–347 *Social Research*, 53(2), 1986.
Frieden, Ken. Freud's *Dream of Interpretation*. Albany: SUNY, 1990.
Frixione, Eugenio. "Sigmund Freud's Contribution to the History of the Neuronal Cytoskeleton," 12–24 *Journal of the History of the Neurosciences*, 12(1), March 1, 2003.
Frosh, Stephen. "Freud and Jewish Identity," 167–178 *Theory & Psychology*, 18(2), April 2008.
Fryxell, Allegra R.P. "Psychopathologies of Time: Defining Mental Illness in Early 20th Century Psychiatry," 3–31 *History of the Human Sciences*, 32(2), April 2019.
Fuks Bernardo, Betty. "Vocation of Exile: Psychoanalysis and Judaism," 7–12 *International Forum of Psychoanalysis*, 8(1), 1999.
Garrigou-Kempton, Émilie. "Dying at the Salpêtrière: Autopsies and the Afterlife of the Hysteric," 123–136 *Esprit Créateur*, 61(1), Spring 2021.
Gauchet, Marcel and Swain, Gladys. *Madness and Democracy: The Modern Psychiatric Universe*. Tr. Catherine Porter. Princeton: Princeton University Press, 1999.
Gay, Peter. *Freud: A Life of Our Time*. New York: Doubleday, 1989.
Gelbin, Cathy S. and Gilman, Sander L. "Introduction" to Their Co-Edited *Cosmopolitanism and the Jews*. Ann Arbor: University of Michigan Press, 2017.
Gelfand, Toby. "Charcot's Response to Freud's Rebellion," 293–308 *Journal of the History of Ideas*, 50(2), April–June 1989).
Gertel, Elliot B. "Fromm, Freud, and Midrash," 429–439 *Judaism*, 48(192), 1999.
Ghisalberti, Giosuè. *Freud, the Contemporary Super-Ego, and Western Morality*. London: Routledge, 2023.
Ghisalberti, Giosuè. *"We Scholars" According to Nietzsche*. New York: Palgrave MacMillan, 2024.
Gilhooley, Dan. "Misrepresentation and Misreading in the Case of Anna O.," 75–100 *Modern Psychoanalysis*, 27(1), 2002.
Gilman, Sander. (Ed). *Hysteria Beyond Freud*. Berkeley: University of California Press, 1993.
Gilman, Sander. *The Jew's Body*. New York: Routledge, 1991.
Gilman, Sander. "Review," 716–717 *Isis* 95(4), 2004.
Gödde, Günter. "Freud and the Nineteenth-Century Sources on the Unconscious," 261–286 *Thinking the Unconscious: Nineteenth-Century German Thought*. Ed. Angus Nicholls and Martin Liebscher. Cambridge: Cambridge University Press, 2010.
Goetz, Christopher G., Bonduelle, Michel, and Gelfand, Toby. *Charcot: Constructing Neurology*. Oxford: Oxford University Press, 1995.
Goetz, Christopher G. "Jean-Martin Charcot (1825–1893)." 374–375 *Journal of Neurology*, 252(3), March 2005.
Golan, Ruth. *Loving Psychoanalysis: Looking at Culture with Freud and Lacan*. London: Routledge, 2006.
Goldbach, Joel and Godley, James A. (Ed). *Inheritance in Psychoanalysis*. Albany: SUNY, 2018.
Gomez, Lavinia. *The Freud Wars: An Introduction to the Philosophy of Psychoanalysis*. London: Routledge, 2005.
Goux, Jean-Joseph. "Freudian Unconscious and Secularization of Judaism," 217–225 *Disciplining Freud on Religion: Perspectives from the Humanities and Sciences*. Ed. Greg Kaplan and William Parsons. Lanham: Lexington Books, 2010.
Greenstein, David. *Roads to Utopia: The Walking Stories in the Zohar*. Stanford: Stanford University Press, 2014.

Gresser, Moshe. *Dual Allegiance: Freud as a Modern Jew*. Albany: SUNY, 1994.
Gluck, Mary. *Popular Bohemia: Modernism and Urban Culture in Nineteenth-Century Paris*. Cambridge: Harvard University Press, 2005.
Guenther, Katja. "The Disappearing Lesion: Sigmund Freud, Sensory-Motor Physiology, and the Beginnings of Psychoanalysis," 569–601 *Modern Intellectual History*, 10(3), 2013.
Gundersen, Ståle. "Freud and the Mind-Brain Problem," 4–12 *The Scandinavian Psychoanalytic Review*, 46(1–2), 2023.
Guntrip, Harry Y. *Personality Structure and Human Interaction: The Developing Synthesis of Psychodynamic Theory*. London: Karnac, 1995.
Gutman, Stephen R. "Hysteria as a Concept: A Survey of Its History in the Psychoanalytic Literature," 182–228 *Modern Psychoanalysis*, 31(2), 2006.
Hacking, Ian. "Do We See Through a Microscope?," 305–322 *Pacific Philosophical Quarterly*, 62(4), October 1981.
Halpern, Werner I. "Review" of Jerry Vitor Diller's Freud's Jewish Identity: A Case Study in the Impact of Ethnicity," 129–131 *Shofar*, 12(3), Spring 1994.
Handelman, Susan A. *The Slayers of Moses: The Emergence of Rabbinic Interpretation in Modern Literary Theory*. Albany: SUNY, 1982.
Hartman, Evelyn T. "An Analysis of Freud's Jewish Identity," 612–616 *Contemporary Psychoanalysis*, 47(4), 2011.
Helperin, David J. "Methodological Reflections on Psychoanalysis and Judaic Studies: A Response to Mortimer Ostow," 183–199 in Mortimer Ostow' *Ultimate Intimacy: The Psychodynamics of Jewish Mysticism*. London: Karnac, 1995.
Herman, David. "Psychoanalysis, Jews and History," 8697 *European Judaism*, 55(1), March 2022.
Hildebrandt, Gerhard, et al. "Georg Büchner, Sigmund Freud and the "Schädelnerven" (Cranial Nerves) – Research on the Brain and Soul in the 19th Century," 1999–2014 *Acta Neurochirurgica*, 156, 2014.
Hirschmüller, Albrecht. *The Life and Work of Josef Breuer: Physiology and Psychoanalysis*. New York: New York University Press, 1989.
Hundley, Michael B. "What Is the Golden Calf?" 559–579 *The Catholic Biblical Quarterly*, 79(4), 2017.
Hunt, Roger. *Freud: A Mosaic*. Newcastle upon Tyne: Cambridge Scholars Publishing, 2012.
Hunter, Dianne. "Hysteria, Psychoanalysis, and Feminism: The Case of Anna O.," 465–488 *Feminist Studies*, 9(3), 1983.
Hurst, Linda C. "What Was Wrong with Anna O.?," 129–131 *Journal of the Royal Society of Medicine*, 75(2), 1982.
Huss, Boaz. *The Zohar: Reception and Impact*. Tr. Yudith Nave. London: The Littman Library of Jewish Civilization, 2008.
Hustvedt, Hasti. *Medical Muses: Hysteria in 19th Century Paris*. London: Bloomsbury, 2011.
Idel, Moshe. *Kabbalah: New Perspectives*. New Haven: Yale University Press, 1988.
Indursky, Alexei Conte and Kveller, Daniel Boianorsky. "Freud and Judaism: Mourning, Trauma, and Transmission," 405–413 *PsicologiaUSP*, 28(3), December 2017.
Jelliffe, Smith Ellie. "Freud and Psychiatry: A Partial Appraisal," 326–340 *The American Journal of Sociology*, 45(3), 1939.

Jennings, Jerry L. "Engaging with the Unknown," *Journal of the History of the Behavioral Sciences*, 60(1), Winter 2024.
Jiraskova, Terezie. "Splitting of the Mind and Unconscious Dynamics," 24–27 *Activas Nervosa Superior*, 56(1/2), 2014.
Johansson, Per Magnus and Punzi, Elizabeth. "Jewishness and Psychoanalysis – The Relationship to Identity, Trauma and Exile. An Interval Study," 140–152 *Jewish Culture and History*, 20(2), 2019.
Johnston, Adrian. *Prolegomena to Any Future Materialism. Volume One: The Outcome of Contemporary French Philosophy*. Evanston: Northwestern University Press, 2013.
Johnston, Adrian and Malabou, Catherine. *Self and Emotional Life: Philosophy, Psychoanalysis, and Neuroscience*. New York: Columbia University Press, 2013.
Jordynn, Jack. "A Pedagogy of Sight: Microscopic Vision in Robert Hooke's *Micrographia*," 192–209 *Quarterly Journal of Speech*, 95(3), May 1999.
Justice-Malloy, Rhona. "Charcot and the Theatre of Hysteria," 133–139 *Journal of Popular Culture*, 28(4), Spring 1995.
Kaplan, Robert M. "O Anna: Being Bertha Pappenheim – historiography and Biography," 62–68 *Australasian Psychiatry*, 12(1), 2004.
Kaplan, Robert M. "Soaring on the Wings of Wind: Freud, Jews, and Judaism," 318–325 *Australasian Psychiatry*, 17(4), August 2009.
Karlsson, Gunnar. *Psychoanalysis in a New Light*. Cambridge: Cambridge University Press, 2012.
Kauders, Anthony D. "From Place to Race and Back Again: The Jewishness of Psychoanalysis Revisited," 72–87 *Space and Spatiality in Modern German-Jewish History*. Ed. Simone Lässig and Miriam Rürup. New York: Berghahn, 2017.
Kimball, Meredith. "From "Anna O." to Bertha Pappenheim: Transforming Private Pain into Public Action," 20–43 *History of Psychology*, 3(1), 2000.
Koehler, Peter. "About Medicine and the Arts: Charcot and French Literature at the fin-de-siècle," 27–40 *Journal of the History of Neuroscience*, 10(1), 2001.
Koerber, Amy. *From Hysteria to Hormones: A Rhetorical History*. Philadelphia: Penn State University Press, 2008.
Kohler, George Y. *Kabbalah Research in the Wissenschaft des Judentums (1820–1880): The Foundation of an Academic Discipline*. Munich: De Gruyter Oldenbourg, 2019.
Koyré, Alexandre. *From the Closed World to the Infinite Universe*. Baltimore: The Johns Hopkins University Press, 1957.
Kradin, Richard. *The Parting of the Ways: How Esoteric Judaism and Christianity Influenced the Psychoanalytic Theories of Sigmund Freud and Carl Jung*. Brighton: Academic Studies Press, 2016.
Krohn, A. *Hysteria: The Elusive Neurosis*. New York: International Universities Press, 1978.
Kronman, Anthony T. *Confessions of a Born-Again Pagan*. New Haven: Yale University Press, 2016.
Kuhn, Thomas. *The Structure of Scientific Revolutions*. 2nd editon. Chicago: The University of Chicago Press, 1970.
Kuriloff, Emily A. *Contemporary Psychoanalysis and the Legacy of the Third Reich: History, Memory, Tradition*. New York: Routledge, 2014.
La Bere, Ann and Feingold, Mordechai. *French Medical Culture in the Nineteenth Century*. Leiden: Brill, 1994.

Lakritz, Isaac. "Judaism and Freud," 225–227 *Tradition: A Journal of Orthodox Jewish Thought*, 15(1–2), Spring/Summer 1975.
Langs, Robert. *Science, Systems and Psychoanalysis*. London: Routledge, 1992.
Lather, Marie. *The Aesthetics of Artifice: Villiers's L'Ève Future*. Chapel Hill: The University of North Carolina Press, 1996.
Latour, Bruno. "Coming out as a philosopher," 599–608 *Social Studies of Science*, 40(4), 2010.
Leonard, Miriam. *Socrates and the Jews: Hellenism and Hebraism from Moses Mendelssohn to Sigmund Freud*. Chicago: The University of Chicago Press, 2012.
Lepoutre, Thomas and Villa, François. "Freud and Charcot: Freud's Discovery and the question of diagnosis," 345–368 *International Journal of Psychoanalysis*, 90(2), 2015.
Levenson, Edgar A. *The Fallacy of Understanding and the Ambiguity of Change*. Hillsdale: Routledge, 2005.
Lewis, Aaron. "Freud's Ironically Jewish Science: Commentary on Paper by Jill Salberg," 219–231 *Psychoanalytic Dialogues*, 17(2), 2007.
Lipsitt, Don R. "In Freud's Pocket: A Totem of Medical Ambivalence?," 738–751 *American Imago*, 77(4), Winter 2020.
Loewenberg, Peter. *Fantasy and Reality in History*. Oxford: Oxford University Press, 1995.
Lorentz, Elizabeth. "Jewish Women and Intersectional Feminism: The Case of Bertha Pappenheim," 24–50 *Feminist German Studies*, 29(1), 2023.
Lynch, William T. *Solomon's Child: Method in the Early Royal Society of London*. Stanford: Stanford University Press, 2001.
Mace, C.J. "Hysterical Conversion: I: A History," 369–377 *British Journal of Psychiatry* 161, 1992.
Machado, Bruno J and Auxéméry, J. "From Epileptic Hysteria to Psychogenic Non Epileptic Seizure: Continuity or Discontinuity for Contemporary Psychiatry?," *European Journal of Trauma and Dissociation*, 5, 2021.
MacMillan, Malcolm. *Freud Evaluated: The Completed Arc*. Cambridge: The MIT Press, 1997.
Manzo, Silvia. "Francis Bacon: Freedom, Authority, Science," 245–273 *British Journal for the History of Philosophy*, 14(2), 2006.
Marchese, Frank J. "An Overlooked Sexual Element in the Breuer-Anna O. Case," 261–276 *North American Journal of Psychology*, 20(2), 2018.
Marshall, Jonathan. "Dynamic Medicine and Theatrical Form at the fin de siècle: A Formal Analysis of Jean-Martin Charcot's Pedagogy, 1862–1893," 131–153 *Modernism/modernity*, 15(1), 2008.
Matley, David. "Philology as Kabbalah," 13–28 *Kabbalah and Modernity: Interpretations, Transformations, Adaptations*. Ed. Boaz Huss, Mario Pasi, Kocku von Stuckrad. Leiden: Brill, 2010.
Mayer, Andreas. *Sites of the Unconscious: Hypnosis and the Emergence of the Psychoanalytic Setting*. Chicago: The University of Chicago Press, 2013.
McCarthy, John A. *Remapping Reality: Chaos and Creativity in Science and Literature: Goethe – Nietzsche – Grass*. Amsterdam: Rodopi, 2006.
Meghnagi, David. "A Cultural Event within Judaism," 57–70 *Freud and Judaism*. Ed. David Meghnagi. London: Karnac, 1993.
Meiring, Henry James. "Darwing of the Mind: Freud's Darwinian Image," 171–187 *Imagining the Darwinian Revolution: Historical Narratives of Evolution from the*

*Nineteenth Century to the Present.* Ed. Ian Hesketh. Pittsburgh: University of Pittsburgh Press, 2022.

Merskey, Harold. "Anna O. Had a Severe Depressive Illness," 185–194 *The British Journal of Psychiatry*, 161(2), August 1992.

Neusner, Jacob. *The Way of Torah: An Introduction to Judaism.* Encino, California: Dickenson Publishing Company, Inc., 1974.

Nussbaum, Martha. *The Fragility of Goodness.* Chicago: The University of Chicago Press, 1986.

Olafson, Frederick A. *Naturalism and the Human Condition: Against Scientism.* London: Routledge, 2001.

Ostow, Mortimer. *Ultimate Intimacy: The Psychodynamics of Jewish Mysticism.* London: Routledge, 1995.

Parisi, Thomas and Leonard D. Goodstein. "Why Freud Failed: Some Implications for Neurophysiology and Sociobiology," 235–245 *The American Psychologist*. Vol. 42(3), 1987.

Perkins,-McVey, Matthew. "Critical Localization and the Nerve Cell: Freud's work in Meynert's Psychiatry Clinic," *History of Psychology*, 2024.

Petocz, Agnes. "The Scientific Status of Psychoanalysis Revisited," 145 *Philosophy, Science, and Psychoanalysis: A Critical Meeting.* Ed. Simon Boag, Linda A.W. Brakel, Vesa Talvitie. London: Routledge, 2015.

Philipps, Adam. *Becoming Freud: The Making of a Psychoanalyst.* New Haven: Yale University Press, 2014.

Phillips, Denis. "Francis Bacon and the Germans: Stories from When Science Meant Wissenschaft," 378–394 *History of Science*, 53(4), December 2015.

Pichel, Beatriz. "From Facial Expressions to Bodily Gestures: Passions, Photography and Movement in French 19th Century Sciences," 27–48 *History of the Human Sciences*, 29(1), 2016.

Pierce, Jennifer L. "The Relation Between Emotion Work and Hysteria: A Feminist Reinterpretation of Freud's *Studies on Hysteria*," 255–270 *Women's Studies*, 16 (3–4), 1989.

Pomata, Gianni. "Observation Rising: The Birth of an Epistemic Genre, 1500–1650," 45–80 *Histories of Scientific Observation.* Chicago: The University of Chicago Press, 2011.

Quin, Grégory and Bohuon, Anaïs. "Muscles, Nerves and Sex: The Contradictions of the Medical Approach to Female Bodies in Movement in France, 1874–1914," 172–186 *Gender and History*, 24(1), 2012.

Quinodoz, Jean-Michel. *Reading Freud: A Chronological Exploration of Freud's Writings.* Tr. David Alcorn. London: Routledge, 2005.

Rancière, Jacques. *The Emancipated Spectator.* Tr. Gregory Elliott. London: Verso, 2009.

Reitter, Paul. "Rereading Freud's Moses (Again)," 11–24 *The Germanic Review*, 83(1), 2008.

Reijzer, Hans. *A Dangerous Legacy: Judaism and the Psychoanalytic Movement.* Tr. Jeannette Ringold. London: Karnac, 2011.

Renish, N., et al. "Jean-Martin Charcot: Pioneer of Neurology," 1–6 *Cureus*, 16(8), 2024.

Richards, Arnold D. "Freud's Jewish Identity and Psychoanalysis as a Science," 987–1003 *Journal of the American Psychoanalytic Association*, 62(6) 2014.

Richards, Robert J. *The Tragic Sense of Life: Ernest Haeckel and the Struggle Over Evolutionary Thought.* Chicago: The University of Chicago Press, 2008.

Robbins, Michael. "The Primary Process: Freud's Profound Yet Neglected Contribution to the Psychology of Consciousness," 186–197 *Psychoanalytic Inquiry*, 38(3), 2018.

Rolnik, Eran J. *Freud in Zion: Psychoanalysis and the Making of Modern Jewish Identity*. London: Karnac, 2012.

Rosenzweig, Franz. *On Jewish Learning*. Ed. N. N. Glatzer. New York: Schocken Books, 1955.

Rubenstein, Richard L. "Freud and Judaism: A Review Article," 39–44 *The Journal of Religion*, 47(1), 1967.

Rudnytsky, Peter L. *Rescuing Psychoanalysis from Freud and other Essays on Re-vision*. London: Karnac, 2011.

Sadger, Isidor. *Recollecting Freud*. Ed. Alan Dundes. Tr. Johanna Micaela Jacobsen and Alan Dundes. Madison: The University of Wisconsin Press, 2005.

Salberg, Jill. "Hidden in Plain Sight: Freud's Jewish Identify Revisited," 197–217 *Psychoanalytic Dialogues*, 17(2), 2007.

Sanz Giancola and C. Alvarez Garcia. "Hysteria: A History of Conceptual and Clinical Pathomorphosis," 545–546 *European Psychiatry*, 65(1), 2022.

Schabert, Gerhard. "Freud and Evolution," 295–312 *History and Philosophy of the Life Sciences*, 31(2), 2009.

Schäfer, Peter. "The Triumph of Pure Spirituality: Sigmund Freud's Moses and Monotheism," 381–406 *Jewish Studies Quarterly*, 9(4), 2002.

Schaper, Eva. "Aristotle's Catharsis and Aesthetic Pleasure," 131–143 *The Philosophical Quarterly*, 18(71), April 1968.

Schauer, Frederick. *The Proof: Uses of Evidence in Law, Politics, and Everything Else*. Cambridge: Harvard University Press, 2022.

Sharpe, Matthew and Faulkner, Joanne. *Understanding Psychoanalysis*. London: Routledge, 2008.

Schickore, Jutta. *The Microscope and the Eye: A History of Reflections, 1740–1870*. Chicago: The University of Chicago Press, 2007.

Schermer, Victor L. *Meaning, Mind, and Self-Transformation: Psychoanalytic Interpretations and the Interpretation of Psychoanalysis*. London: Karnac, 2014.

Schuler, Romana Karla. *Seeing Motion: A History of Visual Perception in Art and Science*. Berlin: De Gruyter, 2015.

Schneider, Stanley and Berke, Joseph H. "Freud's Meeting with Rabbi Alexander Safran," 1–15 *Psychoanalysis and History*, 12(1), 2010.

Schneider, Stanley and Berke, Joseph H. "The Oceanic Feeling, Mysticism and Kabbalah: Freud's Historical Roots," 131–156 *Psychoanalytic Review*, 95(1), February 2008.

Schniedewind, William M. "The History of Classical Hebrew: From the invention of the alphabet to the Mishnah," *Religion Compass*, 13(4), 2019.

Scholem, Gershom (Ed). *Zohar: The Book of Splendor*. New York: Schocken Books, 1963.

Schonbar, Rosalea A. and Beatus, Helena R. "The Mysterious Metamorphoses of Bertha Pappenheim: Anna O. Revisited," 59–78 *Psychoanalytic Psychology*, 7(1), 1990.

Schorske, Carl E. "Freud: The Psychoarchaeology of Civilizations," 5–24 *The Cambridge Companion to Freud*. Ed. Jerome Neu. Cambridge: Cambridge University Press, 1991.

Schultheiss, Katrin. "The Internal Image: Mind and Brain in the Age of Charcot," 23–46 *Modern Intellectual History*, 18(1), 2021.

Scull, Andrew. Hysteria: *The Disturbing History*. Oxford: Oxford University Press, 2009.

Segal, Julia. *Phantasy in Everyday Life: A Psychoanalytic Approach to Understanding Ourselves*. London: Karnac, 1995.

Shapira, Michal. "The New History of Psychoanalysis: Towards a Richer and More Nuanced Narrative," 227–231 *Modern Intellectual History*, 17(1), 2020.
Showalter, Elaine. *Hystories: Hysterical Epidemics and Modern Media*. New York: Columbia University Press, 1997.
Sirotkina, Irina. "Review," 303–305 *British Journal for the History of Science*, 39. Iss. 141, Jun. 2006.
Skues, Richard A. *Sigmund Freud and the History of Anna O.: Reopening a Closed Case*. New York: Palgrave, 2006.
Slavet, Eliza. "Immaterial Materiality: The 'Special Case' of Freud's Theory of Jewishness," 353–382 *Jewish Studies Quarterly*, 15(4), 2008.
Smadja, Eric. *Freud and Culture*. London: Karnac, 2015.
Smith, David L. *Approaching Psychoanalysis: An Introductory Course*. London: Karnac, 1999.
Snelling, David. *Philosophy, Psychoanalysis and the Origin of Meaning: Pre-Reflective Intentionality in the Psychoanalytic View of the Mind*. London: Routledge, 2017.
Solm, Mark. "An Introduction to the neuroscientific works of Sigmund Freud," 1–35 *The Pre-Psychoanalytic Writings of Sigmund Freud*. Ed. Barford, Duncan, Geerardyn, Filip, van de Vijer, Gertrudis. London: Karnac, 2002.
Sorell, Tom. *Scientism: Philosophy and the Infatuations with Science*. London: Routledge, 1991.
Steiner, John. *Psychic Retreats: Pathological Organizations in Psychotic, Neurotic and Borderline Patients*. London: Routledge, 1993.
Strauss, Leo. *Jewish Philosophy and the Crisis of Modernity: Essays and Lectures in Modern Jewish Thought*. Albany: SUNY, 1997.
Sulloway, Frank J. *Freud, Biologist of the Mind: Beyond the Psychoanalytic Legend*. Cambridge: Harvard University Press, 1979.
Swenson, Carol. "Freud's Anna O.: Social Work's Bertha Pappenheim," 149–163 *Clinical Social Work Journal*, 22(2), 1994.
Symington, Neville. *The Blind Man Sees: Freud's Awakening and Other Essays*. London: Karnac, 2004.
Symington, Neville. *A Healing Conversation: How Healing Happens*. London: Routledge, 2006.
Tait, Peta. "Performing Neurology: The Dramaturgy of Dr. Jean-Martin Charcot," 217–239 *Australasian Dram Studies*, 71, October 2017.
Tasca, Cecilia, et al. "Women and Hysteria in the History of Mental Health," 110–119 *Clinical Practice and Epidemiology in Mental Health*, 8(1), 2012.
Tauber, Alfred I. "Freud's Philosophical Path: From a Science of the Mind to a Philosophy of Human Being," 32–43 *The Scandinavian Psychoanalytic Review*, 32, 2009.
Tauber, Alfred I. *The Reluctant Philosopher*. Princeton: Princeton University Press, 2010.
Thienhaus, Ole J. "Jewish Time: Ancient Practices, Hellenistic and Modern Habits, Freud's Reclaiming," 442–449 *Judaism*, 48, 1999.
Vogel, Wolfgang H. and Berke, Andreas. *Brief History of Vision and Ocular Medicine*. Amsterdam: Kugler Publications, 2009.
Vogel, Ladislaus Z. "Freud's Early Clinical Work," 94–101 *American Journal of Psychotherapy*, 48(1), Winter 1994.
Wade, Nicholas J. "Ernst Brücke on Stereoscopic Vision," 159–164 *Strabismus*, 30(3), 2022.
Walton, Douglas. "Francis Bacon: Human Bias and the Four Idols," 385–389 *Argumentation*, 13(4), November 1999.

Walusinki, Olivier. "Jean-Martin Charcot's Lesson on Parkinson's disease," 604–605 *Revue Neurologique*, 173(10), December 2017.

Waraich, Manny and Shah, Shailesh. "The Life and Work of Jean-Martin Charcot (1825–1893): 'The Napoleon of Neuroses'," 48–49 *Journal of the Intensive Care Society*, 19(1), 2018.

Webster, Jamieson. *Conversion Disorder*. New York: Columbia University Press, 2018.

Weeks, S.V. Francis Bacon's Doctrine of Idols: A Diagnosis of 'Universal Madness'," 1–39 *British Journal for the History of Science*, 52(1), March 2019.

Weinert, Friedel. *Copernicus, Darwin, and Freud: Revolutions in History and Philosophy of Science*. Oxford: Wiley-Blackwell, 2008.

Weiss, Dieter G., Jirikowski, Günther, Reichelt. "Microscopic Imaging: Interference, Intervention, Objectivity," 35–54 *Traces: Generating What Was There*. Ed. Bettina Bock von Wülfingen. Berlin: De Gruyter, 2017.

Weiss, Tzahi. *Sefer Yesirah and Its Contexts: Other Jewish Voices*. Philadelphia: University of Pennsylvania Press, 2018.

Westen, Drew. "The Scientific Legacy of Sigmund Freud: Toward a Psychodynamically Informed Psychological Science," 333–371 *Psychological Bulletin*, 124(3), 1998.

Westerink, Herman. *A Dark Trace: Sigmund Freud on the Sense of Guilt*. Leuven: Leuven University Press, 2013.

White, Deborah Elise. "Studies on Hysteria: Case Histories and the Case Against History," 1035–1049 *MLN*, 104(5), 1989.

Whitebook, Joel. *Freud: An Intellectual Biography*. Cambridge: Cambridge University Press, 2007.

Whitebook, Joel. "Jacob's Ambivalent Legacy," 139–155 *American Imago*, 67(2), Summer 2010.

Whitebook, Joel. "Our Dual Inheritance: On Psychoanalytic Social Theory Today," 1–14 *American Imago*, 76(1), Spring 2019.

Whitehouse, P. J. "Meynert, Theodore Hermann," 1117 *Encyclopedia of the Neurological Sciences, Second Edition*, 2014.

Wieser, Martin. "From the Eel to the Ego: Psychoanalysis and the Remnants of Freud's Early Scientific Practice," 259–280 *Journal of the History of the Behavioural Sciences*, 49(3), Summer 2013.

Wieser, Martin and Slunecko, Thomas. "Images of the Invisible: An Account of Iconic Media in the History of Psychology," 435–457 *Theory & Psychology*, 23(4), 2013.

Williams, Richard N. and Daniel N. Robinson, *Scientism: The New Orthodoxy*. London: Bloomsbury, 2015.

Wilson, Catherine. *The Invisible World: Early Modern Philosophy and the Invention of the Microscope*. Princeton: Princeton University Press, 1995.

Wilson Smith, Matthew. *The Nervous Stage: Nineteenth-Century Neuroscience and the Birth of the Modern Theatre*. Oxford: Oxford University Press, 2018.

Yerushalmi, Josef Hayim. *Freud's Moses, Judaism Terminable and Interminable*. New Haven: Yale University Press, 1991.

Yilmaz Anil, Yunus. "Ernst Brücke and Sigmund Freud: Physiological Roots of Psychoanalysis," 568–591 *Journal of the History of the Neurosciences*, 31(4), 2022.

Yovell, Yoran. "From Mechanics to Metaphor – On Freud's Struggle with the Biology of the Mind," 513–524 *Journal of the American Academy of Psychoanalysis*, 25(3), September 1997.

Yvens, Jean-Michel. "Catharsis: Psychoanalysis and Its Theatre." Tr. Andreas Weller. 1009–1027 *International Journal of Psychoanalysis*, 92(4), August 2011.
Zaretsky, Eli. *Political Freud: A History*. New York: Columbia University Press, 2015.
Zaretsky, Eli. *Secrets of the Soul: A Social and Cultural History of Psychoanalysis*. New York: Alfred A. Knopf, 2004.

# Index

absences 128, 133, 143; Anna O. 120, 141, 151, 194
acculturation 30
acting-out 158, 188
"Address to the Society of B'Nai Brith" (Freud) 33
advances 77–79
"The Aetiology of Hysteria" (Freud) 169
aggression 134
Amyotrophics lateral sclerosis (ALS) (Charcot's disease) 176
anaesthesia 141–142
anatomy, and psychology 190
ancestry 9
animal sacrifice 54
Anna O. 3, 13–14, 16–18, 35, 73, 85, 95, 99, 108, 111, 117, 120–122, 124–126, 130–132, 134–138, 141–144, 158–159, 163, 169, 177, 181, 184, 191; absences 120, 128, 141, 151, 194; *condition seconde* 145–146, 153; consciousness 138; cure of 156; day-dreaming 152; disturbance of vision 150–151; double-conscience 152; feminist reinterpretation of 132–133, 145; hallucinations 137–138; hallucinatory absence 141; histrionic 156; idols 92; language 143; linguistic problems 140; memories 146–159; perception 139, 141, 144–146; prescriptions 148–149; private theatre 137–139, 178, 187–188, 194, 196; sensory perception 51; split consciousness 139–140, 150, 195; symptoms 134–135, 149–150, 155, 187; talking cure 14–15, 47, 101, 128, 140, 187; transference 147

anti-Semitism 11, 24, 26
archaic heritage 23–37, 163–164; language 44; *see also* heredity
Aristotle 17, 157, 197; catharsis 125, 138–139, 154–155; *Poetics* 14–15, 18, 92, 107, 135, 138, 146–147, 153–155, 187–188, 193–194, 199; recognition 195–196
assimilation 90
assimilationist 11
atheism 45
attacks 128–129
authority 86
*An Autobiographical Study* (Freud) 1, 135, 177, 189–190, 198
autohypnosis 126
autopsies of hysterics 183

back-and-forth 41
Bacon, Francis 7, 75–76, 84, 89–90, 100; "the *Door* or *Gate*" 93; fallacy 98; idols 93–94, 97; idols of the tribe 91–92; "Instance of the Lamp" 92; instances 93; *Novum Organum* 9, 11, 37, 62, 76, 84–86, 90–92, 100; revealing instances 92
bad reception 154
barbarism 24, 57
Bernay, Jacob 152
*Beyond the Pleasure Principle* (Freud) 82–83
bias 98
Bible narrative 59
Bible story 3, 31, 33, 35, 38, 48–49, 58, 81
*Bildung* 4, 18, 20, 63, 88, 166, 183, 195
biological inheritance 36
biology 83, 164

Brentano, Franz 89
Breuer, Josef 17, 95, 106, 108, 117, 119–120, 127, 149, 171; Anna O. 120–121, 131–132, 134–135, 137–140, 145, 147–148, 153, 191; catharsis 125, 138–139, 188; language 143
Brücke, Ernst 101; laboratory 99, 103–104

called 62
canonical hysterics 142
catharsis 125, 138–139, 143, 147, 152–155, 157, 184, 188, 193
cathartic method 101, 130, 138–139
Charcot, Jean-Martin 16, 18, 99; hysteria 180–185; hysterical theatre 195–196; neuropathology 167; obituary of 163–176
Charcot's disease 176
*Civilization and Its Discontents* 57
"The Claims of Science to Scientific Interest" (Freud) 83
coercion 39
*condition seconde* 129, 133, 143; Anna O. 145–146, 153
confession 53
conscious 15; *see also* consciousness
conscious perception 79; *see also* perception
conscious self-perception 4; *see also* perception
consciousness 4–5, 8, 14, 17, 20n3, 26, 31, 48–49, 84, 92, 95, 97, 110, 128, 138, 165–166, 168–169, 171–172; hypnoid consciousness 129; of others 29; *see also* split consciousness
conversion 108, 122, 139
conversion disorder 146
cosmopolitan 11, 27, 30, 62, 198
cosmopolitan history 90
creation 47–48
crypto-biologist 13
cultural transference 23
culture 11, 19, 164, 169

Darwin, Charles 69–70, 81, 87, 121
day-dreaming 126, 137, 152
Decalogue 39, 44
decision 71
defense of psychoanalysis 105–106
degeneracy 197
demonic possession 178, 182; *see also* hysteria

depth-psychology 13, 28, 46, 111, 124, 146, 163, 167
destructive aggression 134
*Die Gesundheit* 63
"Difficulties" (Freud) 5
"A Difficulty in the Path of Psychoanalysis" (Freud) 71
diminution 144
disassociation 167
discourses 9
*disploplia* 133, 144
distortion of self 152
distortions 38
disturbance of vision, Anna O. 150–151
divided consciousness 127; *see also* split consciousness
doctor-patient relationship 121, 135, 187–188
"the *Door* or *Gate*" 93
double vision 144
double-conscience 126–127, 152
drama 138–139, 156–157, 188, 190, 194–195
dreams 123–124, 126
drives 124, 147
drugs: for Anna O. 148–149; effects of 144
dual inheritances 133
dynamic psychiatry 9
"The Dynamics of Transference" (Freud) 25

ego 2, 26, 124, 169; consciousness 172
*The Ego and the Id* (Freud) 35, 49–51
Egyptian hieroglyphics 49
*eidolon* (false appearance) 98
emancipated spectators 193
endopsychic perception 137–138, 173
energy 97
Epicurus 90
essence of humans 33
ethnicity 11, 37
existence 93
experimentation 100
external events, hysteria 123

fallacy 98
familial conflict 153
family history 166
"father" figure 87
fatigue 141
feminist reinterpretation of Anna O. 132–133, 145

free association 41, 48
freedom 86
Frixione, Eugenio 101
"functional" nervous diseases 71
*The Future of an Illusion* (Freud) 31, 39, 60
"The Future Prospects of Psycho-analytic Therapy" (Freud) 171

Galileo 76
gap between knowledge of physiological function and total personality 91
geriatry 164
Goethe 70, 86–87
graven images 24, 35, 49–50, 52, 76
*The Great Instauration* (Freud) 85
group psychology 91–92

Haeckel, Ernst 24, 59
hallucinations 137–138, 143
hallucinatory absence 141
Hebrew alphabet 38, 41, 45–47, 49, 55
Helmholtz, Hermann von 86, 97, 101
hereditarianism 167
heredity 163–164, 166, 169, 175, 197
Hippocratic oath 171
historical transference 45
histrionic, Anna O. 156
Holy Writ 48
human intelligence 72
humanists 78
hypnoid consciousness 129
hypnoid states 128
hypnosis 126–128, 187–188
hysteria 16–18, 87, 106, 117–123, 127, 141, 153, 175–187, 189; attacks 128–129; canonical hysterics 142; critical assessment of 191; images 124–125; reminiscences 126; symptoms 126; *see also* Anna O.
"Hysteria" (Freud) 179
*hysteron* 154–155
hystories 141

identity 26–30, 34, 36–37, 54, 56, 62, 64n6
"idol of the theatre" 99
idolatry 24, 79, 93–94, 190; and neurosis 124
idols 76, 91, 93–94, 97–98, 106
idols of the mind 100
idols of the tribe 91–92
illness 153

images 13, 38, 49–51, 54, 57, 124; hypnosis 128; hysteria 124–125; idolatry 79; *see also* dreams
increase 80
indebtedness 43
inheritance 24, 36, 70, 163; dual inheritances 133
inherited language 129
"Instance of the Lamp" 92
instances 92–93
*instauration* 92
*Instincts and Their Vicissitudes* 151
institutions for the mentally ill 192, 194; *see also* Salpêtrière
instrument-mediated perception 76
intellectual biography 9–10
internal perception 152
interpretation 44
*Interpretation of Dreams* (Freud) 53, 156, 177
inter-relationships 172
*Introductory Lectures on Psychoanalysis* (Freud) 14, 77, 82, 107, 120–121, 135
*Israelitische Bibel* 32

*Jahrbuch* 119
Janet, Pierre 121, 171, 196
Jewish education 26
Jewish science 7–8, 10, 23, 47, 63, 70, 104; *see also* psychoanalysis
Jewishness 11, 26–30, 32, 49, 53, 55; *see also* identity
Judaism 9–10, 26, 32–34, 54, 70

Kabbalah 7, 39–40, 42, 65n9
Kabbalists: Hebrew alphabet 46; language 44

language: Anna O. 143; Hebrew alphabet 38, 41, 45–47, 49, 55; inheritance 129; Kabbalists 44
latent 23, 39, 42, 47, 53, 93, 130
liberalism 57
linguistic problems, Anna O. 140
localization 76
love-transference 154

*macropsia* 133, 144–145
magnification 94
Maimonides 43–44
manifestations 5, 16, 23, 39, 42, 72, 99, 134, 139

materialism 73
medical muses 187
medical scenography 182
medical science 87; *see also* science
medical training 85–89
*Medicina mentis* 97
melancholia 125
memories 125; of Anna O. 146–159
metaphysics 73, 104–105
metapsychology 125
Meynert, Theodor 116
Michelangelo 9, 50, 55, 60
microscopes 75–76, 94–96; as an allegory of perception 99–111
midrash 37
mind-body problem 130
miraculous gift 9
*mitzvot* 38
morality 52
Moses 3, 7, 9, 23, 30, 38, 41, 44–46, 49–50, 53, 56, 58, 60, 70, 87
*Moses and Monotheism* (Freud) 5–6, 24, 26, 32, 34–36, 38, 44–45, 48, 51–52, 54–55, 57–63, 73
"The Moses of Michelangelo" (Freud) 9, 50
Mosheh 53
mourning 125
"Mourning and Melancholia" 126
mysticism 38–40
mythos 35

nationalism 63
*Naturwissenschaft* 69
neologism 141
neurologists 71
neurology 12, 23, 83, 130, 174, 181–183, 187; *see also* Charcot, Jean-Martin
neuropathology 167
neurosis/neuroses 16, 124, 152, 169, 173, 188
*New Introductory Lectures on Psychoanalysis* (Freud) 169
new manifestation 16
new product of science 75
*new science* 74
new scientific discipline 75
*new Torah* 63
Newton, Isaac 86
nosography 173
*Novum Organum* (Bacon) 11, 37, 62, 76, 84–86, 90–92, 100

obituary of Martin Charcot 163–176
objectivity 12
observation 80–83, 100
Oedipal issues 70
Oedipus Complex 188
*Oedipus the King* (Sophocles) 156, 198
"On the History of the Psychoanalytic Movement" (Freud) 119
*On the Origin of Species* (Darwin) 121
ontogenesis 24
optic glasses 93
orthodoxy 86
our perceptions 4
"An Outline of Psychoanalysis" (Freud) 4, 77, 79–80, 83–84, 109
overdetermination 6, 58, 69

*paideia* 88
pan-genderism 132
Pappenheim, Bertha 35; *see also* Anna O.
paralysis agitans 164
Paris 17, 19
Parkinson's disease 164
patriarchs 53
perception 20n3, 48–52, 77, 81, 92, 97, 123–125, 129–130; Anna O. 139, 141, 144–146; conscious perception 79; endopsychic perception 137–138, 173; instrument-mediated perception 76; internal perception 152; microscopes as an allegory of 99–111; self 78; sensory perception 49, 51; veridical perception 103
performances of hysterical patients 192–193
*peripeteia* 189
peripety 157, 197
personal identity, Judaism 26
phantasies 15, 159
philosophy 70–71
photography 190–191; in clinics 185
phylogenesis 5, 24
physical contortions 180
physicalism 71, 97, 178
*physiologia* 90–91
physiology 73
Plato 35
*Poetics* (Aristotle) 14–15, 18, 92, 107, 135, 138, 146–147, 153–155, 187–188, 193–194, 199
politics 57

possession 178, 181
preconditions 6
"Preliminary Communication" (Freud) 14, 35, 118, 121–125, 127–128, 130, 140, 146–147, 168
prescriptions for Anna O. 148–149
private theatre, Anna O. 35, 47, 99, 121, 133, 137–138, 156–158, 165–166, 175, 178, 180–182, 187–188, 194, 196
*The Problem of Anxiety* (Freud) 6
projection 173
psyche 76, 80
psychedelic experience 93
psychiatry, history of 186
psychical 4
"The Psychical Apparatus" (Freud) 76
psychical regression 24; *see also* regression
psychical revelations 23
psychical splitting 14
psychoanalysis 3, 5–7, 9, 11–13, 18–20, 28, 42, 72, 95, 99–100, 150, 152, 169; beginning of 120; birth of 172; defense of 105–106; defined 74; meaning of purpose 73–74; as science 80–85, 87
psychoanalysts 53
psychoanalytic therapy 134
psychological condition 86
psychology 1, 3–4, 19, 71, 78, 86, 94, 172, 197; and anatomy 190; of consciousness 78, 110; depth-psychology 13, 28, 46, 111, 124, 146, 163, 167; therapeutic psychology 131
psychopathology of consciousness 92
"The Psychopathology of Everyday Life" (Freud) 172
psychoscopes 103
"The Psychotherapy of Hysteria" (Freud) 158

*Qara* (Freud) 62
"The Question of Lay Analysis" (Freud) 19

rabbinical elements 37
racial unconscious 67n60
reception 51, 79, 81
recognition 195–196
regression 32, 73
relationships 174; *see also* transferences
relativism 10
religious spirit 111
reminiscences 124, 126, 153
repetition of a scene 158

"Report on My Studies in Paris and Berling" (Freud) 175
repression 71, 125
"The Resistances to Psycho-Analysis" 154
revealing instances 92
revelation 40; Moses 60

Salpêtrière 17, 18, 99, 125, 137, 171, 173, 194; hysterics at 176–187
Salpêtrière doctrine 163
science (*scientia*) 71–72, 75, 78, 81, 88–89, 91–92, 110
science/humanism divide 89
scientific freedom 86
scientific revelations 101–102
scientism 71–72
scopes 93
scribes of Moses 45
secular kabbalist 41
*Sefer Yetzirah* ("Book of Formation" or "Creation") 23, 38, 45
self 2
self-analysis 91–92, 152
self-awareness 188–189
self-formation 87–88, 166
self-involvement 53
self-knowledge 79
self-perception 78
self-recourses 34
self-reflection 156, 189
sense 93
"Sense of Symptoms" (Freud) 135
sensory perception 49, 51
sensory-motor physiology 142, 175
sensualism 93–94
sexual transference 148
"A Short Account of Psychoanalysis" (Freud) 16, 71
sight 80, 86, 93; stereoscopic vision 101
social theory 133
"Some Elementary Lessons in Psychoanalysis" 3
somnambulism 133, 139–140
somnolence 141
spectacles 54, 192–193
spectators 194–195; emancipated spectators 193
speech 157; *see also* language
split consciousness 2, 116–131, 142, 167, 172, 195; Anna O. 138–140, 150
"Splitting of the Ego in the Process of Defense" 2

states of consciousness 14, 17, 119, 143; Anna O. 139–140
stereoscopic vision 101
*The Structure of Scientific Revolutions* 11–12
structures 9
*Studies on Hysteria* (Freud and Breuer) 3, 118–119, 121, 125, 127, 134–135, 144, 146, 154, 158, 185
subjectively conditioned 151–152
super-ego 127
symbolization 151
Symington, Neville 104–105, 177
symptoms: of Anna O. 134–135, 149–150, 155, 187; of hysteria 122–123, 126

talking cure 14–15, 47, 101, 128, 140, 187
Talmud 41
telescope 4, 76, 79, 92, 94, 103
Temple of Science *see* Salpêtrière
Ten Commandments 46
*Tetrapharmakon* 90
theatre 195; *see also* private theatre
theatricality 174
therapeutic psychology 131
"Third Lecture" (Freud) 99
thought 15
*tikkum olan* 38
*Totem and Taboo* 32–33, 50
tragedy 17
transcendent influence 51, 60–61
transference 25–26, 28, 43, 77, 129–130, 148, 150, 169, 174, 193; Anna O. 147; love-transference 154; sexual transference 148; *Übertragung* 56
trans-historical transference 9
treatment of the mentally ill 181

*Übermensch* 32, 59
*Übertragung* 25, 34, 37, 40, 42, 56
unconscious 69, 79, 163, 168, 173; racial unconscious 67n60
The Unconscious (Freud) 77
unconscious representation 151
unconscious self-hypnosis 141; *see also* hypnosis
unknowable 84

veridical perception 103
Vienna General Hospital 72, 85, 88, 116
vision 199; disturbance of 123, 150–151; double vision 144
visual iconography 178

Wieser, Martin 105
*Wissenschaft* 3, 75, 88, 89, 91
*Wissenschaft in Judentums* 43
working-through 125, 158

young science 75

*Zohar* 39–42